To, Dear Father,

Wishing You A Very Happy 85th!!!

Birthday,

With Lots of Love from

Carolyn, Rosie and Meg

X

There is no place like Dartmoor - so hope you enjoy this book!!!

A YEAR ON DARTMOOR

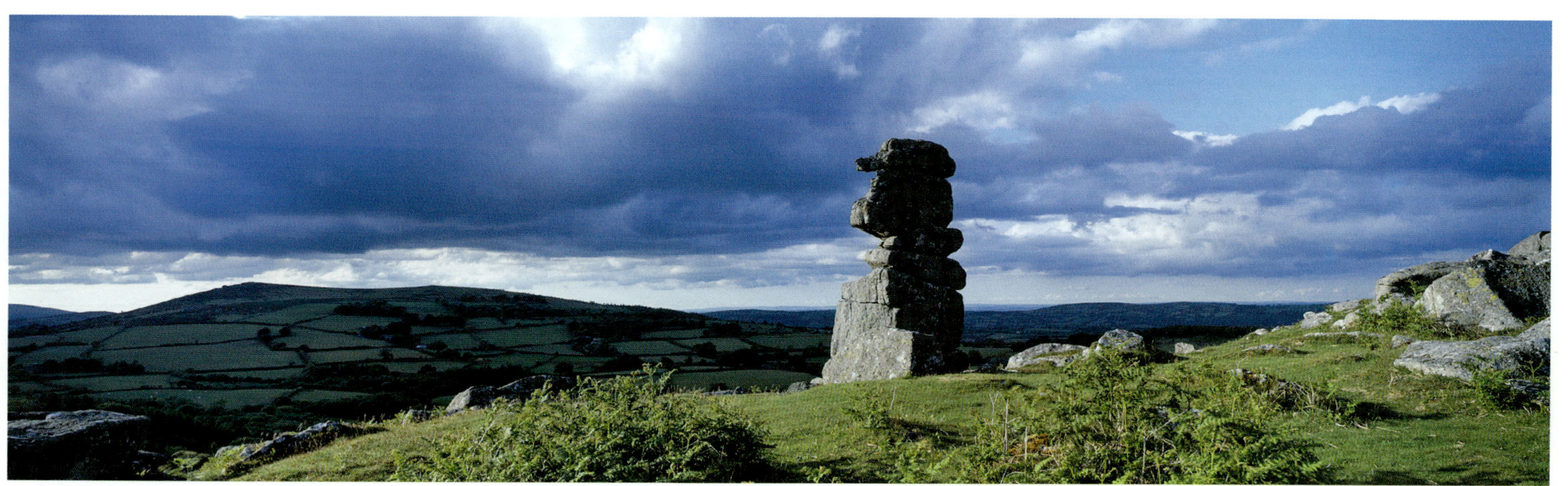

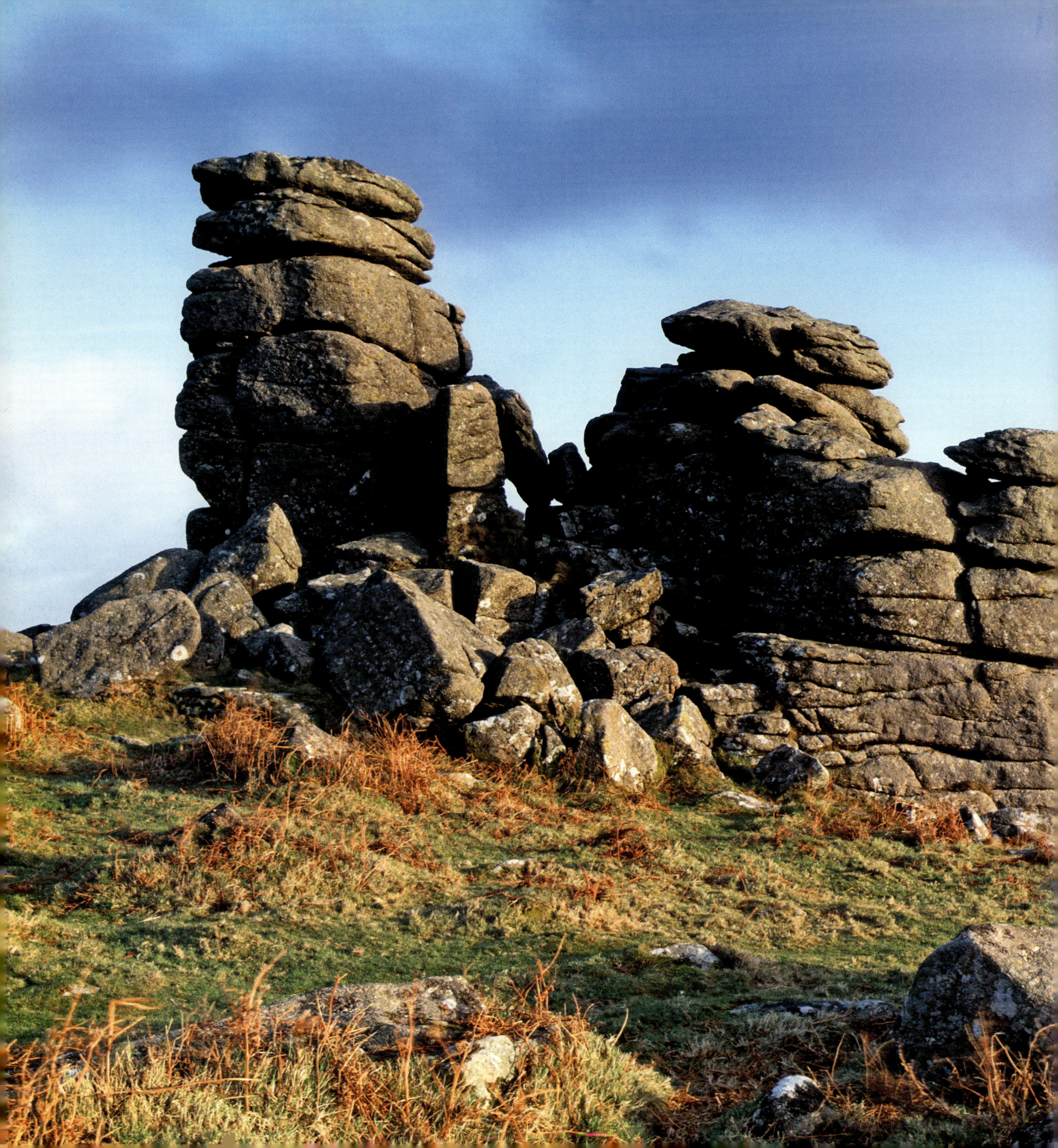

A YEAR ON DARTMOOR

David Entrican

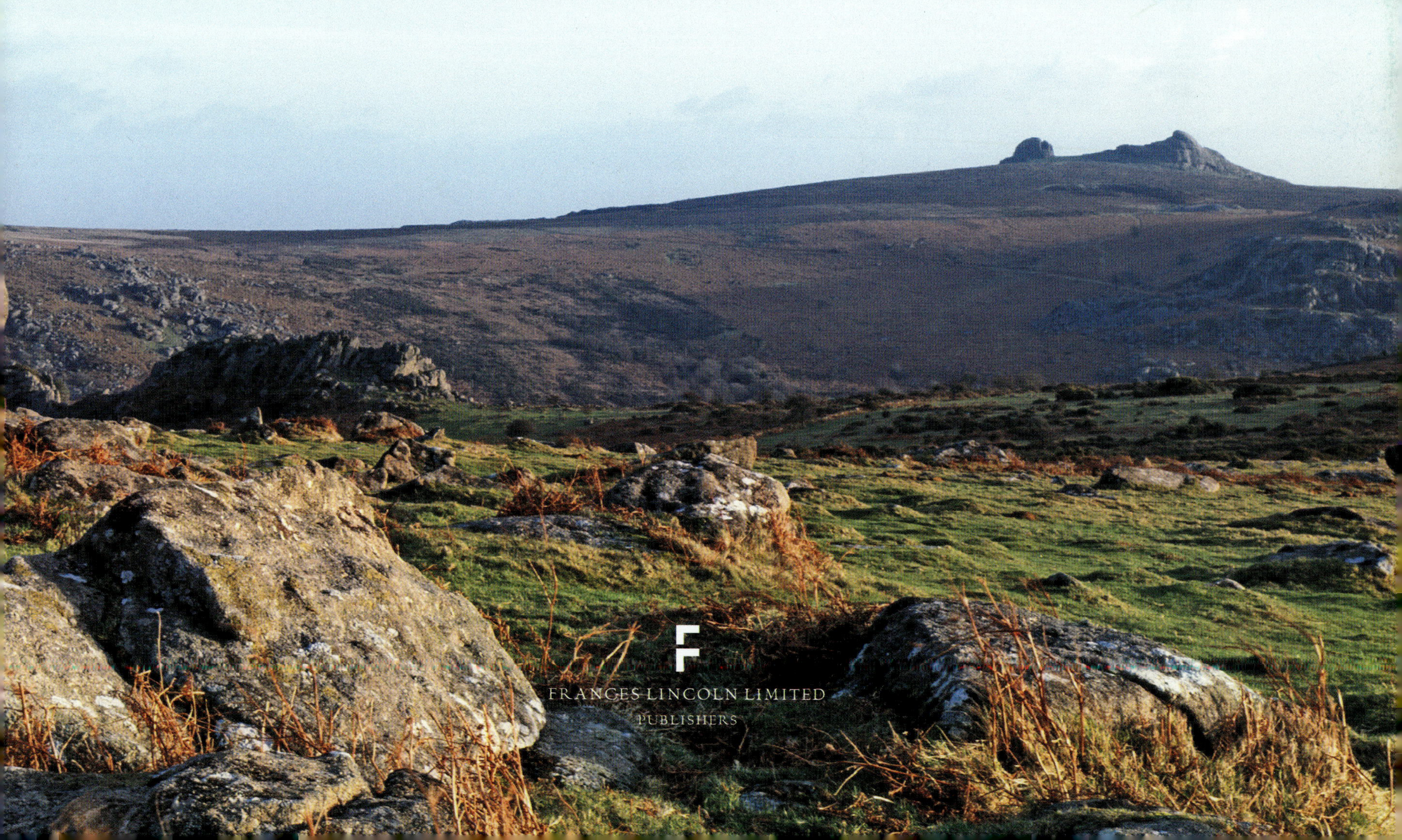

FRANCES LINCOLN LIMITED
PUBLISHERS

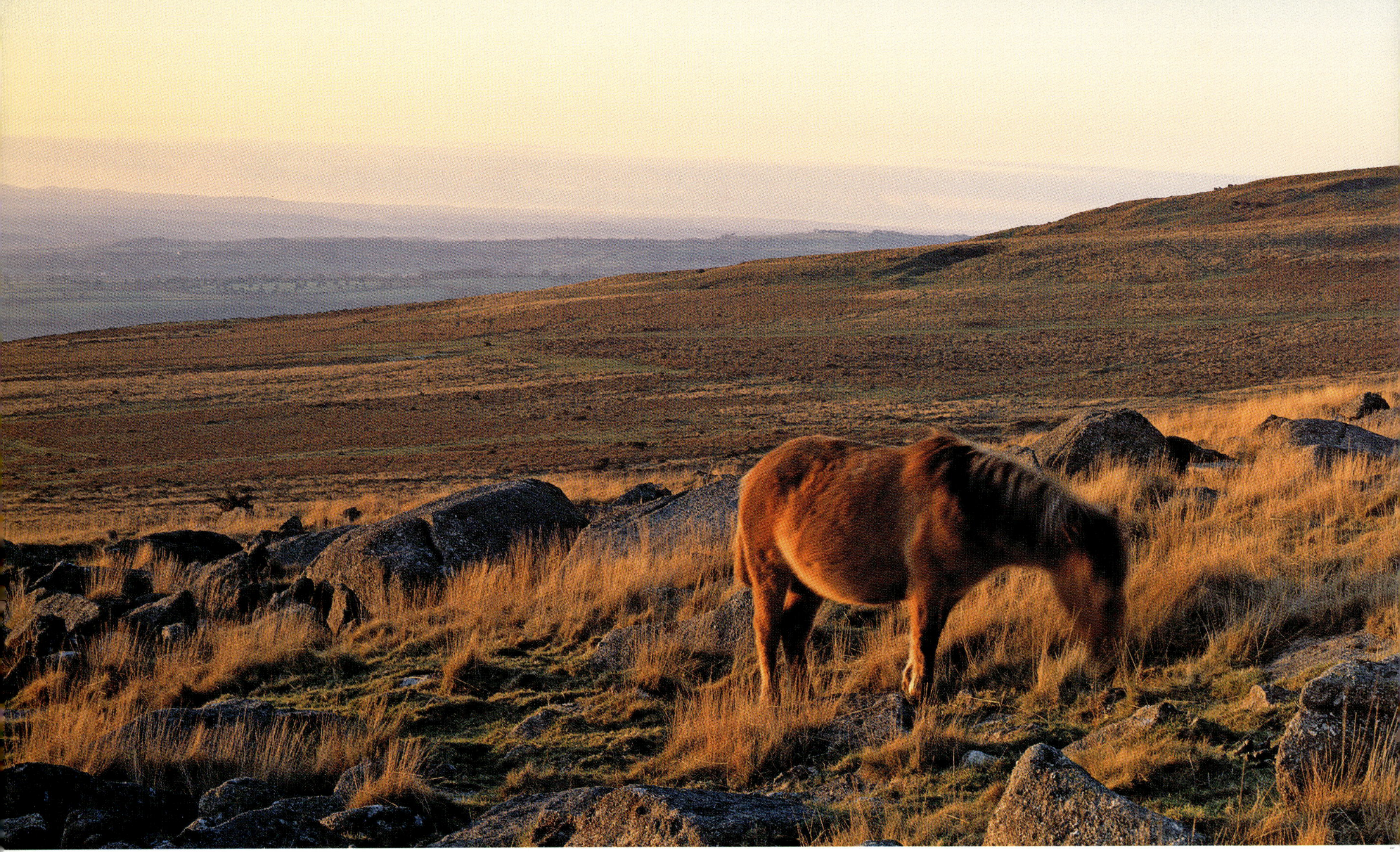

Frances Lincoln Ltd
4 Torriano Mews
Torriano Avenue
London NW5 2RZ
www.franceslincoln.com

A Year on Dartmoor

First Frances Lincoln edition 2008

British Library Cataloguing-in-Publication data
A catalogue record for this book is available from the British Library.

ISBN 13: 978-0-7112-2917-4
ISBN 10: 0-7112-2917-1

Printed and bound in Singapore

9 8 7 6 5 4 3 2 1

above

Dartmoor pony by Cox Tor, Dartmoor.

page 1

Bowerman's Nose, Hayne Down, Dartmoor.

pages 2–3

Haytor Rocks from Hound Tor, Dartmoor.

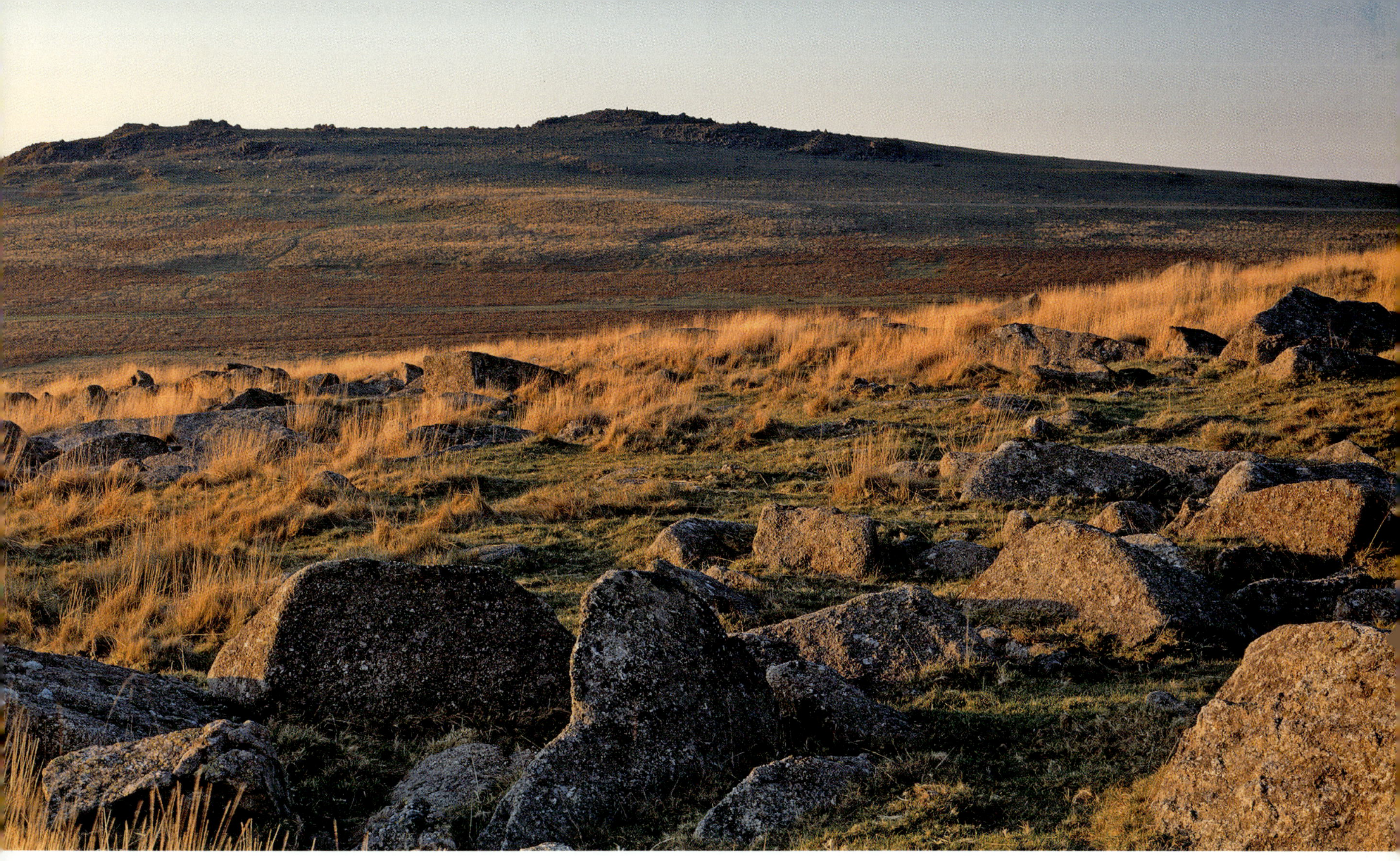

For Kath

CONTENTS

Preface 6

Introduction 7

Winter 9

Spring 41

Summer 63

Autumn 95

Photographic notes 118

Photographic Information 118

Acknowledgements 128

PREFACE

The panoramic format is a window on the world and its ability to embrace the essence of the landscape is well documented. When David's photographs of Dartmoor arrived in the post, I knew instantly that his work was authoritative.

Apart from the quality of light and his beautifully balanced compositions there was something about the work, which was deceptively simple. I say deceptively, because the panoramic format despite its power to amaze is unforgiving in the wrong hands. Simplicity requires depth and this collection of images is testimony to David's passion for part of the world with which he is deeply connected.

From personal experience, I know of the challenges faced by photographers when working with this format in areas which are not mountainous and I think that David must be commended for producing such a stunning collection of images of Dartmoor. I wish him every success with this book.

Colin Prior
Jan 2008

Pink sunset, Great Staple Tor, Dartmoor.

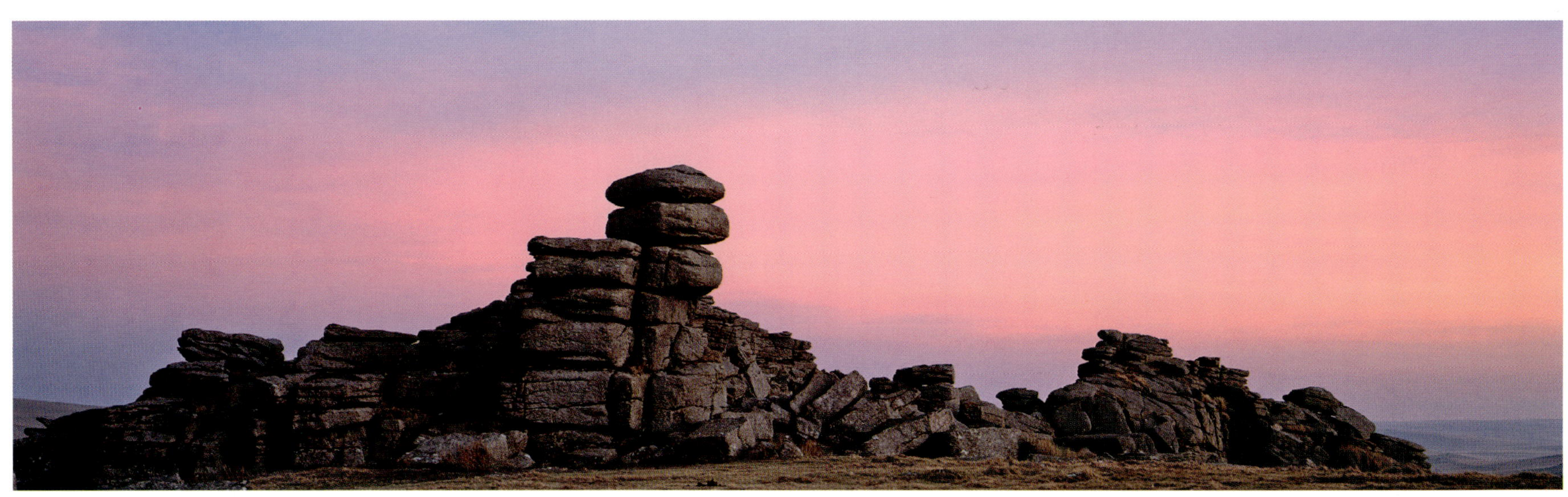

INTRODUCTION

Taking its name from the river Dart formed by the East and West Dart rivers converging at Dartmeet, Dartmoor sits poised above the lowlands of Devon which surround it. The 954 square kilometres of unyielding granite plateau are dotted with tors, dense peat bogs and stocky trees stubbornly adhering to the scoured earth.

Dartmoor can present a mask of barren wilderness to the uninitiated. But for those willing to explore, the moor unfolds the secrets of its seasonal changes, revealing faces of spectacular colour, inspiring light and landscapes distinctly marked over time by the shared presence of humans, wildlife and natural elements alike.

Moving to Devon a few years ago, I was initially captivated with the moor's rugged windswept tors, ancient woods, and valleys, rivers and waterfalls. In photographing this book, I've explored deeper beneath the surface of this pensive moor, and found it to be an even more inspiring place than I could have envisaged.

One end of a spine of granite running in a south-westerly direction to the Scilly Isles, Dartmoor was formed by the magma from the Earth's crust which, when cooled, cast the hills covered with granite rocks resulting in the many tors seen today.

Bronze age settlements are common, with many remains of hut circles, stone circles and crosses still to be found across the moor. Much of Dartmoor was cleared of trees by these early settlers. Industry continued on the moor with tin mining and quarrying of granite which finally ended with the closure of Merrivale quarry in 1997. Most of the marks of these industries have been quietly absorbed and integrated into the landscape.

Parts of Dartmoor have been used as a military firing range for over 200 years and are still in use today, with lights and flags to mark these areas. The army run an annual event called the Ten Tors challenge where teams of walkers spend two days hiking and camping across the moor.

Receiving national park status in 1951, the moor is popular with walkers and horse riders due to its largely unrestricted access. It also provides natural areas for climbing and canoeing. The pursuit of letterboxing is popular, with thousands of hidden containers holding a rubber stamp and a visitors' book for successful finders to collect the stamp. Clues describing their location are found in other letterboxes or on the internet.

Dartmoor's elevation results in much higher rainfall than the surrounding land, giving rise to a vast network of streams and rivers and the hazard of bogs, where rainfall has not drained from peaty areas. Snow too, whilst not very common in the south west of England can occasionally fall on Dartmoor, bringing hordes of excited children and sledges to the slopes of Haytor.

Covering such a vast and changeable area, and with over 160 Tors, not to mention the rivers and forests, I quickly realised I was not going to be able to fully document the whole of Dartmoor for this book. Consequently, I have chosen some of my favourite locations, including some of the popular hotspots and some less visited places in order to give an authentic feel of the vast variety of the area.

Despite my travels on Dartmoor over a couple of years I still feel that I've barely scratched the surface. The more I search, the more interesting places are to be found. Much more than just a number of hills with rocks stacked on top, I would urge you to get your walking boots on and do some exploring if you can.

Enjoying days of sunshine and showers as well as fog, snow, biting cold winds and hail, I have watched in wonder as the landscape has changed over the seasons. My hope is that the photographs contained in this book convey something of the natural beauty that I have witnessed on this majestic moor.

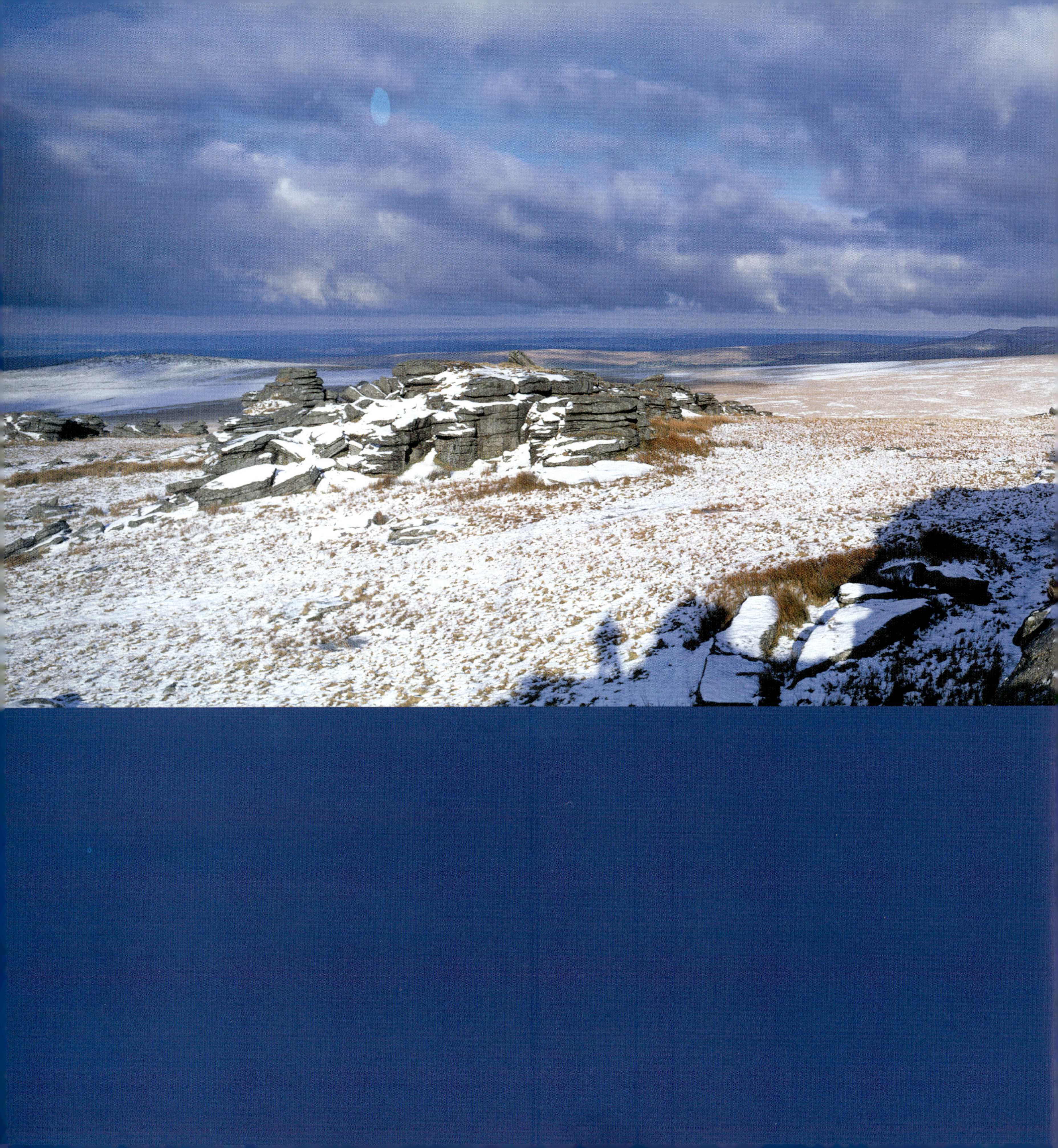

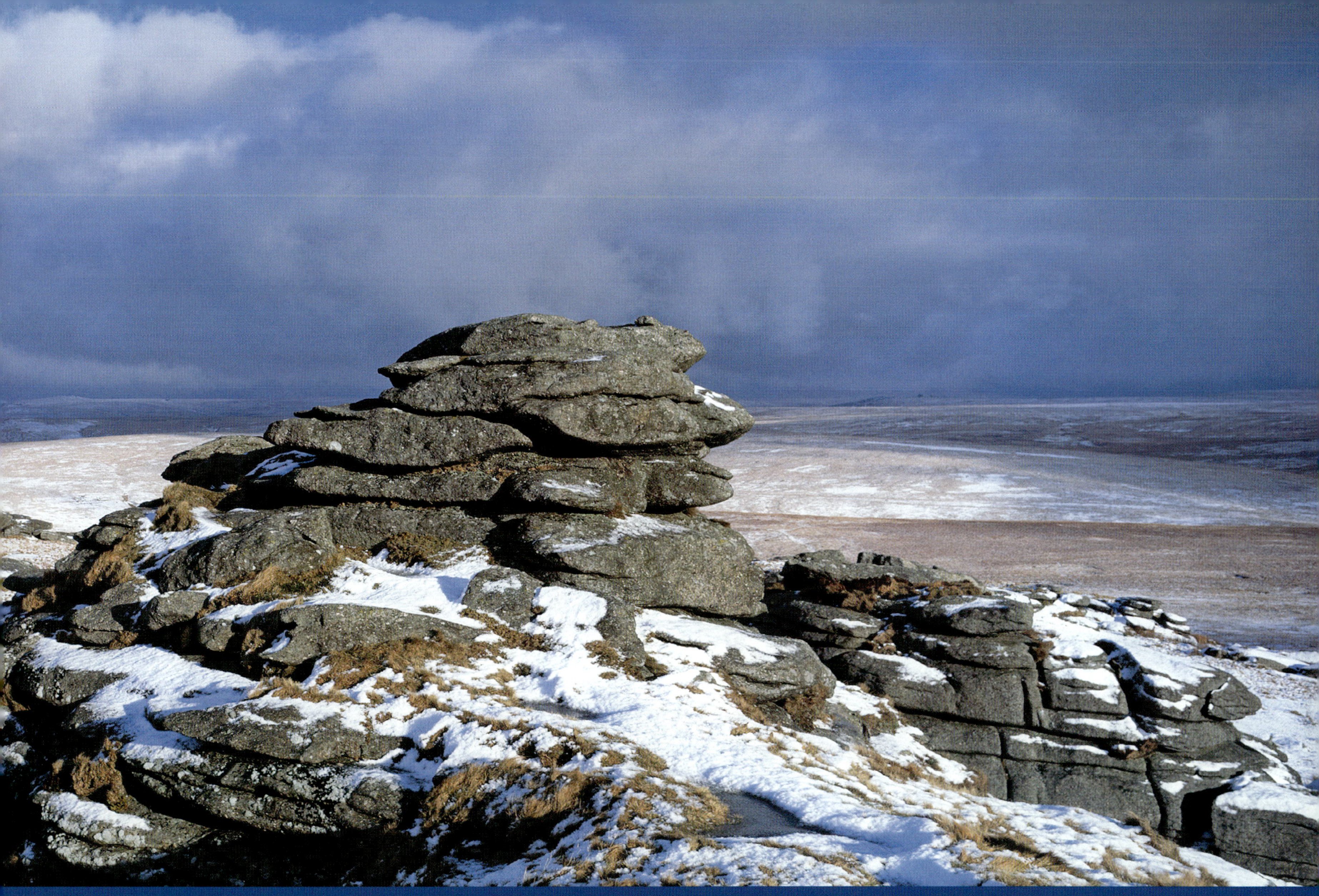

Winter

Looking north from the summit of Great Mis Tor, the briefest of glimpses of morning sunlight illuminates the rocks and snow-covered moors. Although Dartmoor is one of the best places in Devon to see some winter snow, the whole region's proximity to the sea and its southerly latitude mean that it is not a very common sight. Neighbouring tors Staple and Roos can be seen without snow on the same day on the next page.

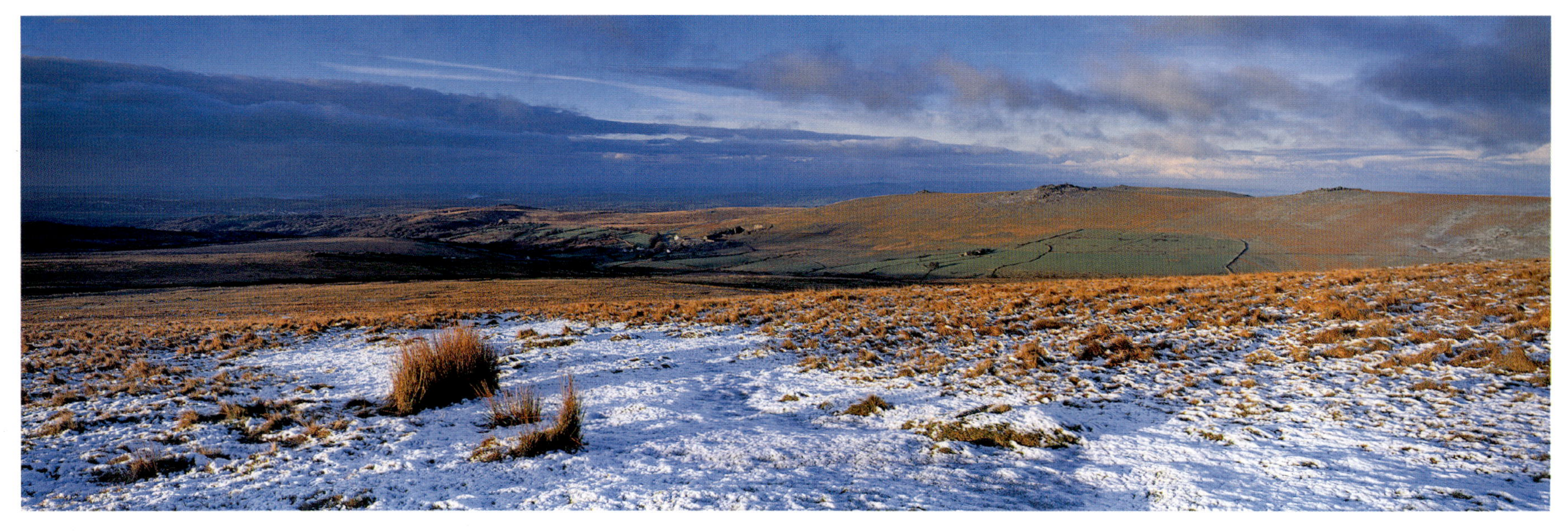

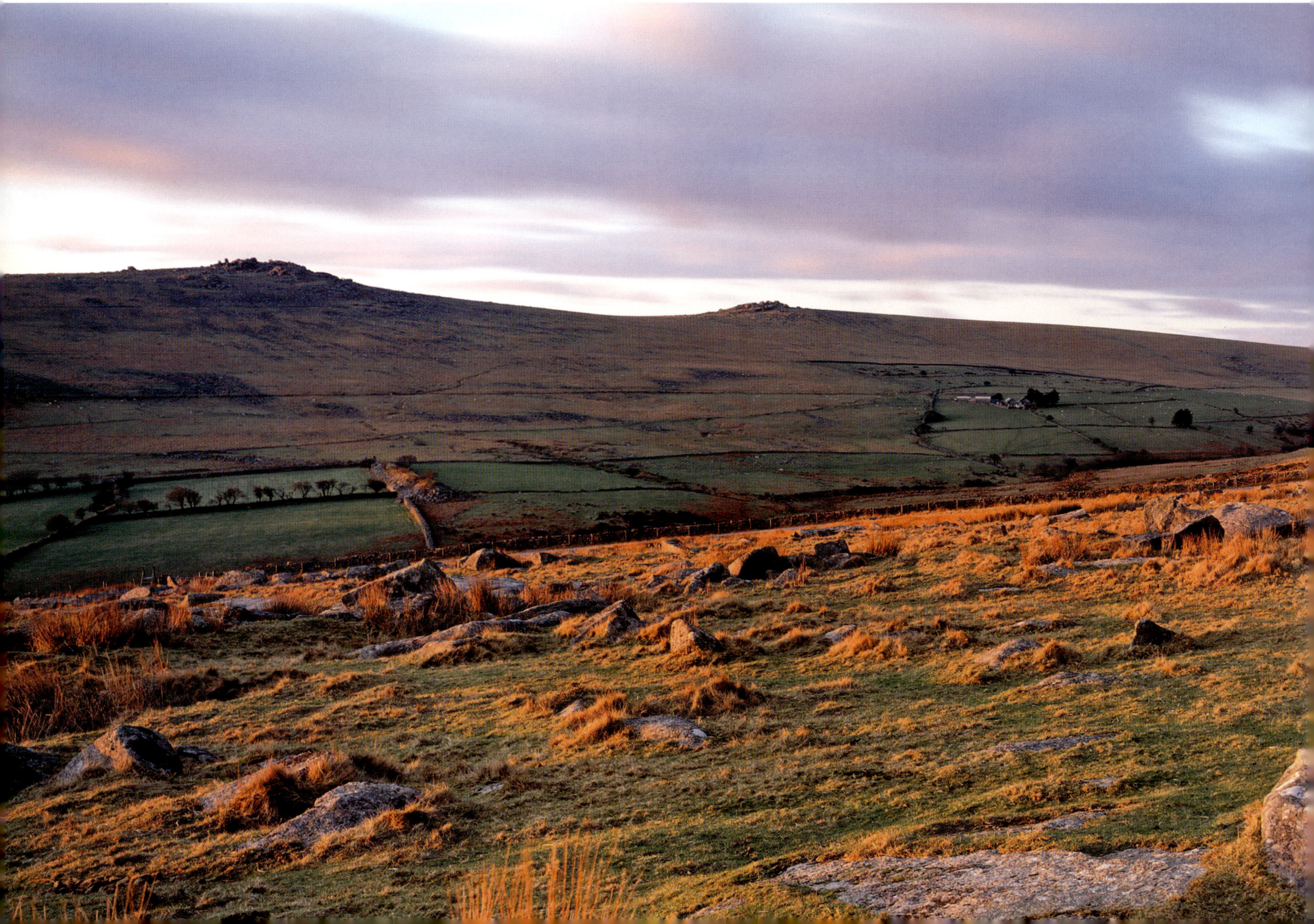

Staple and Roos tors seen from the snowy slopes of Great Mis Tor.

Picked out by the warm coloured light at sunset, this remarkable round stone disc lies surrounded by the ruins of ancient hut circles and stone rows. Great Mis Tor slopes smoothly down towards Merrivale.

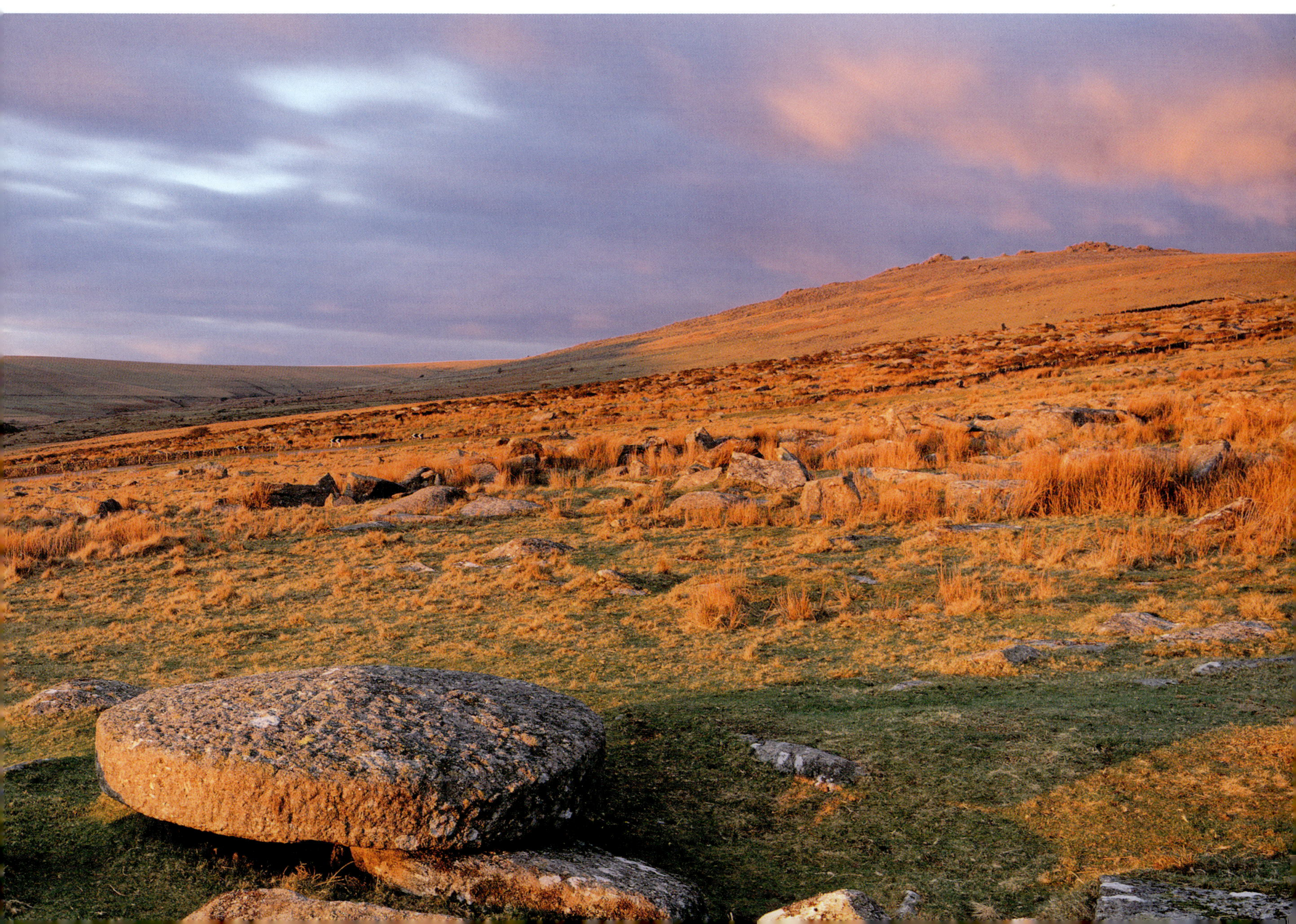

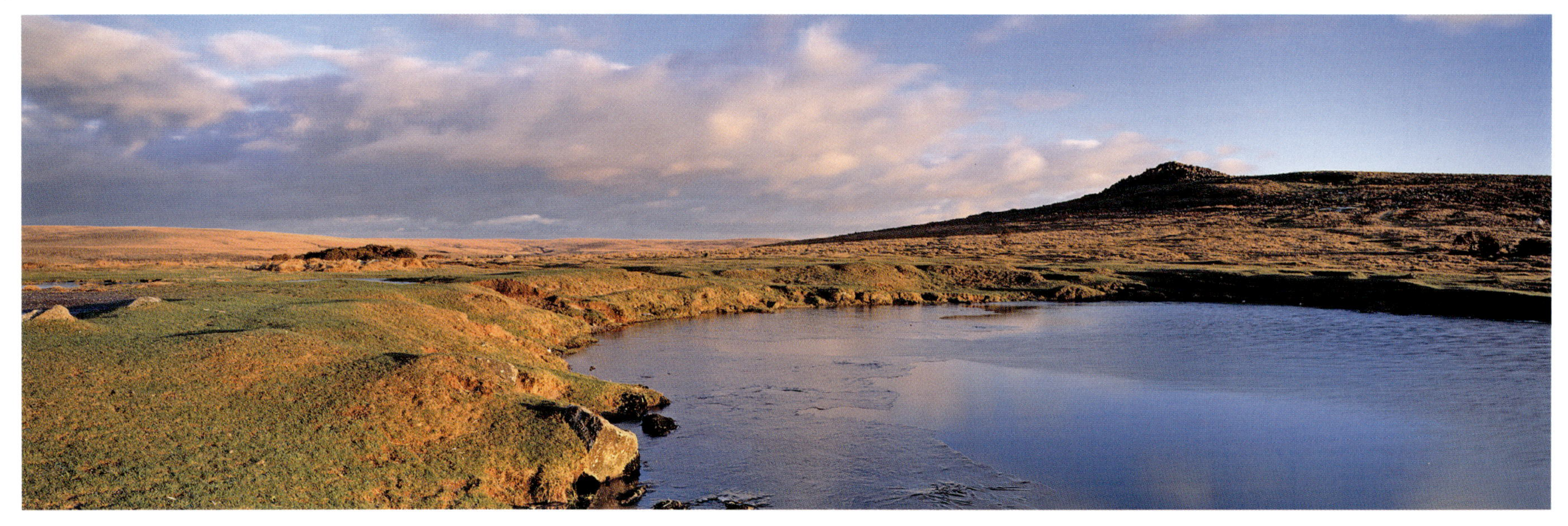

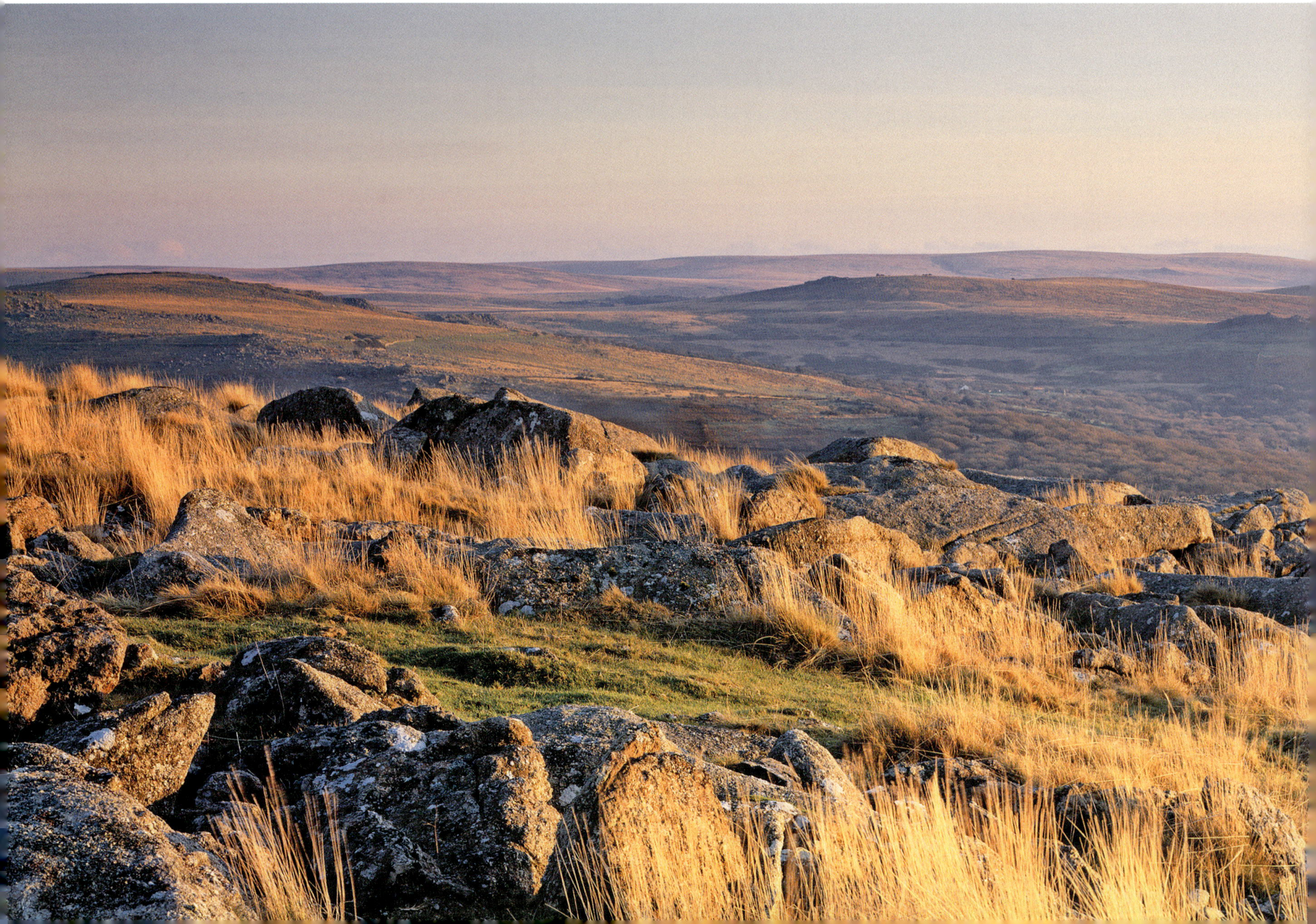

Evening sunlight at Sharpitor.

Despite the freezing winter, the late afternoon sunlight suggests a warm glow in the rocks and grasses on the side of Staple Tor, as the wild ponies graze the hillside in small groups.

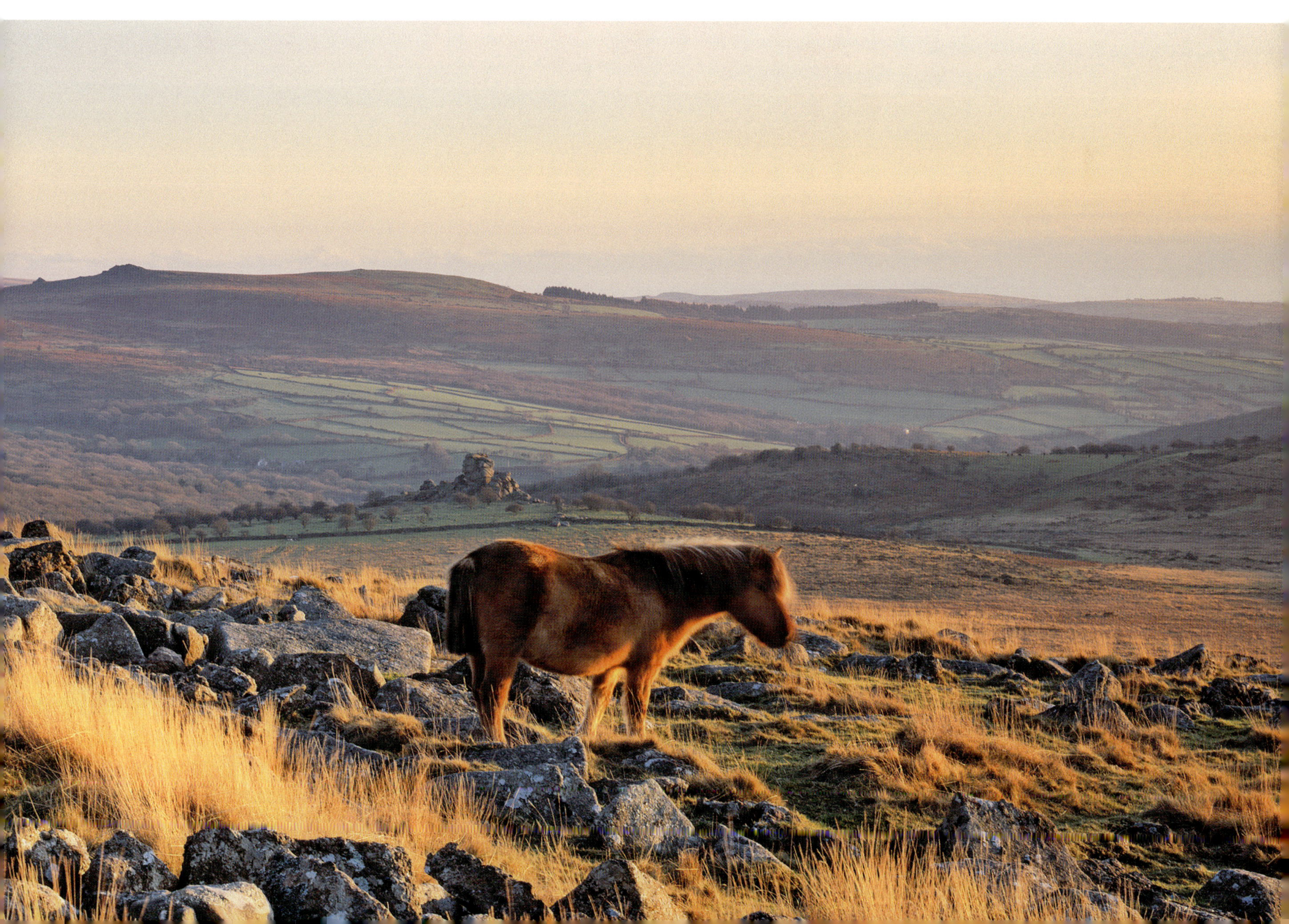

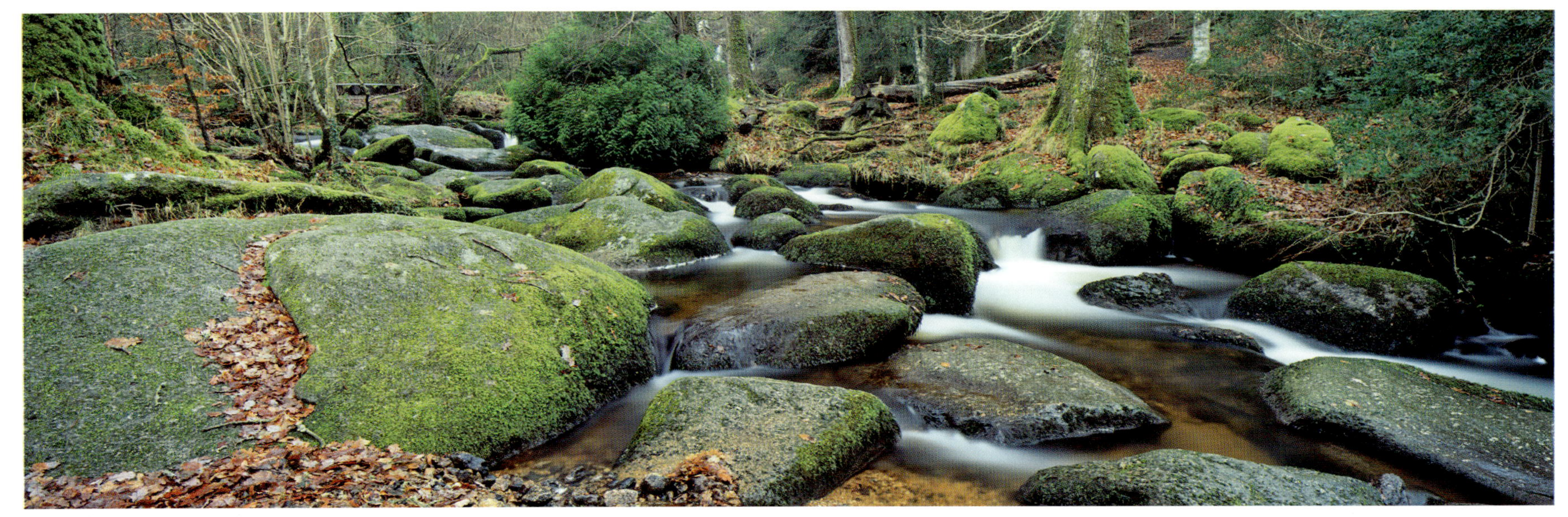

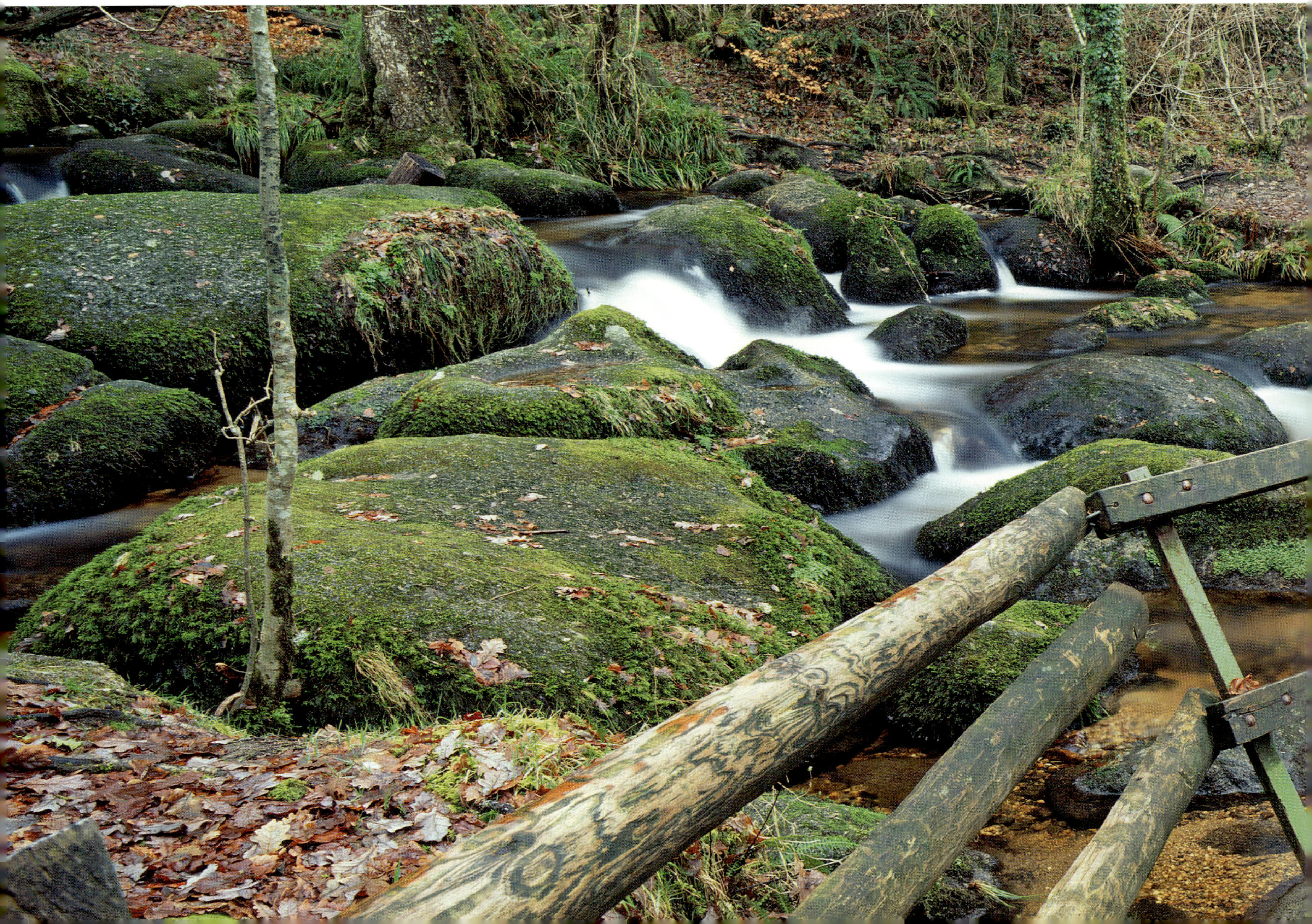

Becka Brook gently flows through Houndtor Woods. A step of faith is needed to cross this rickety footbridge. Its ravaged condition suggests that the river isn't always this calm.

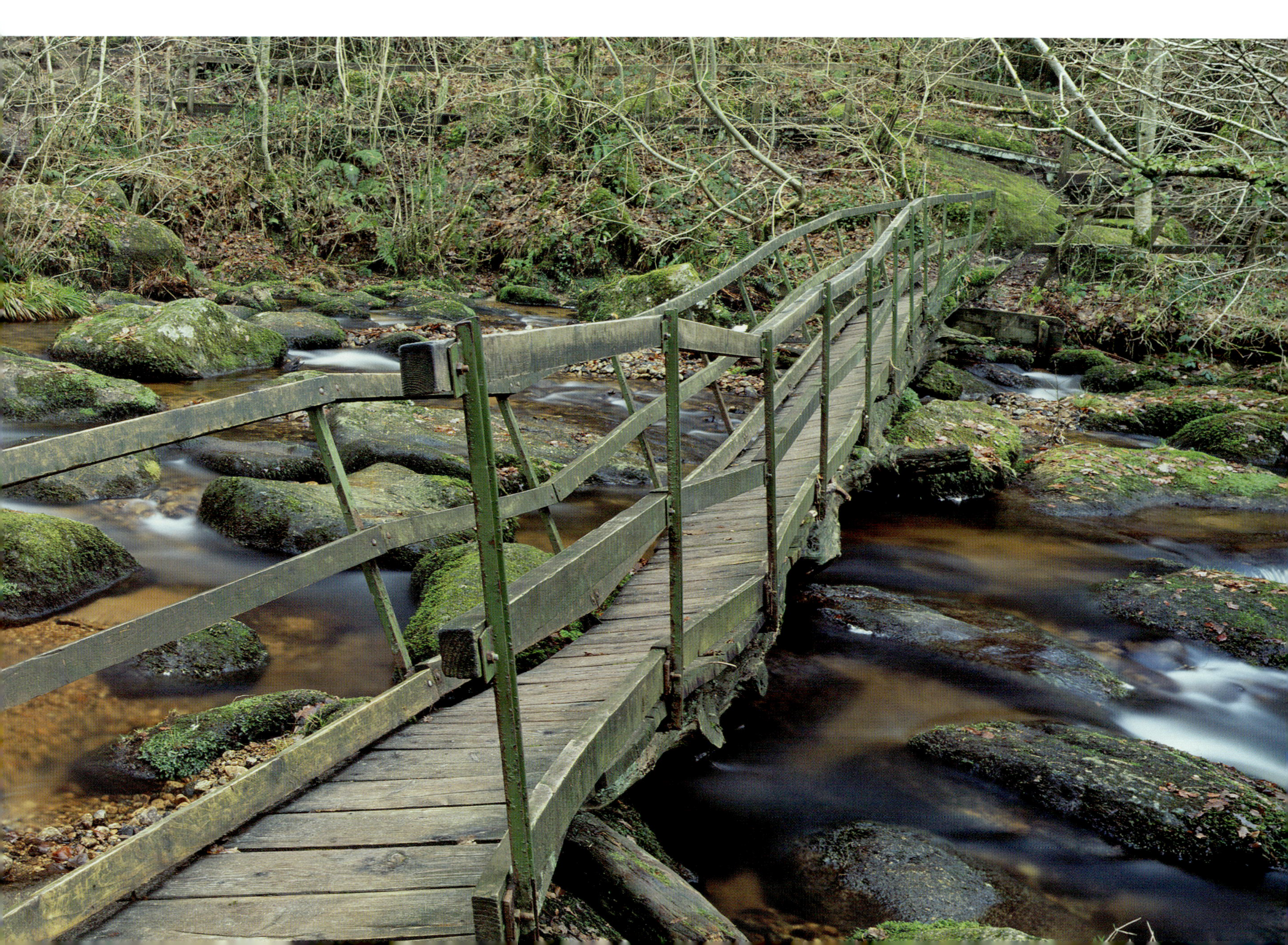

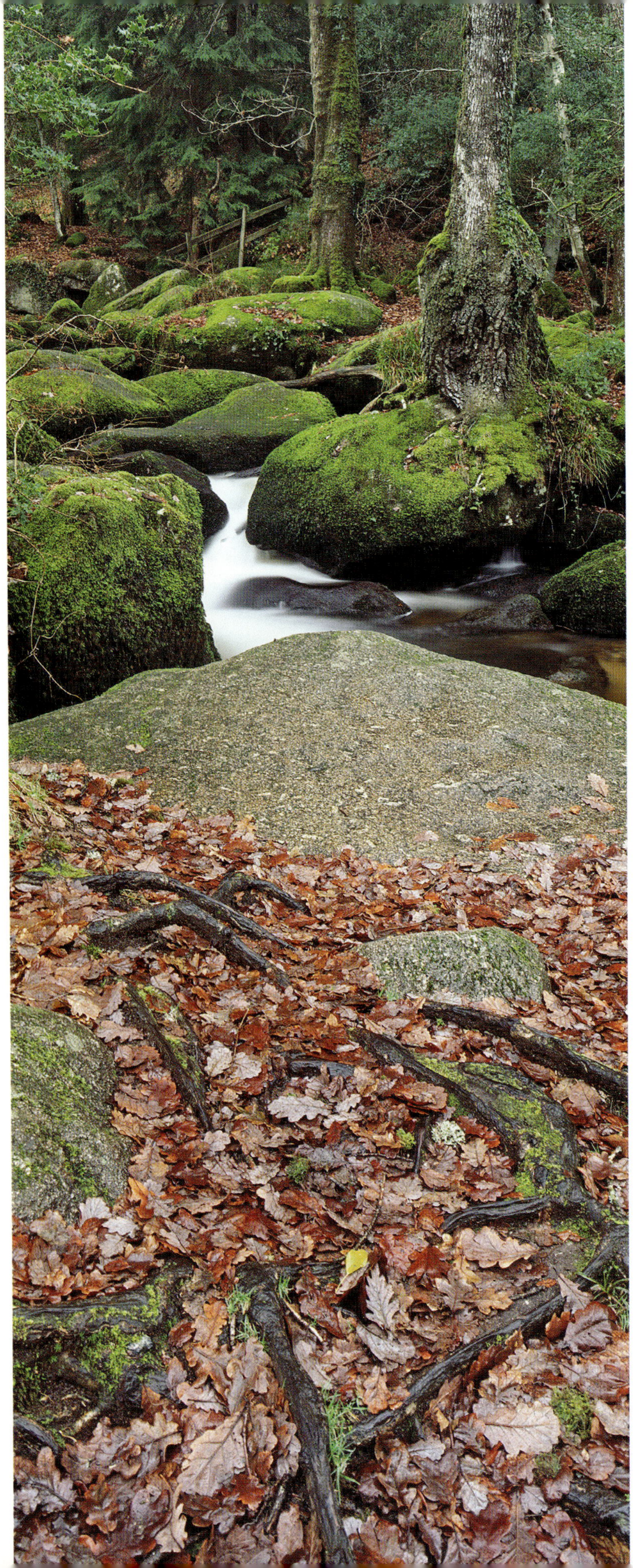

Moss-covered rocks line Becka Brook as it flows towards Bovey Tracy. The roots of trees weave in and out of dry leaves to create a tapestry as they grasp the rocks for stability.

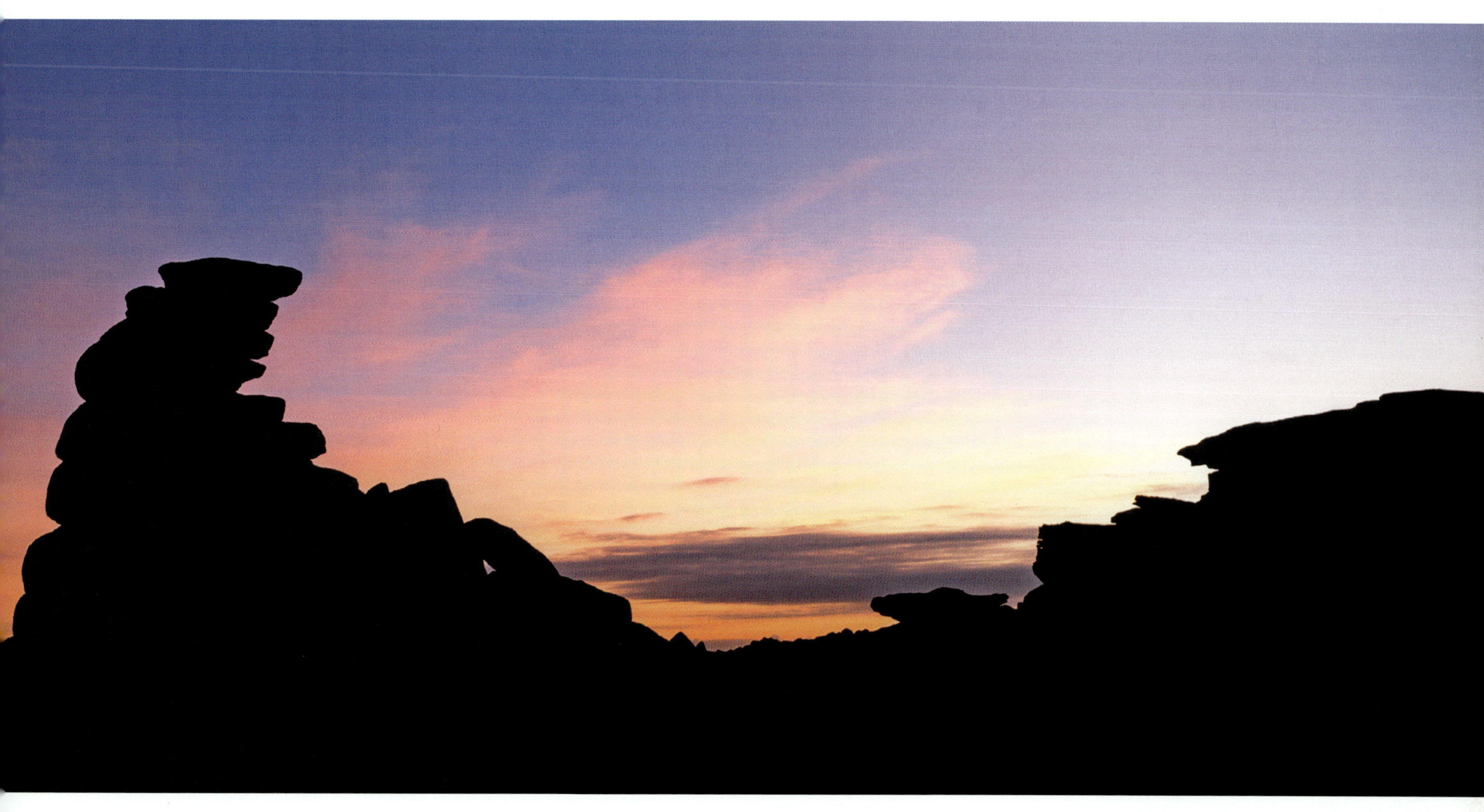

Last light of a winter's day produces a stunning display of colours in the clouds, silhouetting Staple Tor.

Granite rocks lie strewn across the slopes of Sharpitor, looking towards Leather Tor in the evening sunlight.

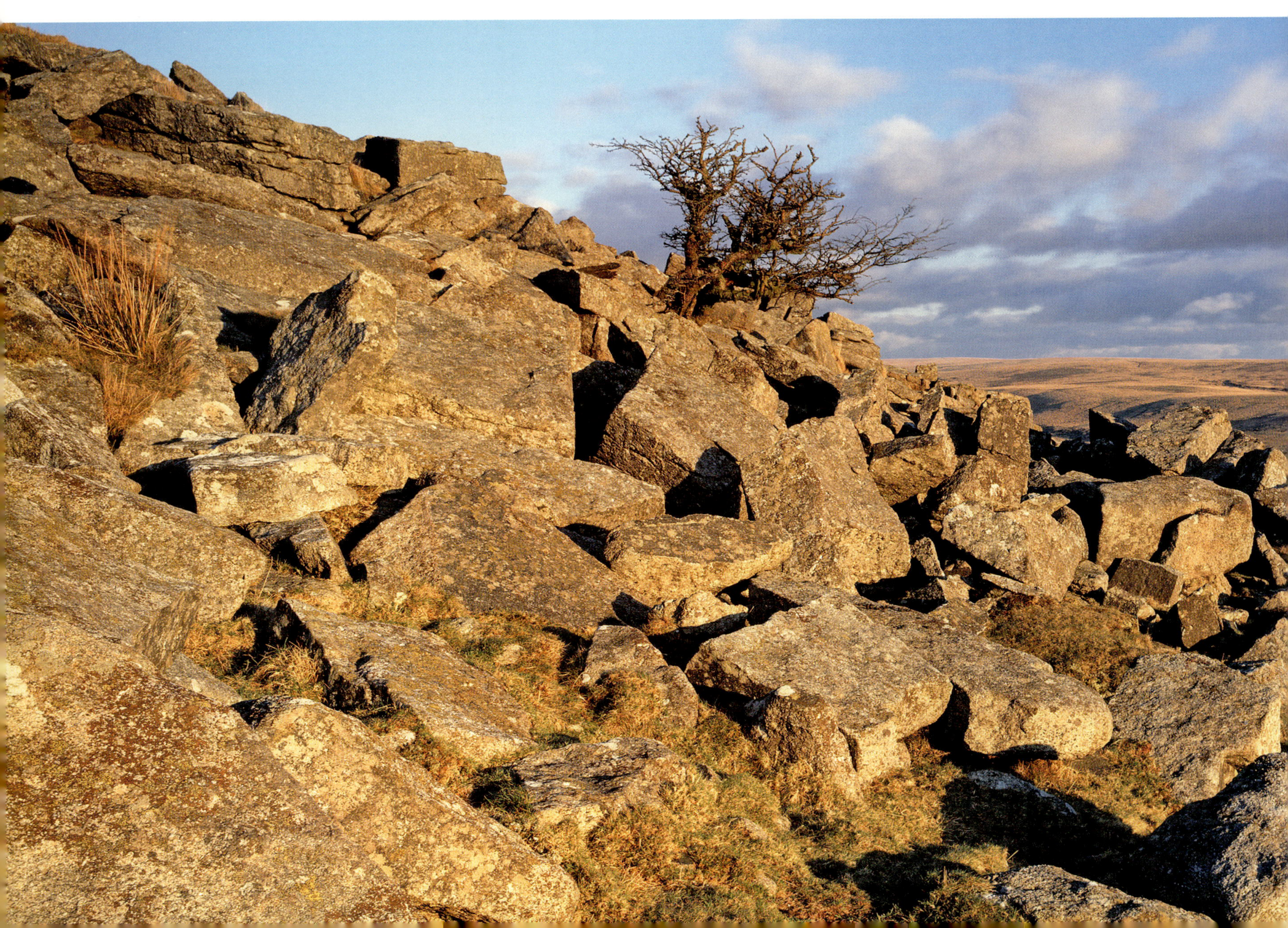

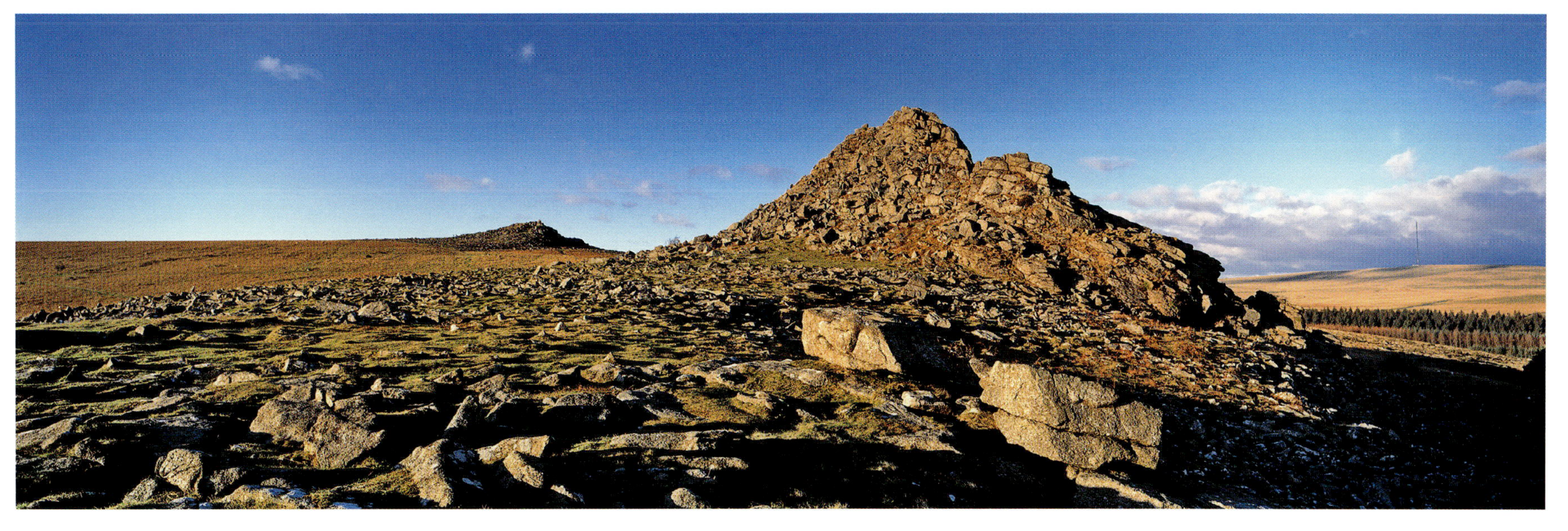

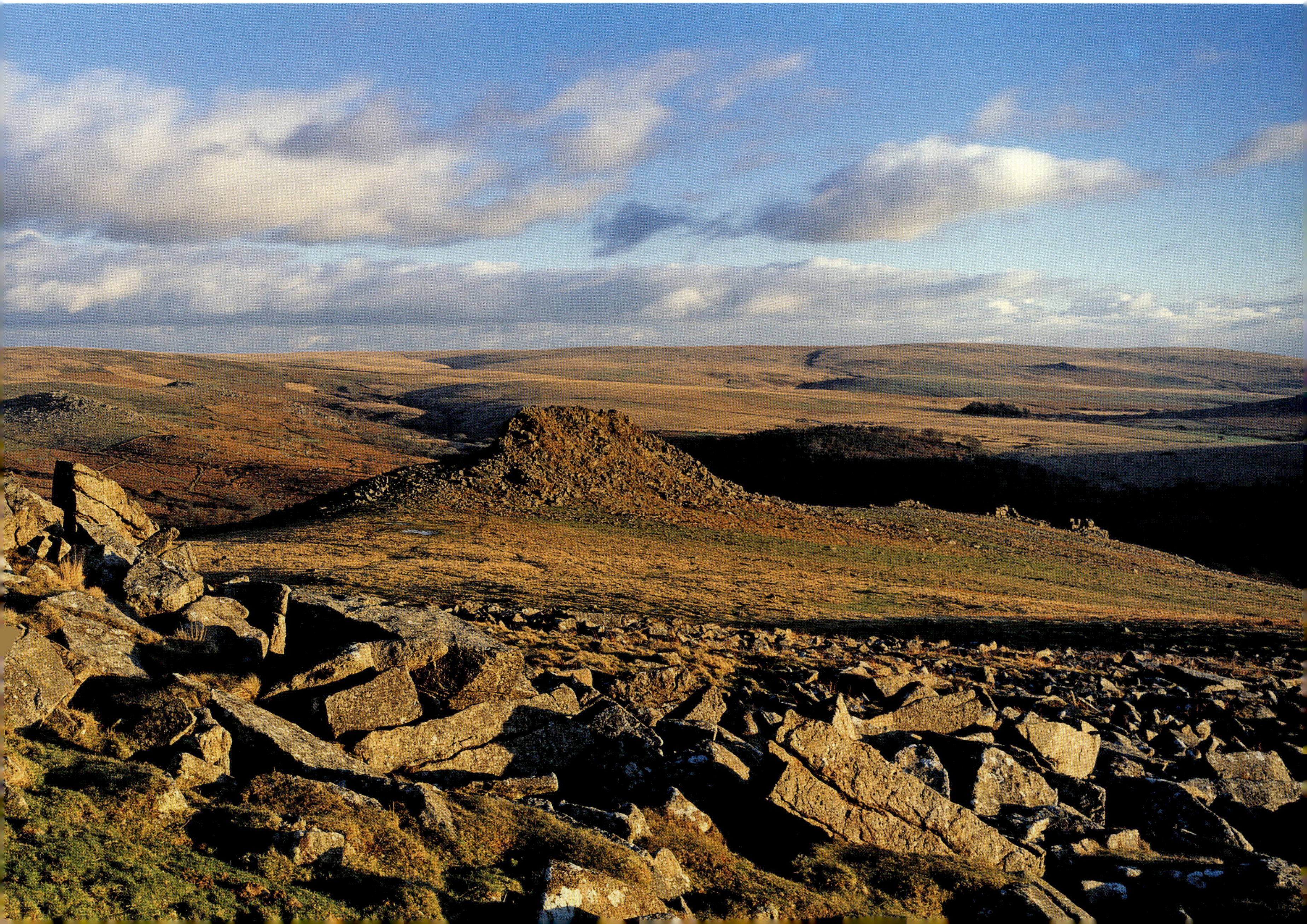

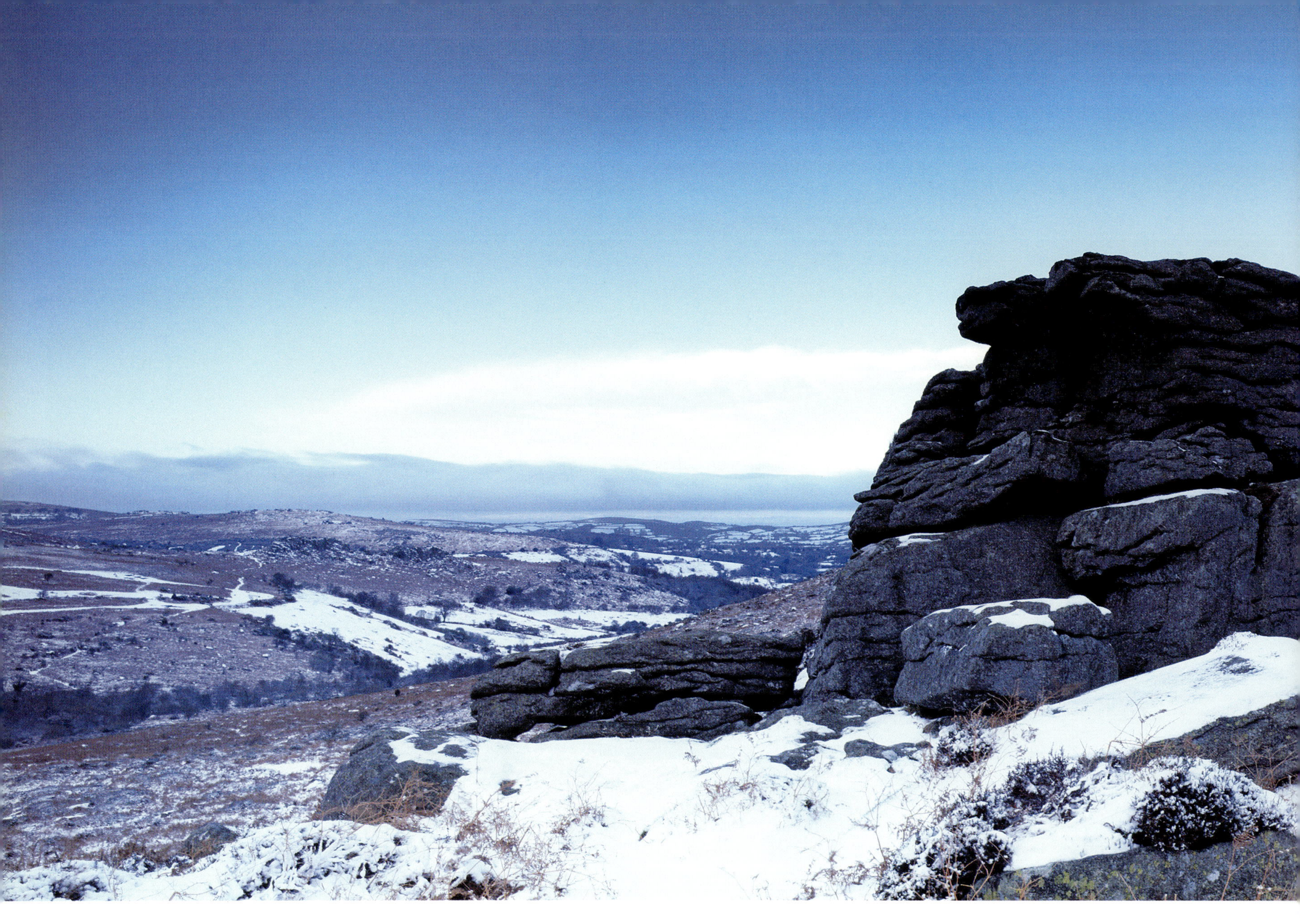

This windswept hawthorn tree between Saddle Tor and Haytor is a favourite haunt of mine. The tree survives in what can be a bleak setting, facing out towards Great Hound Tor in the distance. Both of these photographs were taken in winter: one in the afternoon with a thin blanket of snow, and the other on a crisp morning with the sun's weak rays warming the rocks and bracken.

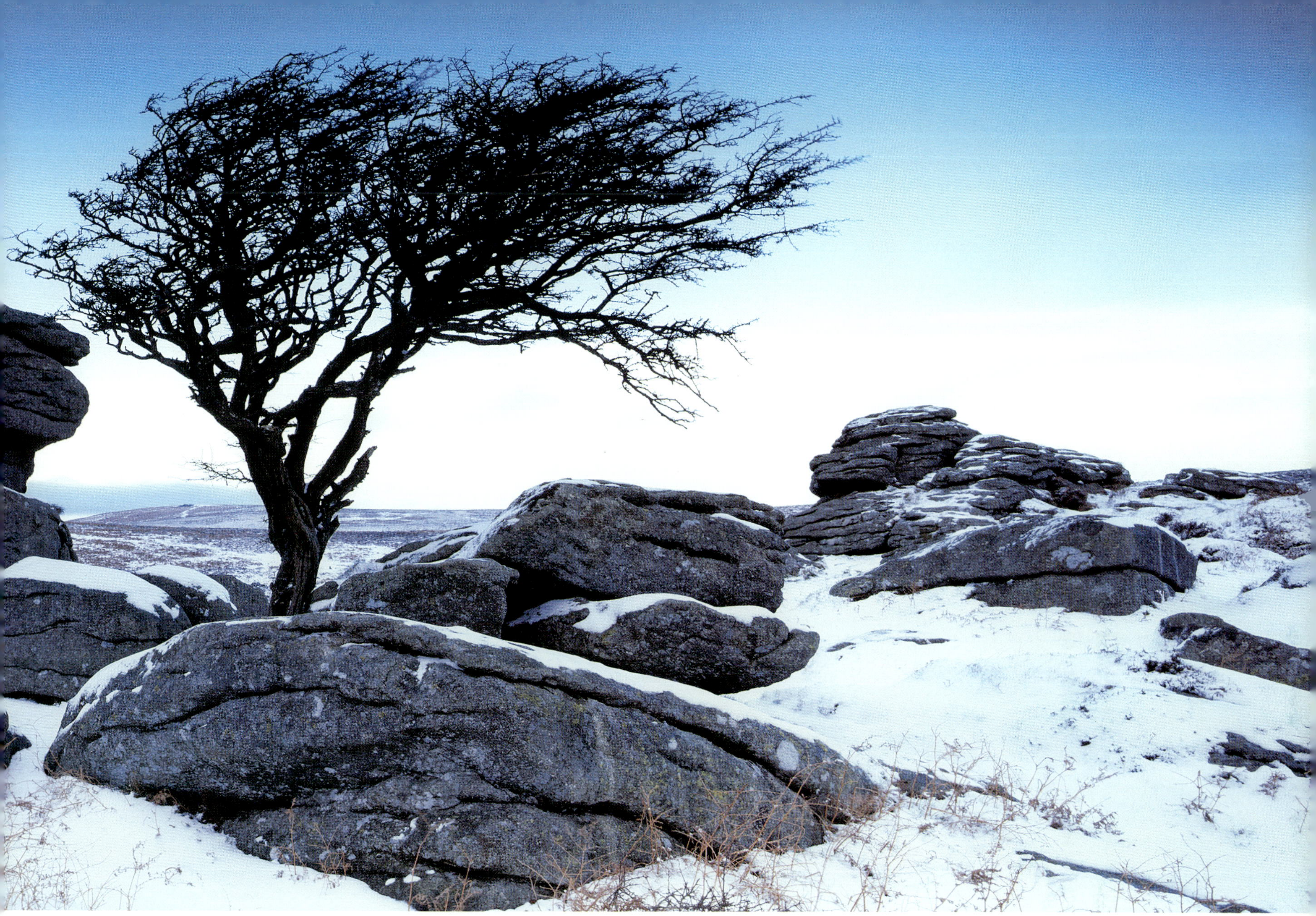

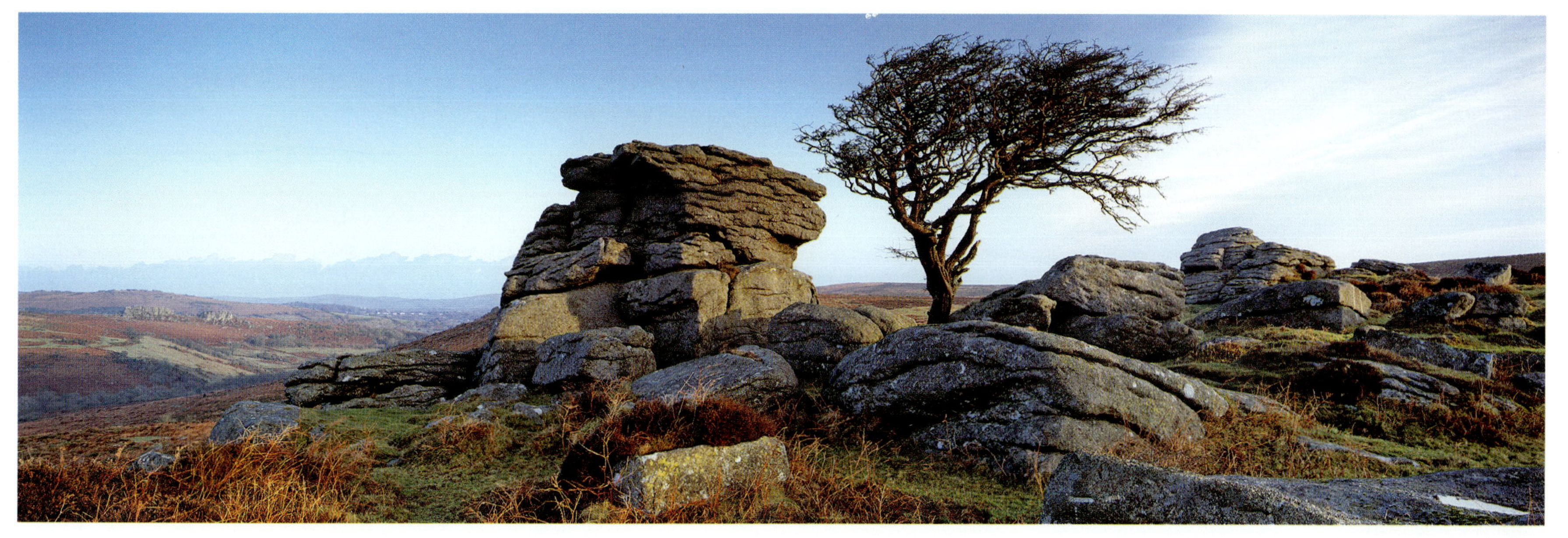

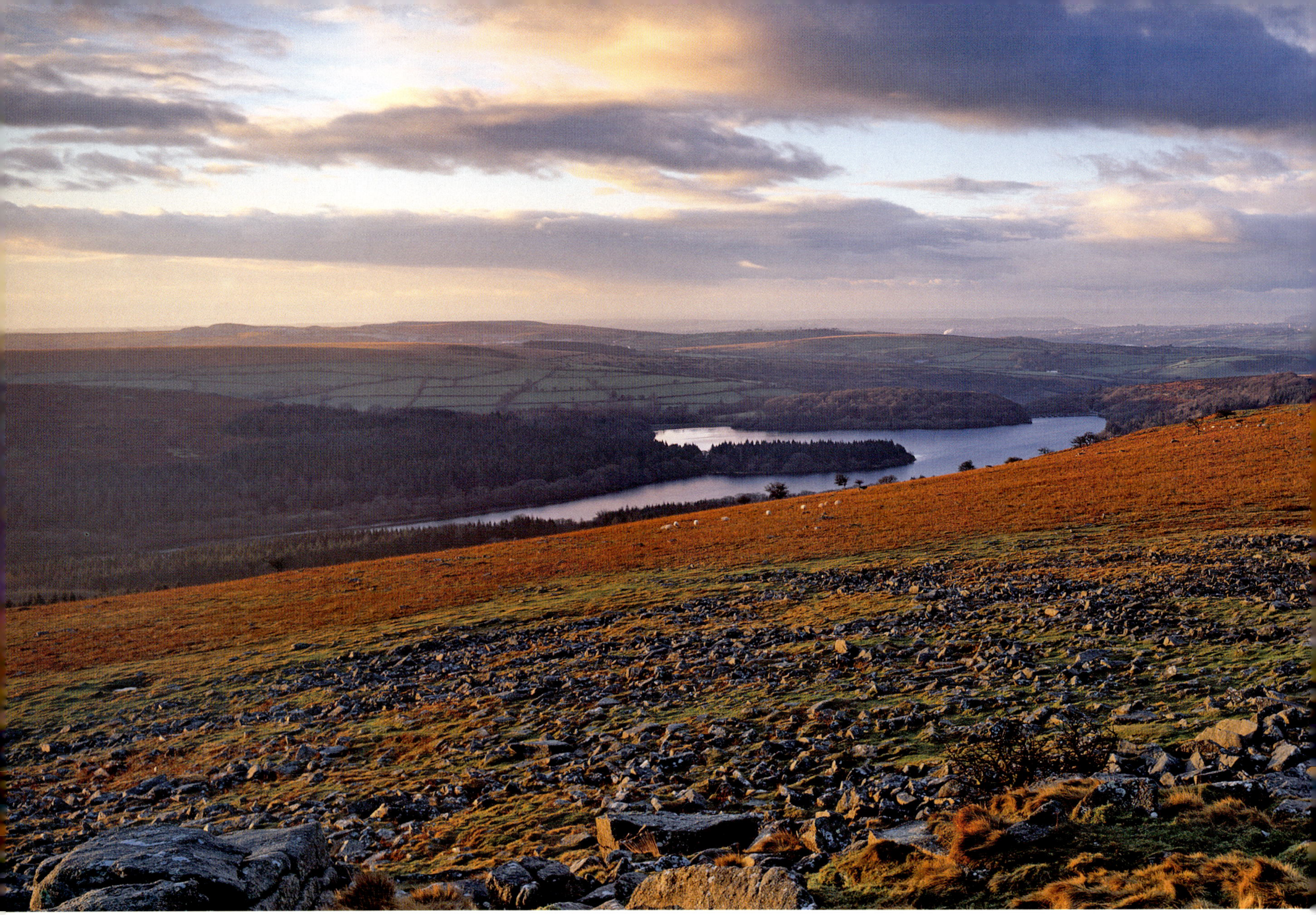

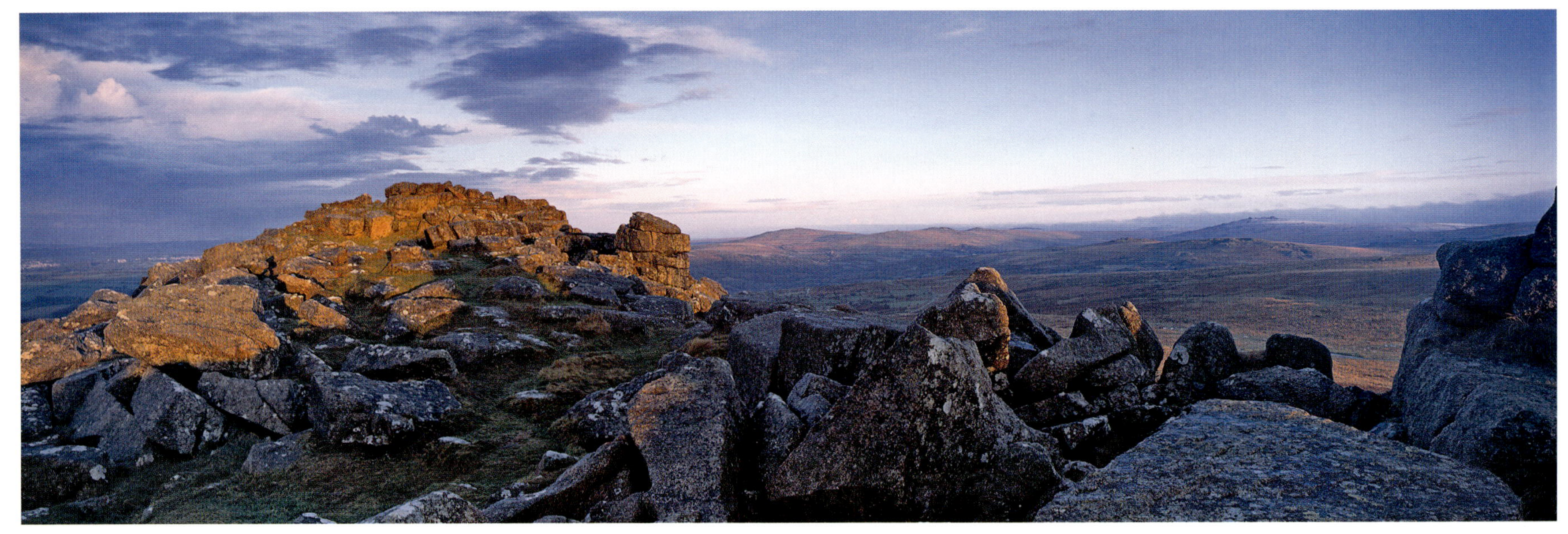

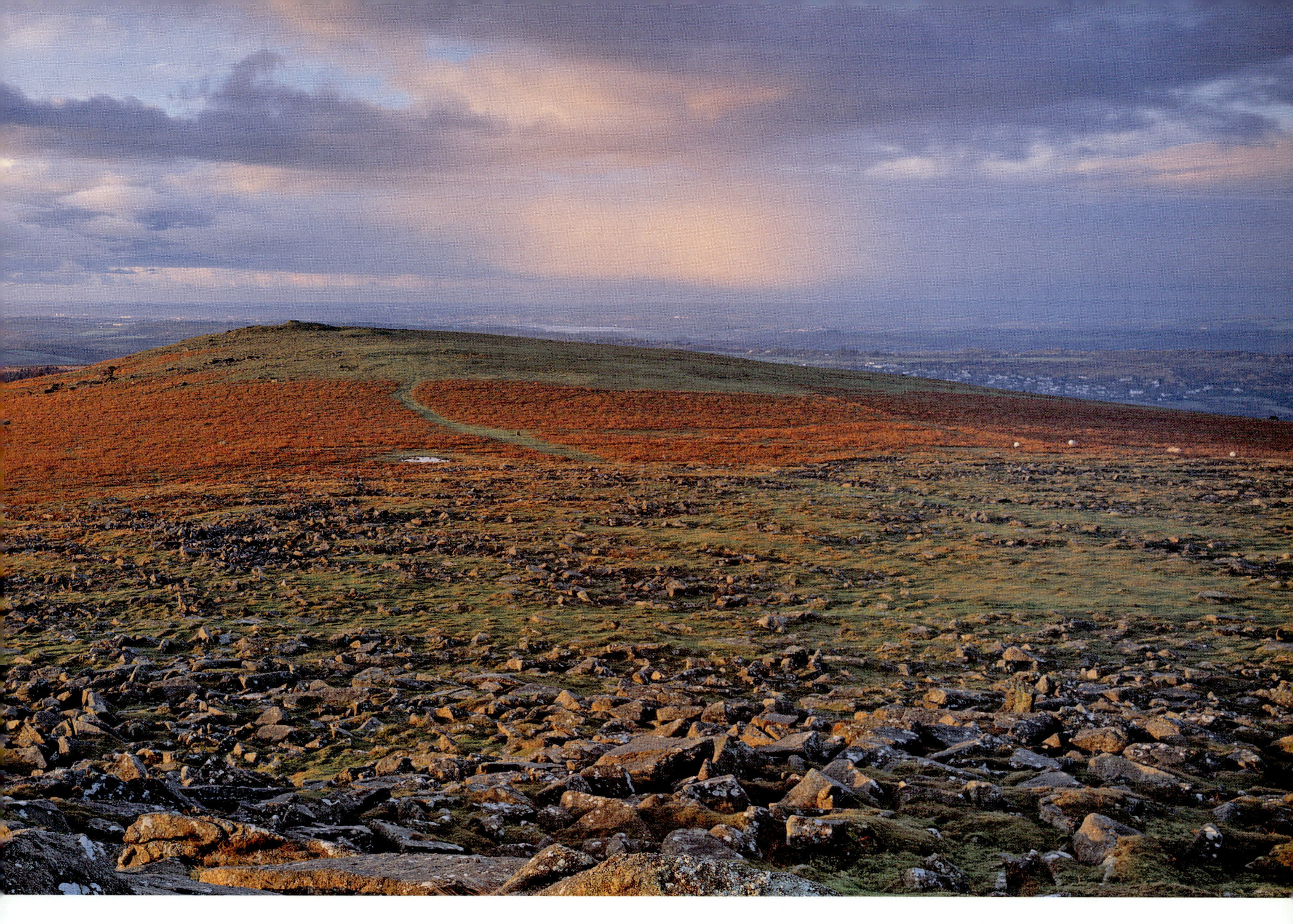

Looking south across Peak Hill, the brilliance of the clouds is reflected in the shining surface of Burrator Reservoir. In the distance the city of Plymouth wakes at the start of another day.

After a climb in the dark to the top of Sharpitor near Burrator Reservoir, the reward is a glimpse of the first rays of sunlight picking out the rocky summit. Clouds move quickly south in the strong wind on the crisp, cold January morning to create a constantly changing outlook.

On the summit of Heckwood Tor
a rounded granite rock sits perfectly
balanced as if placed intentionally.
A hardy tree defies the elements and
clings onto life in the rocky landscape.

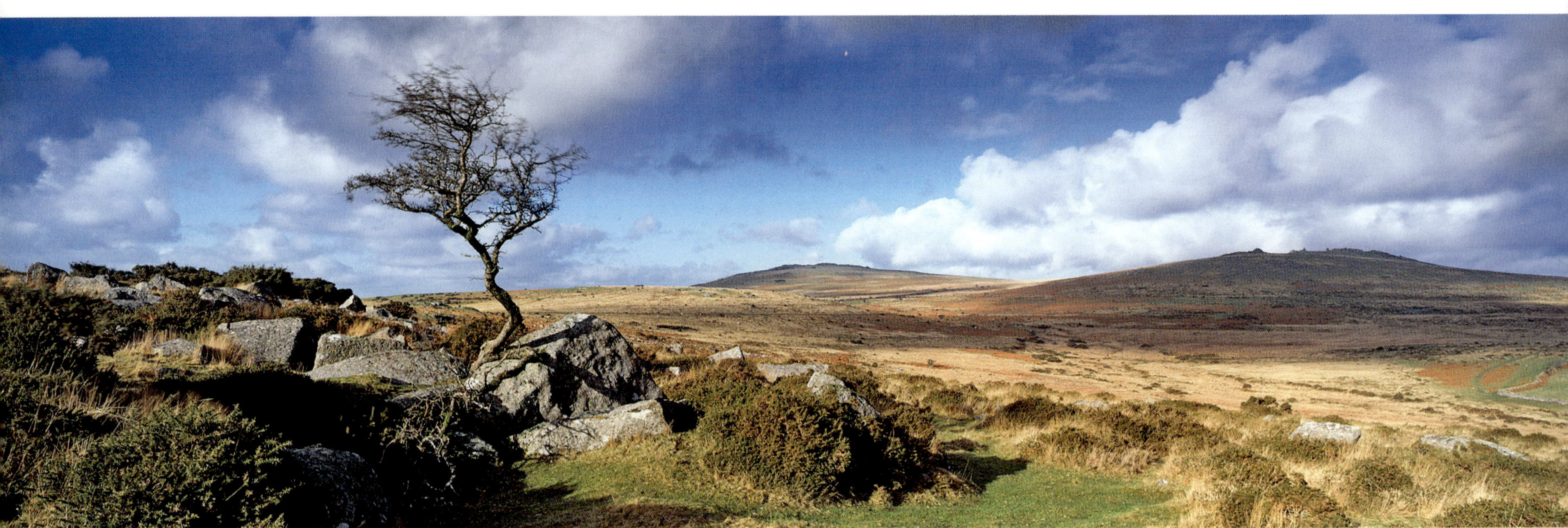

On the side of Heckwood Tor
a small lonely tree clings to life
amongst rocks and grasses.
Cox Tor and Great Staple Tor
appear behind as the landscape is
dappled with sunlight and shadow
from the clouds above.

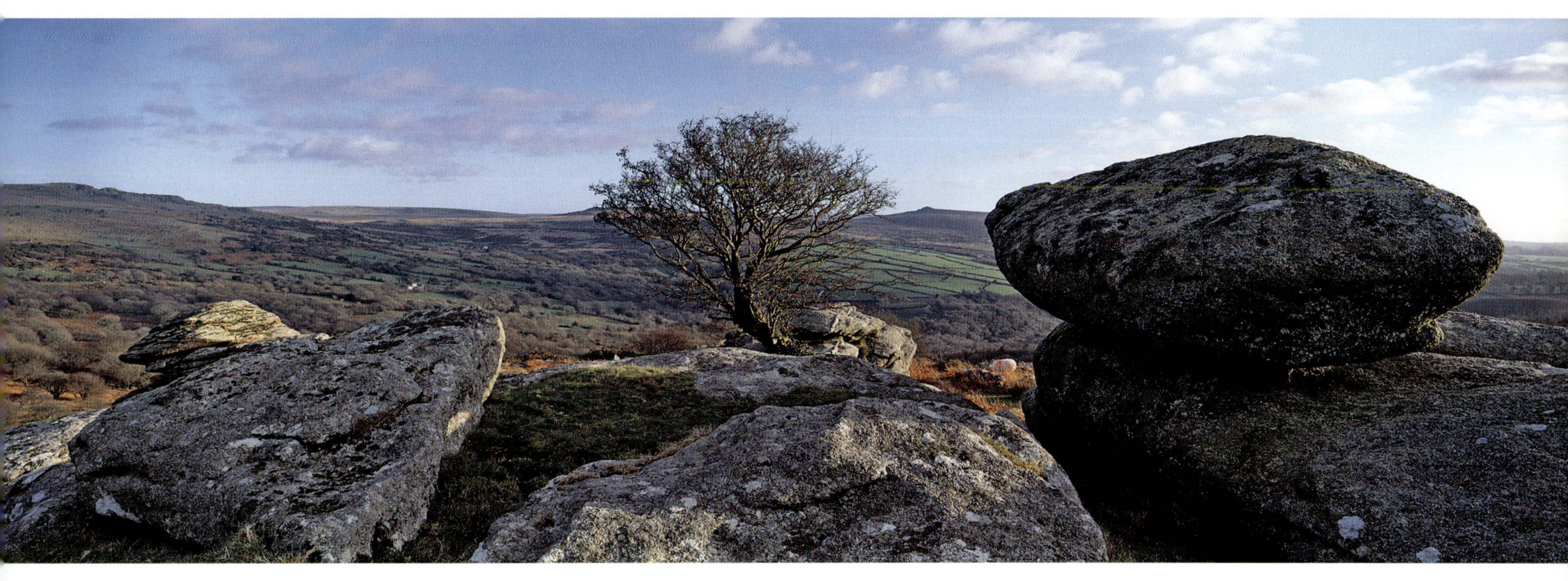

A giant rock found at Roos Tor near Tavistock has balanced in this way for hundreds of years. Dramatic rock formations like this give Dartmoor its identity and charm. Looking east towards the higher summit of Great Mis Tor on a crisp winter's day.

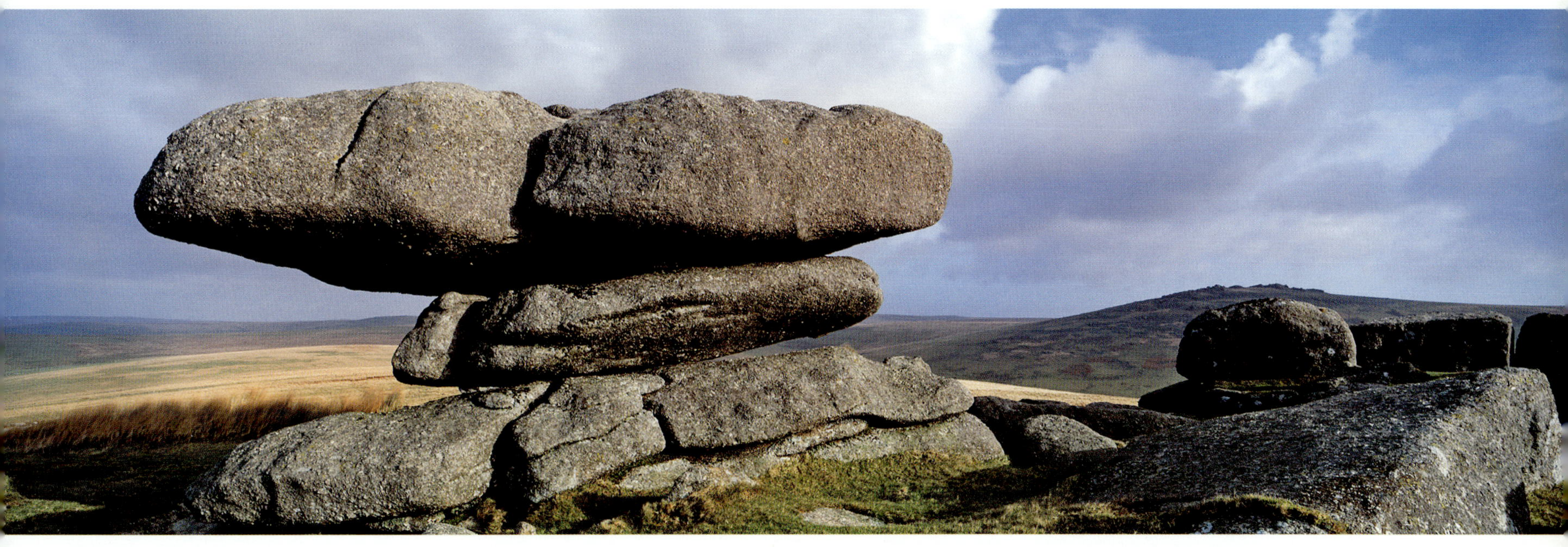

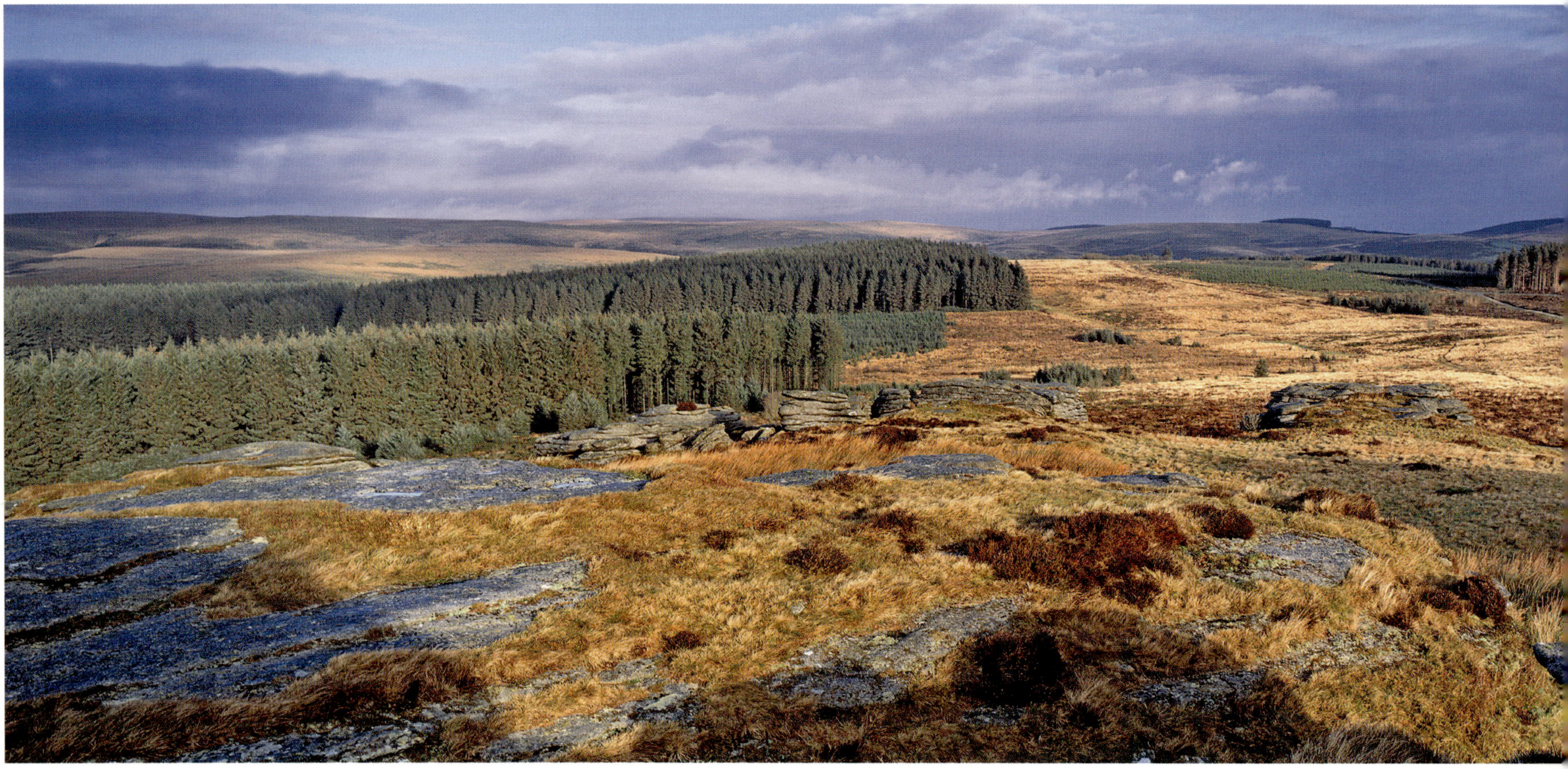

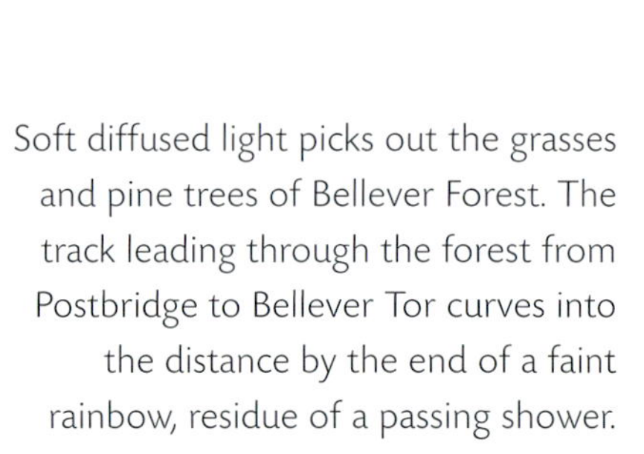

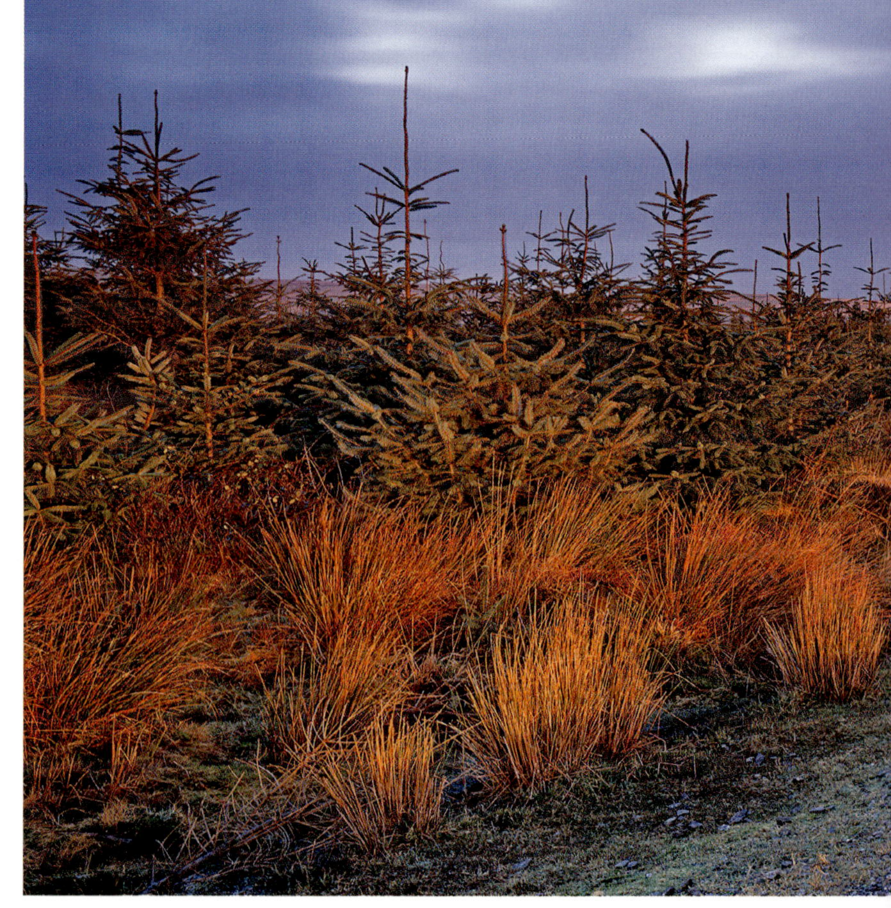

Soft diffused light picks out the grasses and pine trees of Bellever Forest. The track leading through the forest from Postbridge to Bellever Tor curves into the distance by the end of a faint rainbow, residue of a passing shower.

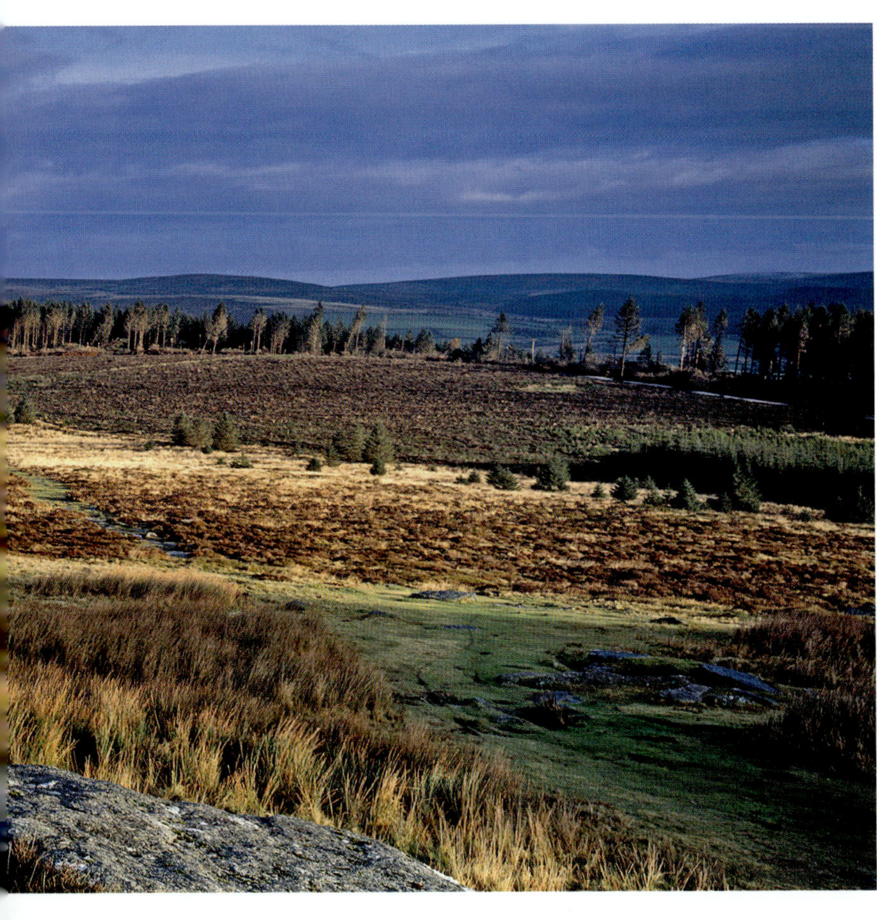

A view of Bellever Forest taken from Bellever Tor. In years gone by, much of Dartmoor was covered in forest before it was cleared by the earliest settlers. Bellever is one place where trees stand again as new timber is farmed by the Forestry Commission.

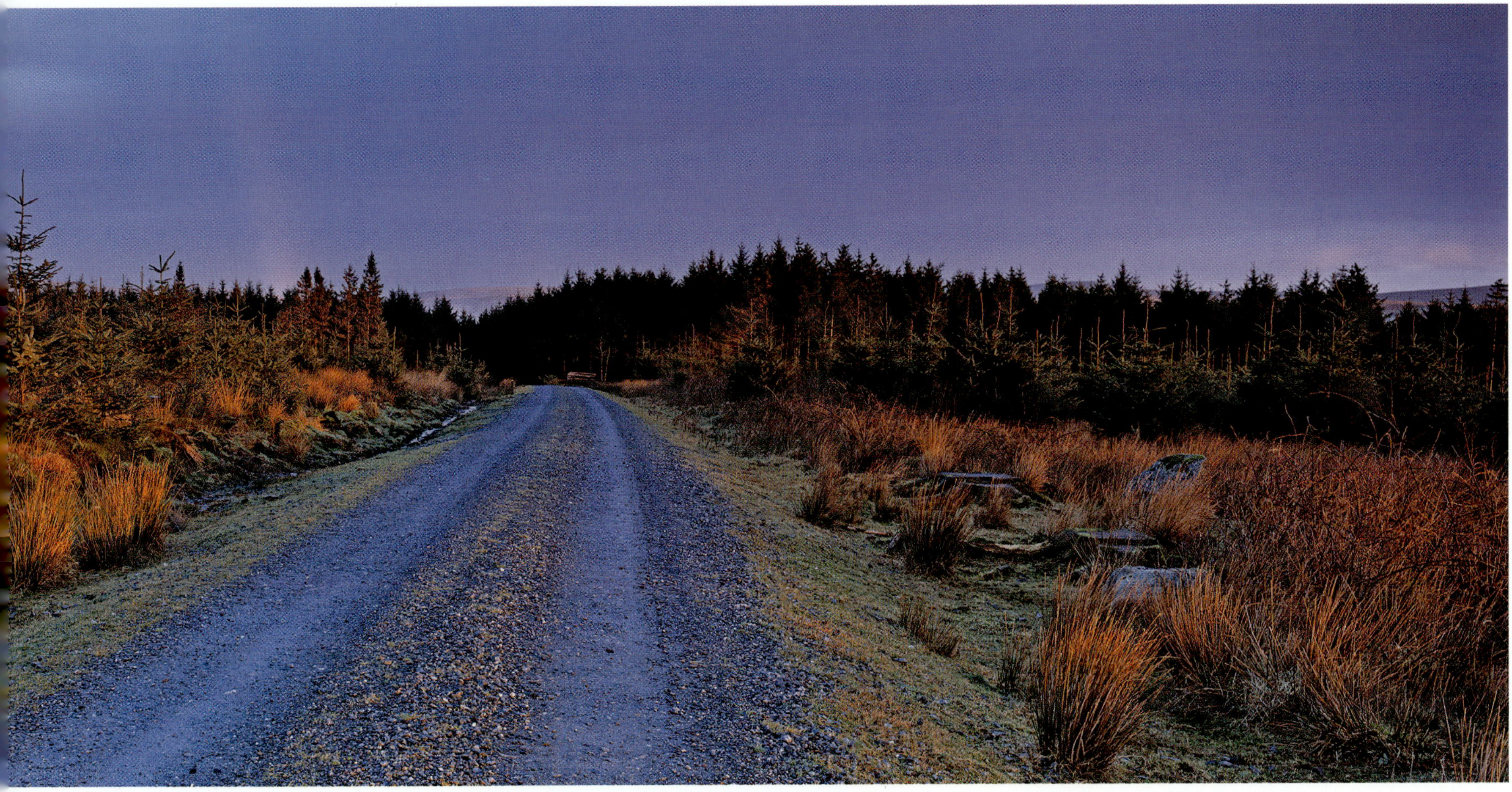

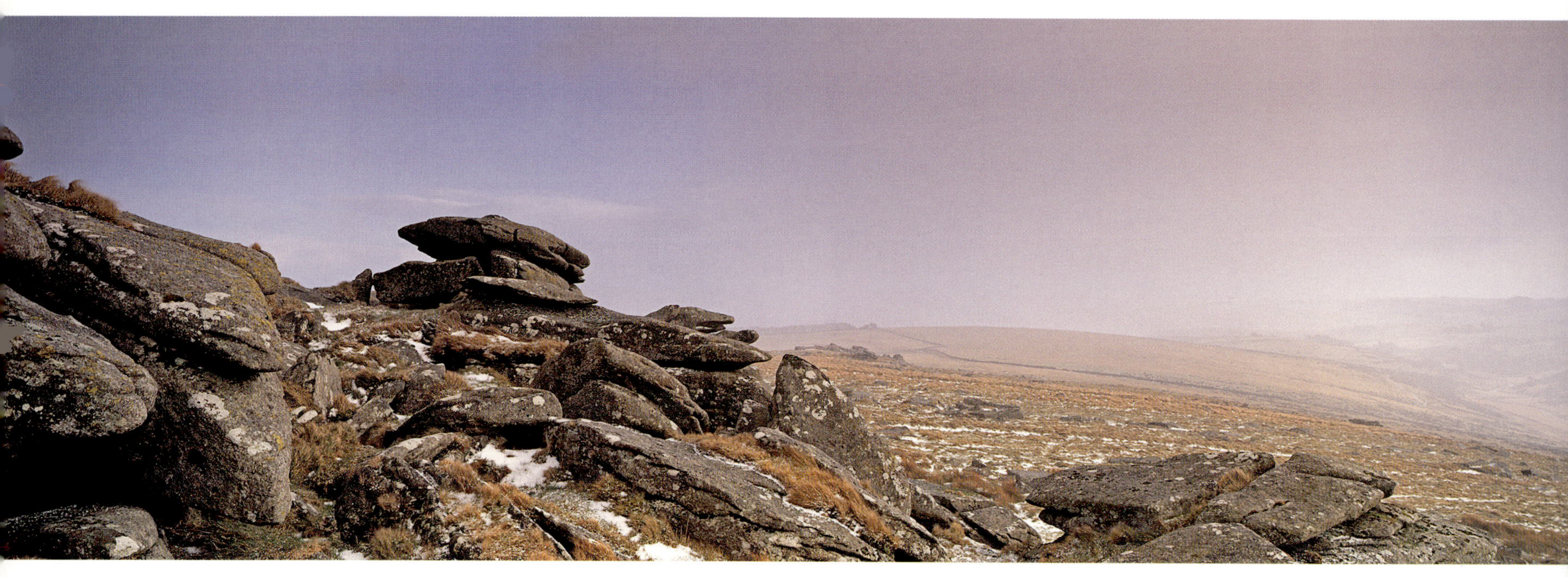

A small dusting of snow and hail sits amongst the tufts of yellow grasses at Hollow Tor near Princetown. Dark clouds dominate the day, with some glimpses of sunlight through breaks in the clouds.

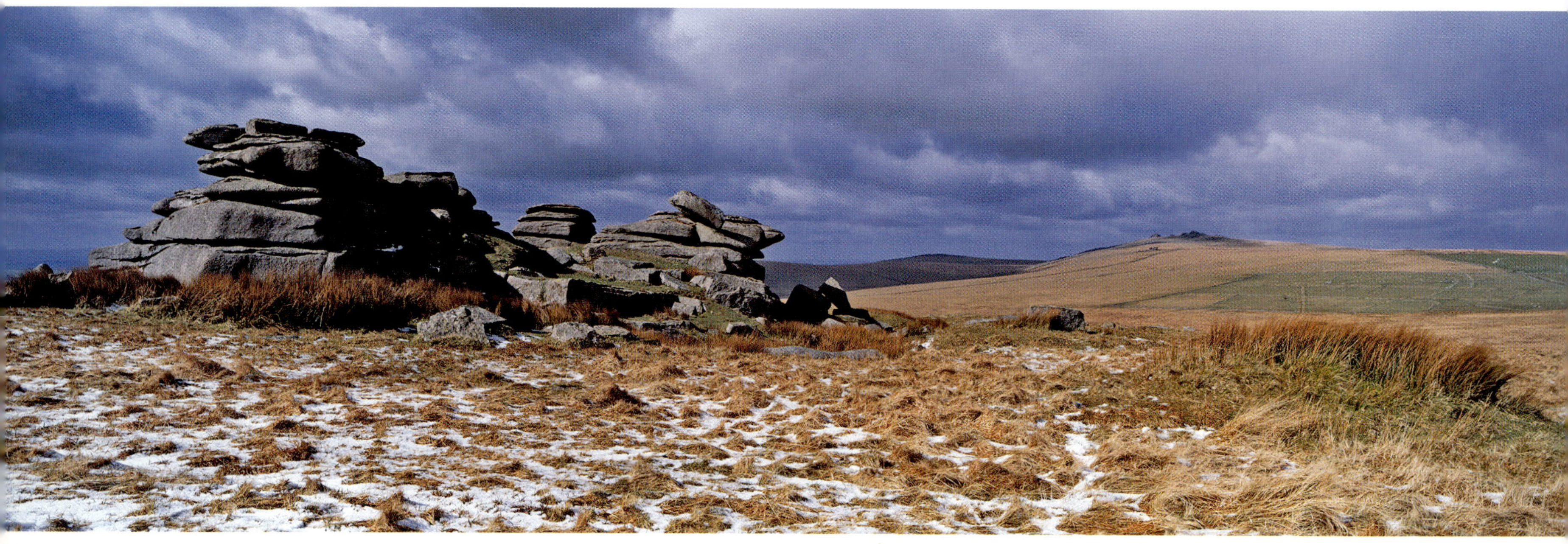

A hailstorm sweeps over Littaford Tor near Wistman's Wood and Two Bridges.

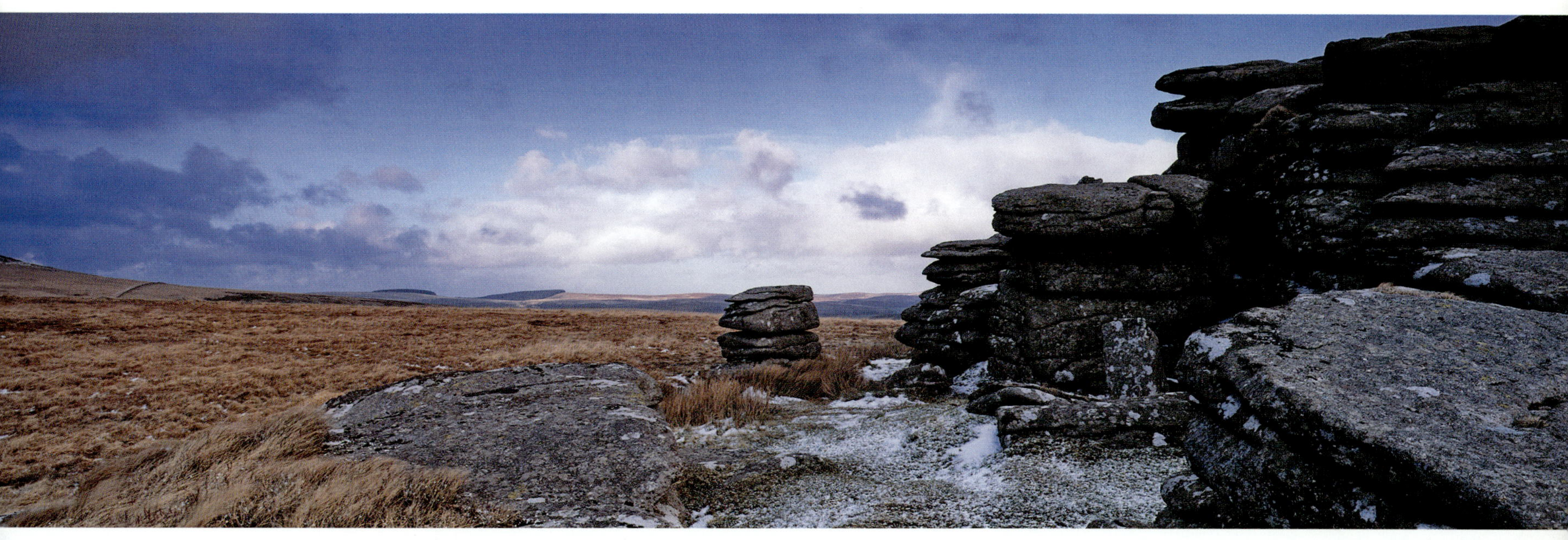

A passing shower of hailstones leaves a white sprinkling at Littaford Tor on a chilly winter afternoon. The same location is transformed just a few months later with the fresh summer growth and warm sunlight, see page 77.

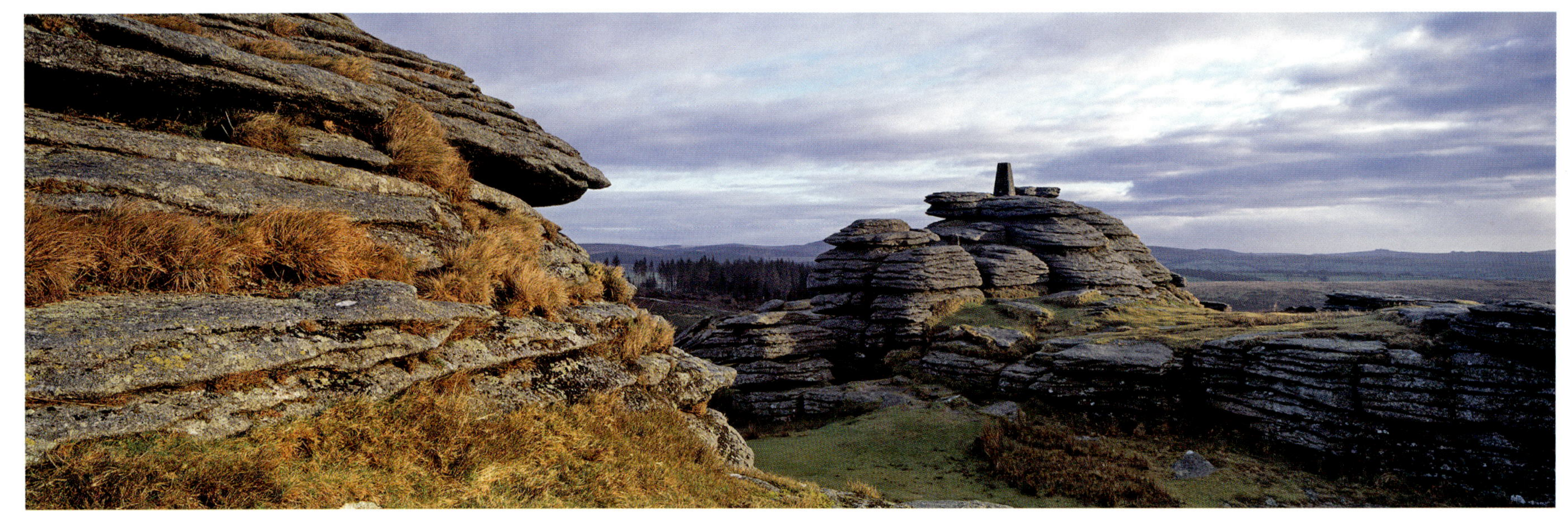

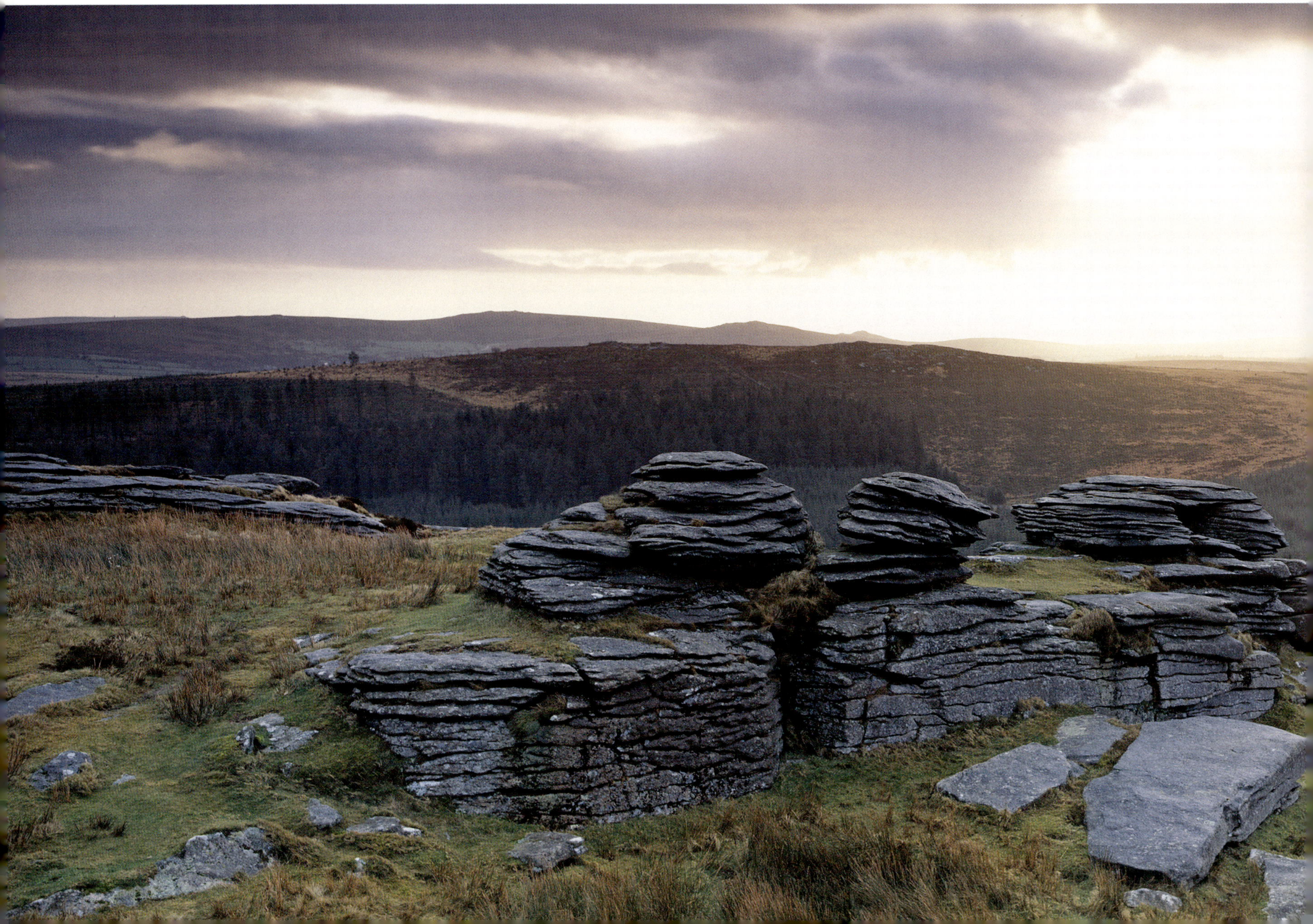

A triangulation pillar, or trig point, marks the summit of Bellever Tor near Postbridge. Used for surveying purposes, it remains a useful marker for hikers and walkers.

The view south from Bellever Tor. Wild ponies can be seen grazing on the slopes of Bellever from the footpath that meanders down towards the West Dart River and Dartmeet.

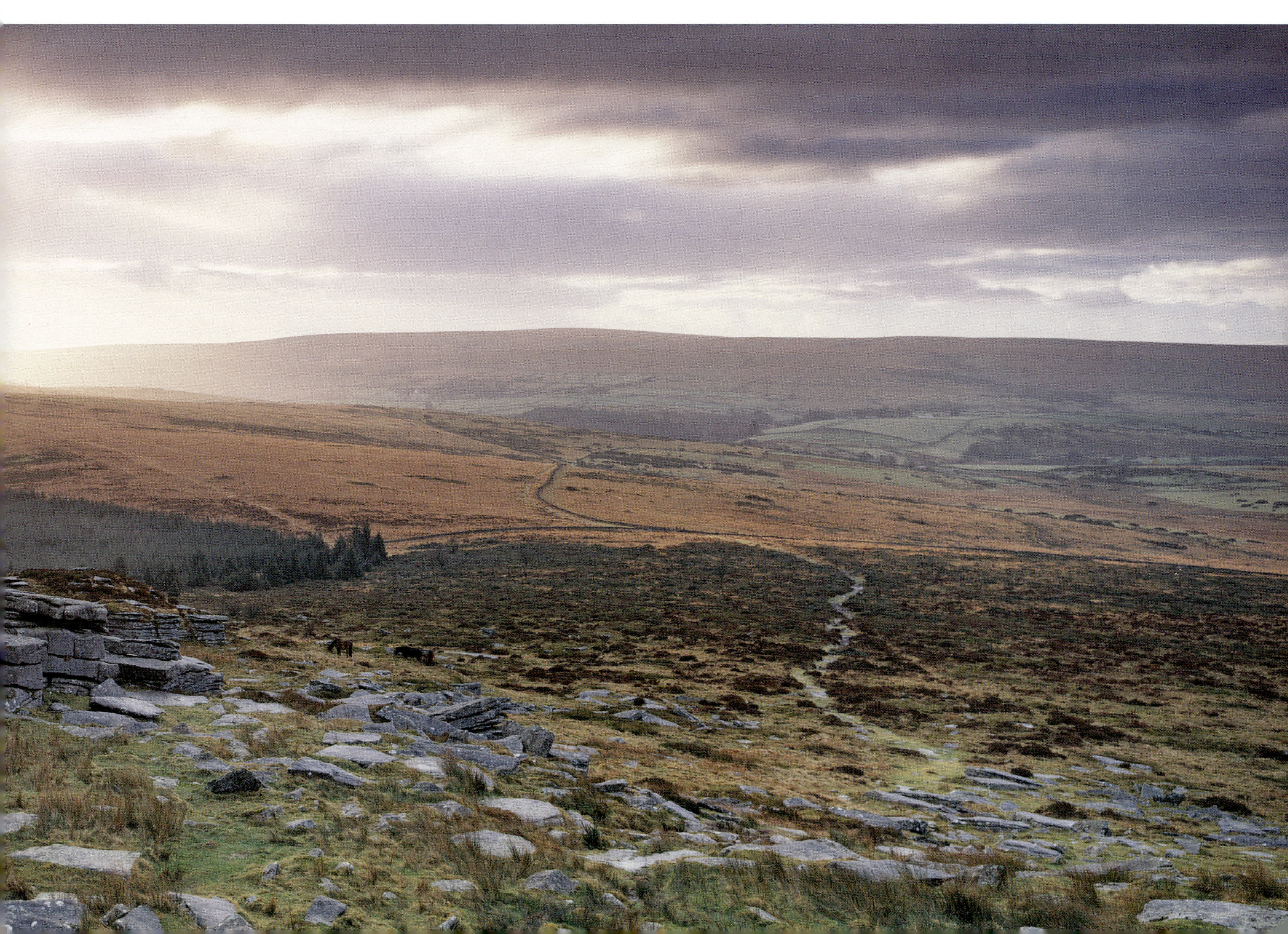

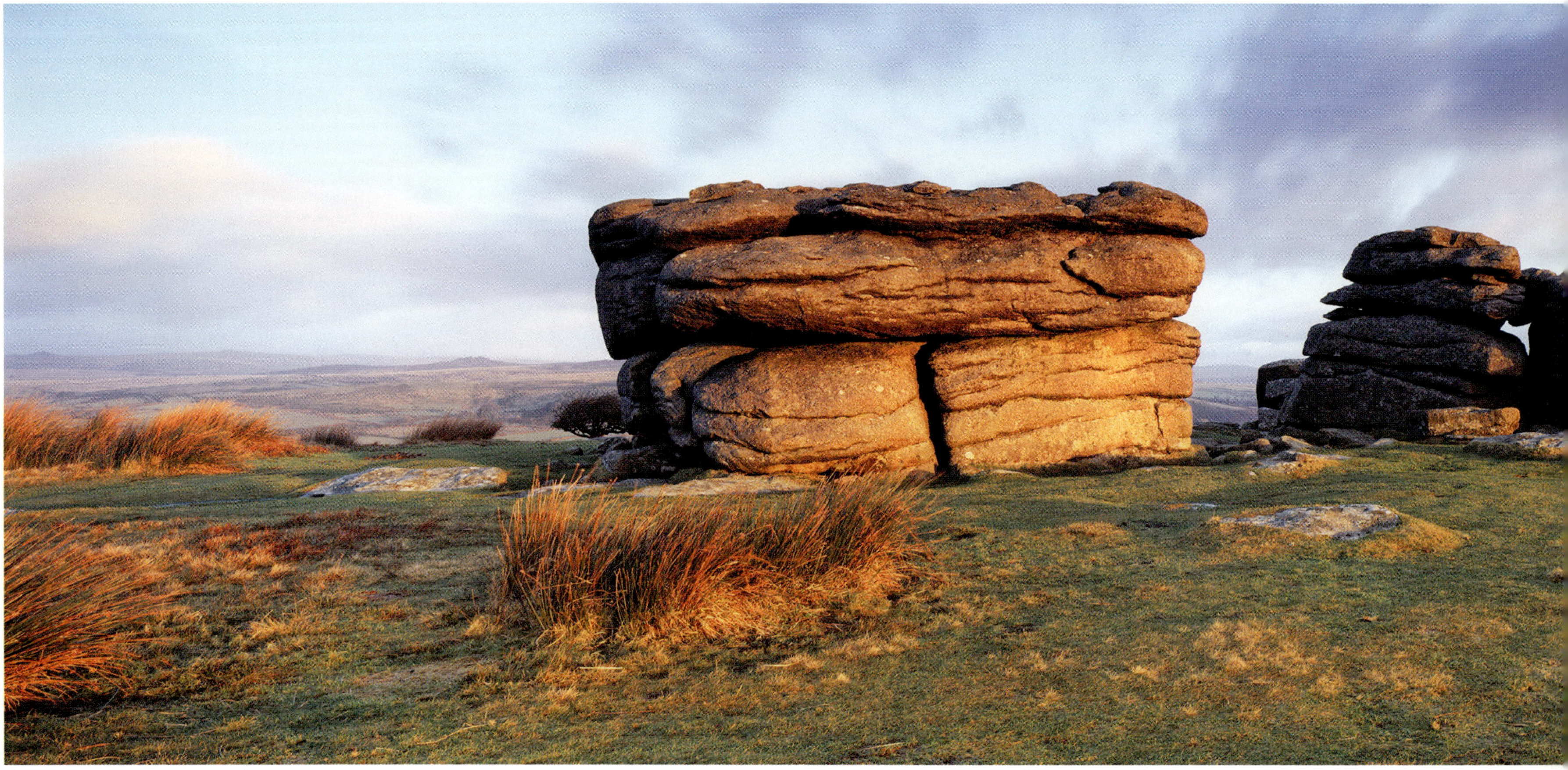

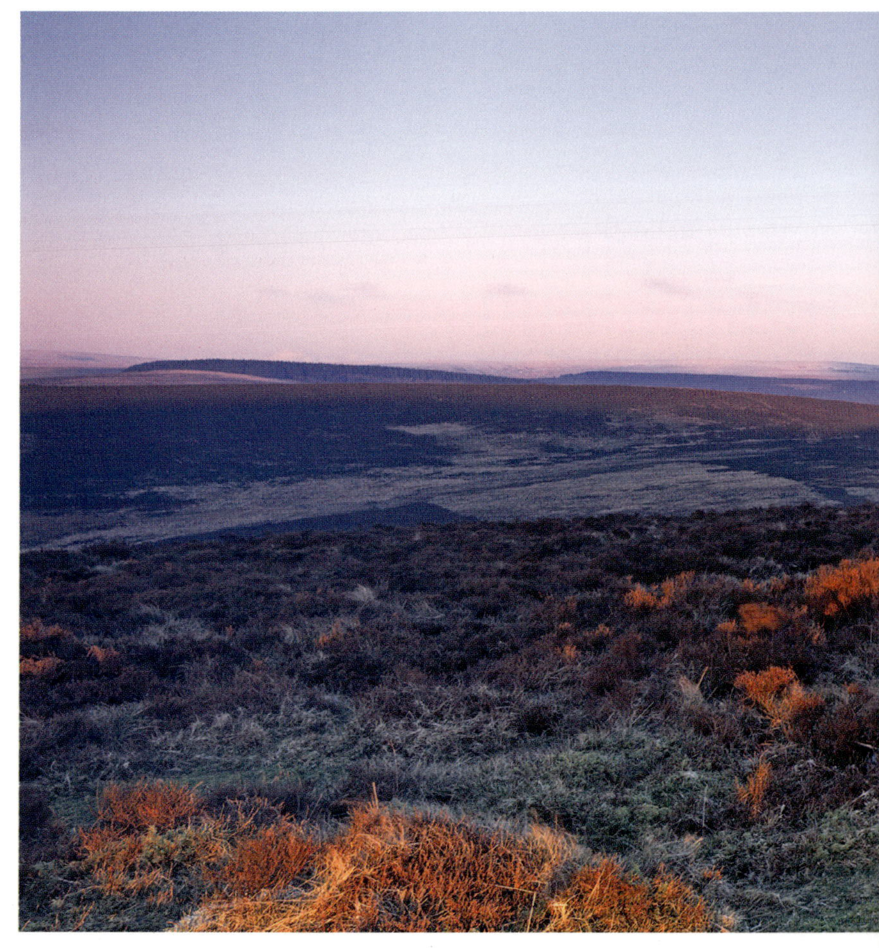

Pastel tones at sunrise fill the sky above Hookney Tor beside the prehistoric Grimspound stone circle.

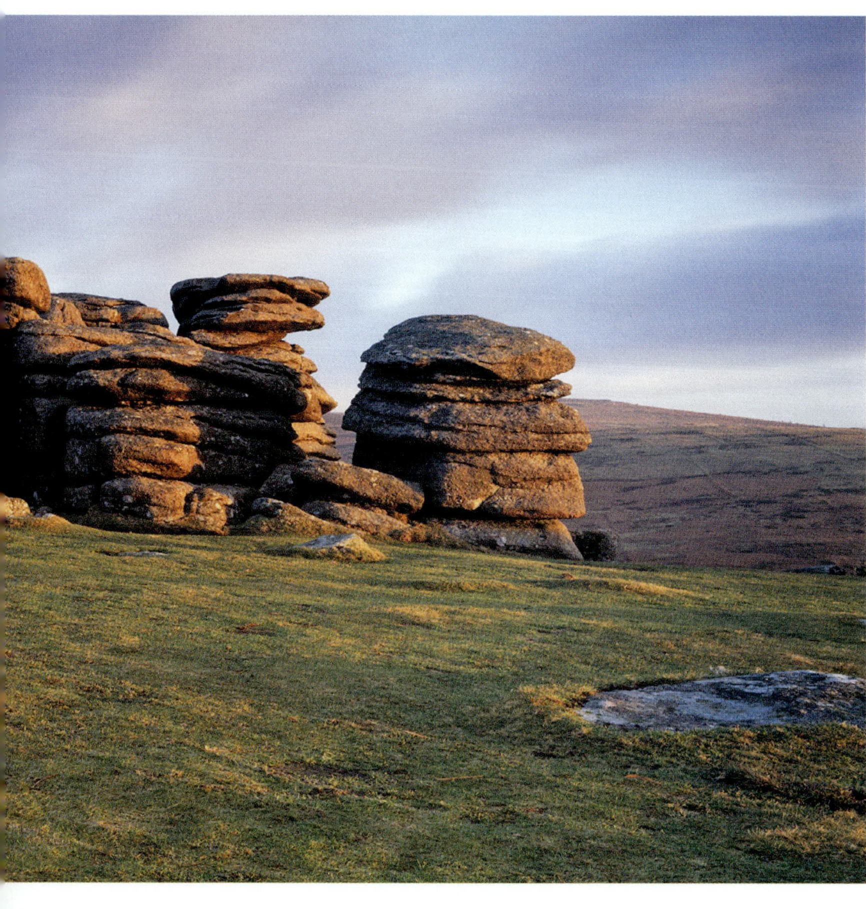

A blustery start to the day at Combestone Tor sends clouds scurrying across the sky. The morning sunlight attempts to warm the stones on this winter's day near Hexworthy.

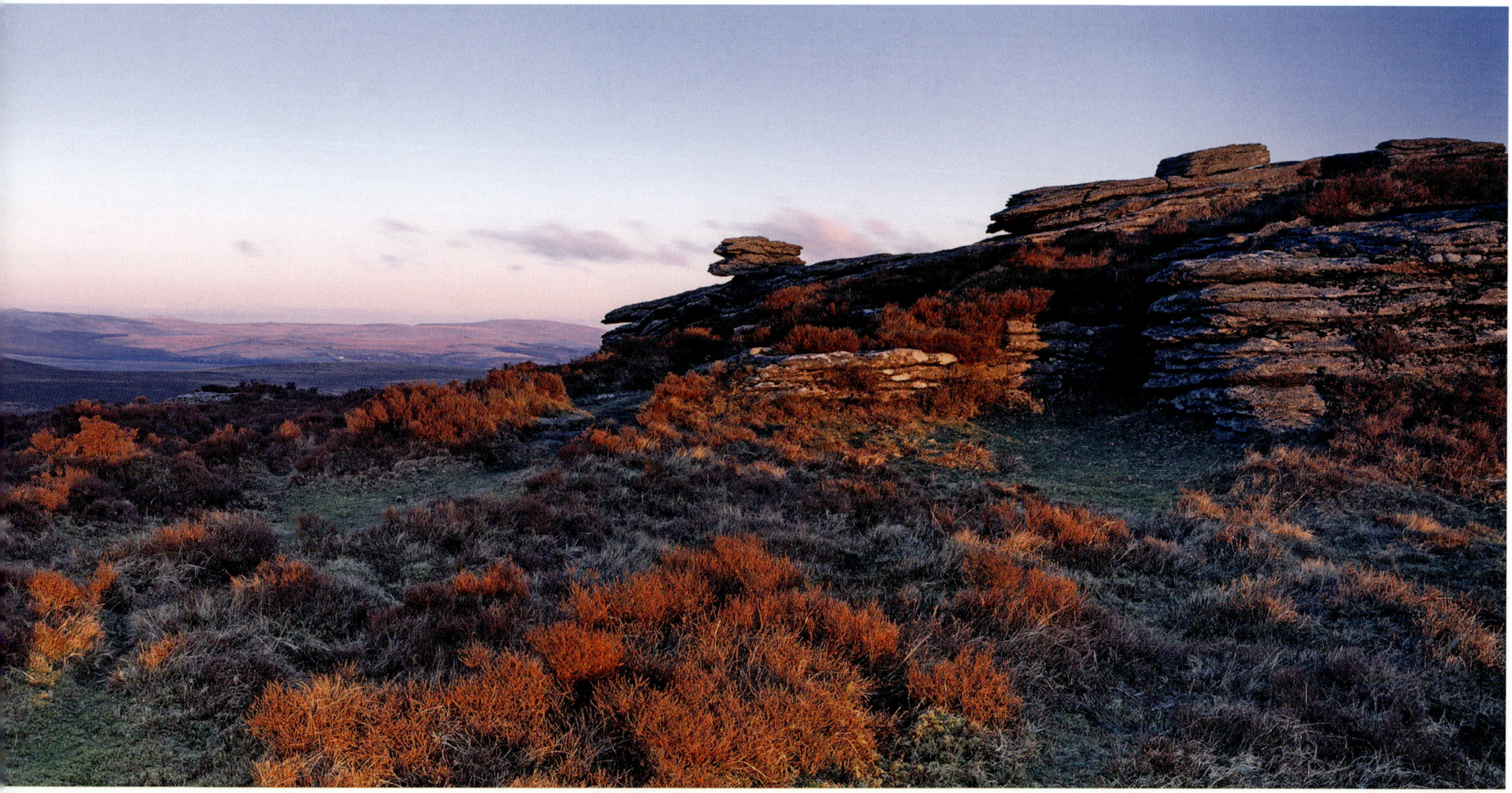

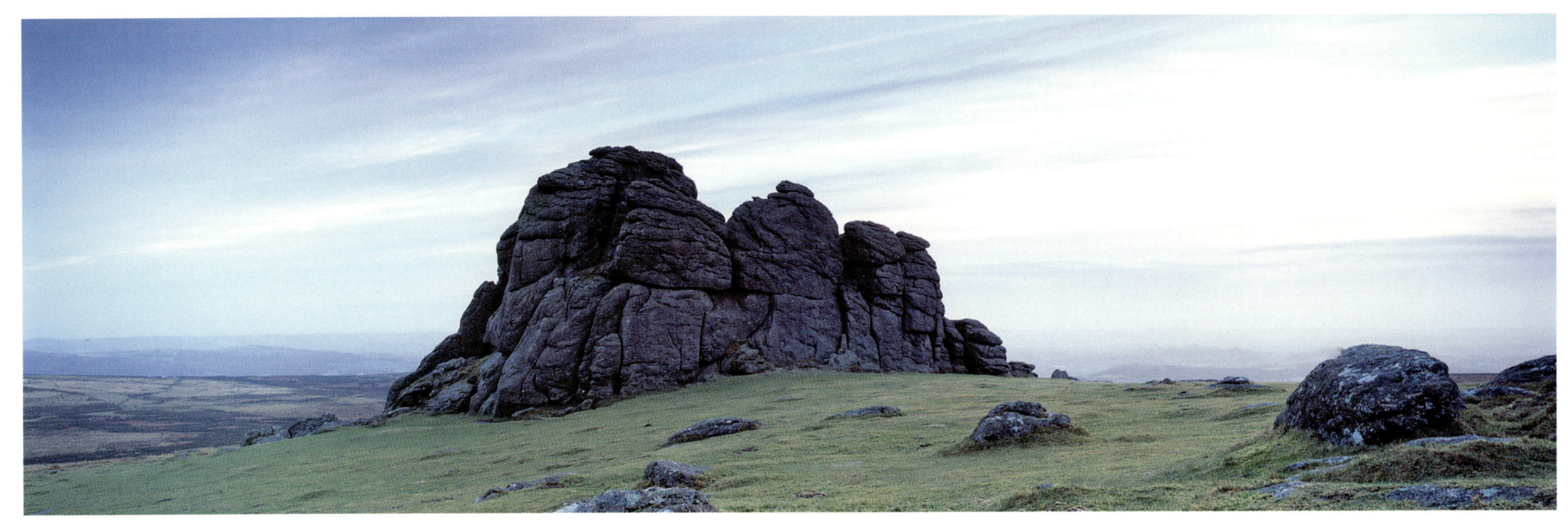

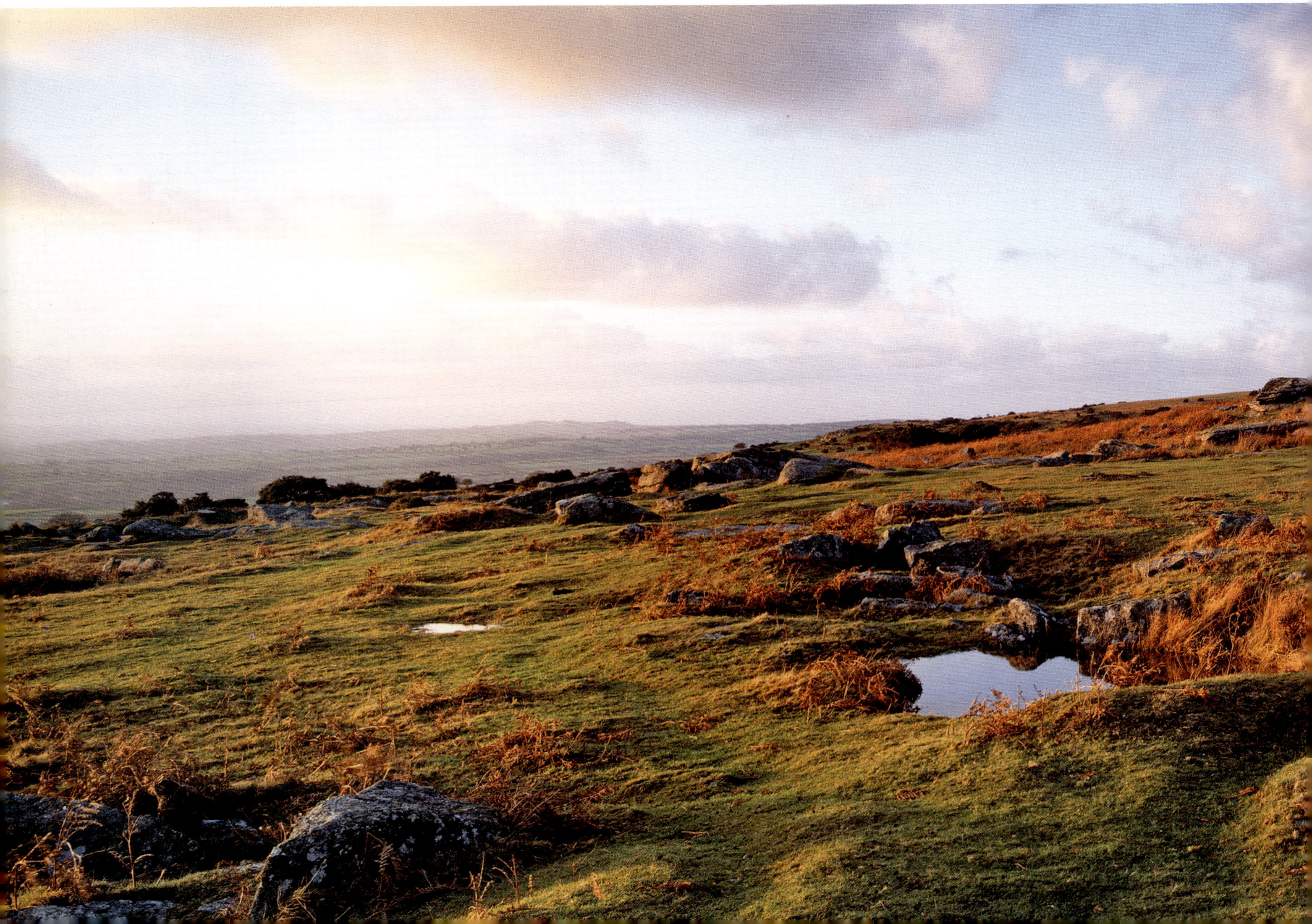

Haytor Rocks at dawn.

The last warm rays of sunlight, reflected in the scattered clouds, brush the tops of the rocks and orange ferns on Feather Tor.

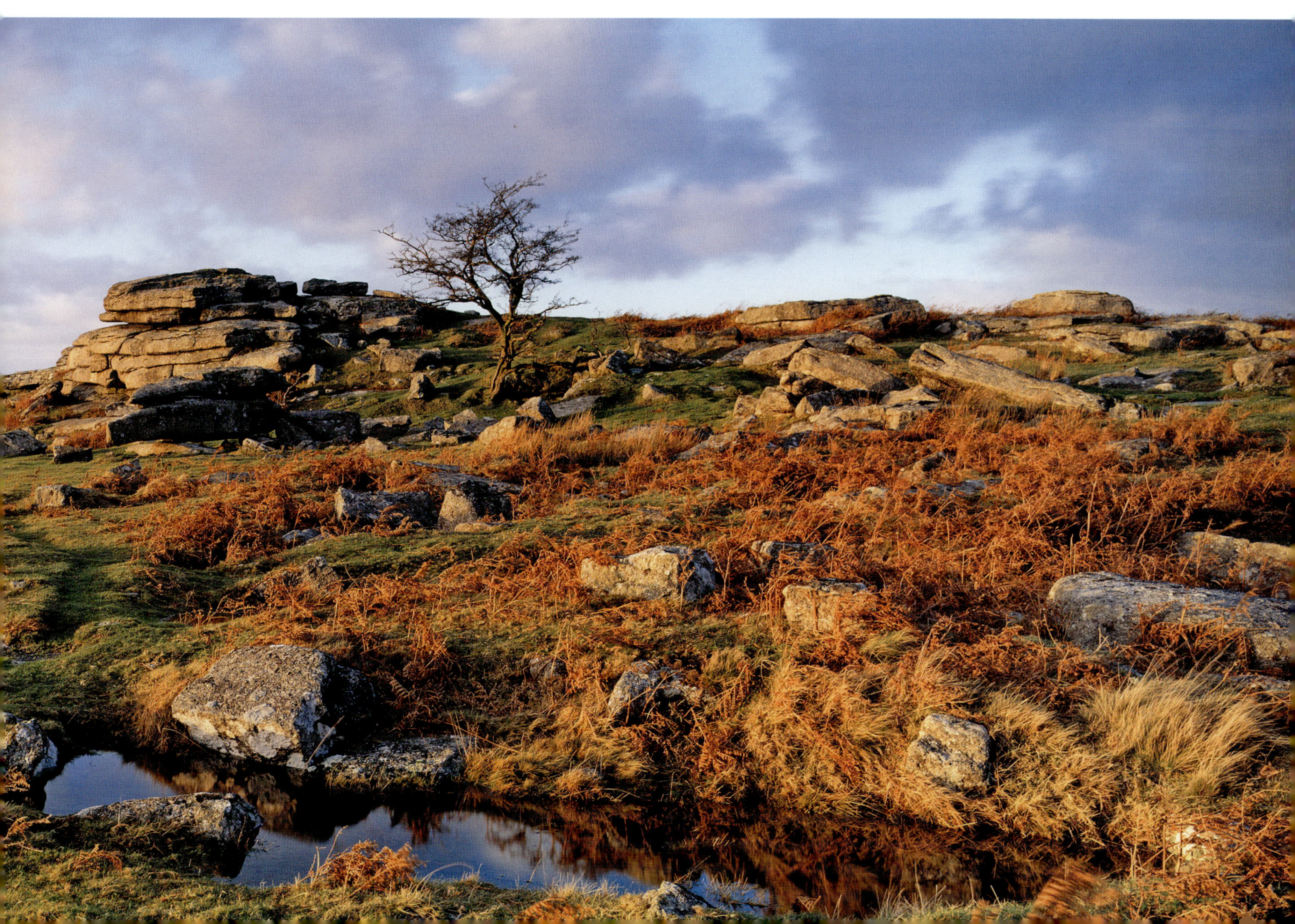

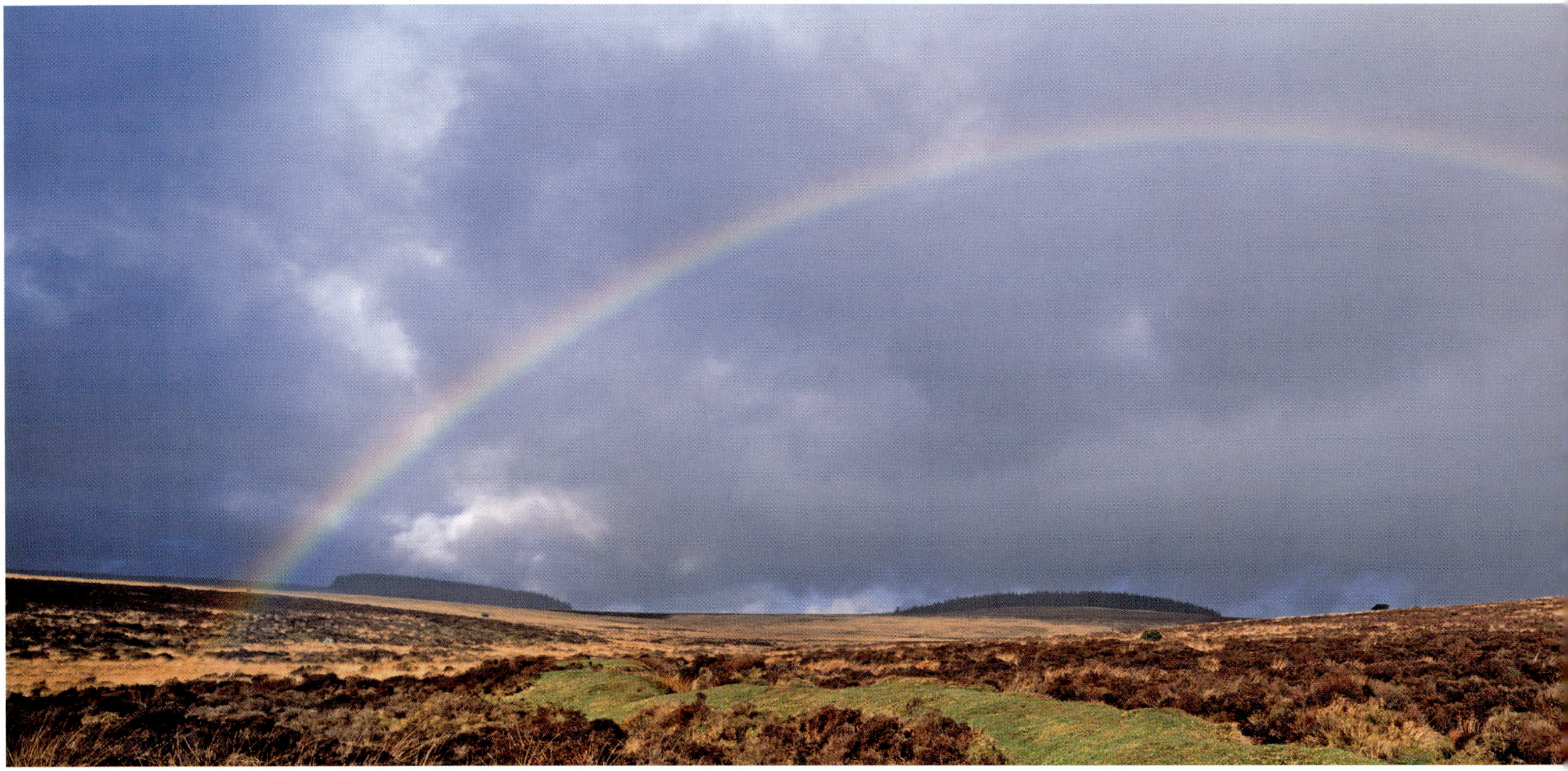

The distant trees at Soussons Down and Headland Warren viewed from Birch Tor. Sweeping scars across the moor reveal Headland Warren's extensive history of mining.

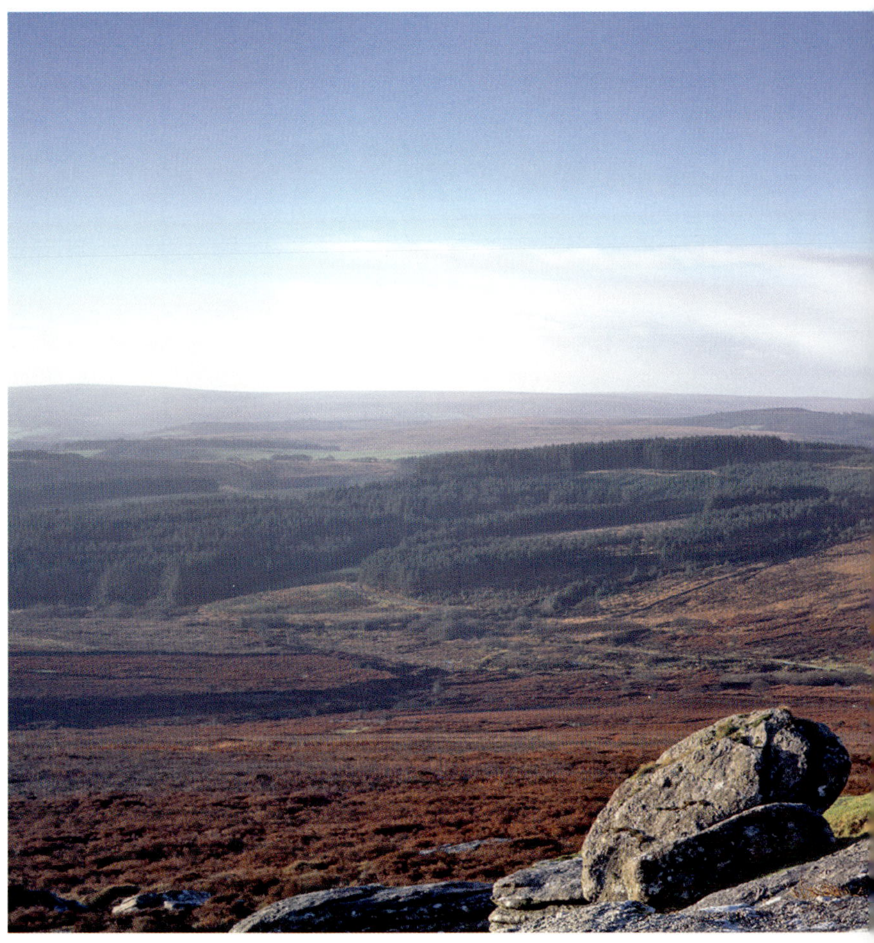

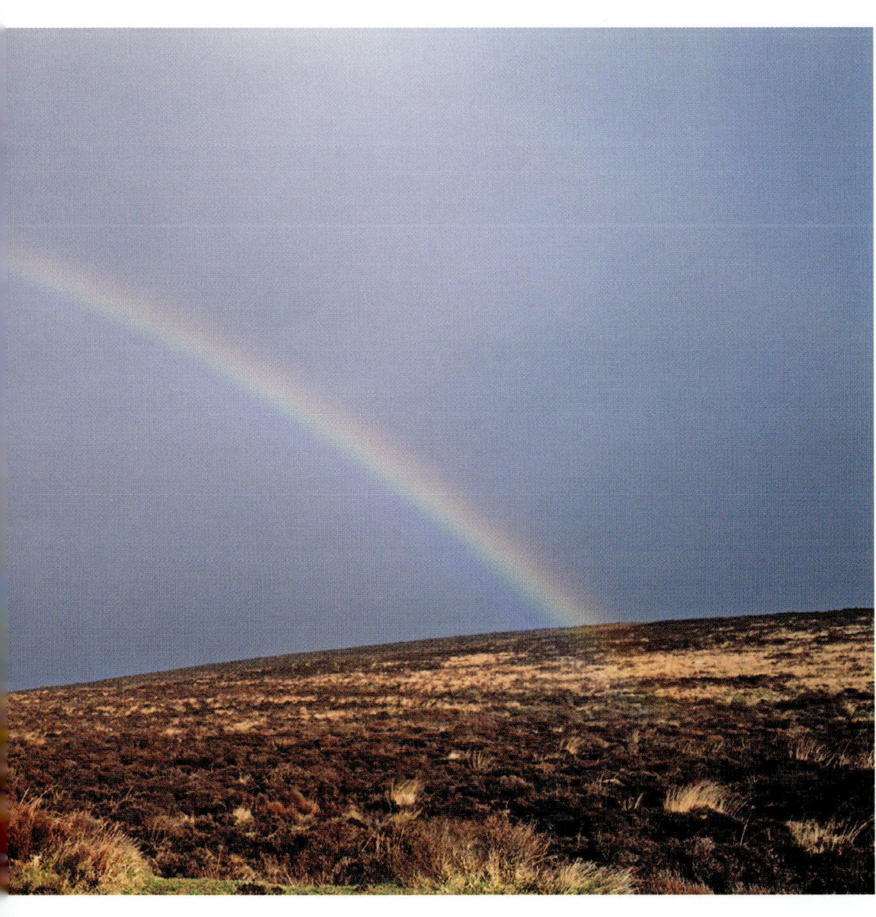

On a windy January morning, a break in the clouds results in this spectacular rainbow arching above Fernworthy Forest for a few precious moments, before the next shower of hailstones and rain hits.

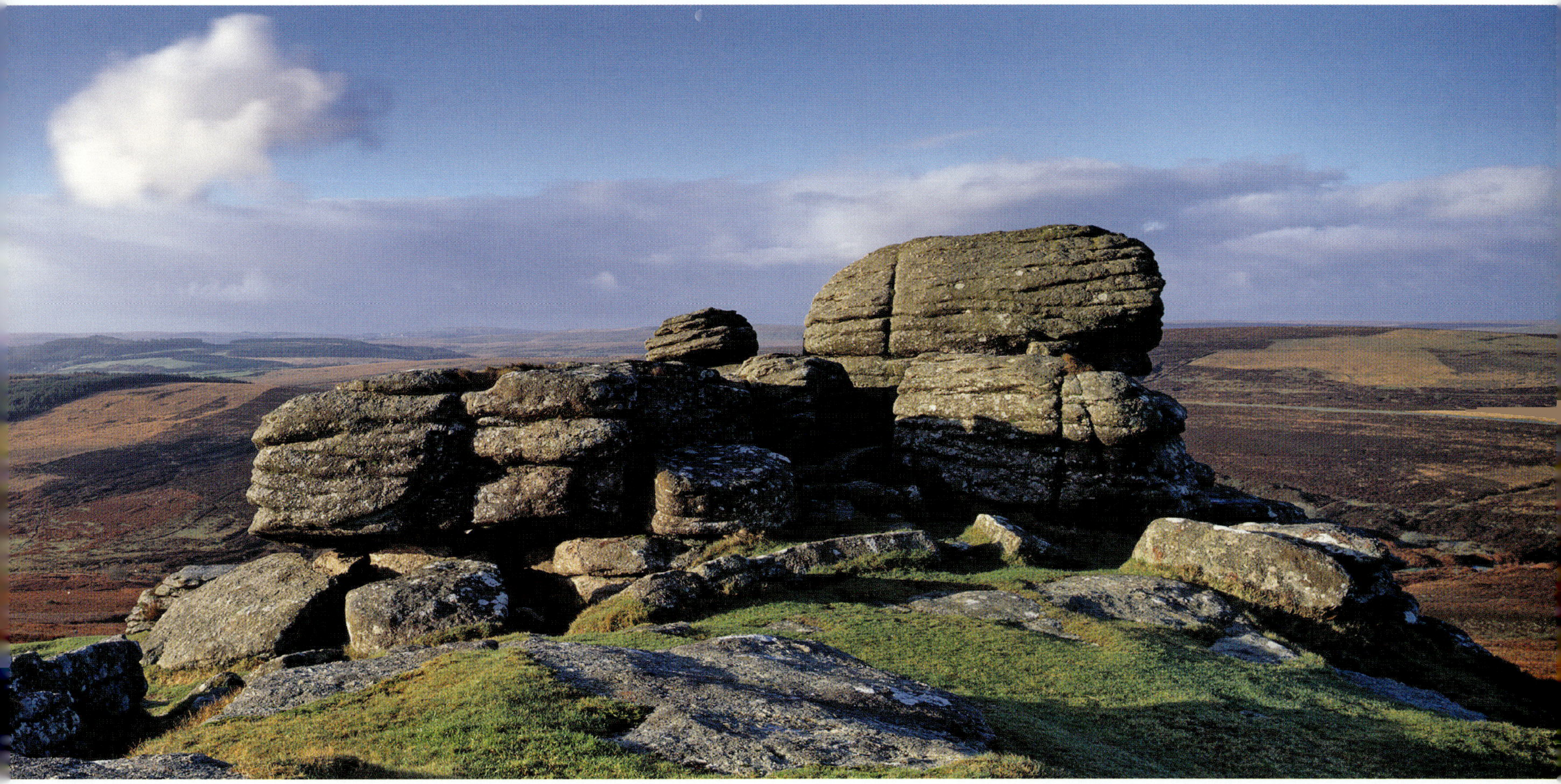

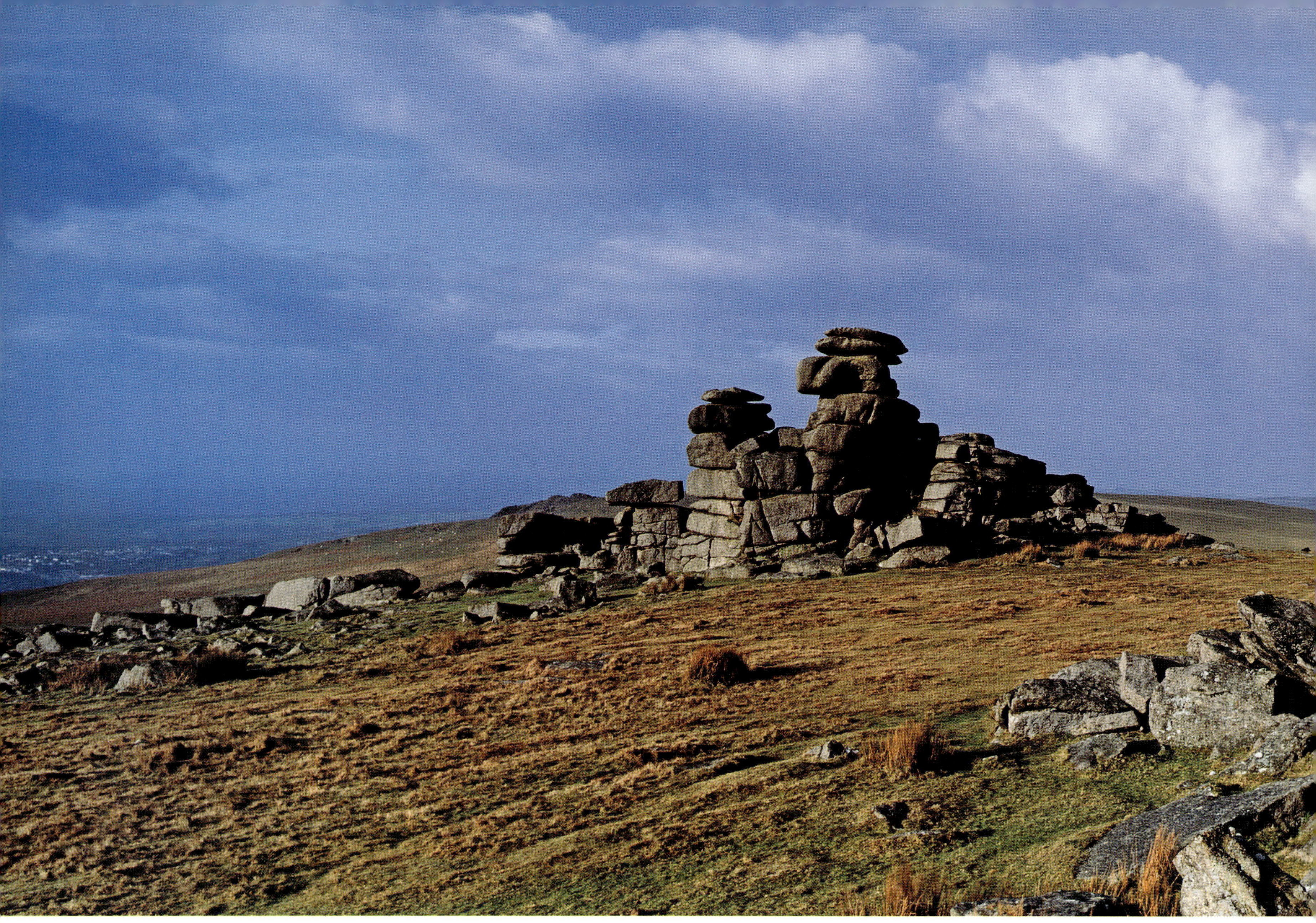

Curious stacks of granite create interesting shapes on Staple Tor, between Merrivale and Tavistock on a cold and windy winter's morning.

Granite rock formation at Staple Tor.

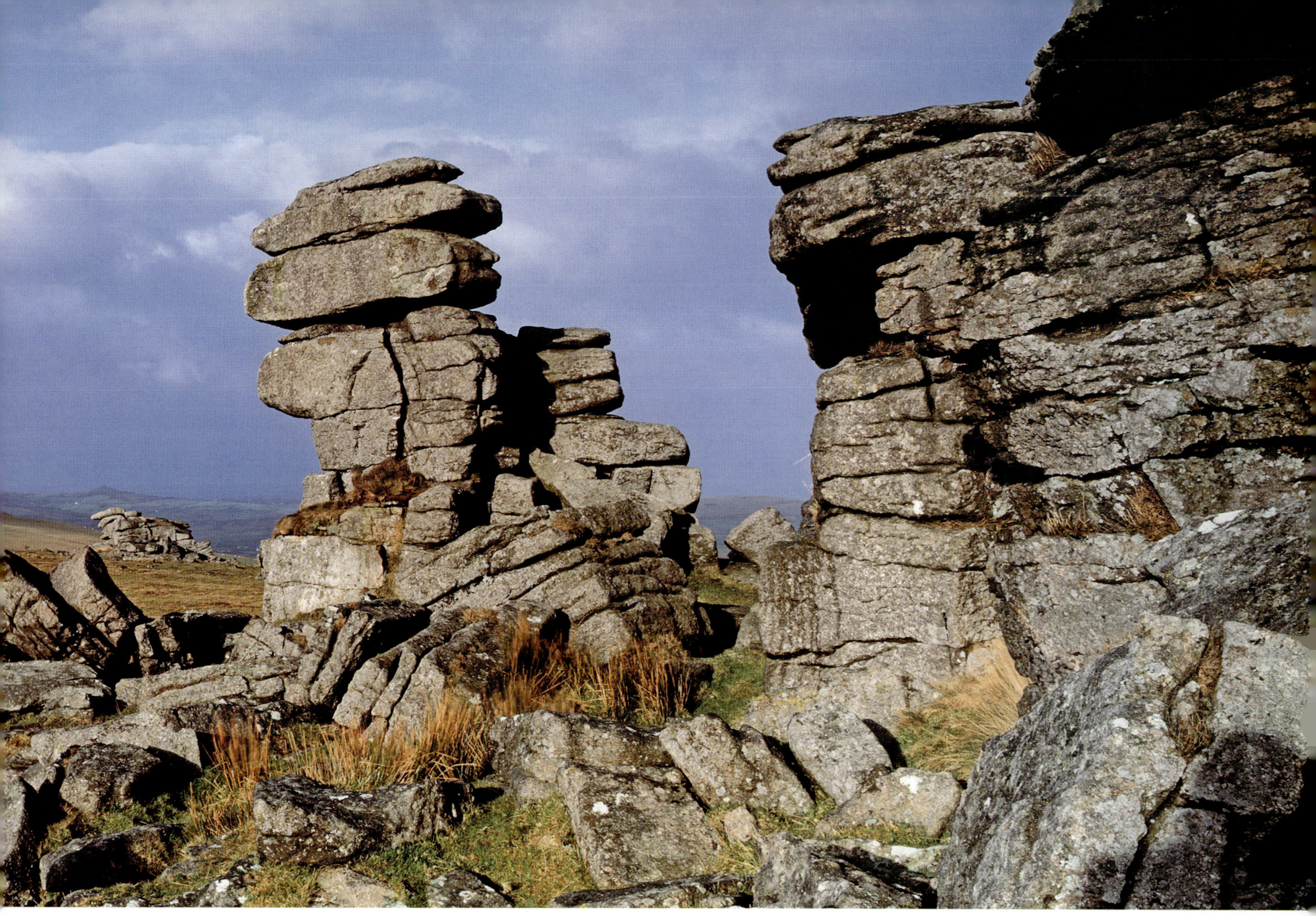

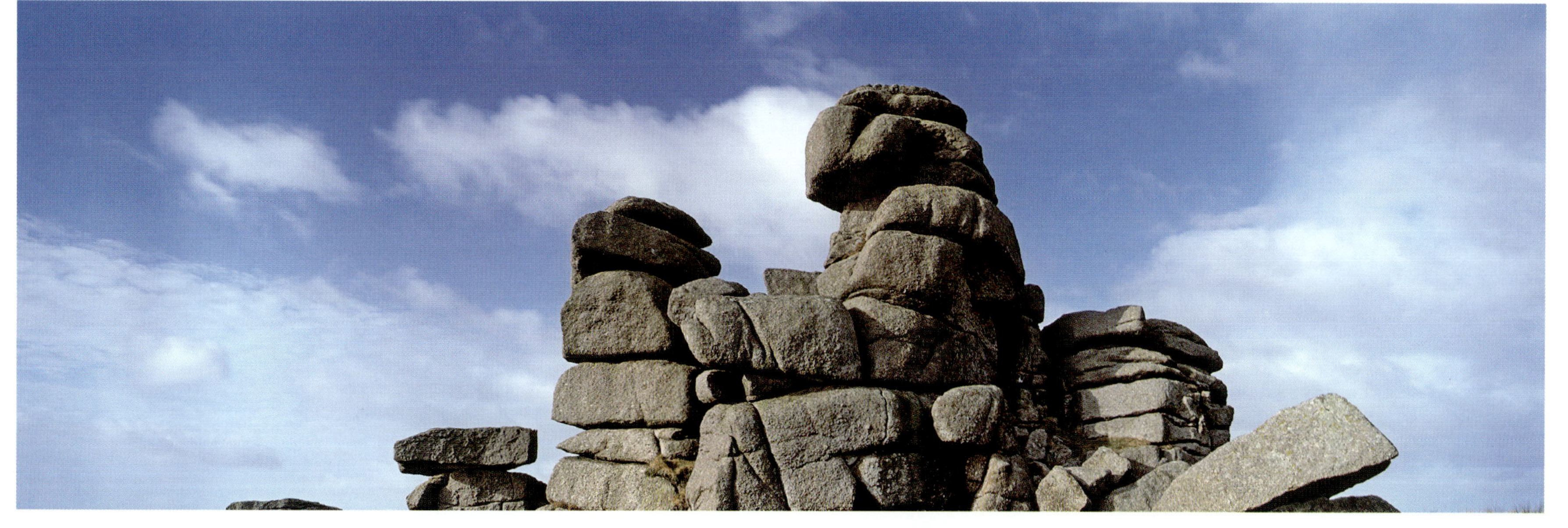

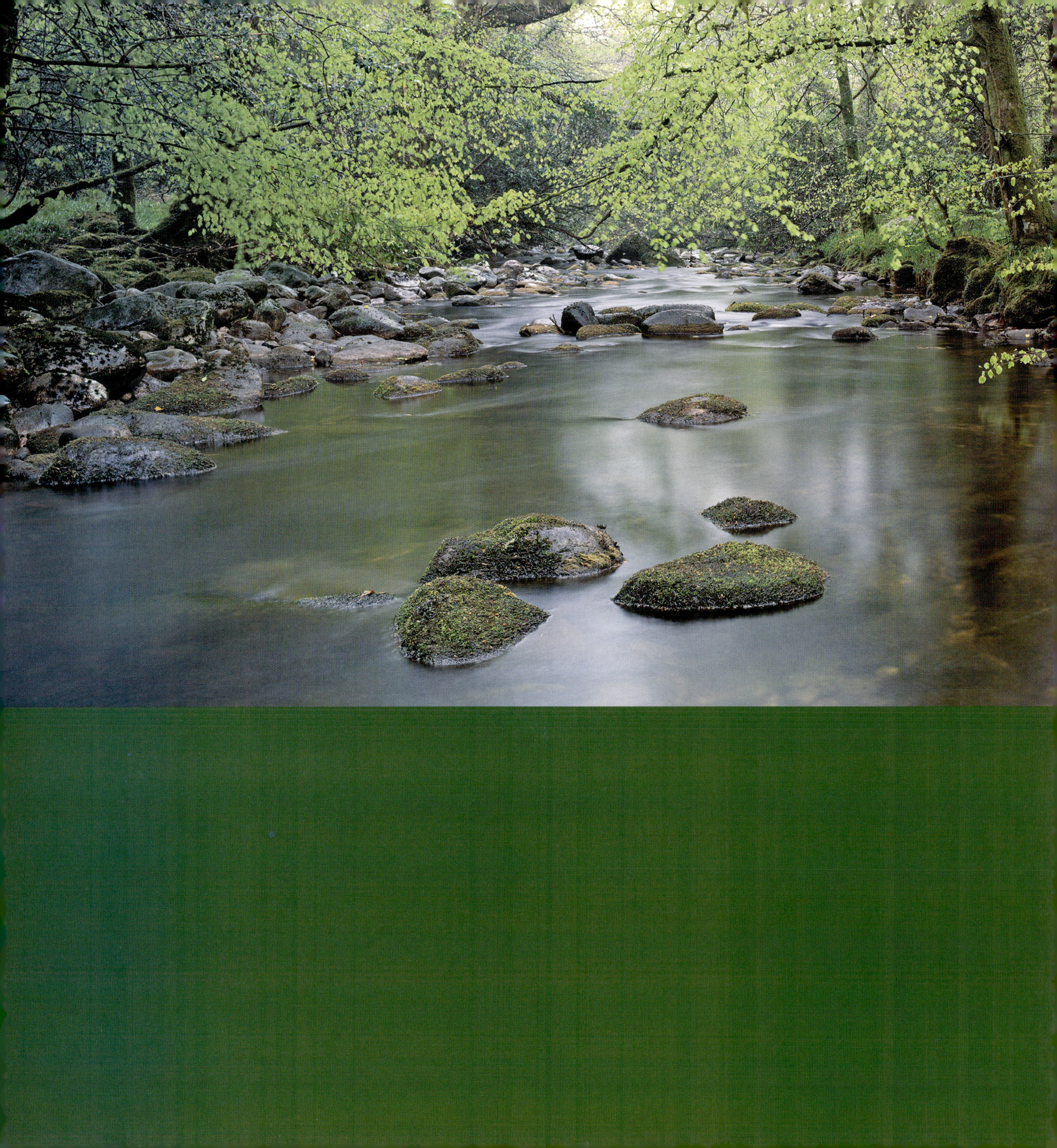

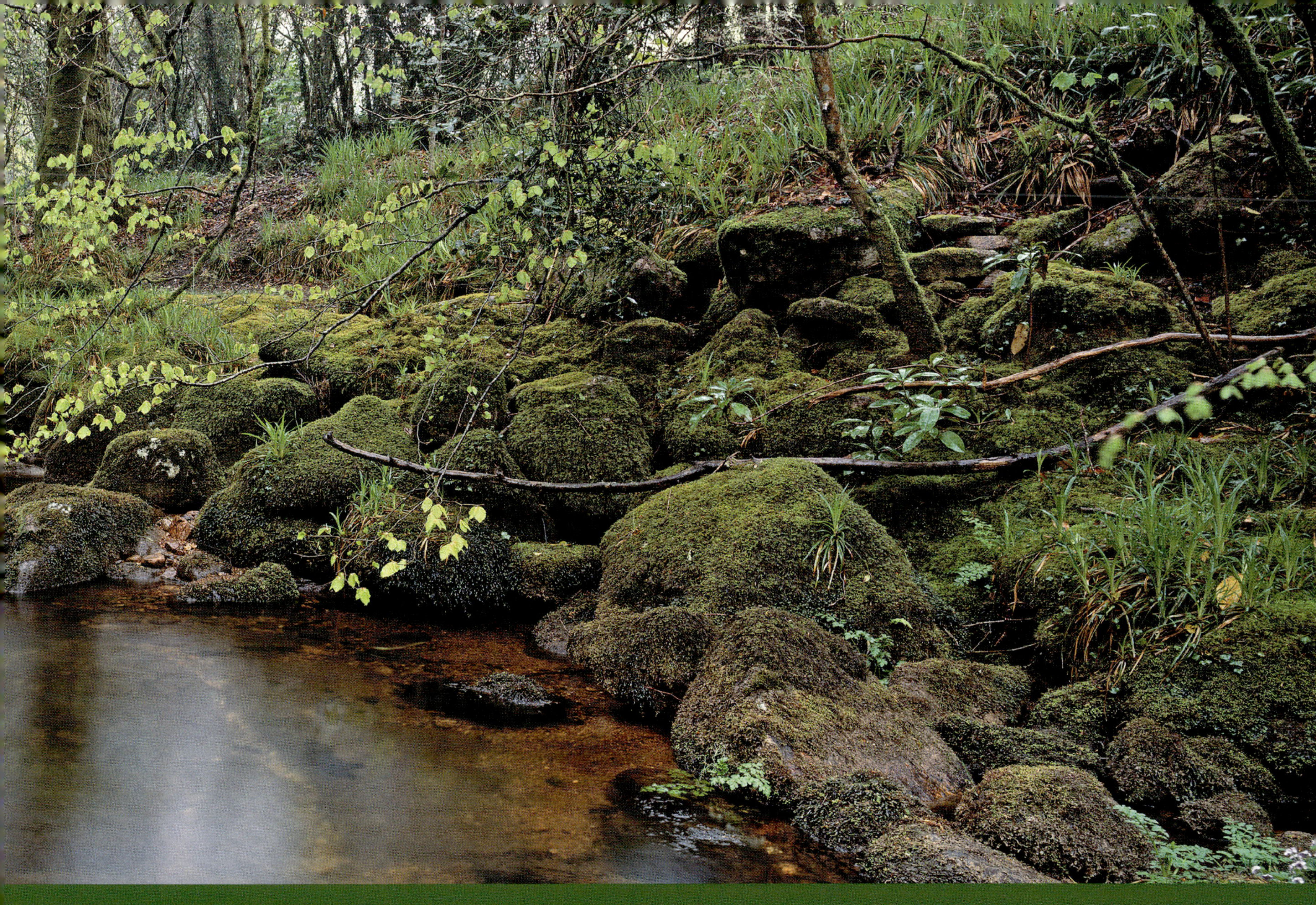

Spring

Beech trees cast their branches of fresh spring leaves over the steady flowing water of the river Avon near Shipley Bridge.

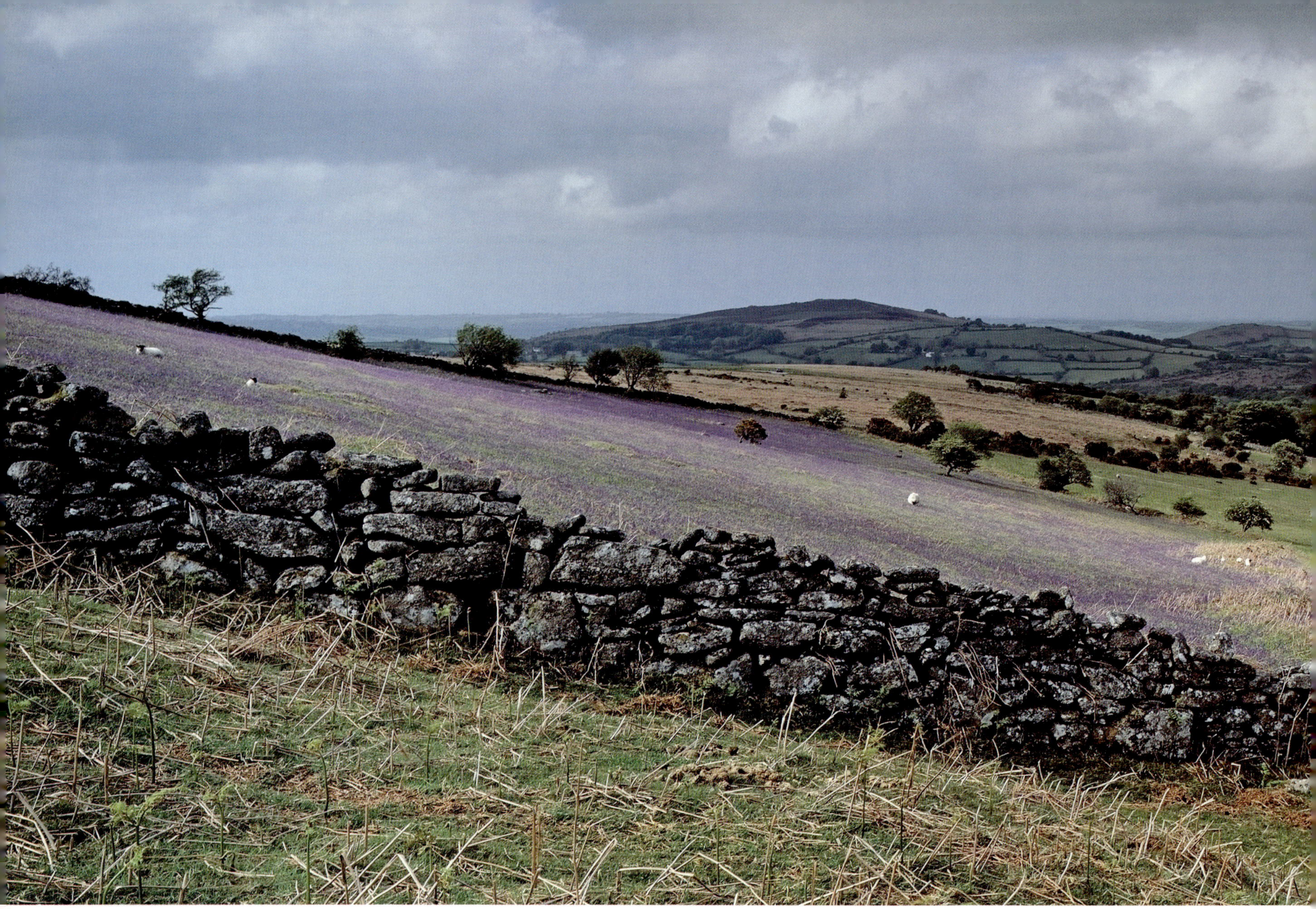

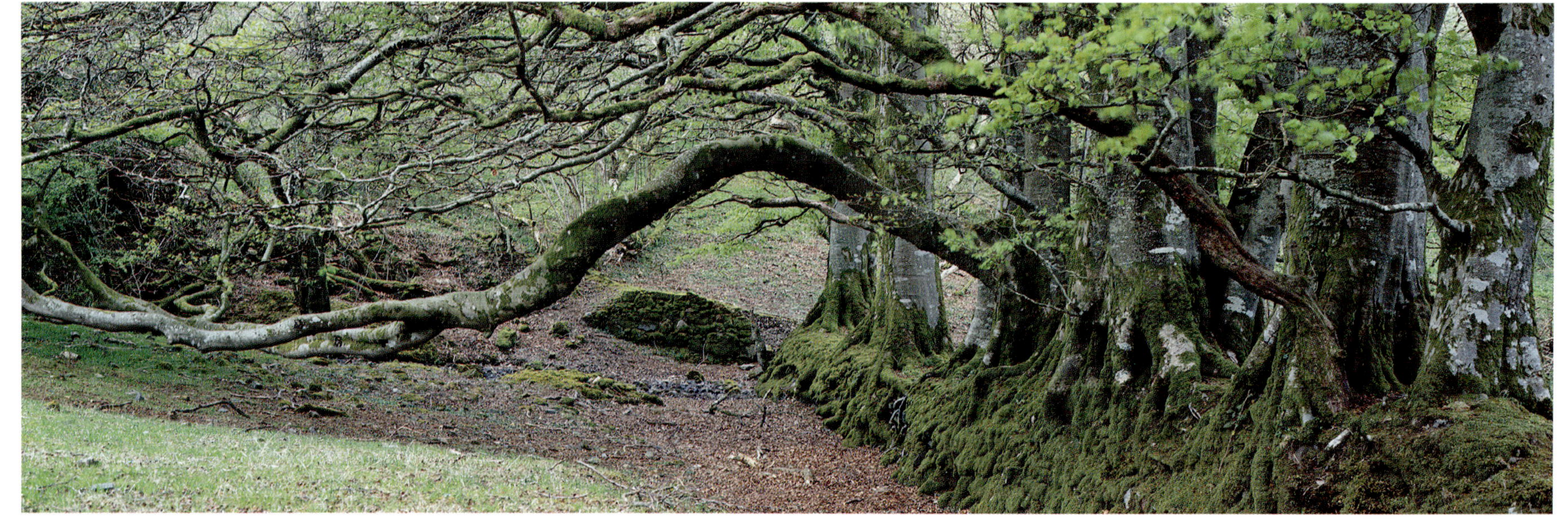

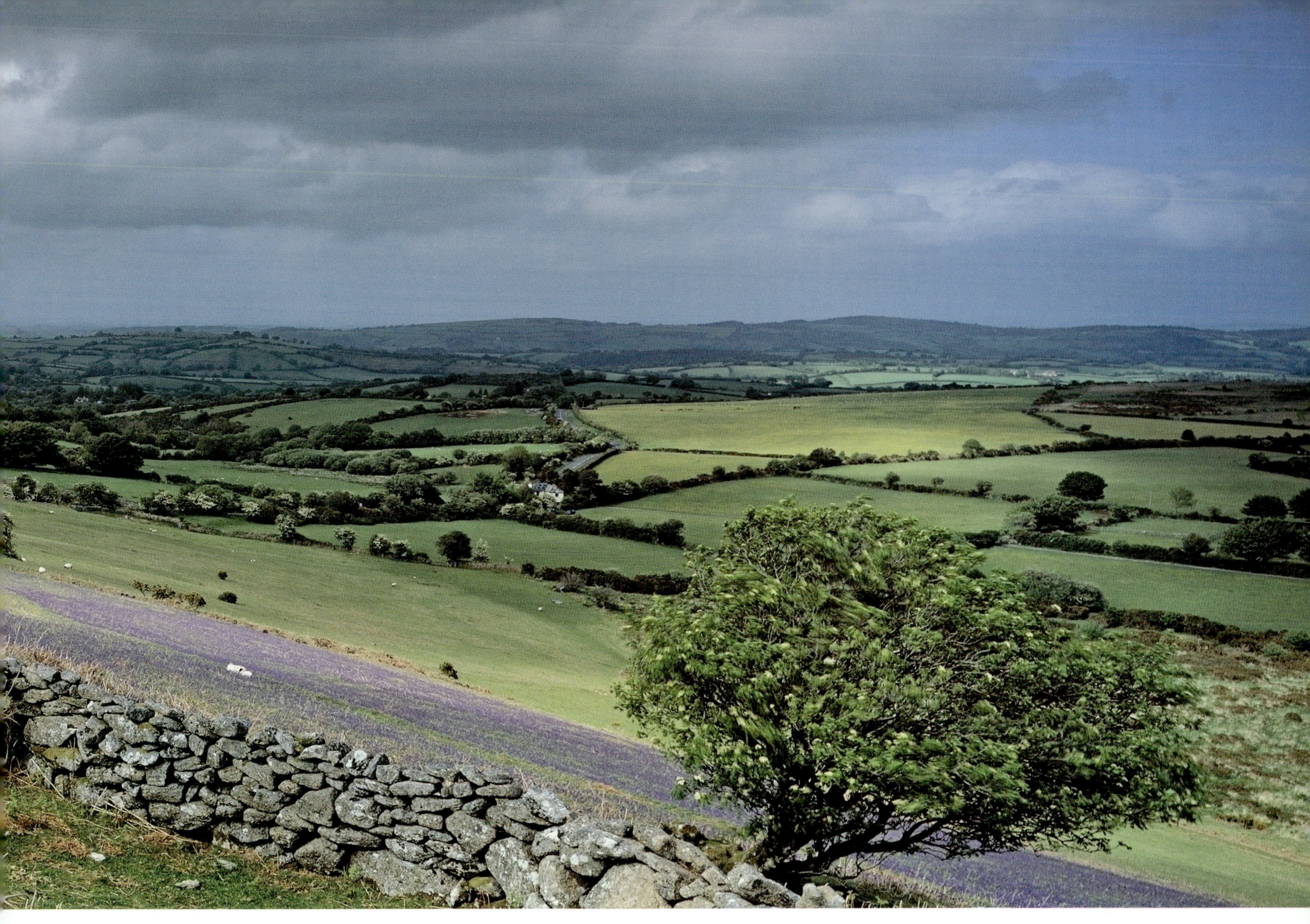

Sheep graze in a sloping meadow of bluebells on the edge of the higher moor as it relaxes into rolling hedge-lined fields and dwellings near Moretonhampstead.

Trees line a mossy drystone wall near Meldon Reservoir in north Dartmoor.

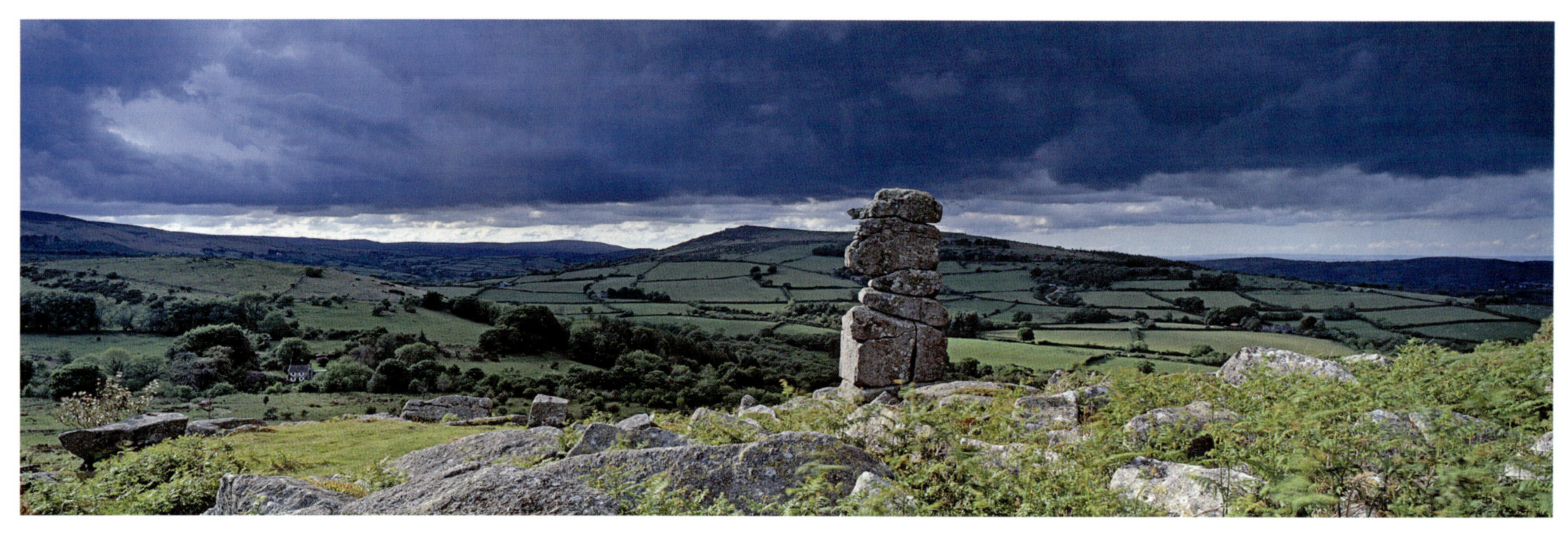

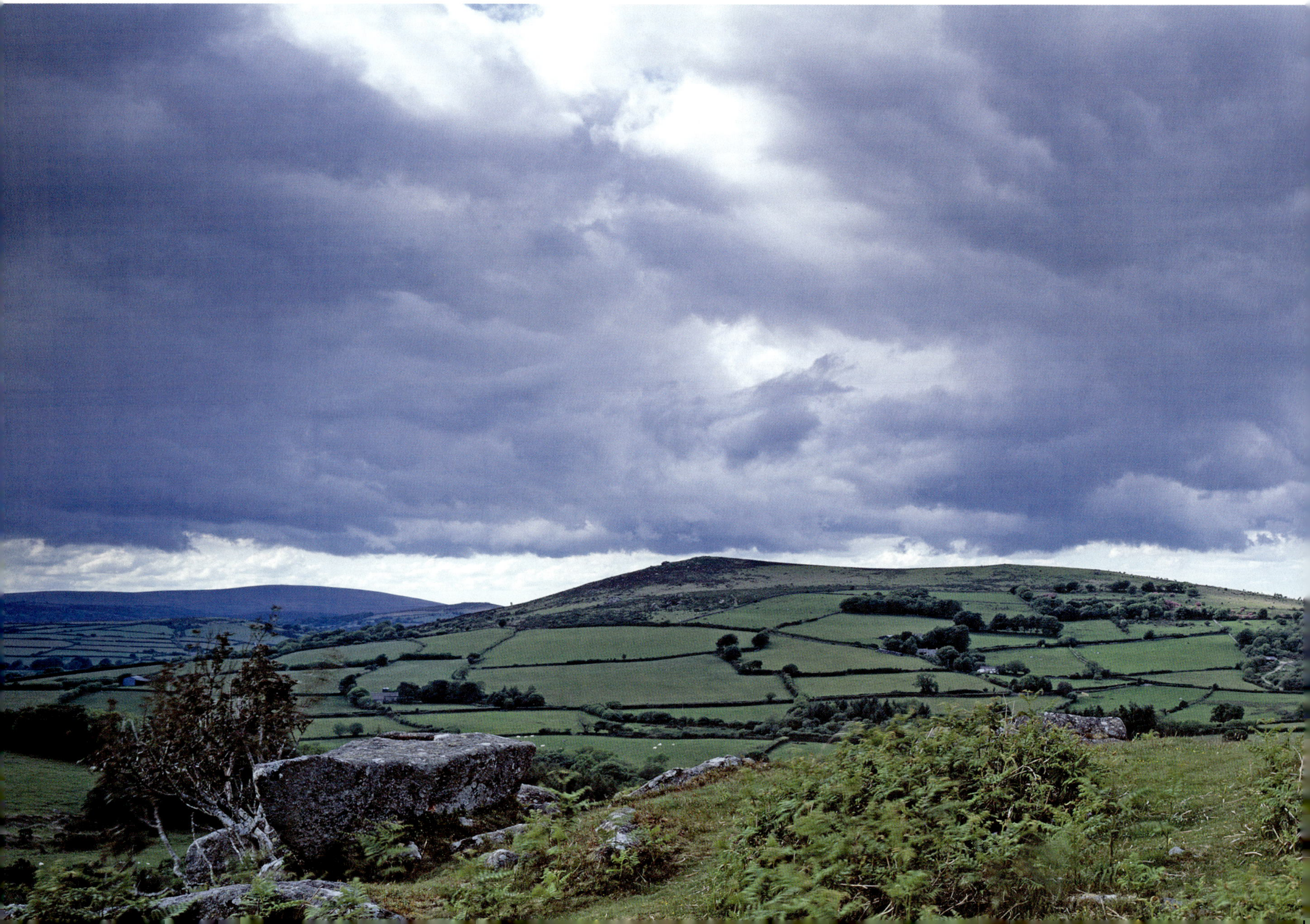

Not far from Hound Tor the dramatic rock stack known as Bowerman's Nose perches on the hillside at Hayne Down. The stack, formed of five blocks of weathered granite nearly 40 feet or 12 metres high, has long attracted visitors and myths alike. Formerly a favourite with climbers, the stack is now off-limits for climbing due to erosion.

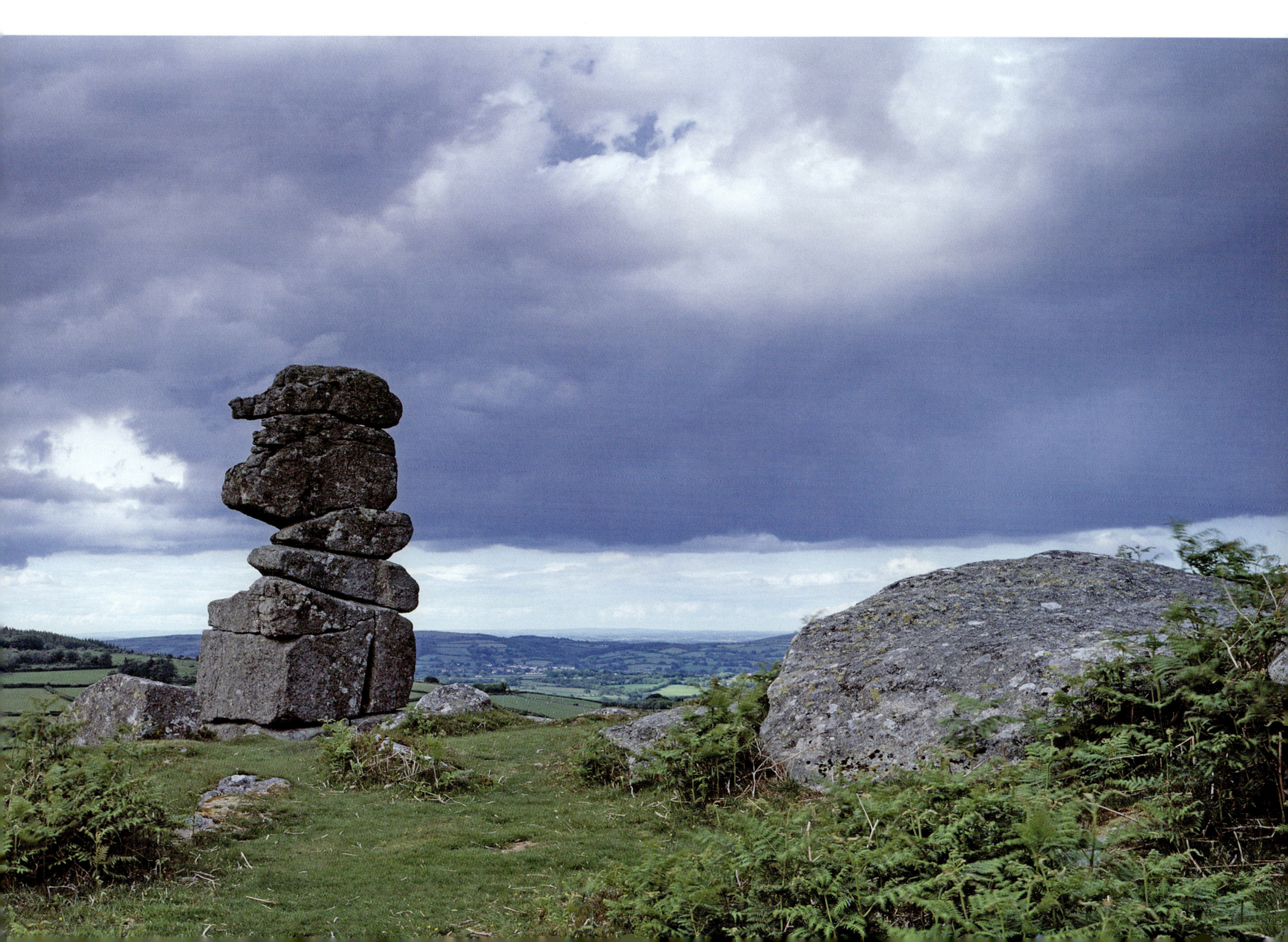

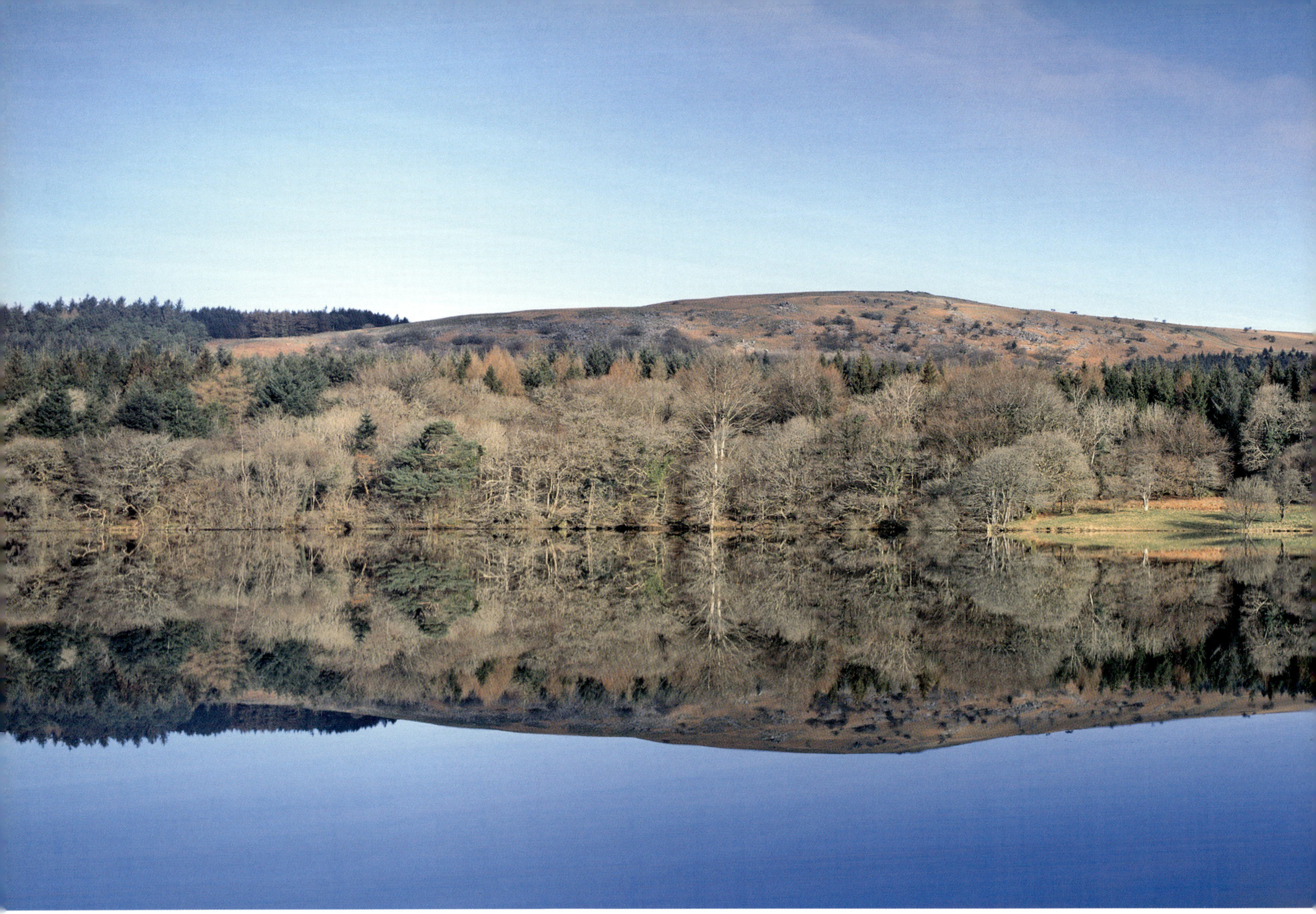

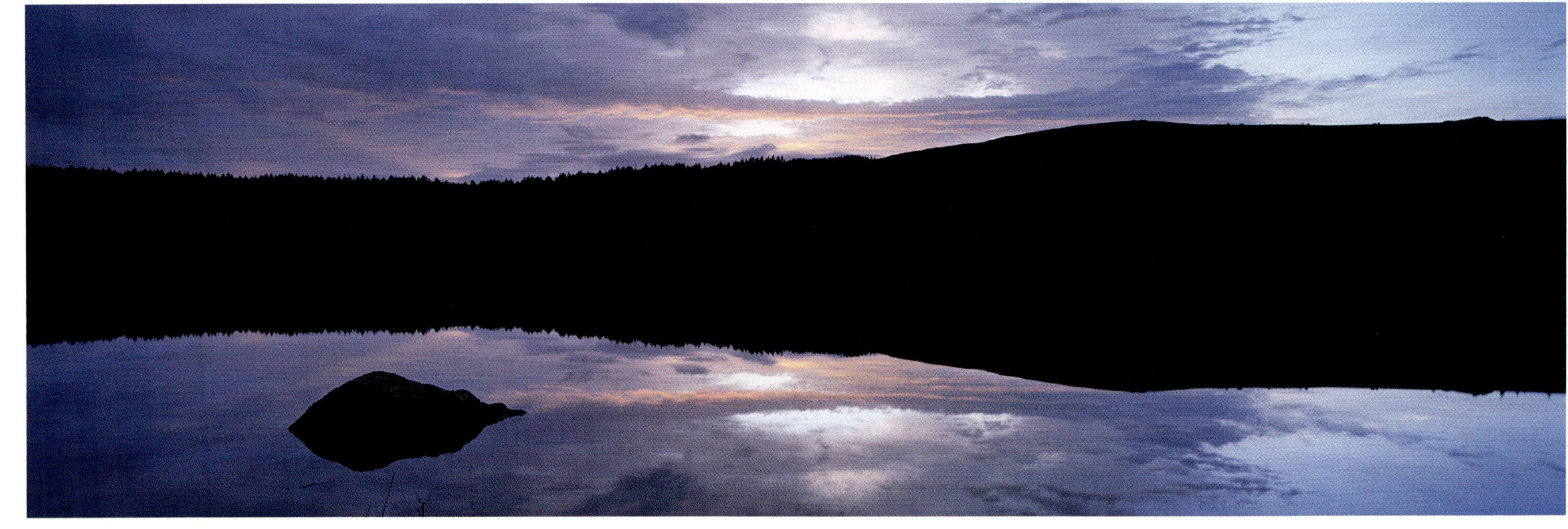

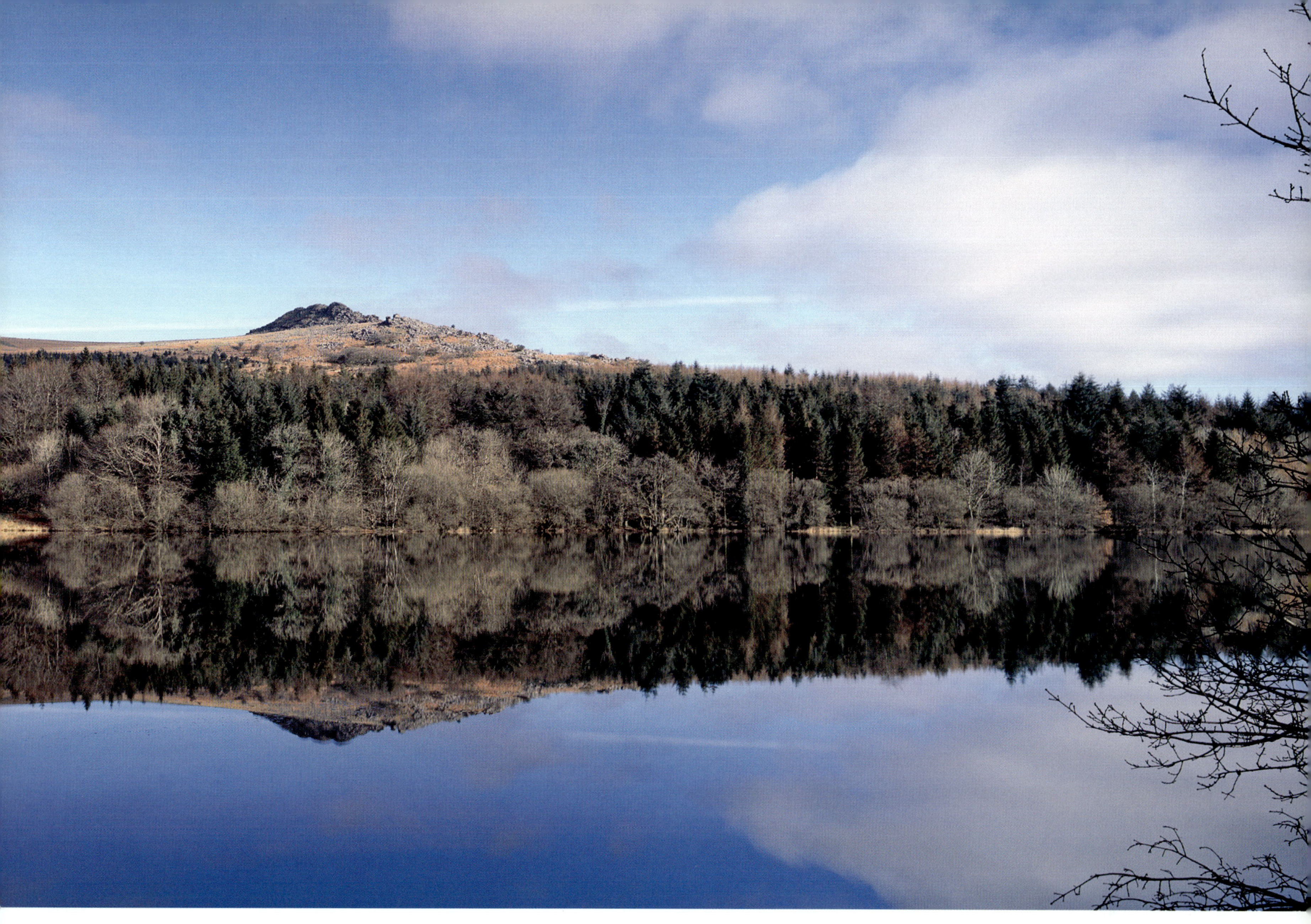

A still spring morning provides a mirror-like reflection of Peak Hill, Sharpitor and Leather Tor in the waters of Burrator Reservoir, which supply the city of Plymouth with water.

The beauty of the spring sunset is reflected in the sheltered waters of Burrator Reservoir.

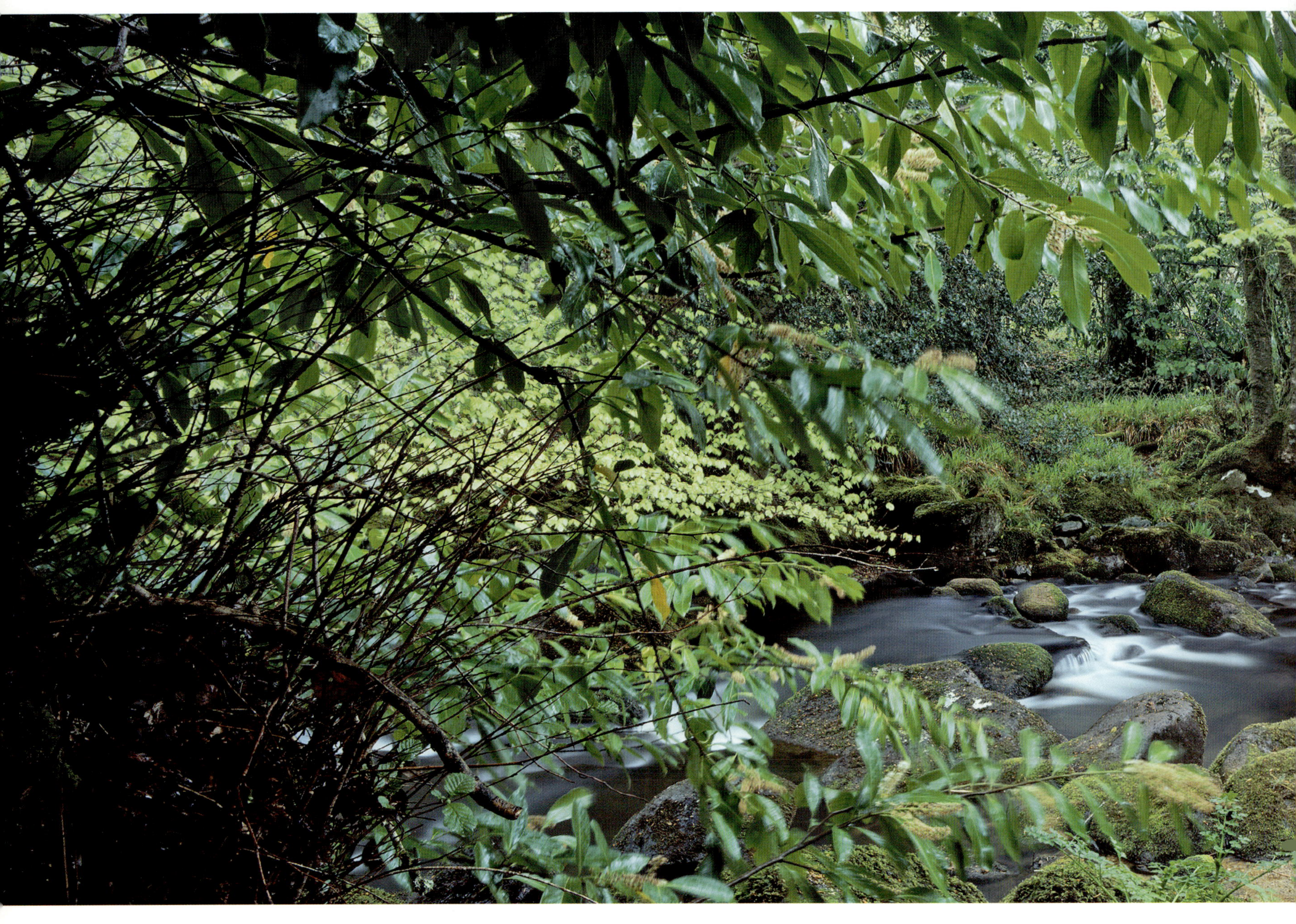

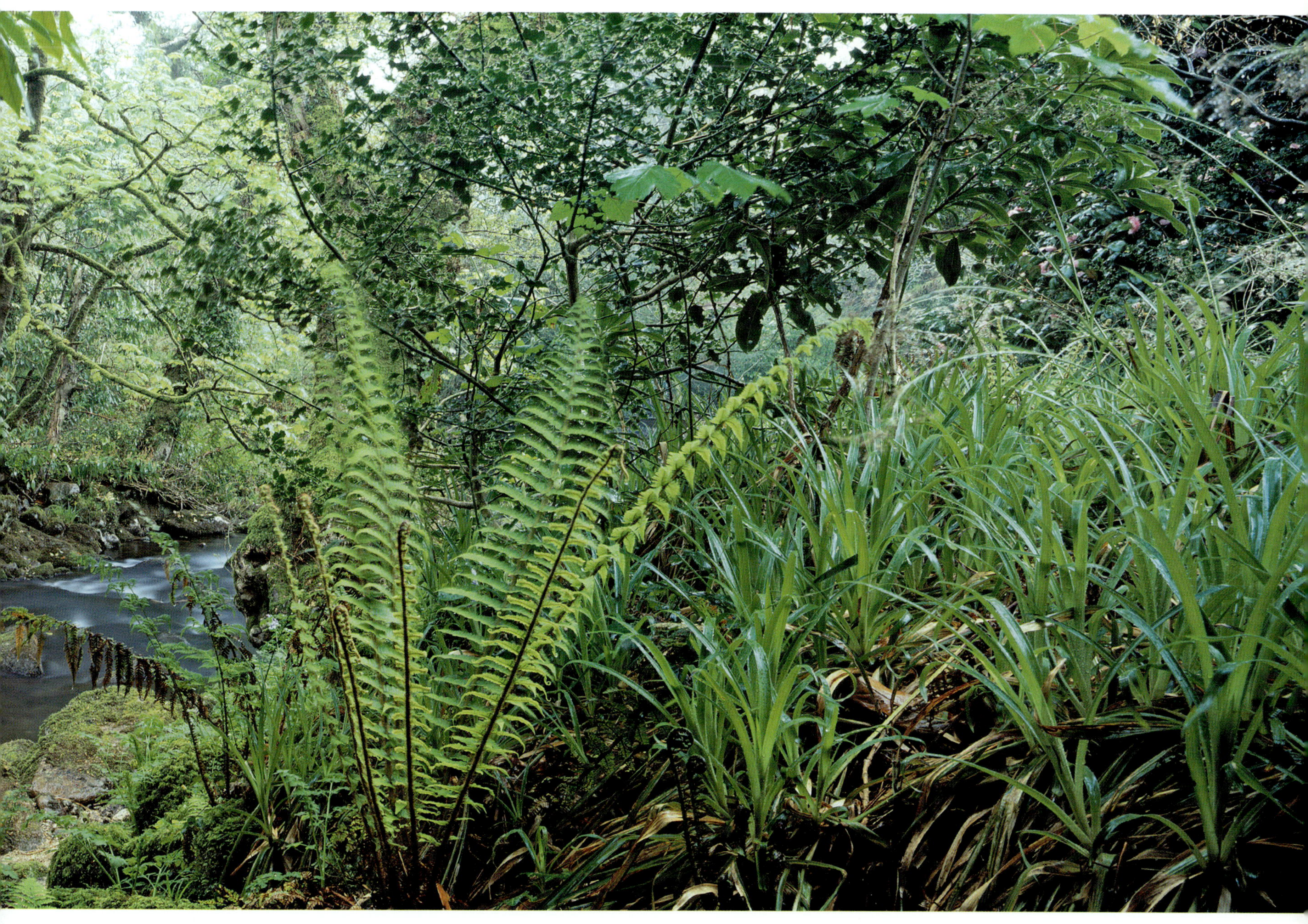

Lush greens appear in the spring with the sumptuous growth of ferns and new leaves beside the babbling waters of the river Avon.

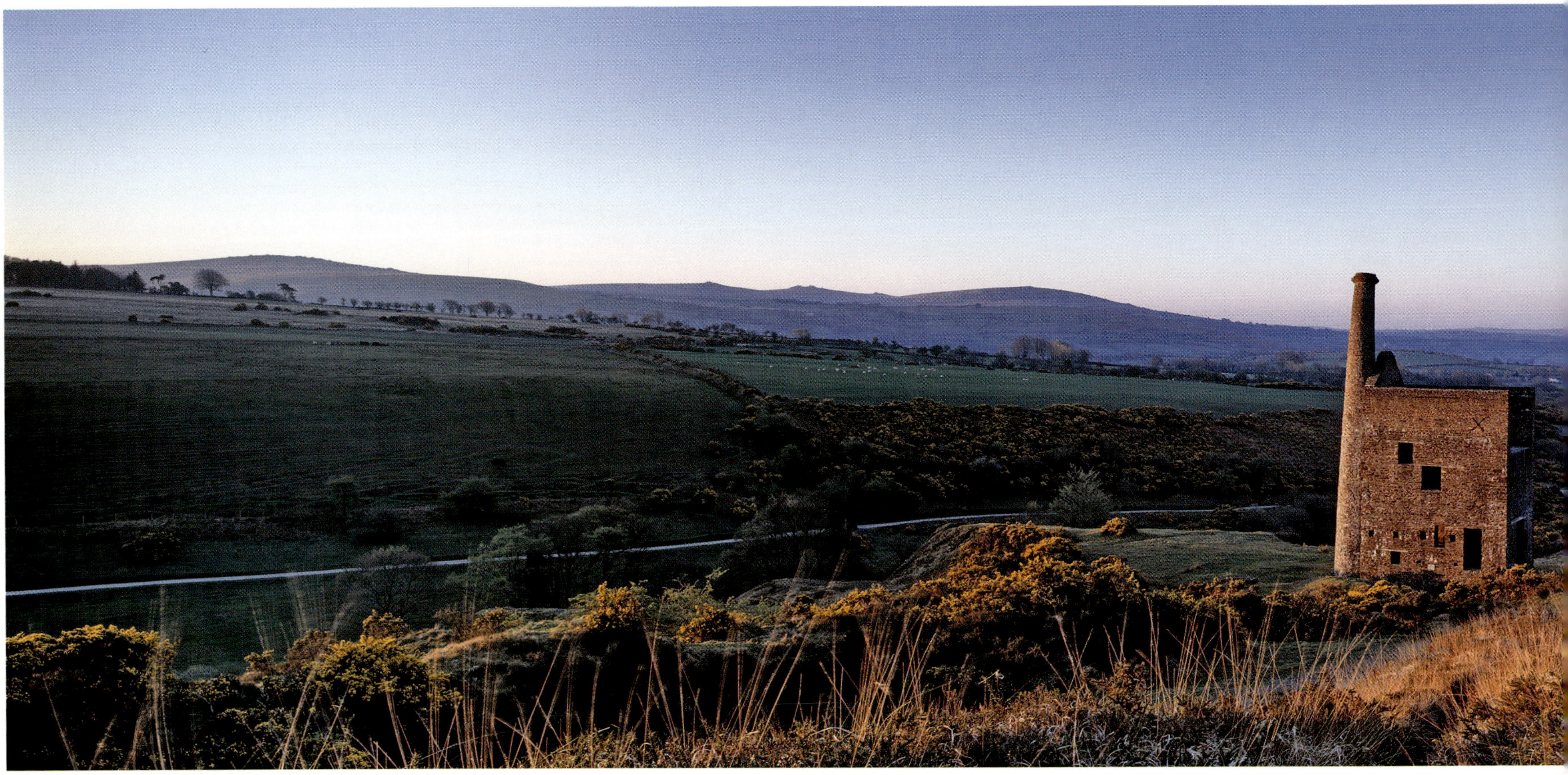

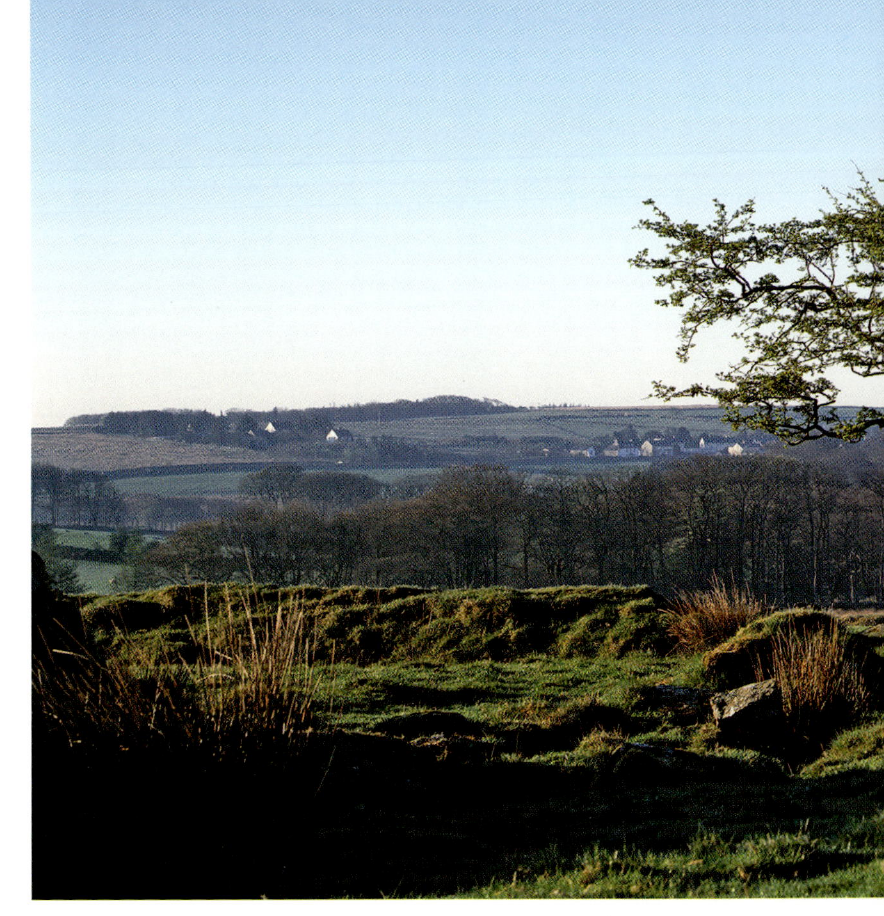

The early morning sunlight reflects from the stone walls of Dartmoor Prison in Princetown. Built in 1806 to house prisoners of the Napoleonic Wars, the prison took three years to complete. During the late 1800s it became known for holding some of the country's most notorious criminals. Still in use as a prison today, it no longer houses any high risk prisoners but emphasises training and rehabilitation.

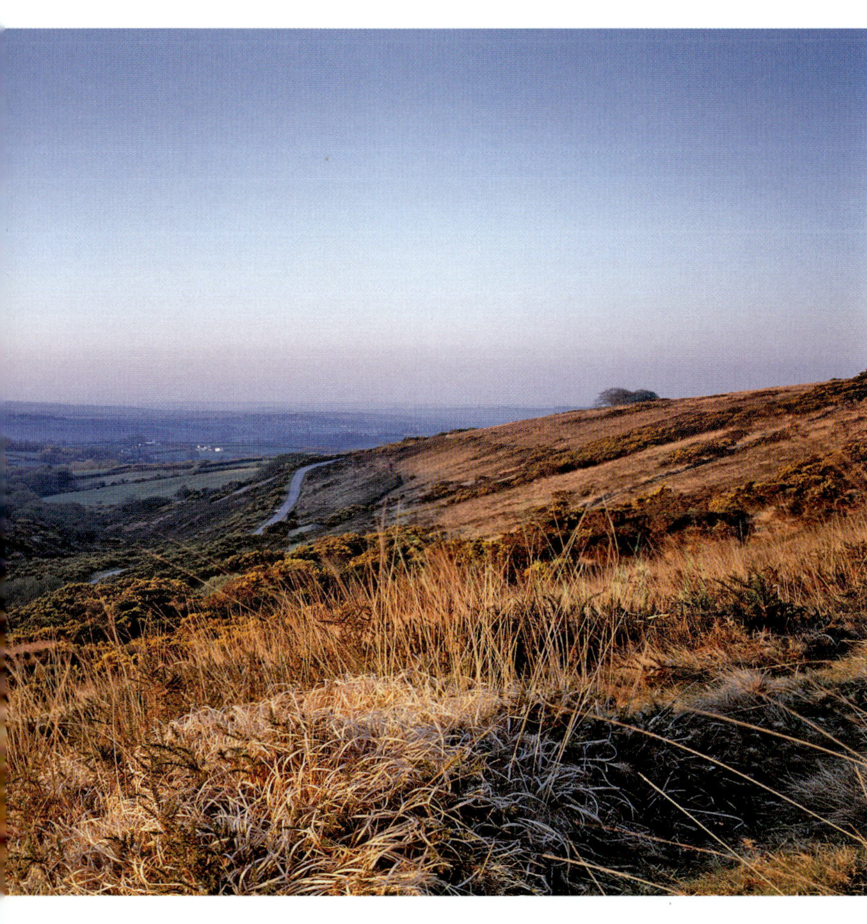

The road between Okehampton and Tavistock provides a clear view of the engine house of Wheal Betsy Mine, situated near Mary Tavy. The mine, employing 128 workers at its peak, finally closed in 1877 after a long history yielding vast quantities of silver as well as some zinc and lead. Seen here in the soft light of a spring sunrise, the mine is the best preserved on Dartmoor and is now owned by the National Trust.

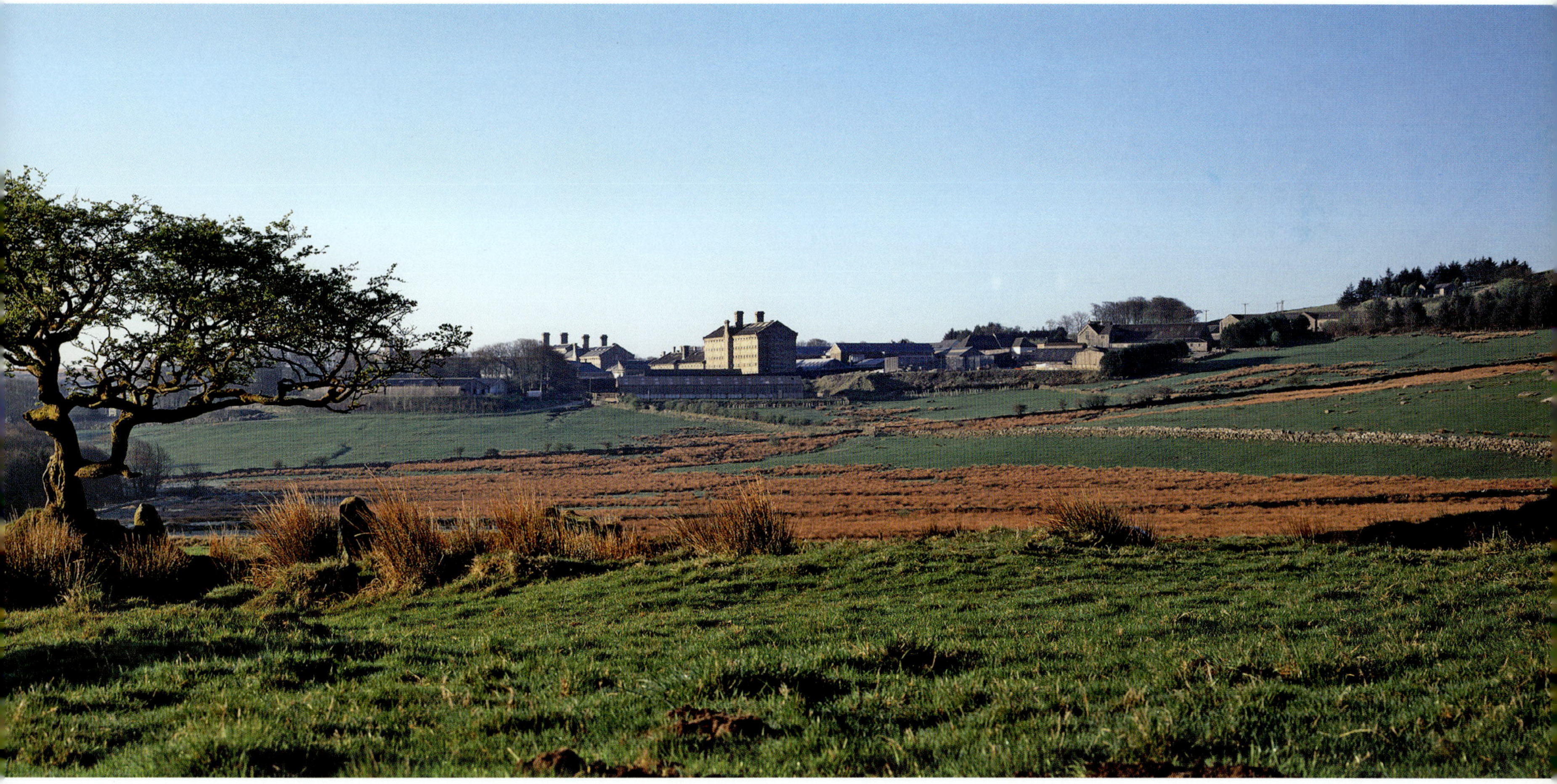

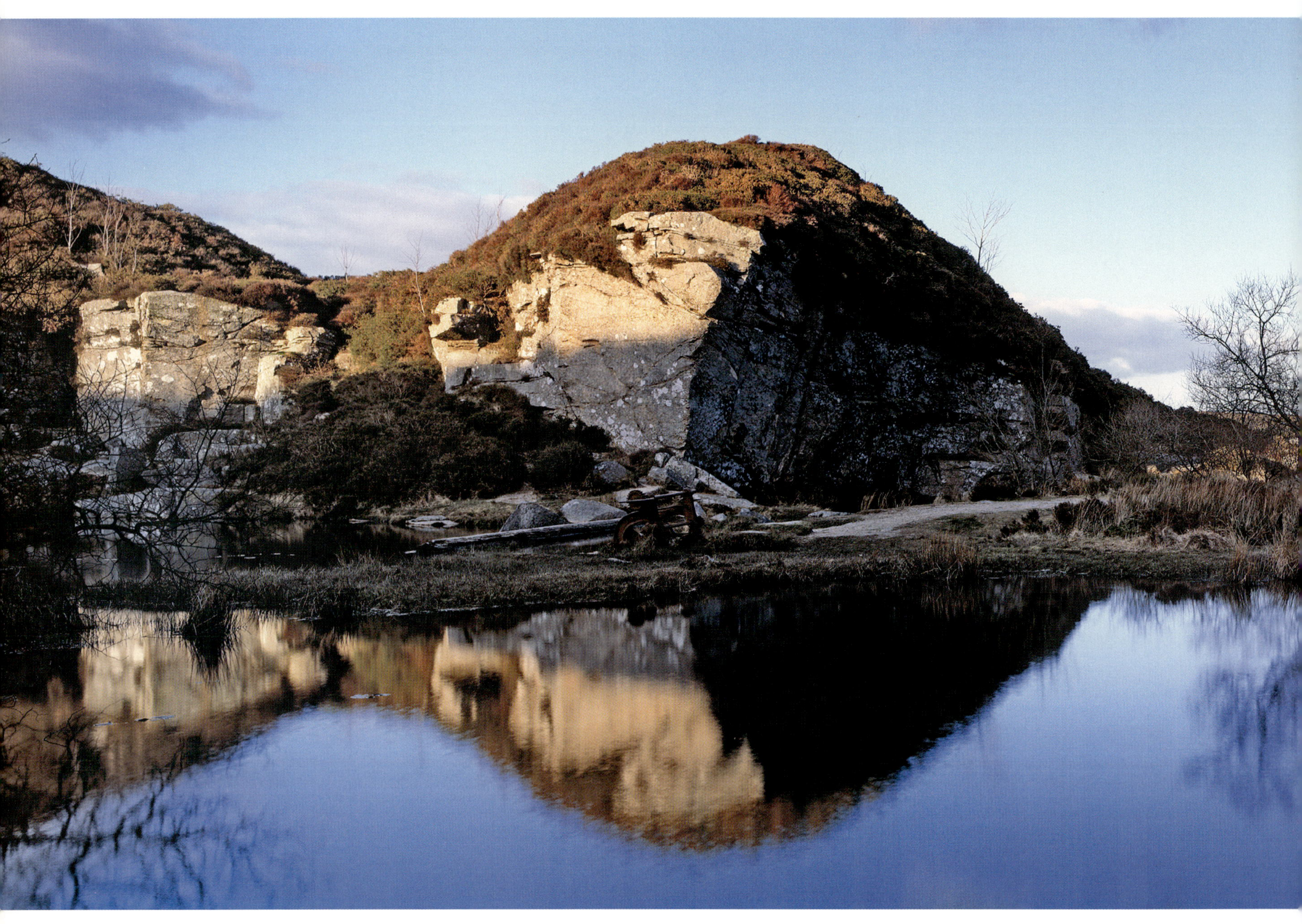

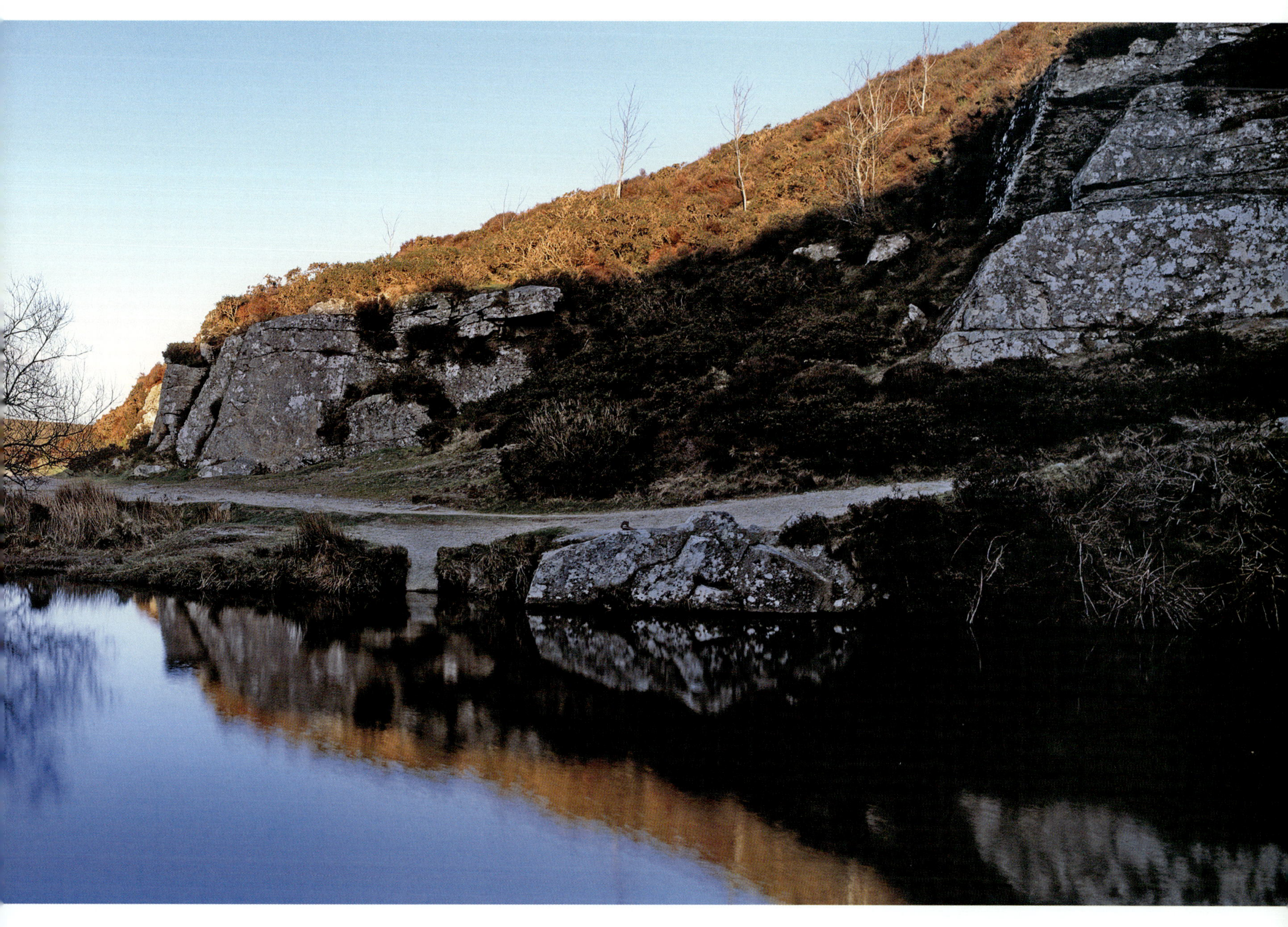

Reflections in the still waters at
Haytor Quarry.

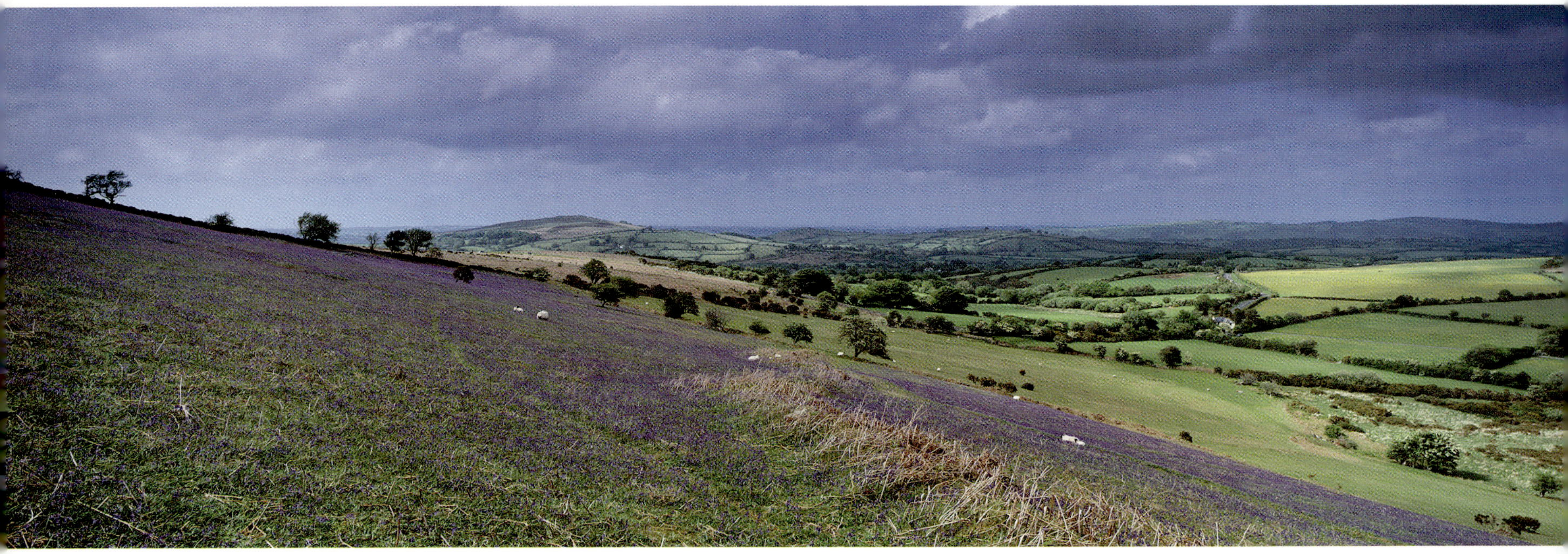

Bluebells beside Greator Rocks.

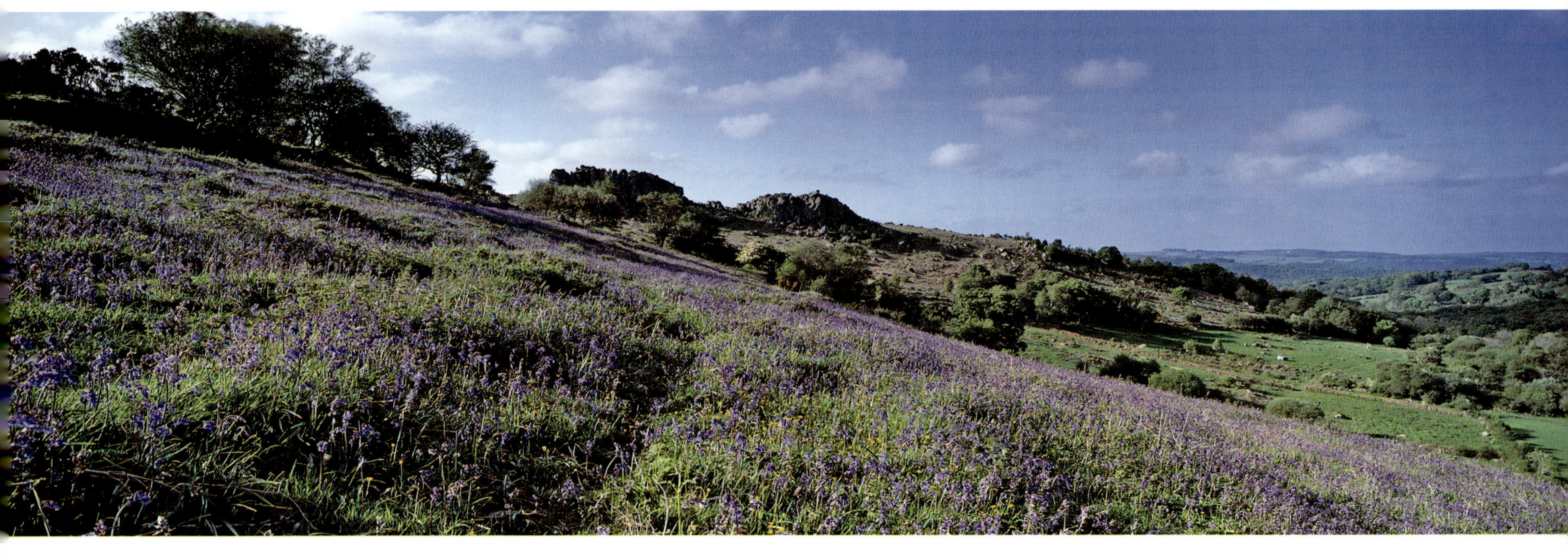

Sheep graze amongst bluebells near North Bovey.

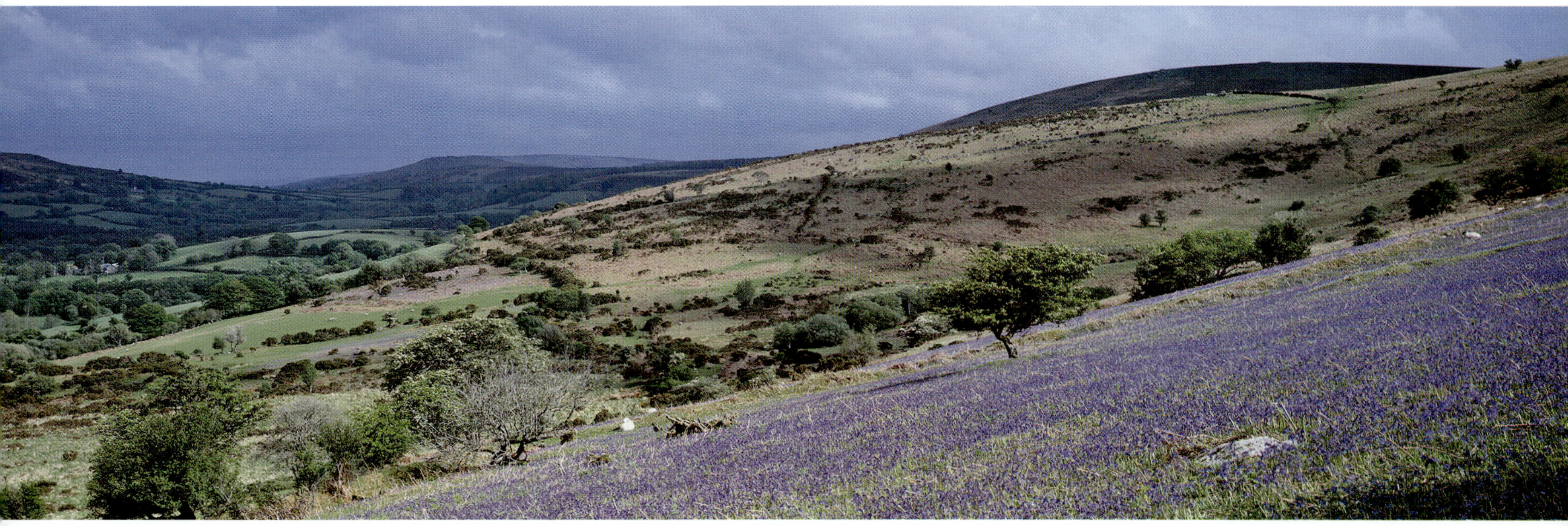

A field of bluebells add colour to the view across Dartmoor's hills.

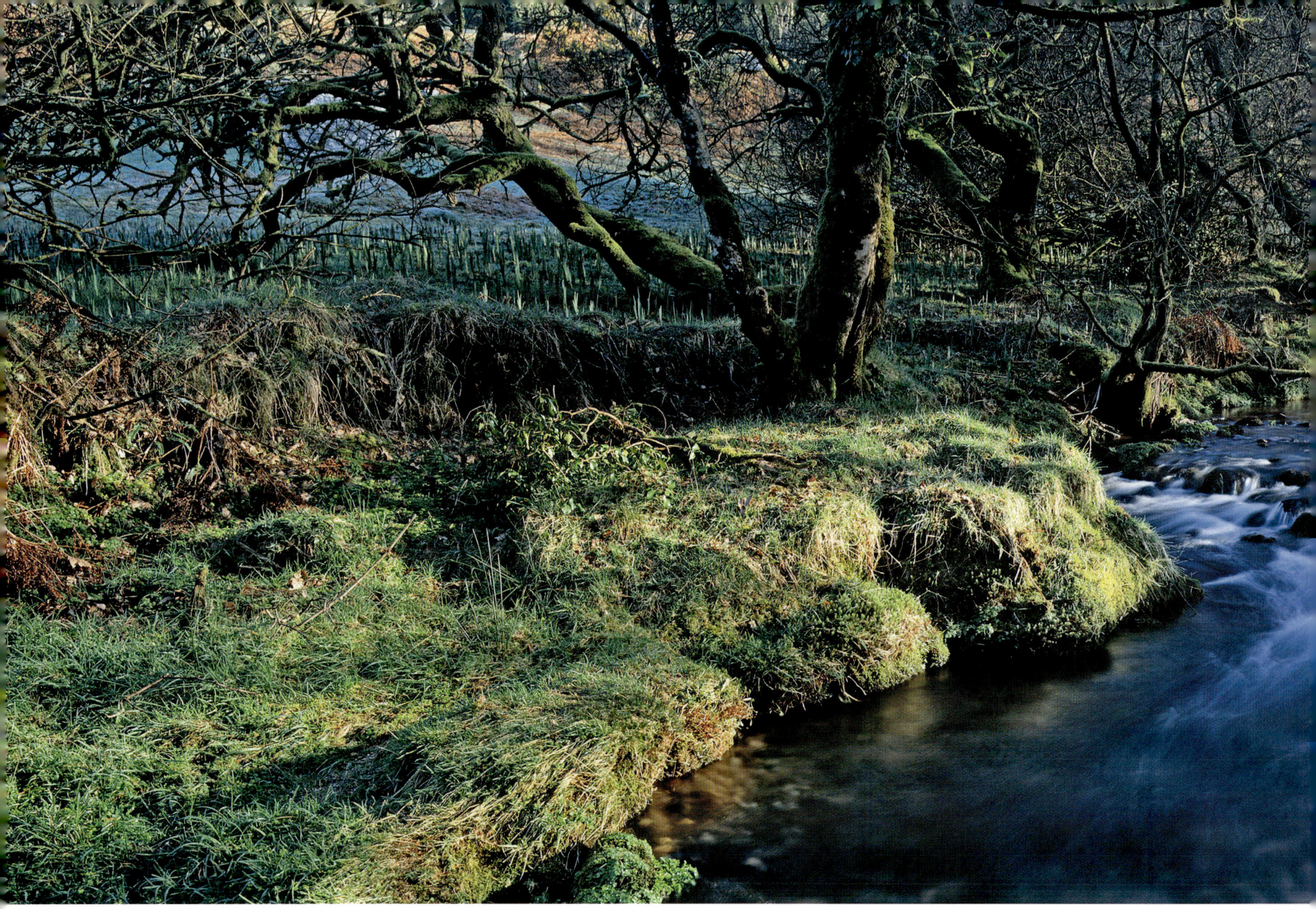

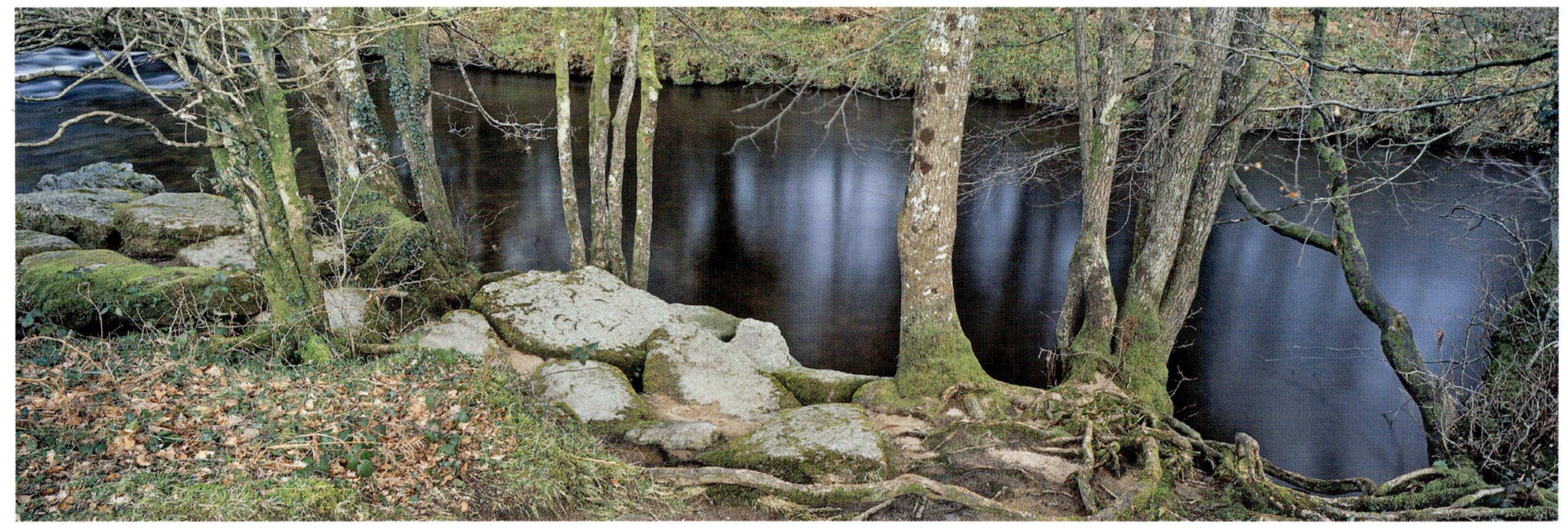

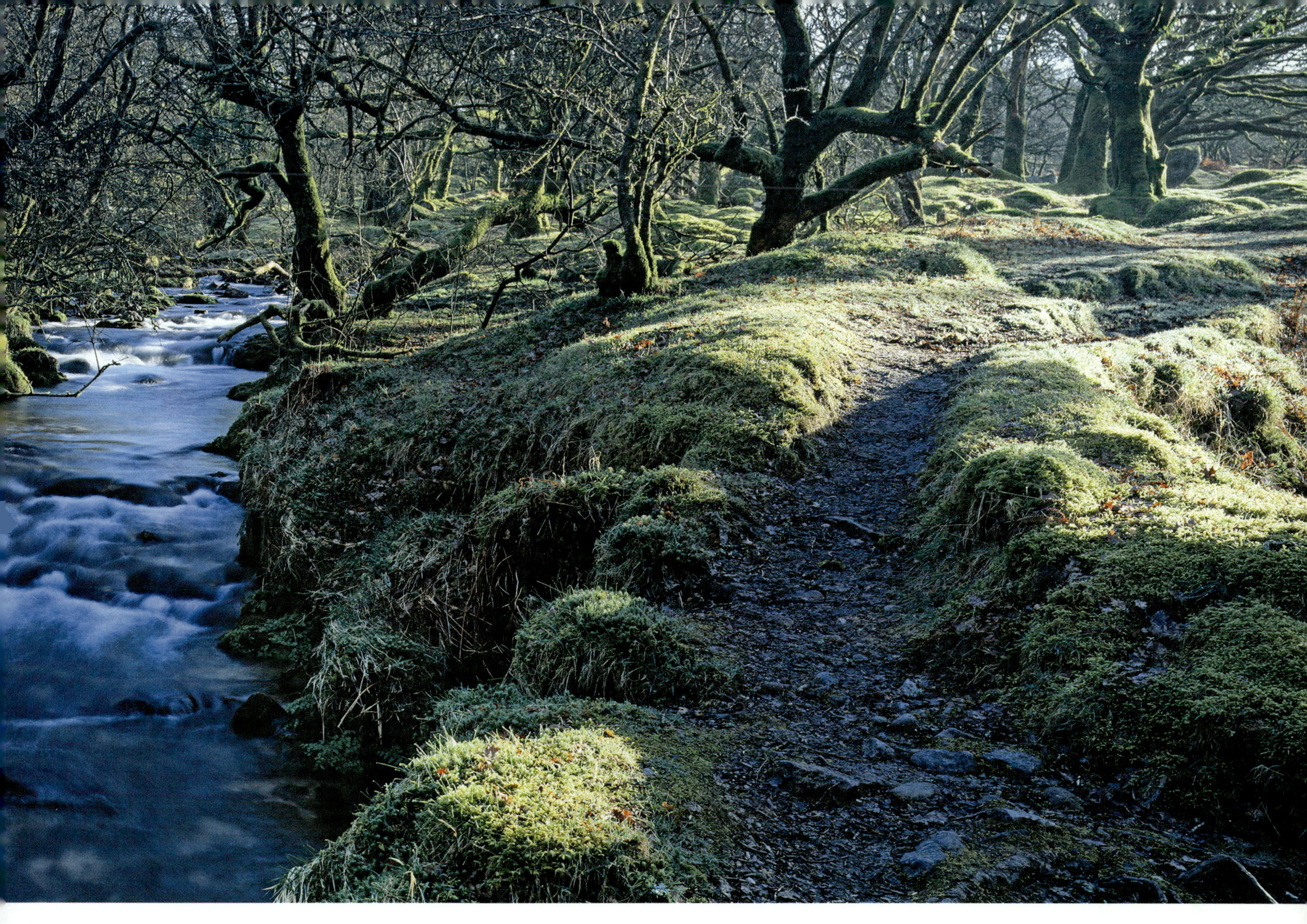

The fast-flowing stream curiously named Newleycombe Lake babbles in the spring morning sunshine en route to Burrator Reservoir near Plymouth.

Tangled roots line the river Dart near Newbridge Marsh.

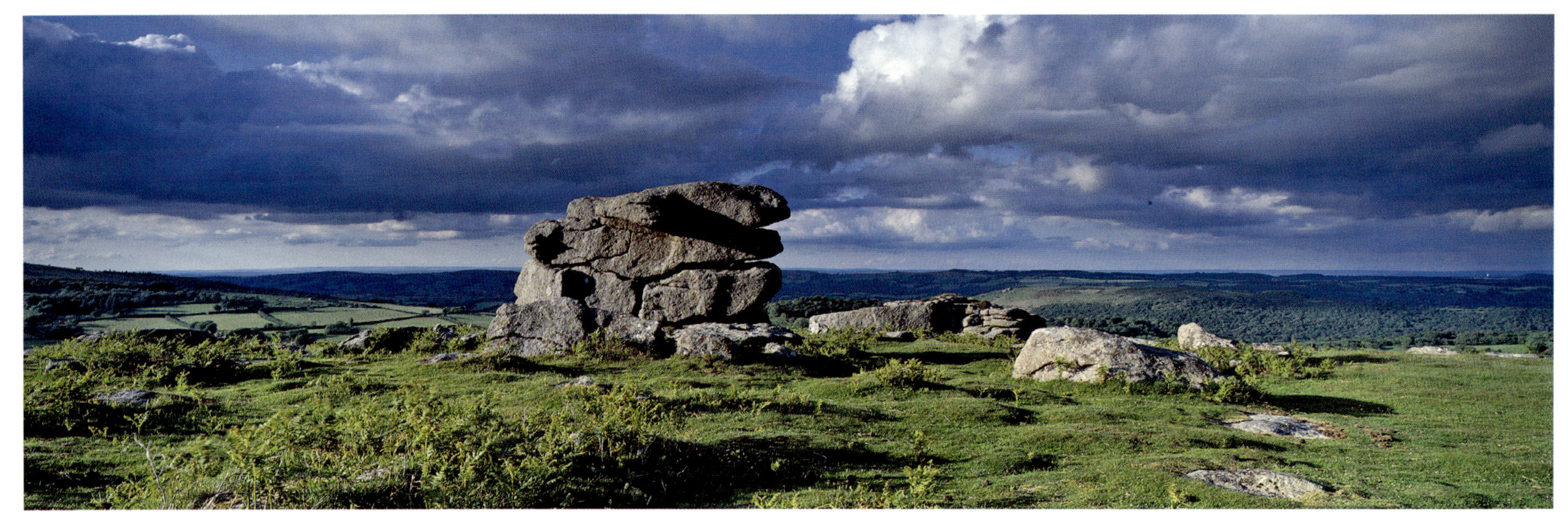

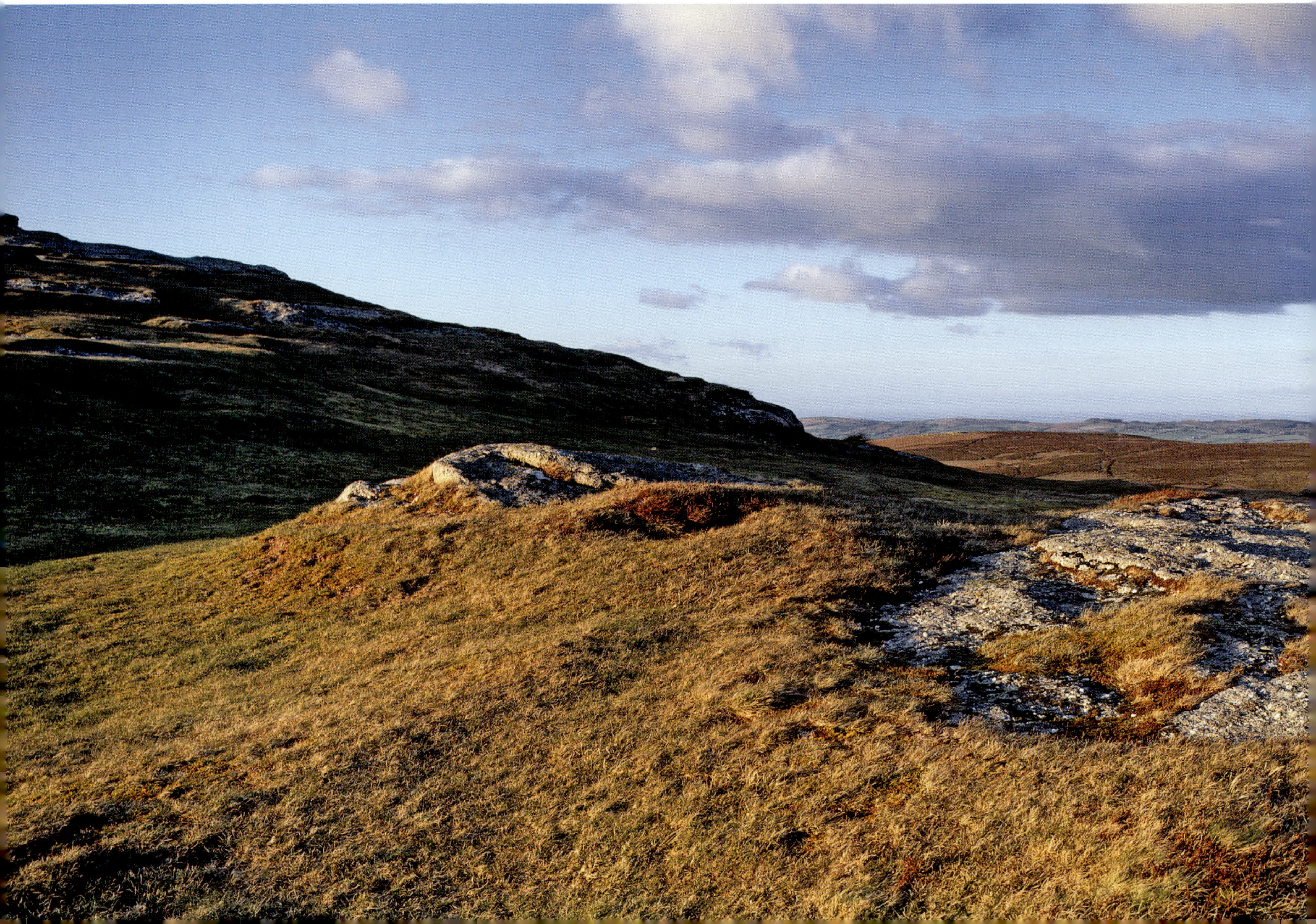

Rocks on the summit of Hayne Down, above Bowerman's Nose, catch the afternoon sunlight.

A low sun rakes long shadows across the popular Haytor, highlighting differing textures of the tough grass and rough granite underfoot.

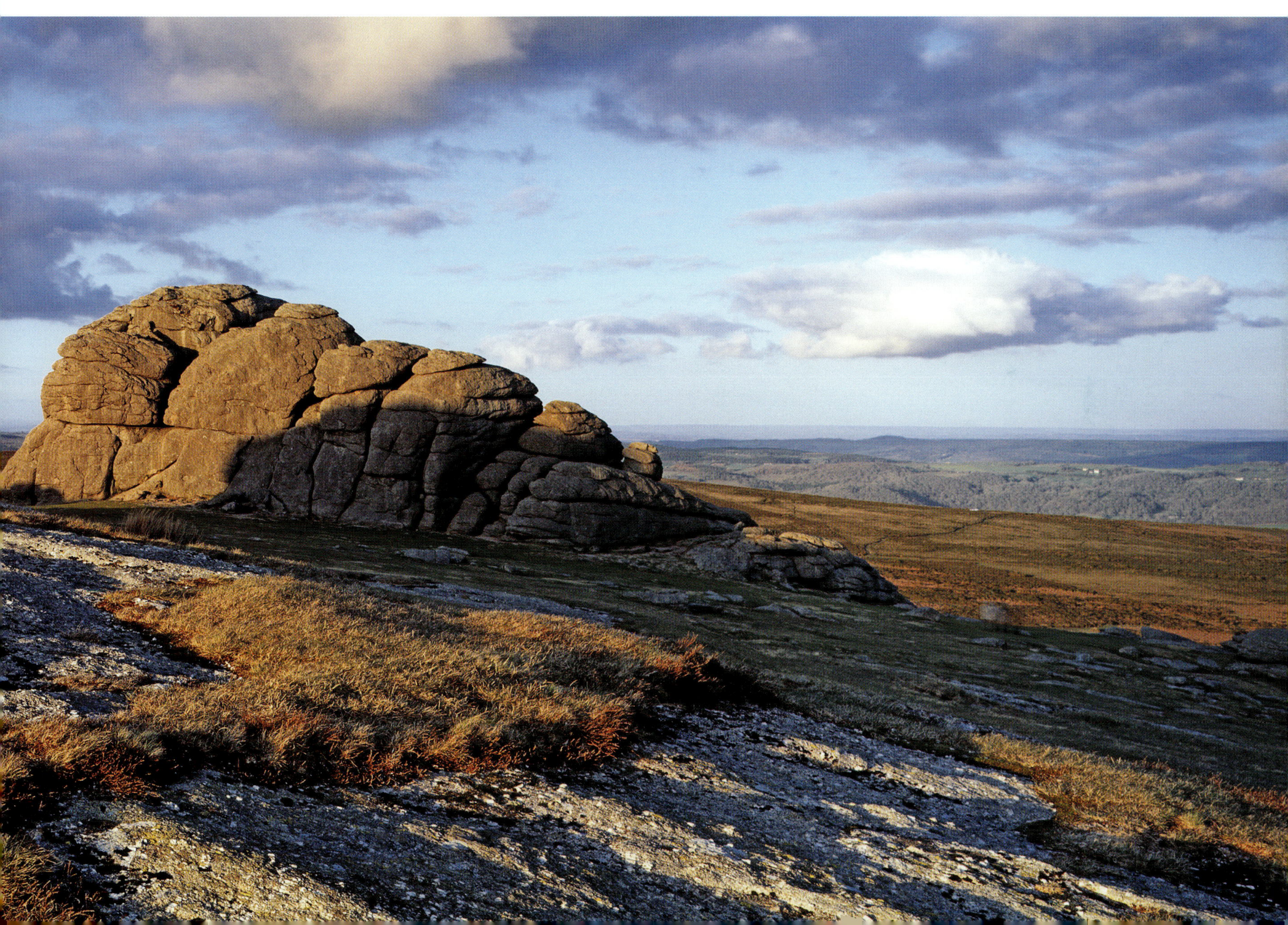

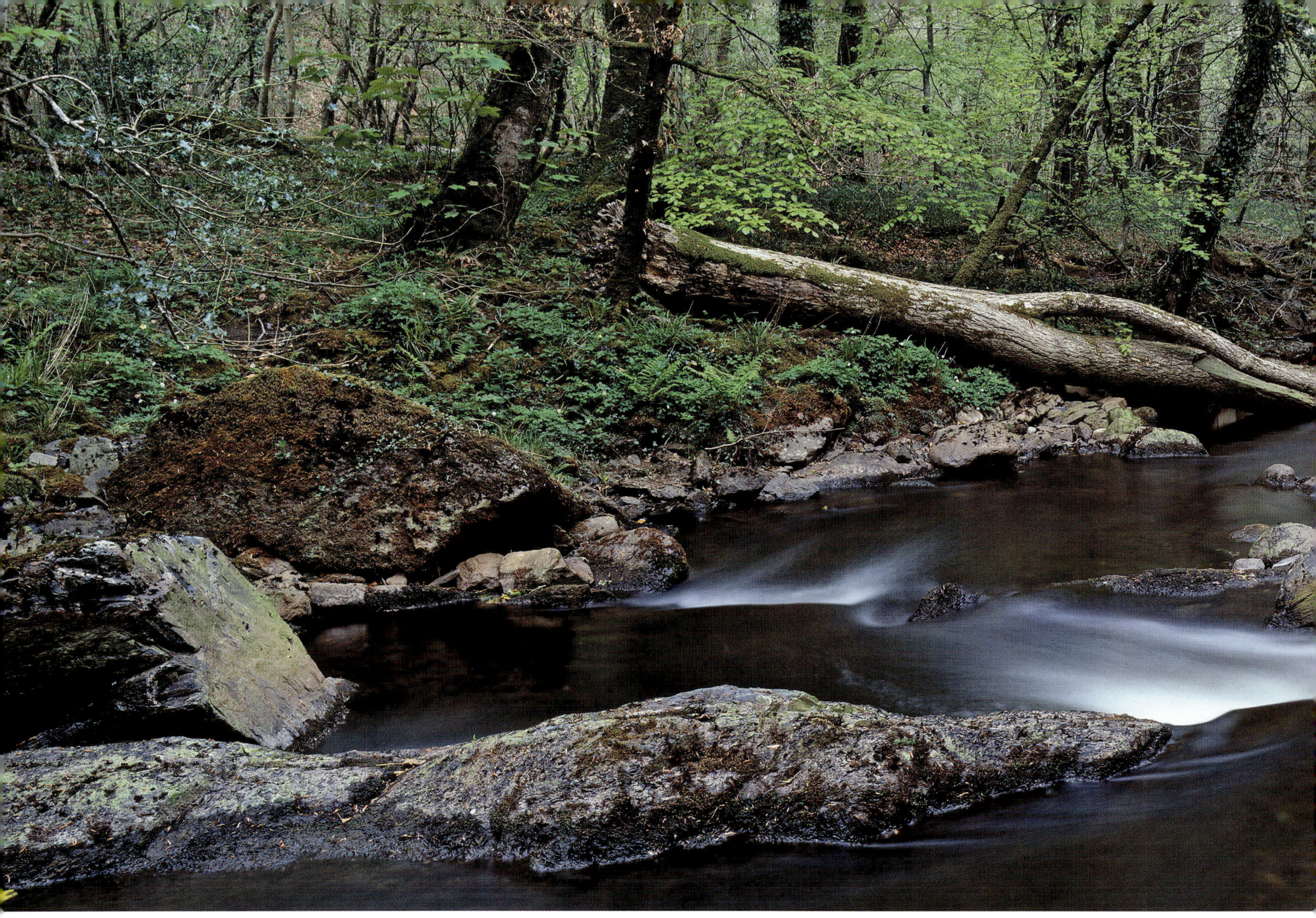

Fallen trees and branches line the West Okement River flowing from Meldon Reservoir in the north of the moor.

Lime green leaves signal new growth in the woods beside the river.

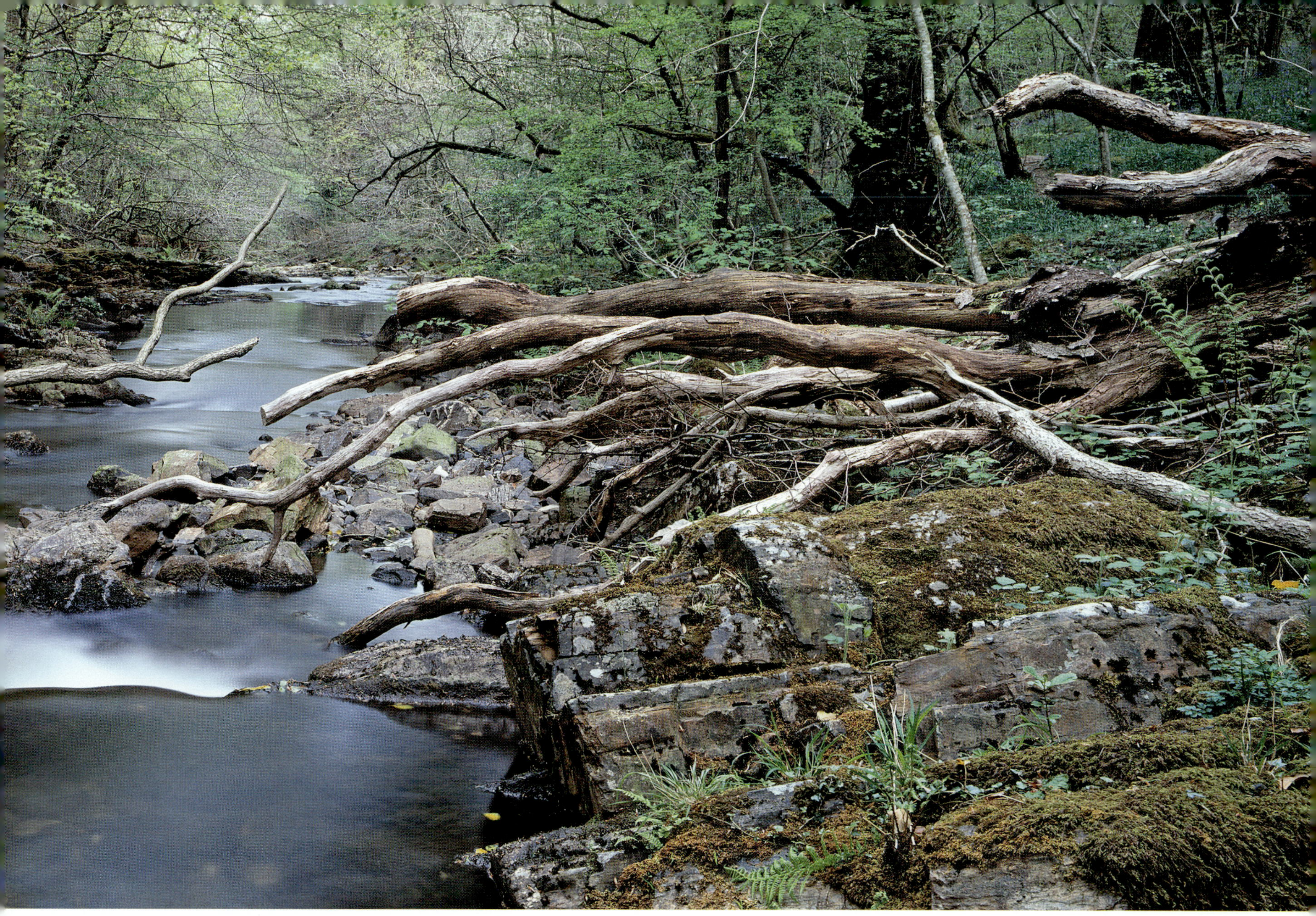

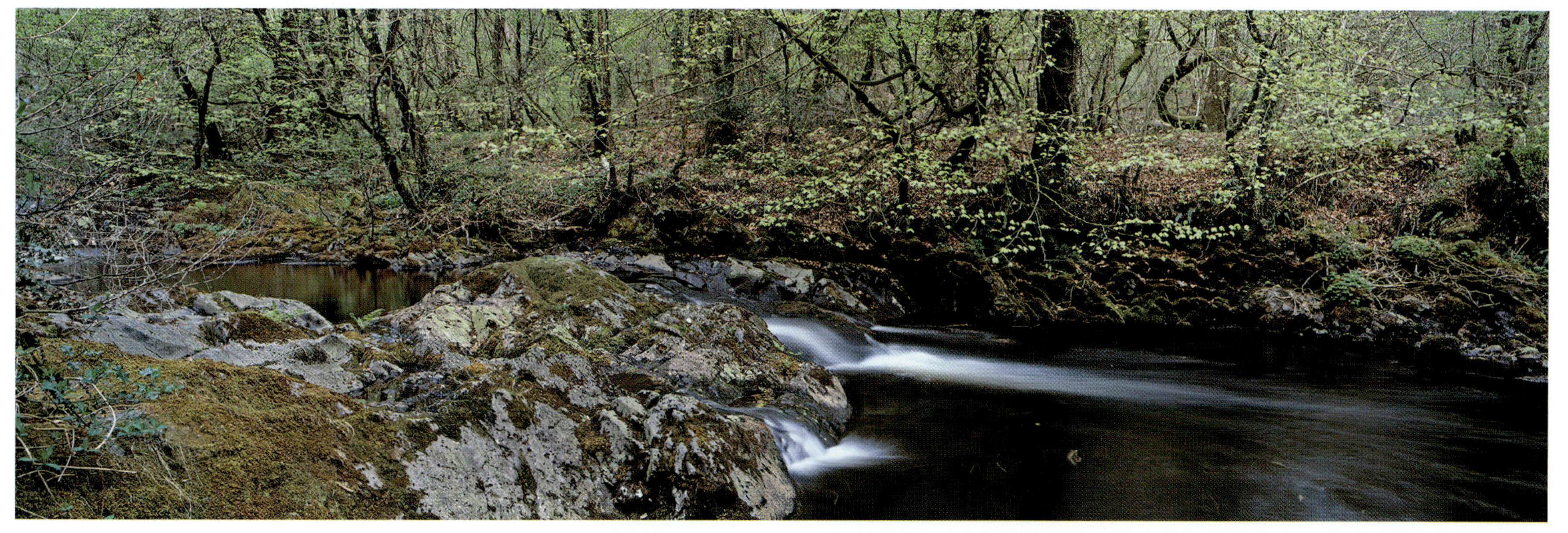

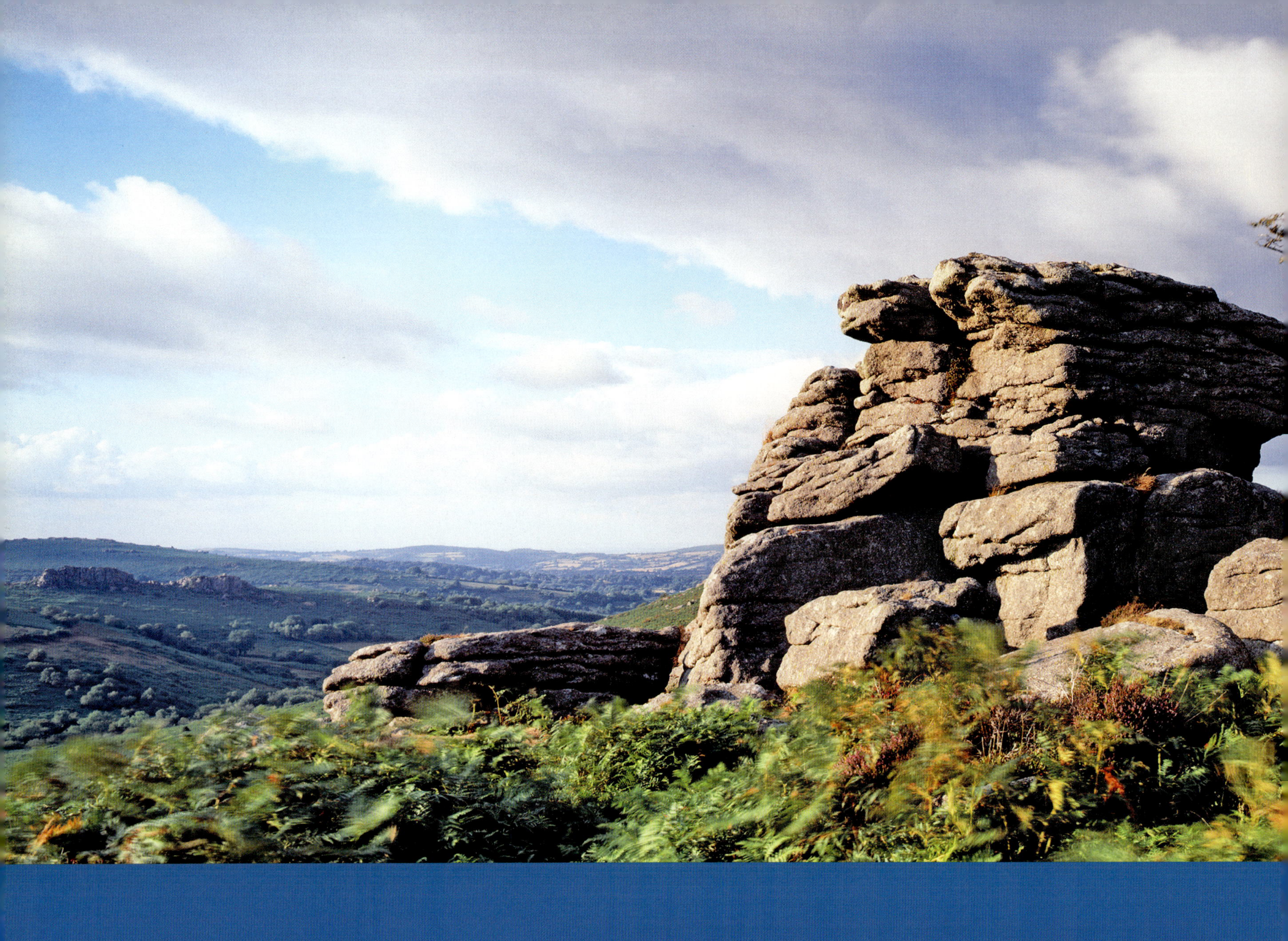

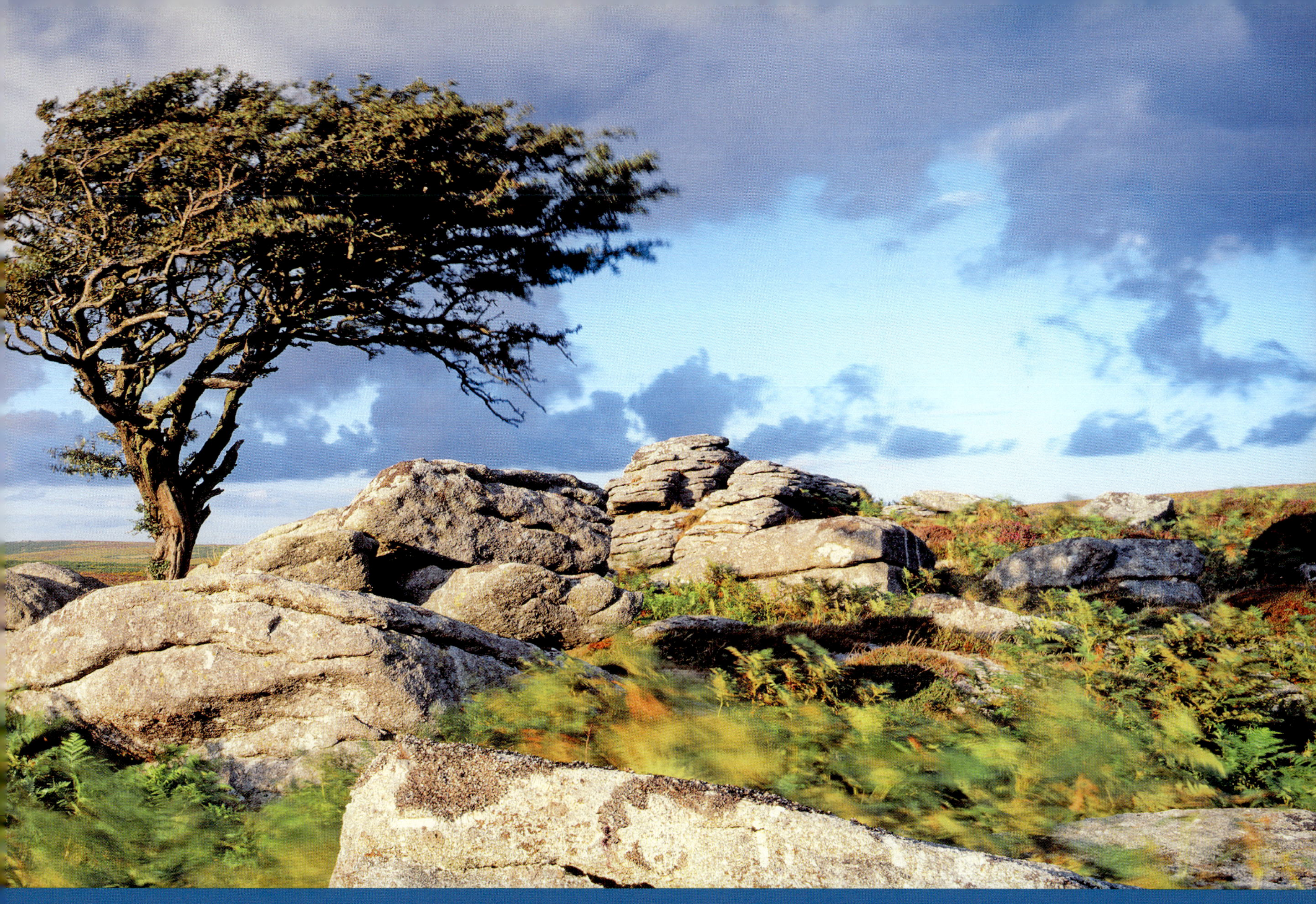

Summer

A blustery day on the moor. Evening sunlight creates a warm glow on the rocks under the dramatic cloudscape above. Vibrant greens of the ferns bring a lively summer display of colour to the landscape.

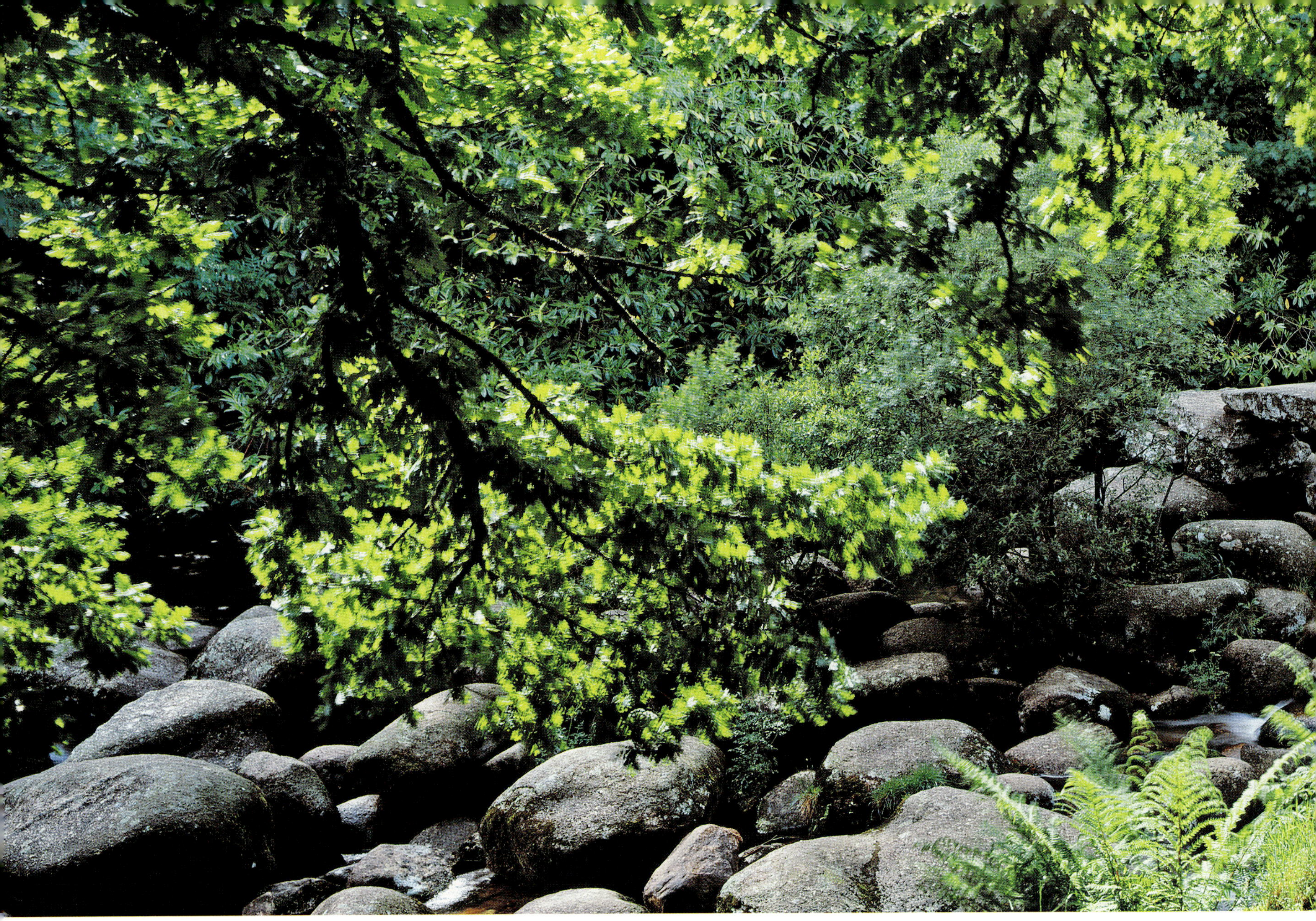

Dartmeet finds its name from the meeting of the East Dart and West Dart rivers. Two bridges span it here: this ancient ruined clapper bridge encircled by luminous foliage and a more modern stone arched bridge.

Overhanging branches and lush green leaves frame the fast-flowing waters of the East Dart.

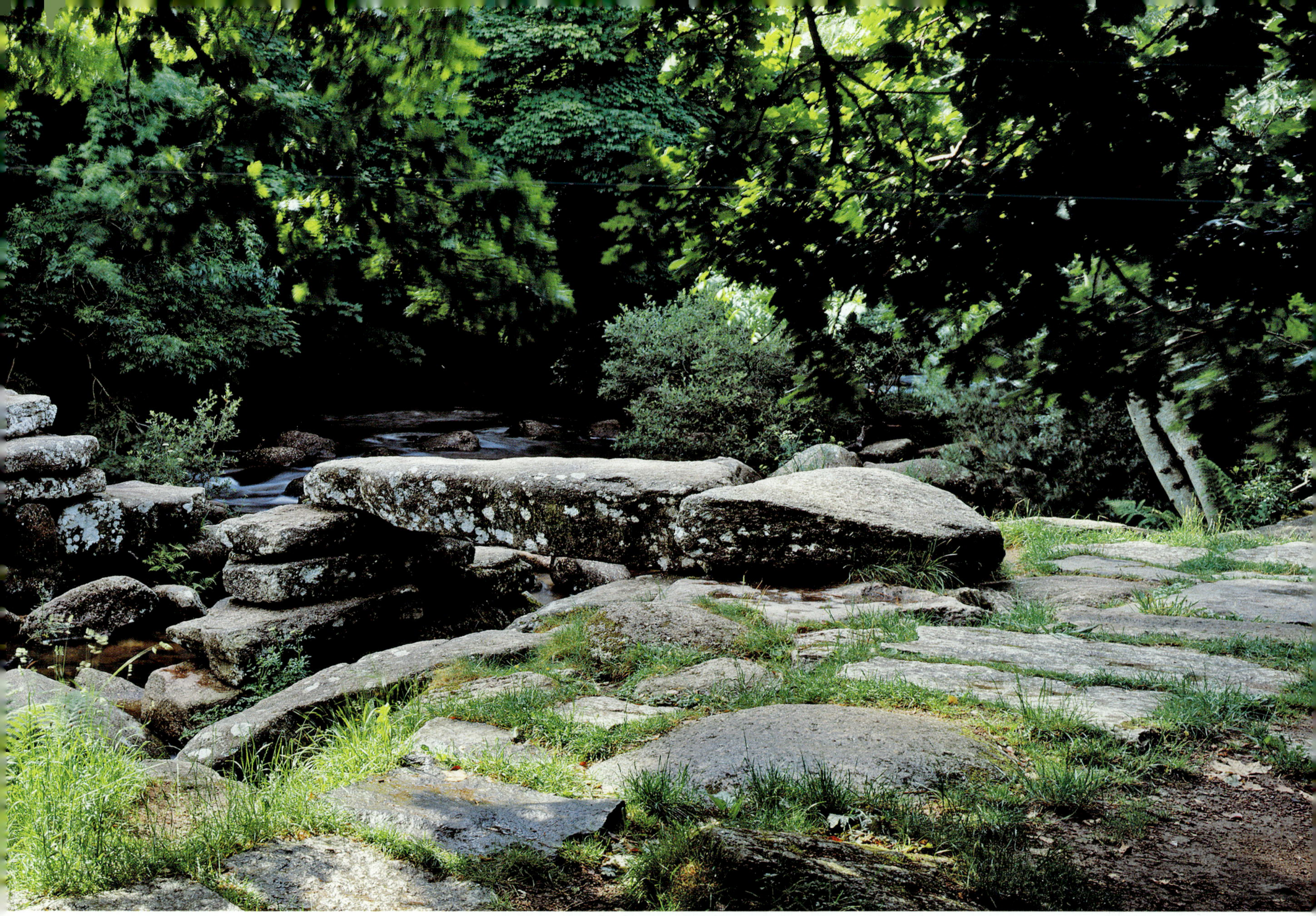

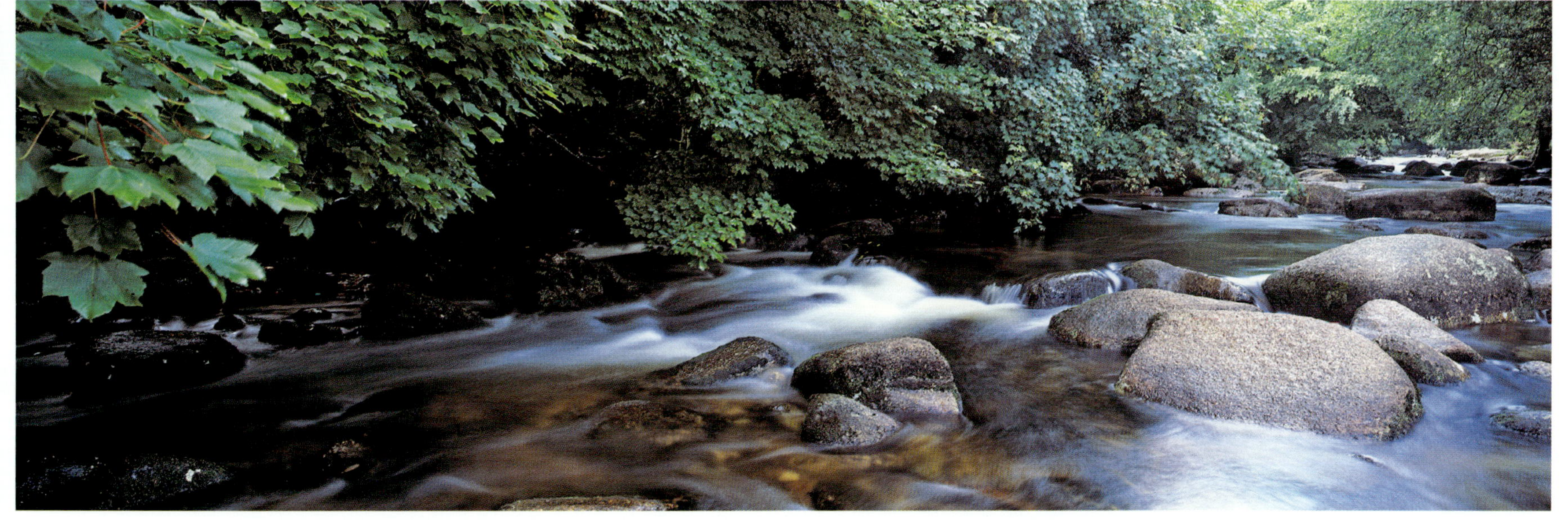

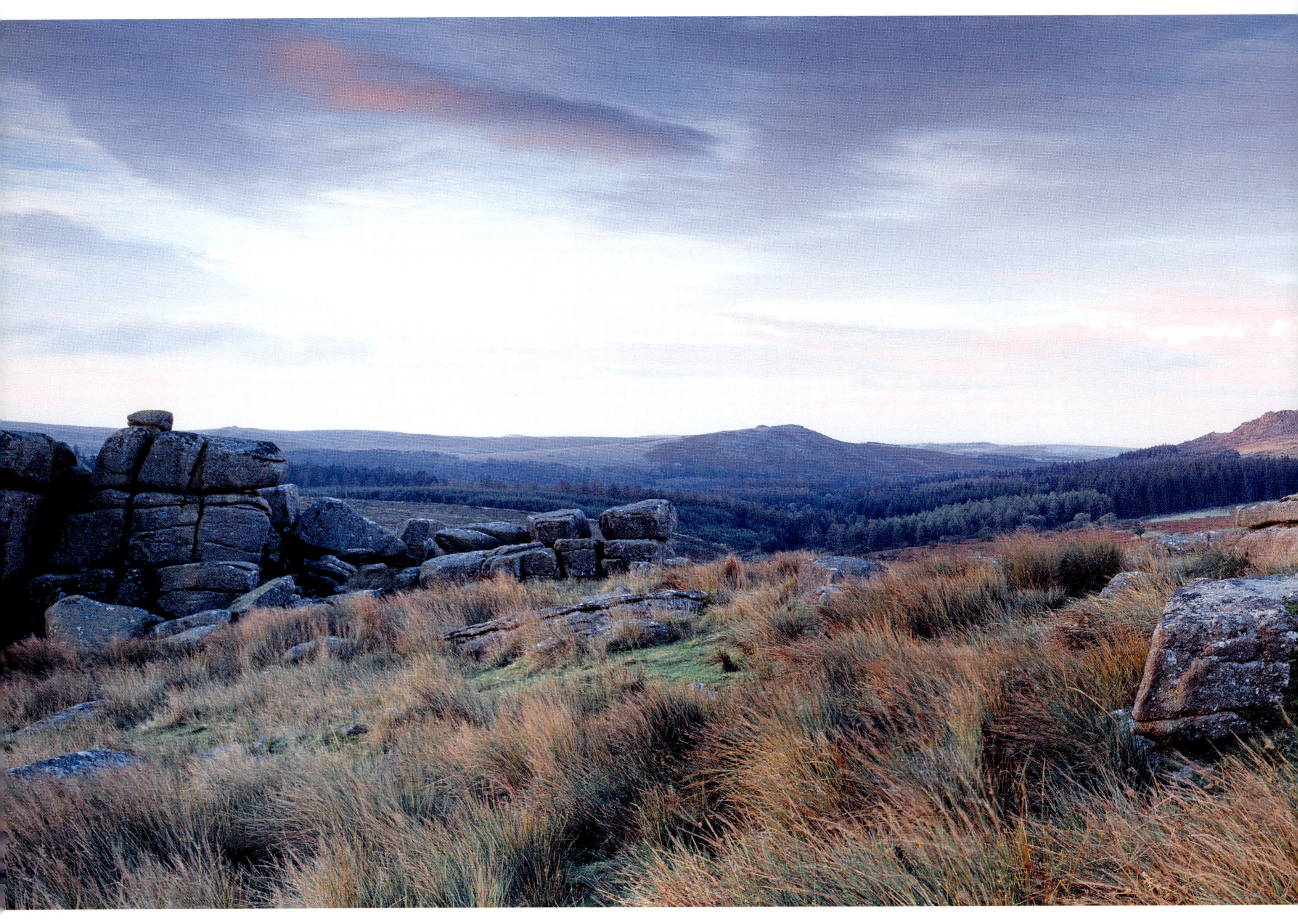

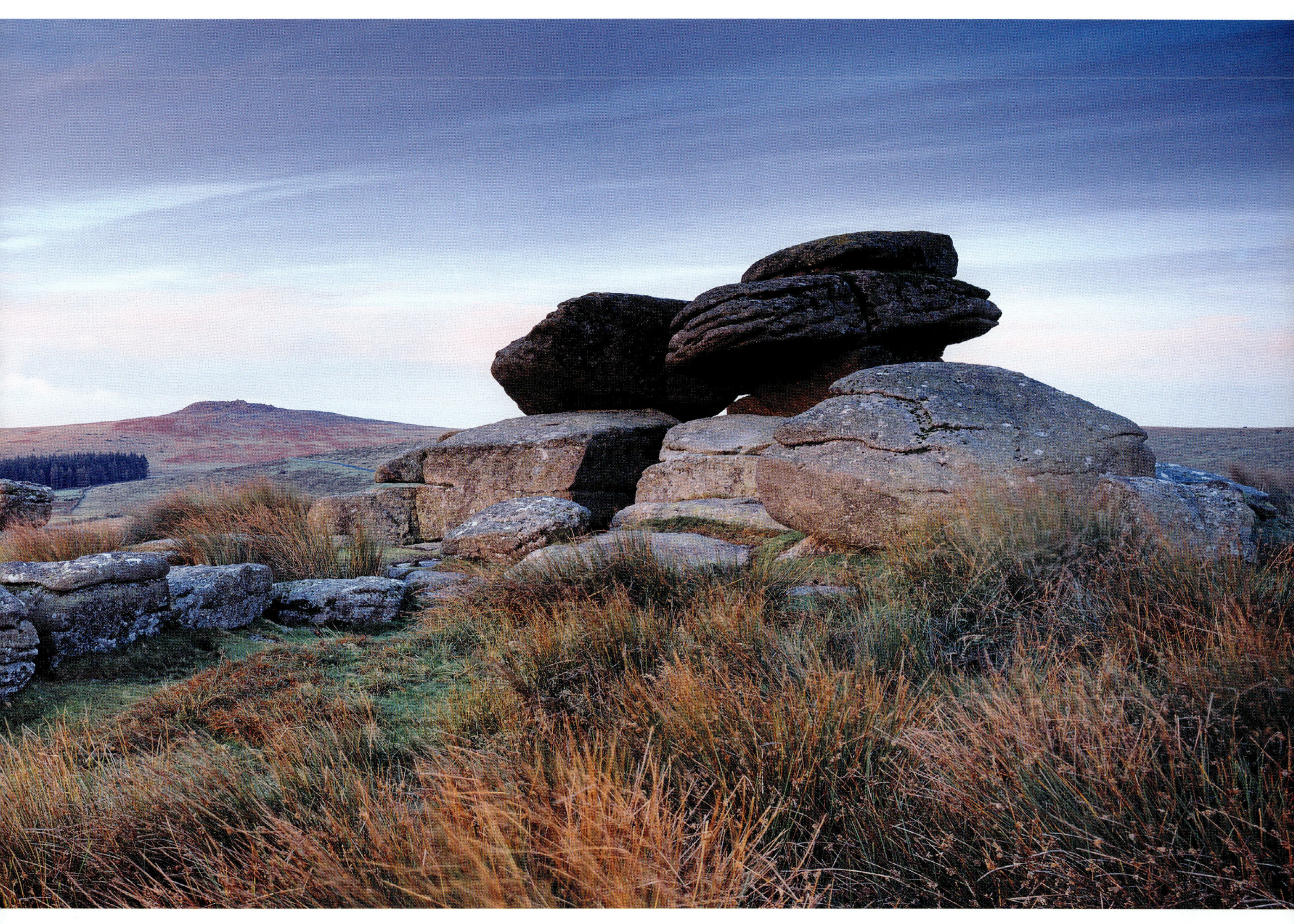

Soft hues from the morning sunrise are reflected by the rocks and grass surrounding Black Tor, looking towards the distant Leather Tor.

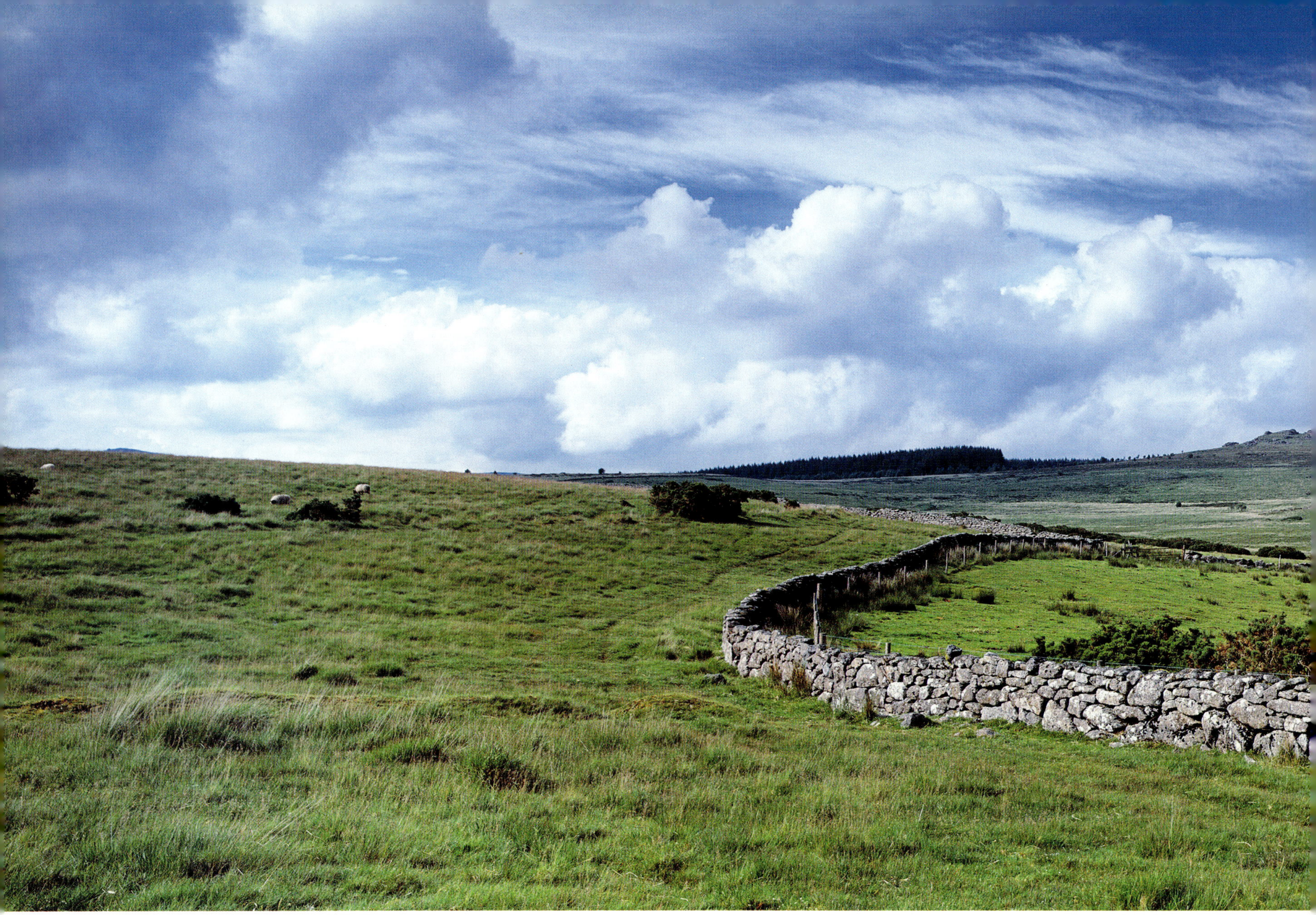

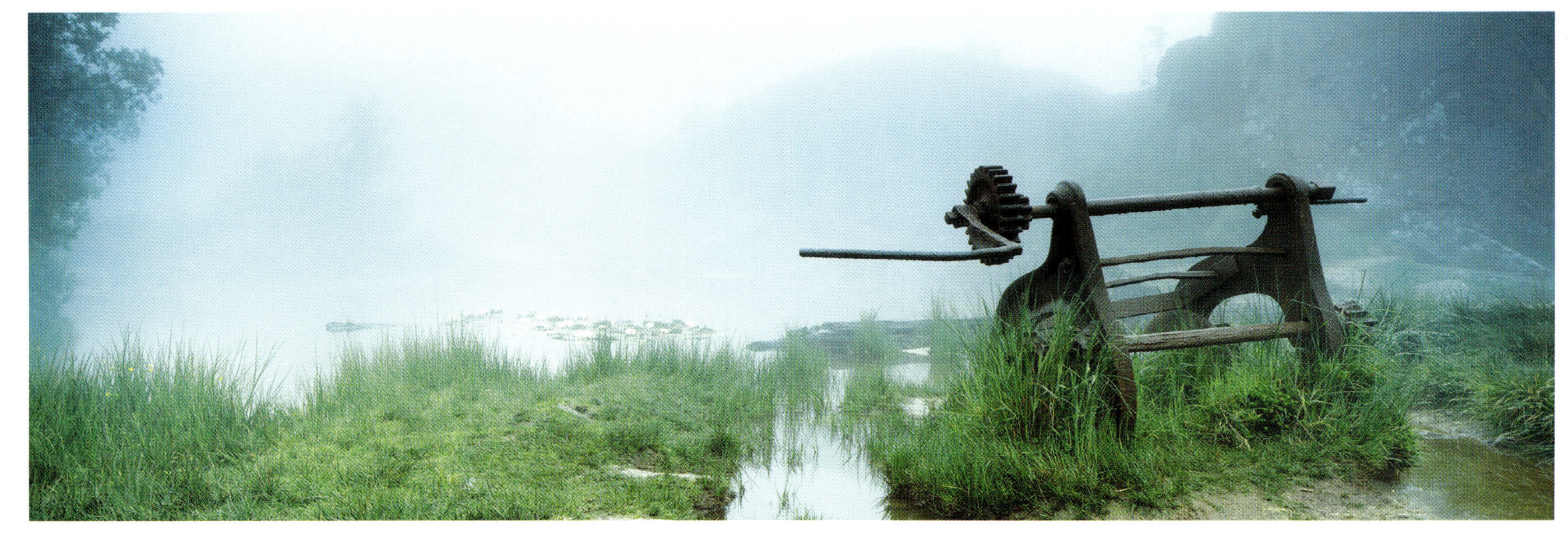

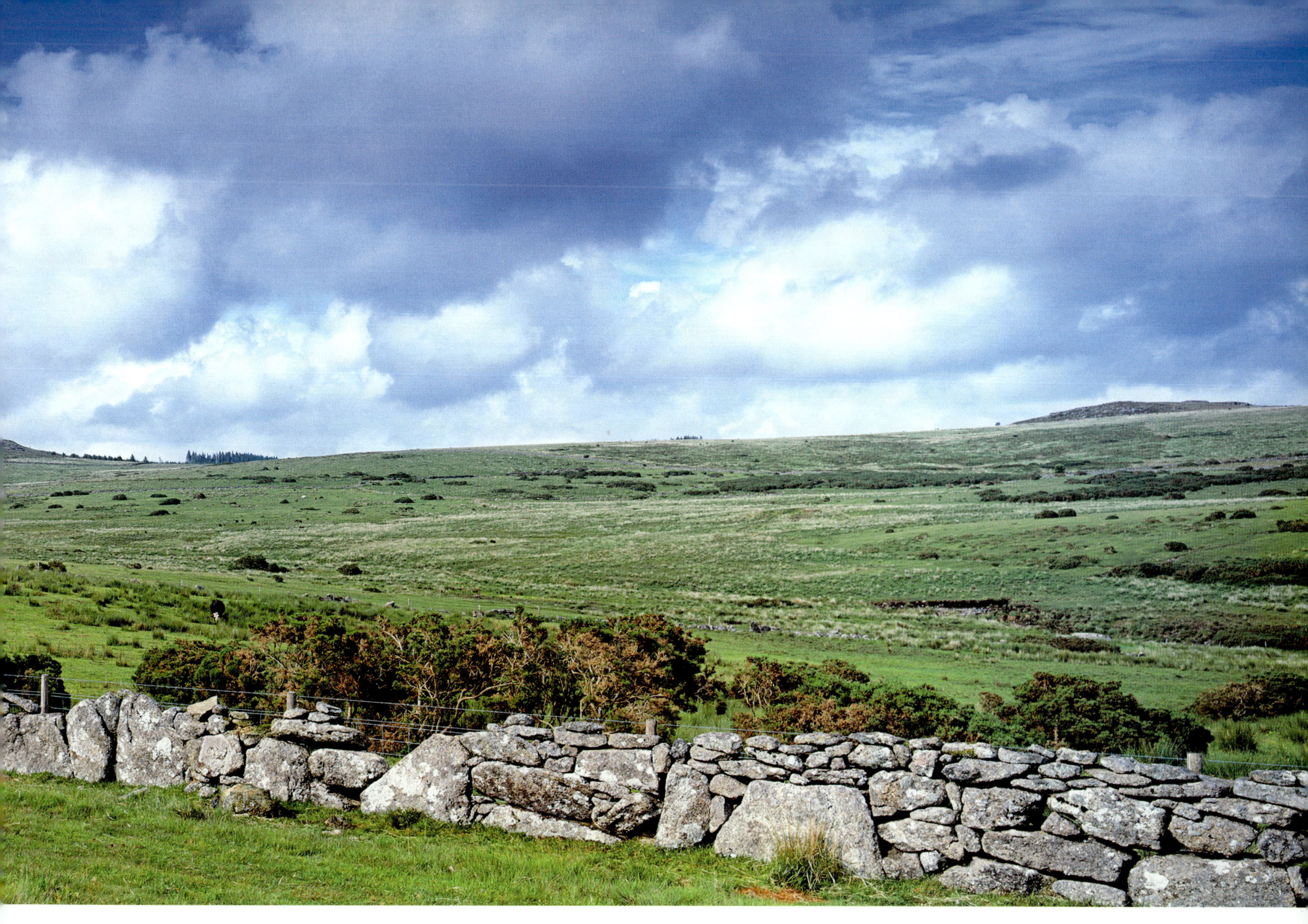

Fog swirls around rusted machinery at Haytor Quarry. Granite blocks were mined here from around 1820 and transported on a specially constructed granite railway ten miles to the sea, where they were loaded onto ships for distribution. Haytor granite was famous for its ability to resist pressure, making it a popular choice for many building projects. Now disused and steeped in water with lilies floating serenely on the surface, the quarry makes a tranquil setting.

Fluffy cumulus clouds crowd the sky above Bellever Tor and Laughter Tor to the right. The granite drystone walls still winding over miles of the moor are a long-standing testament to the skilled craftsmanship of their construction.

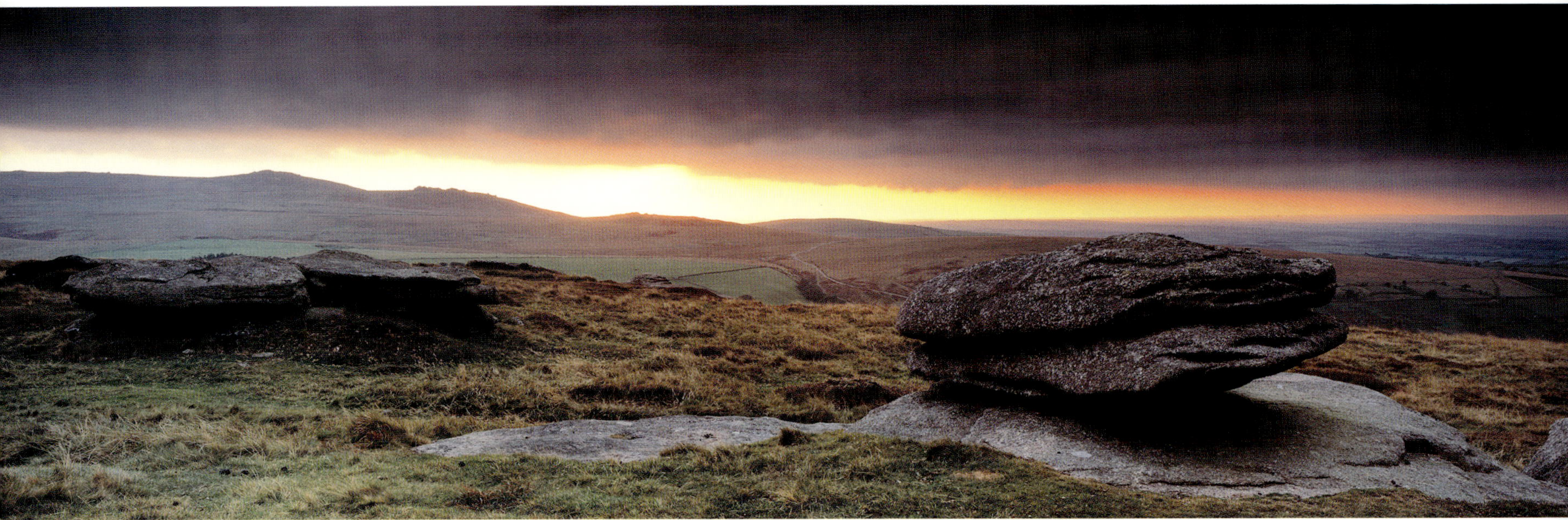

The ascending peaks of Rowtor, West Mill Tor and Yes Tor step skywards as the setting sun slips down through the foreboding clouds above Belstone Tor.

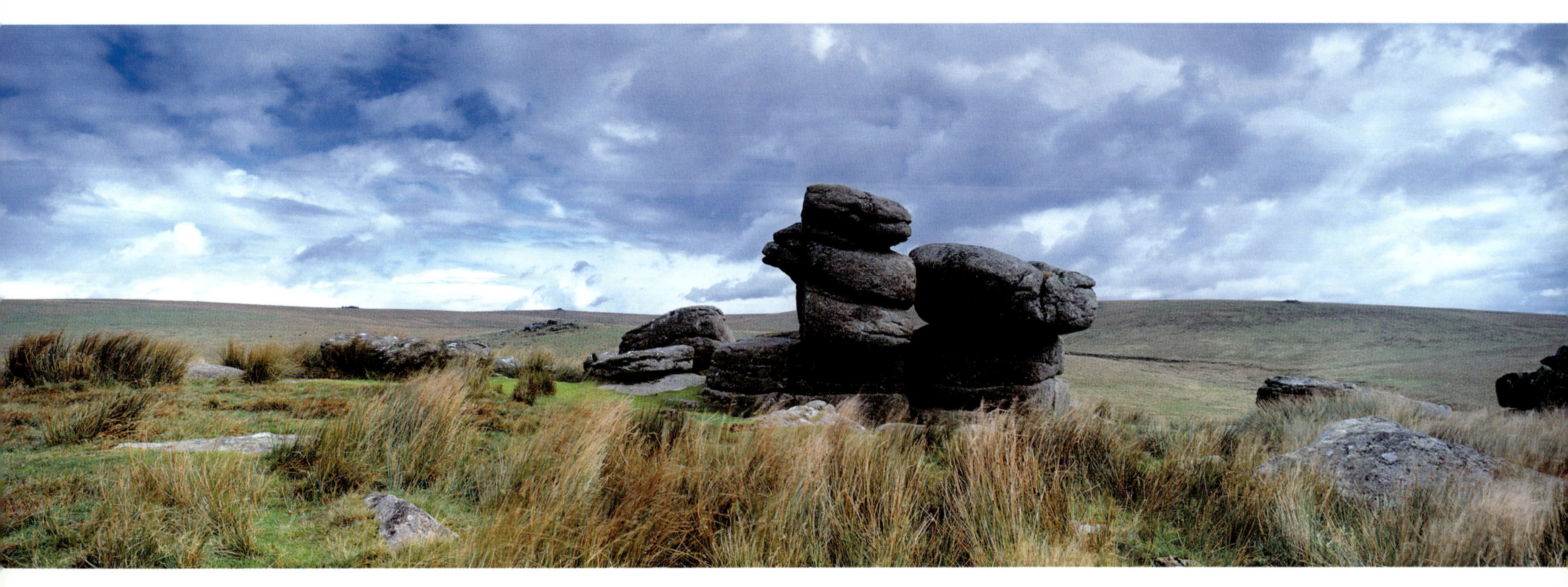

Descending the slopes around Littaford Tor, these lichen-covered granite stacks glow orange in the fading sunlight. The lichen happily grows where most plants would not survive the bleak conditions.

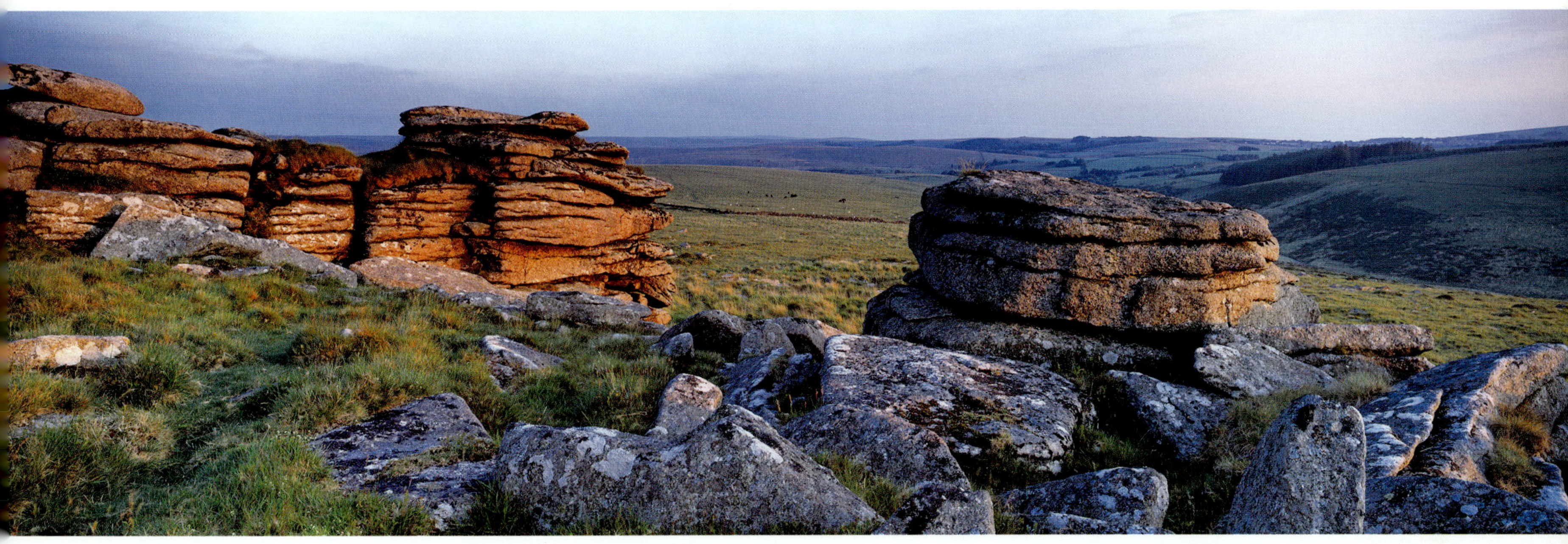

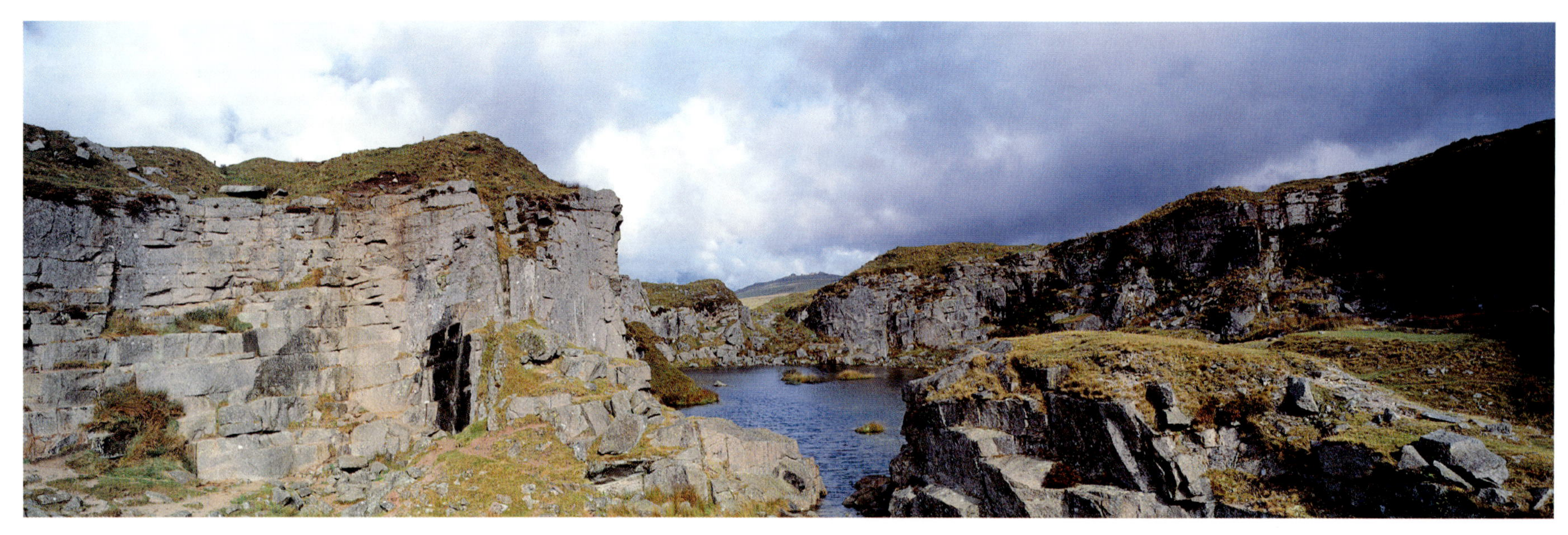

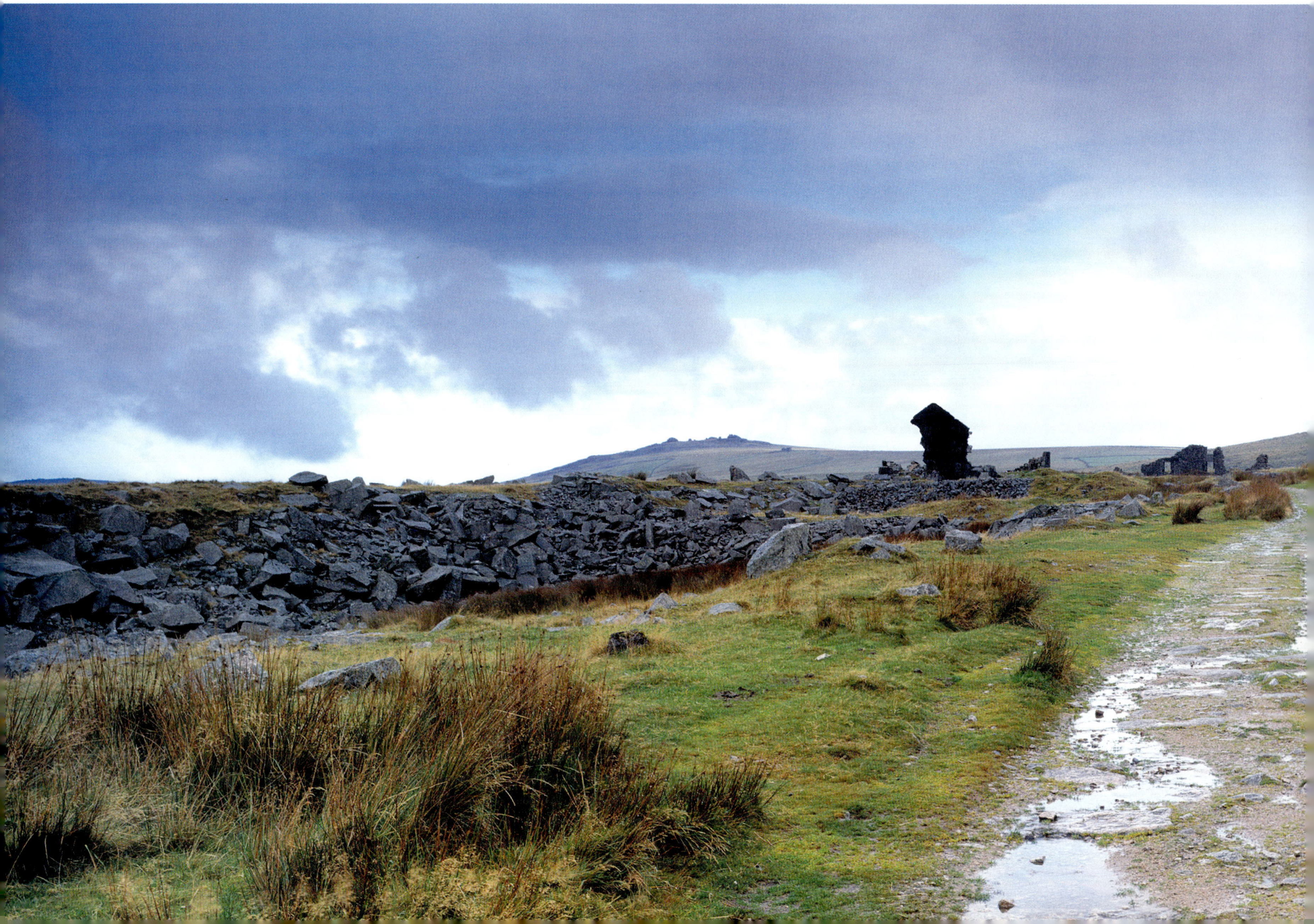

Down this stony track – once a railway line – lies the abandoned quarry of Foggintor. One of Dartmoor's largest quarries, it employed huge numbers of local people, and provided some of the granite used in the construction of London Bridge. Still an impressive sight, the quarry, now surrounded by ruins of buildings, is a popular location for climbing and abseiling.

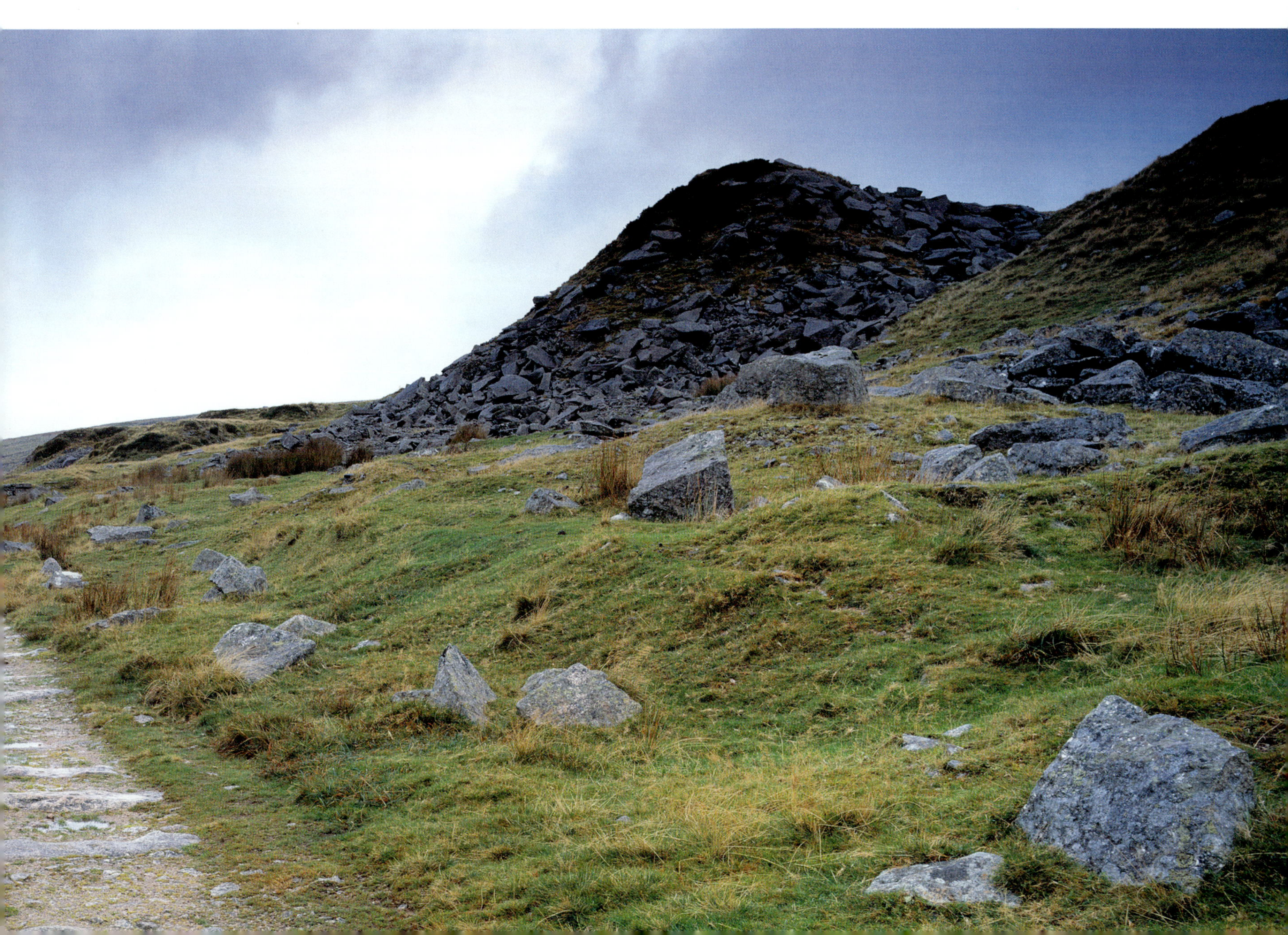

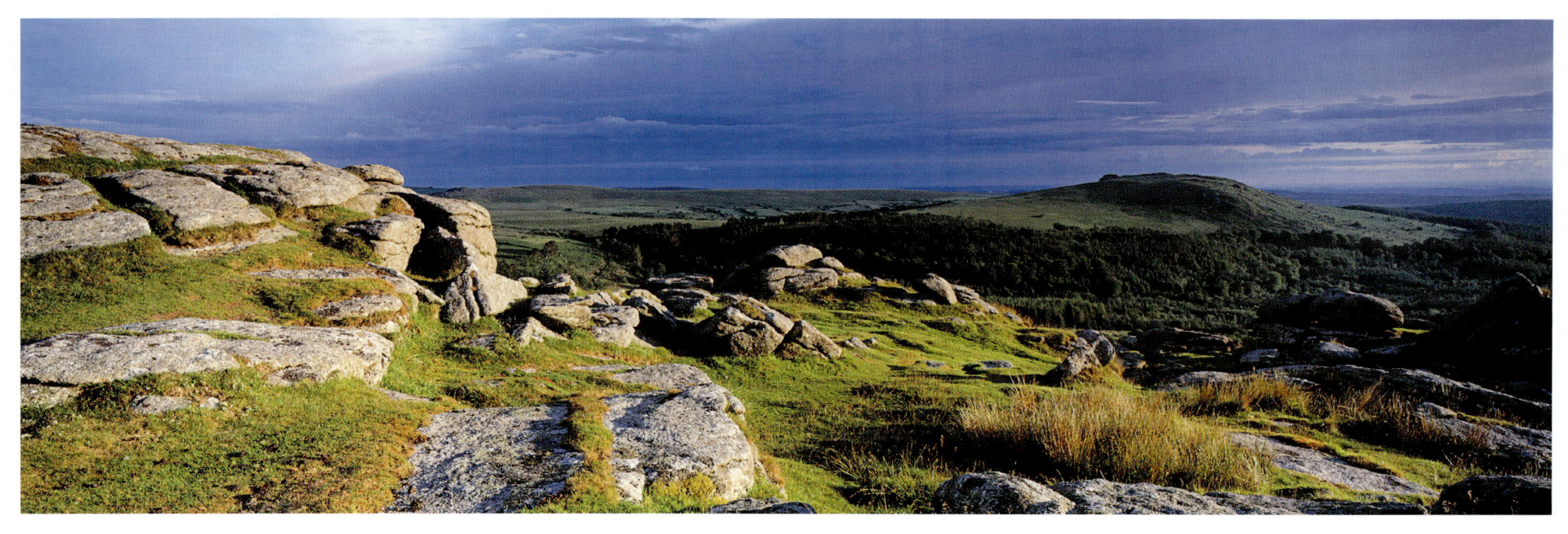

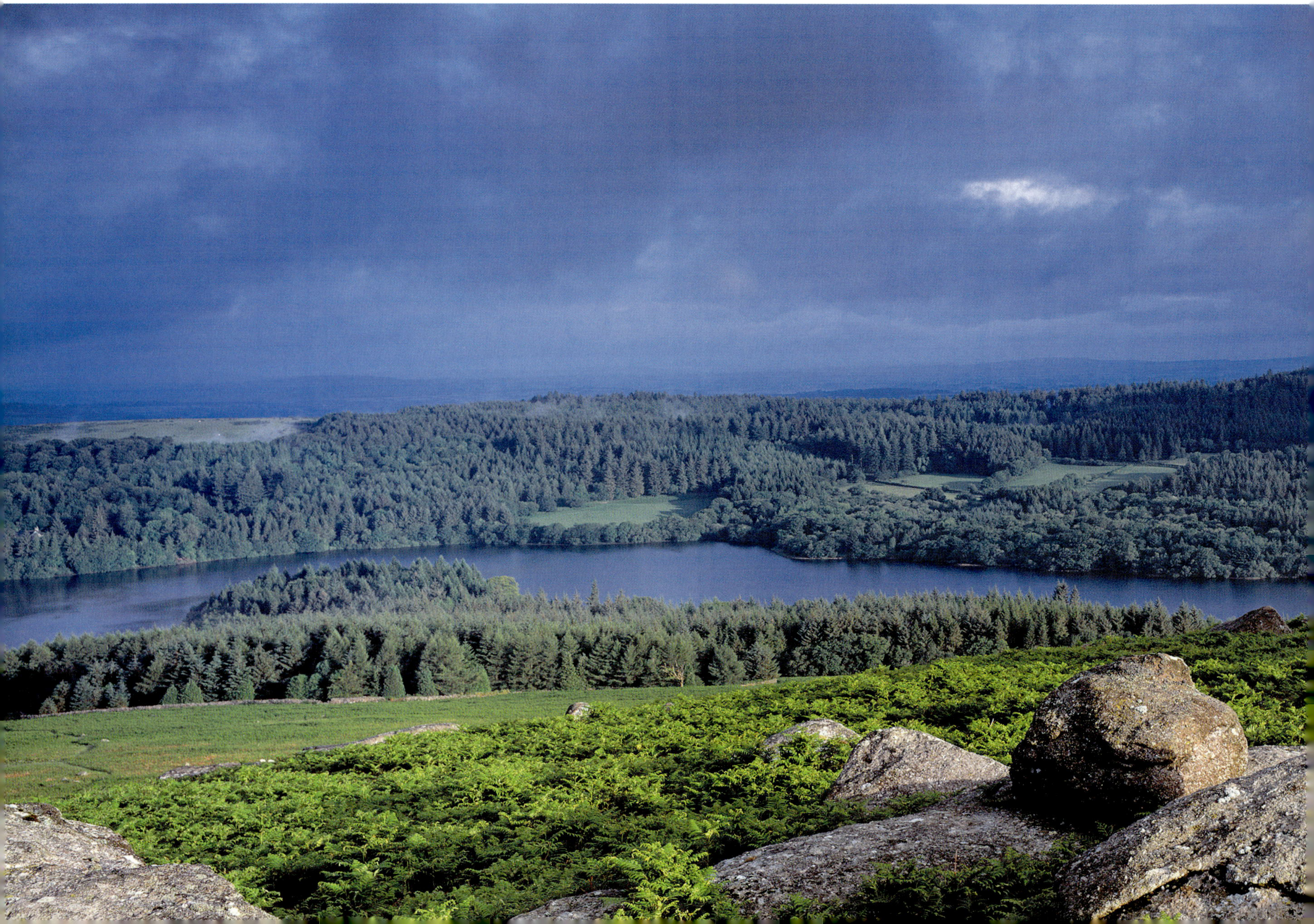

This picture was taken using the last light of the day from the summit of Down Tor. The view looks past Sheeps Tor towards the southern edge of the moor, stretching down to Plymouth.

The view across Burrator Reservoir as seen from the summit of Sheeps Tor. The rocky tops of Leather Tor and Sharpitor can be seen to the right.

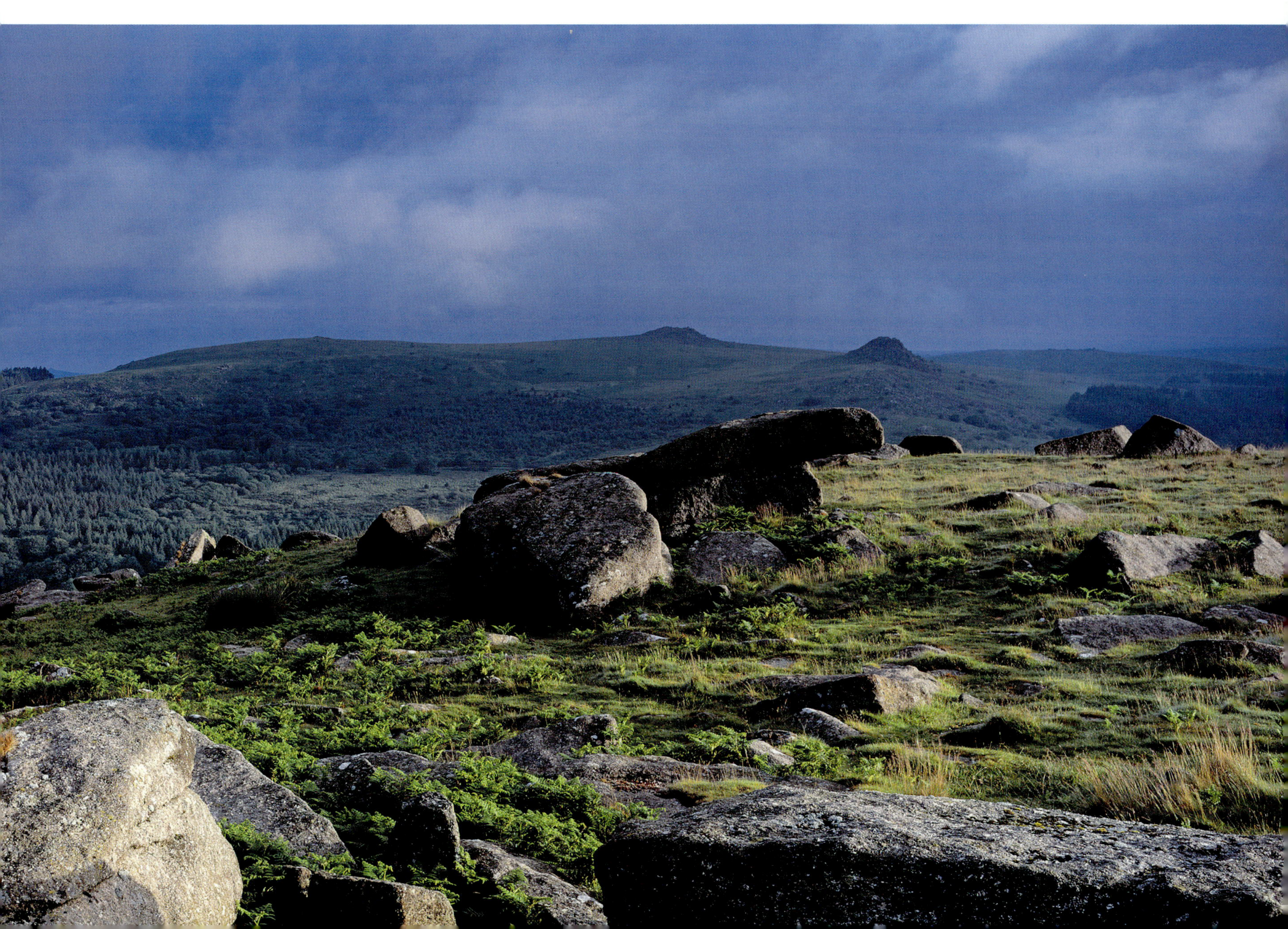

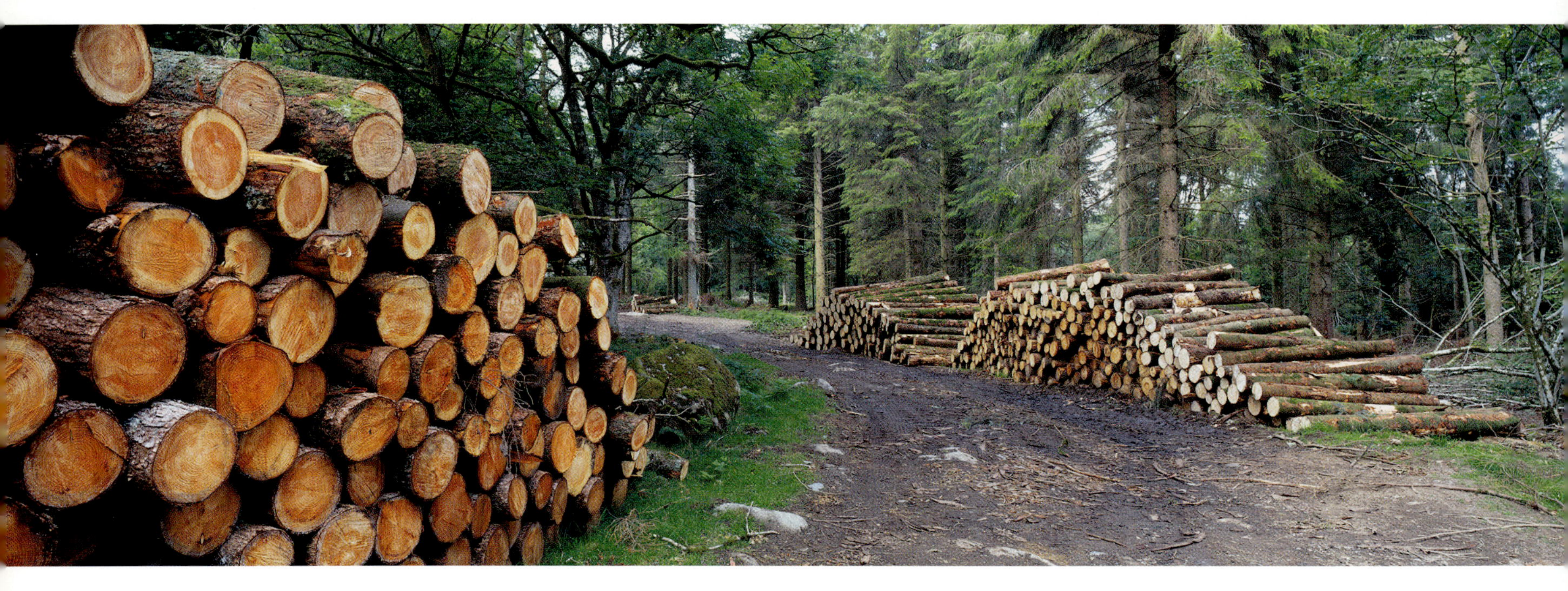

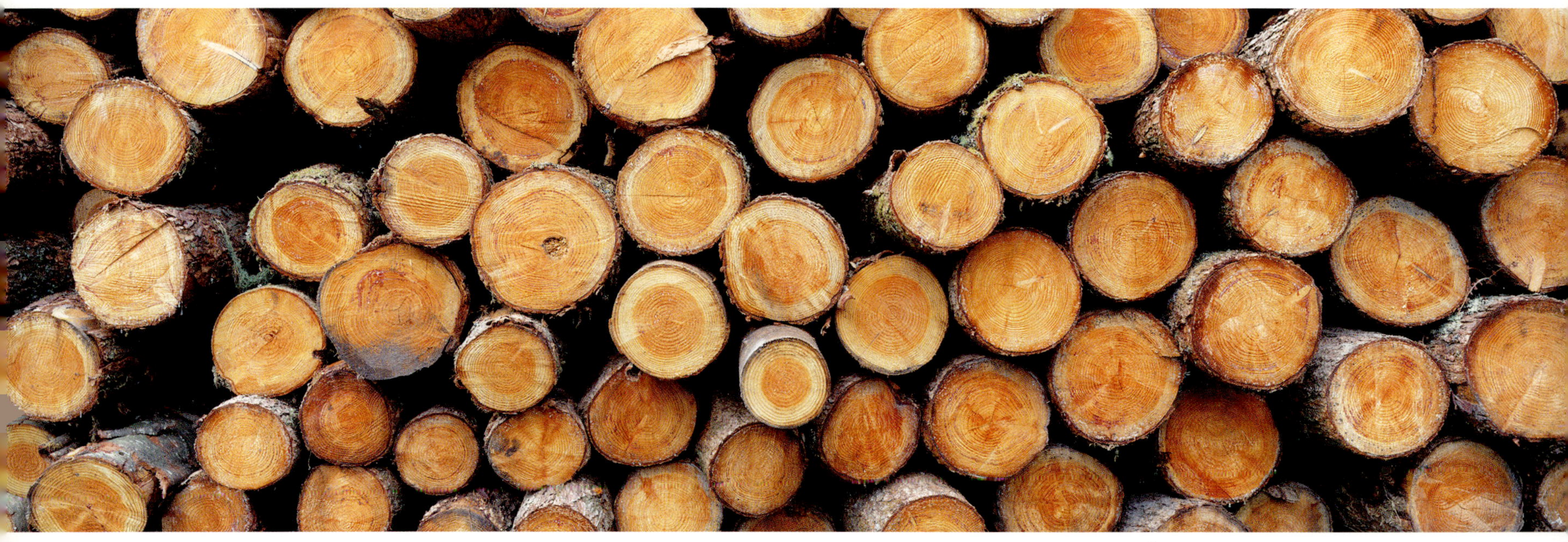

Stacked timber in woods beside Burrator Reservoir.

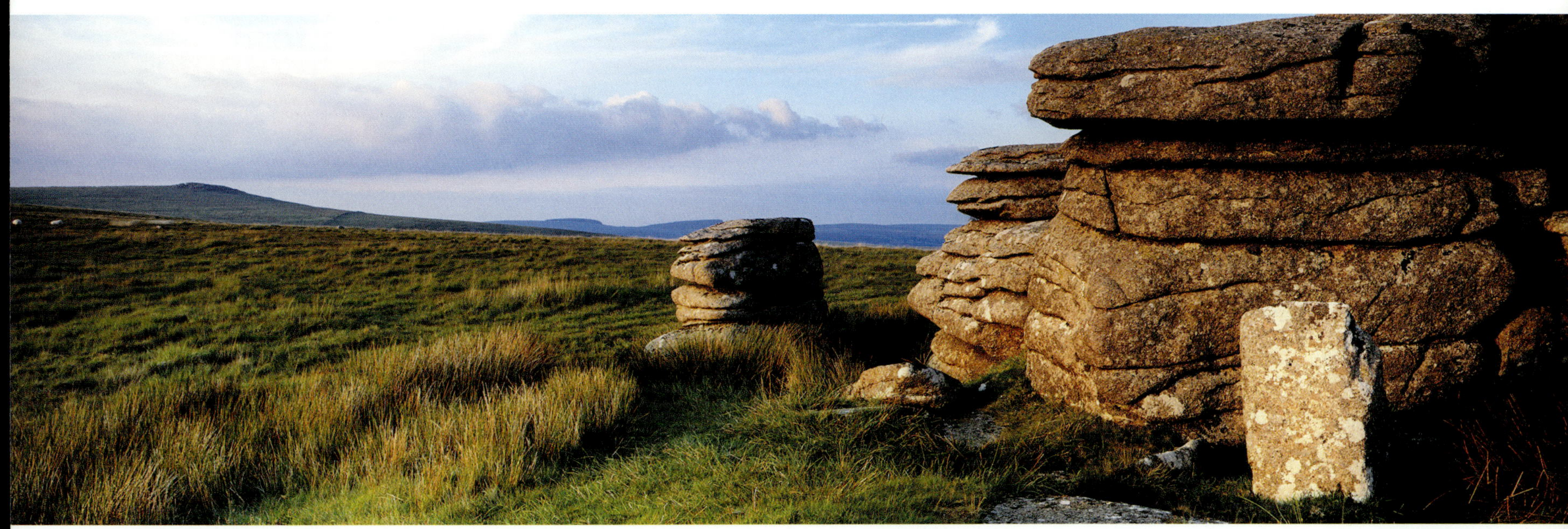

Facing north from Littaford Tor. On this day the tor seems peaceful, bathed in the warm summer sun, in stark contrast to a previous visit in the bitingly cold wind and hail of winter, see page 29.

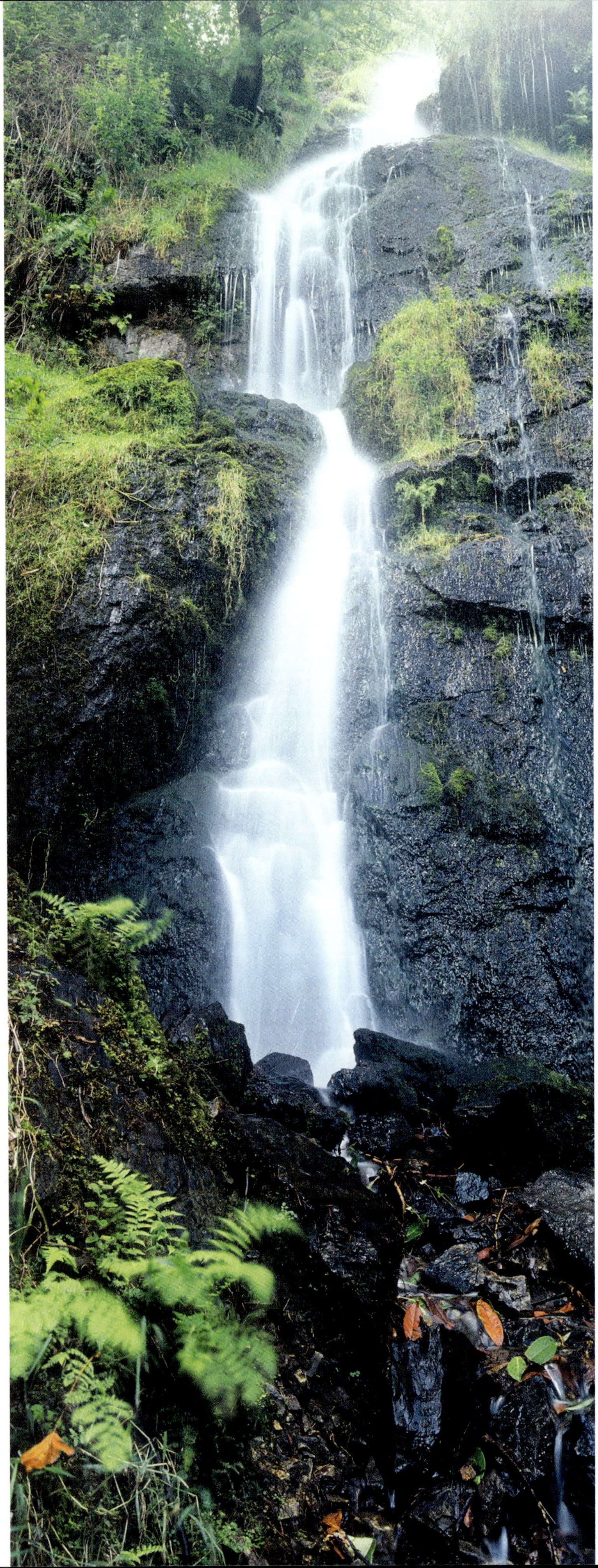

This dramatic cascading waterfall on the river Teign is known as Canonteign Falls. Reputed to be the highest waterfall in England at 220 feet or 67 metres, the river drops down several further falls before continuing along the picturesque Teign Valley.

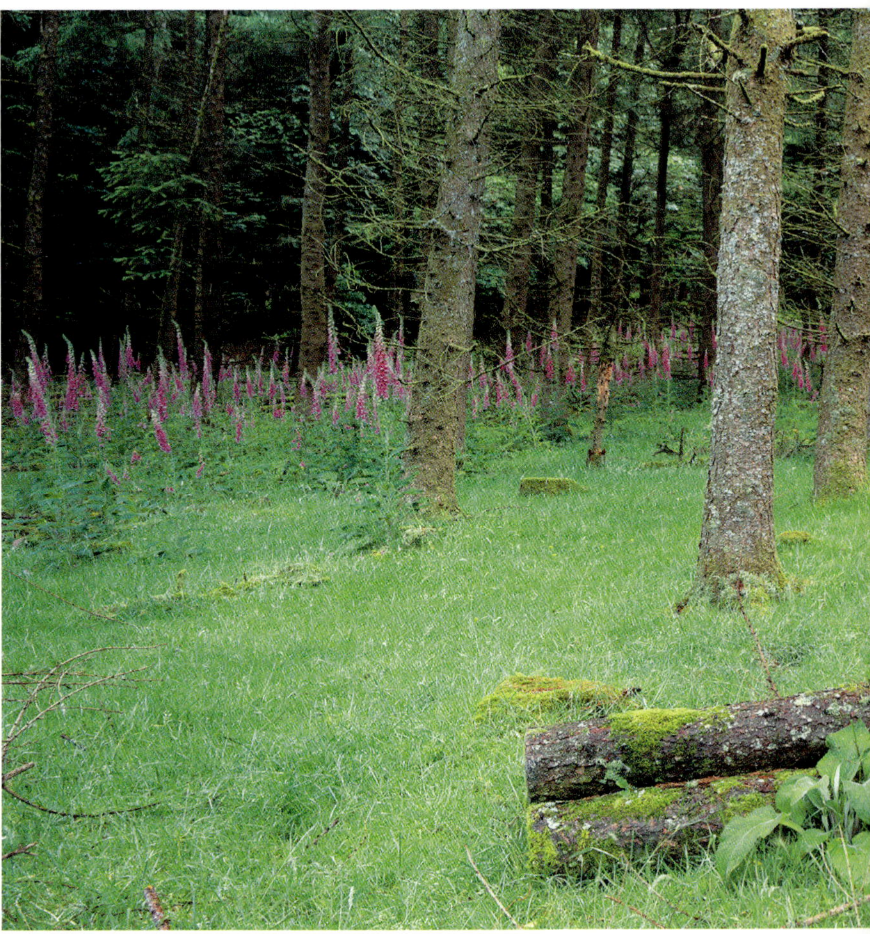

Foxgloves grow amongst the pine trees in woods next to Burrator Reservoir. The lush greens and vibrant pinks are at their most resplendent in the rain.

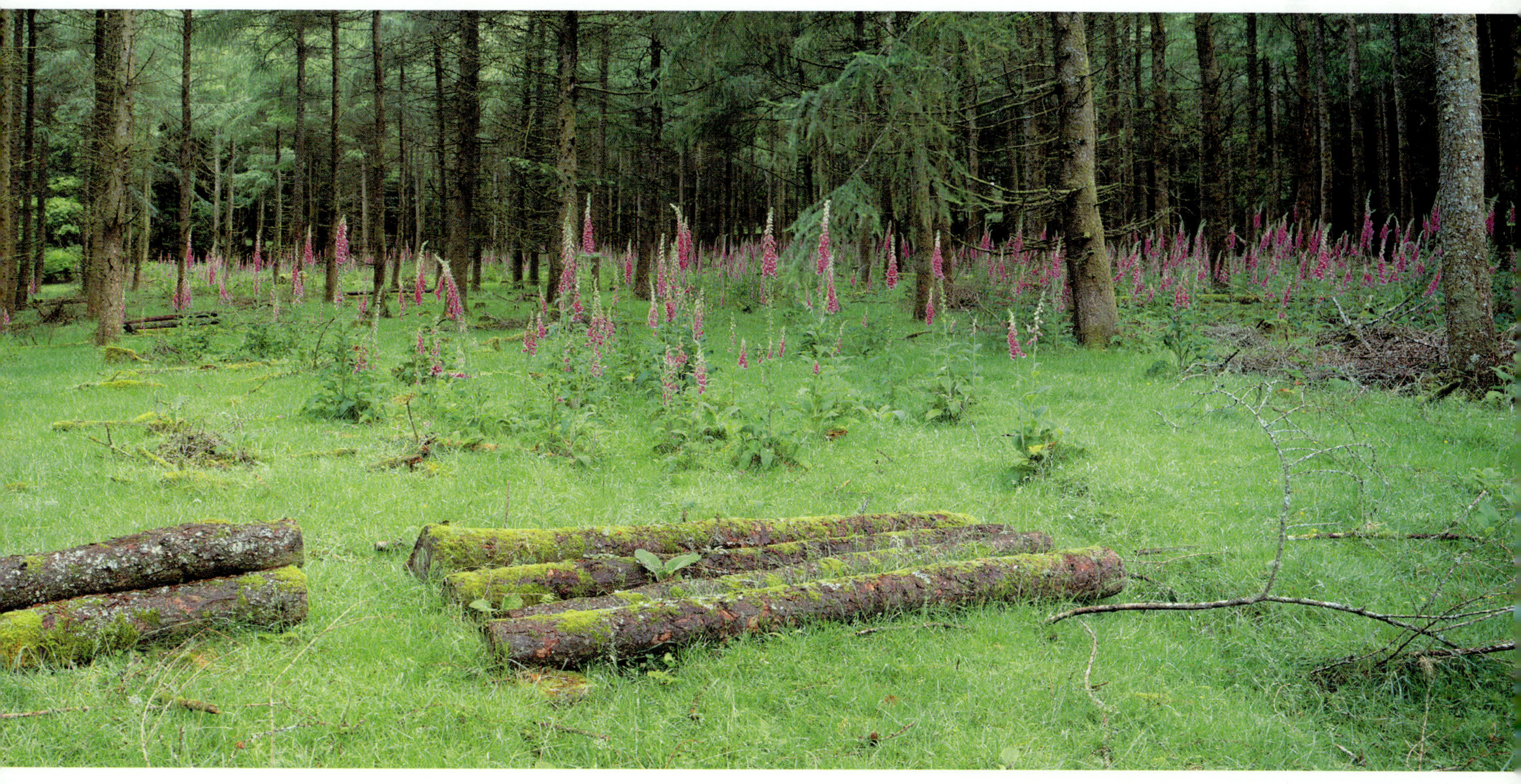

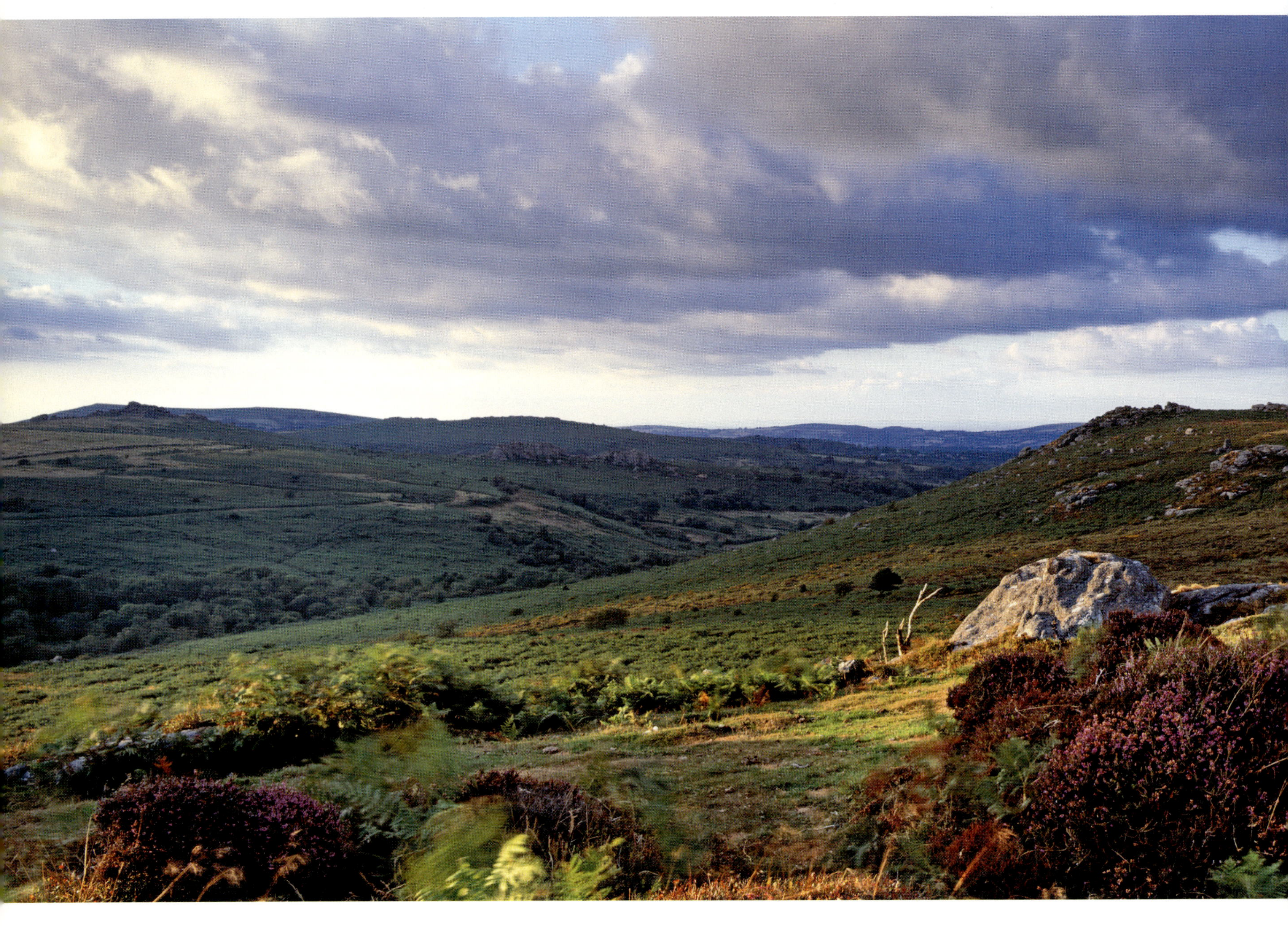

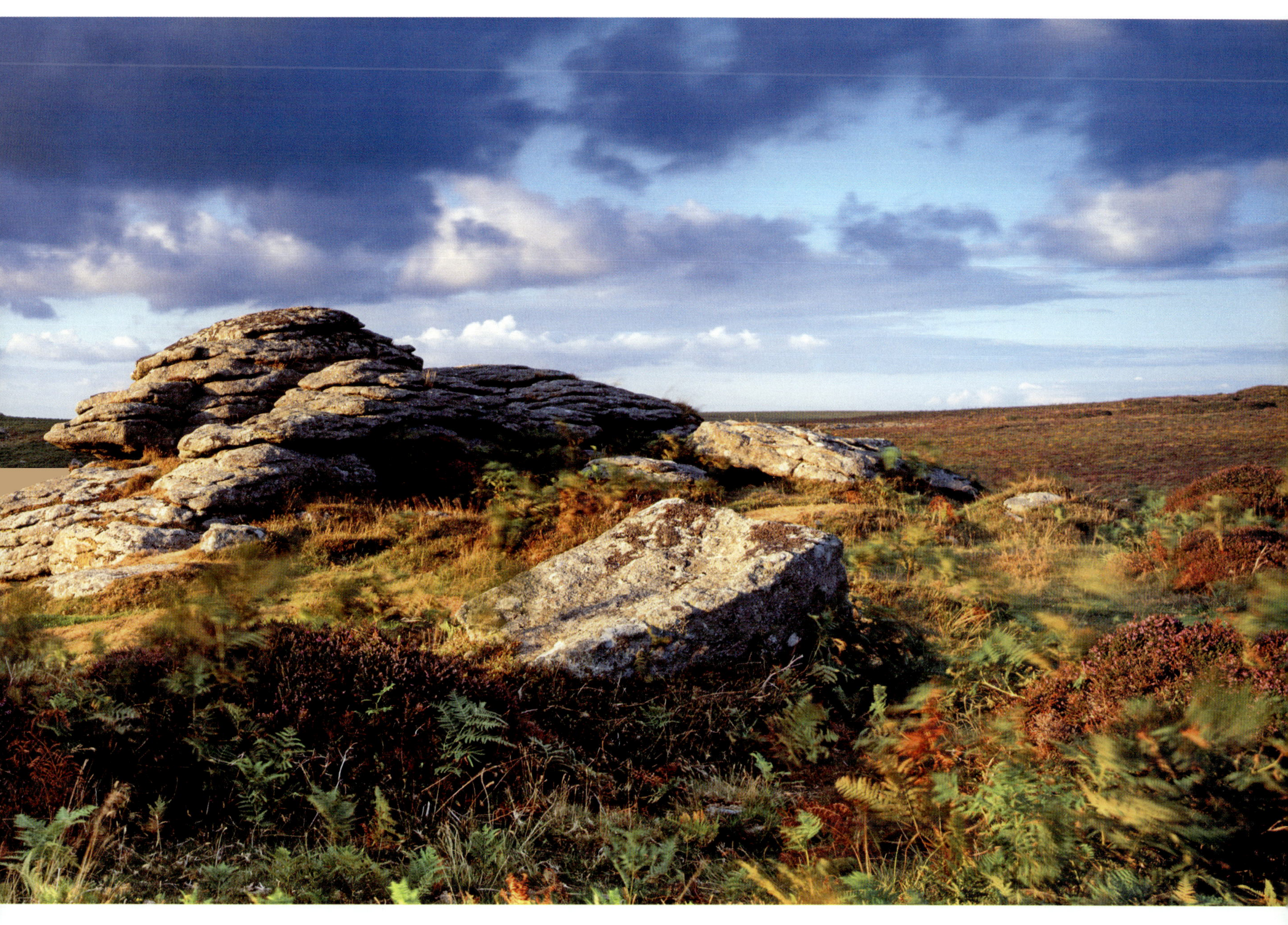

Wild light, Saddle Tor. A shaft of light forces its way through the clouds to give a striking view, looking north towards Holwell Tor and the hills beyond.

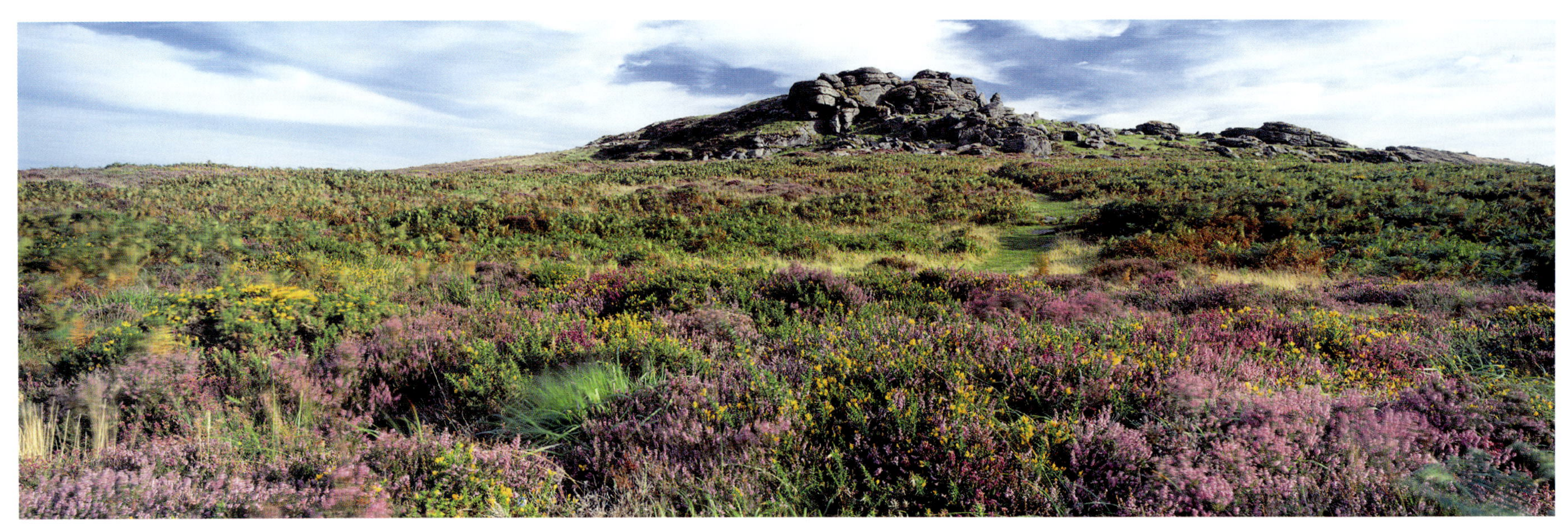

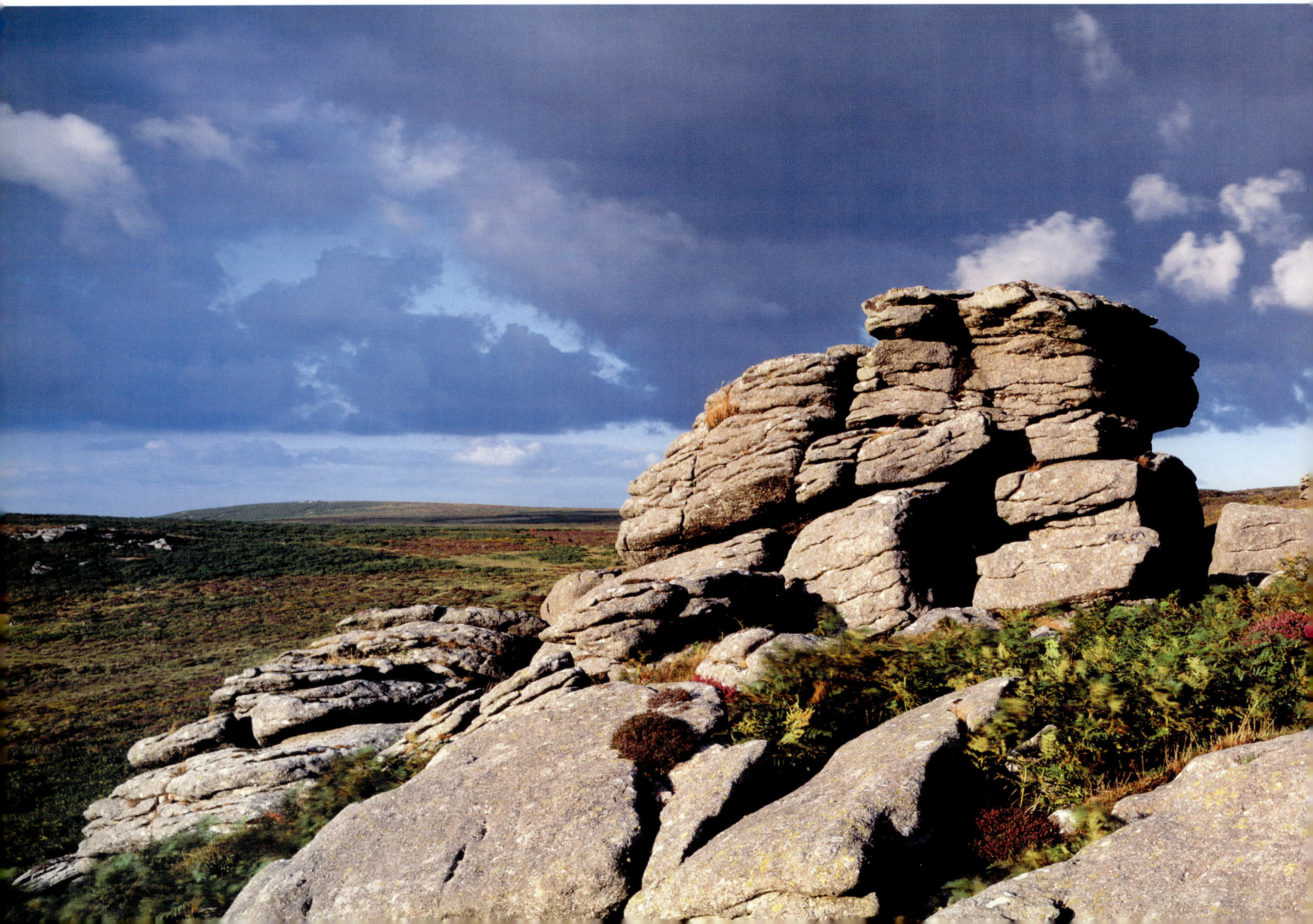

Heather and gorse cover the moor next to Saddle Tor in the height of summer.

A strong wind ruffles the ferns surrounding the granite rocks and lone hawthorn tree as dark clouds pass overhead near Haytor.

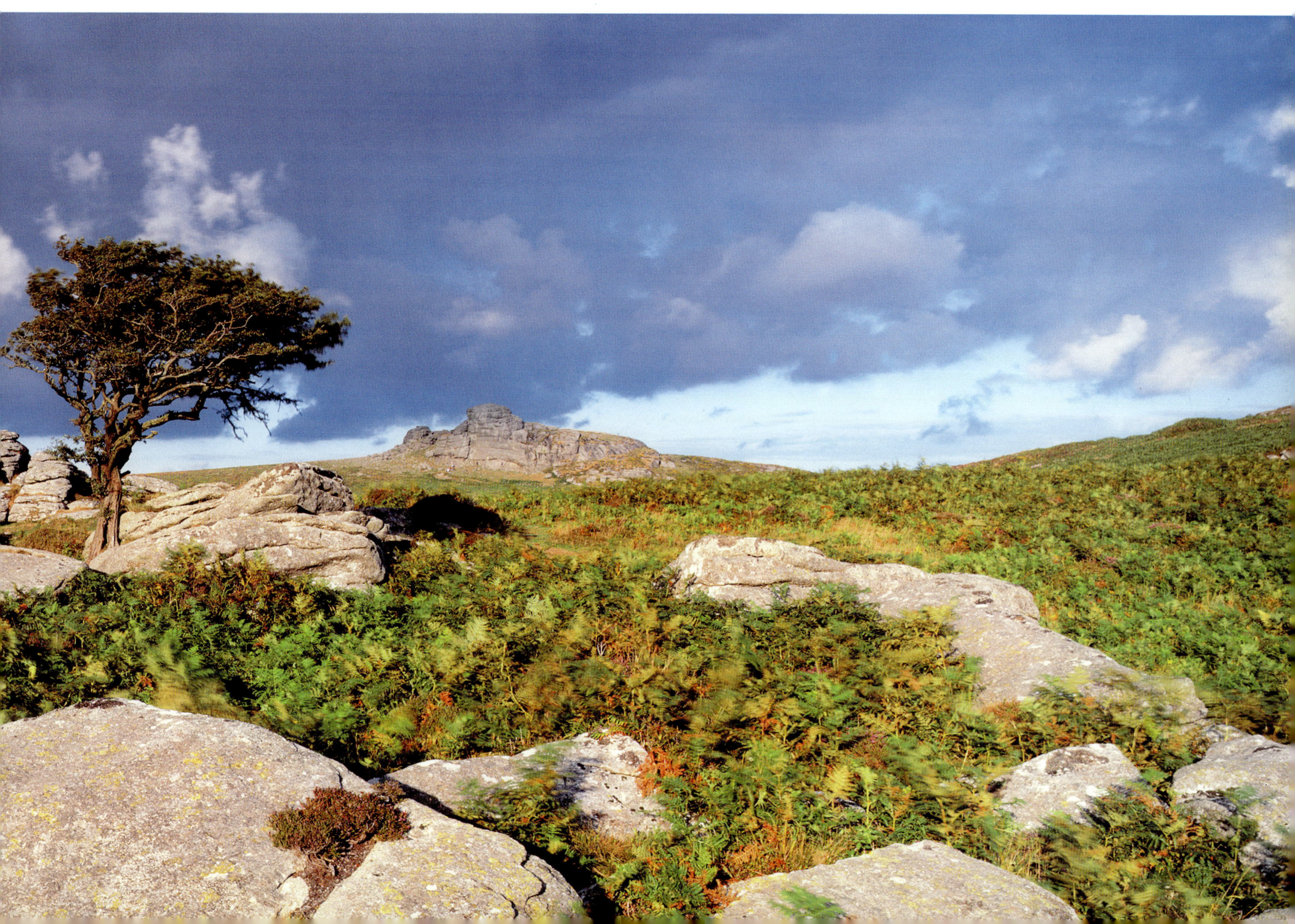

The angle of evening light picks out the grass tufts and granite rocks strewn across this part of the moor near Ivybridge. Looking into the distance highlights the contrast between the low-lying lush farmland and the bleakness of the higher moor.

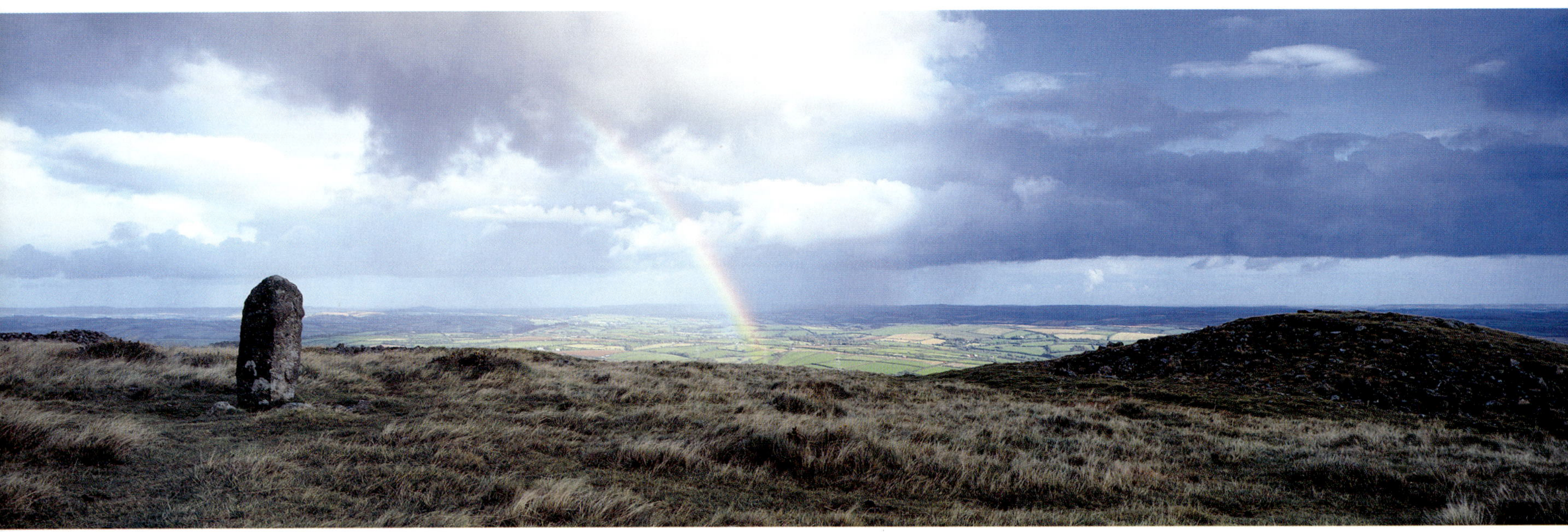

A passing rain shower casts a momentary rainbow against the backdrop of dramatic clouds above Western Beacon, known locally as Ivybridge Beacon. The sunlight brings out a rich patchwork of colours in the fields bordering Dartmoor.

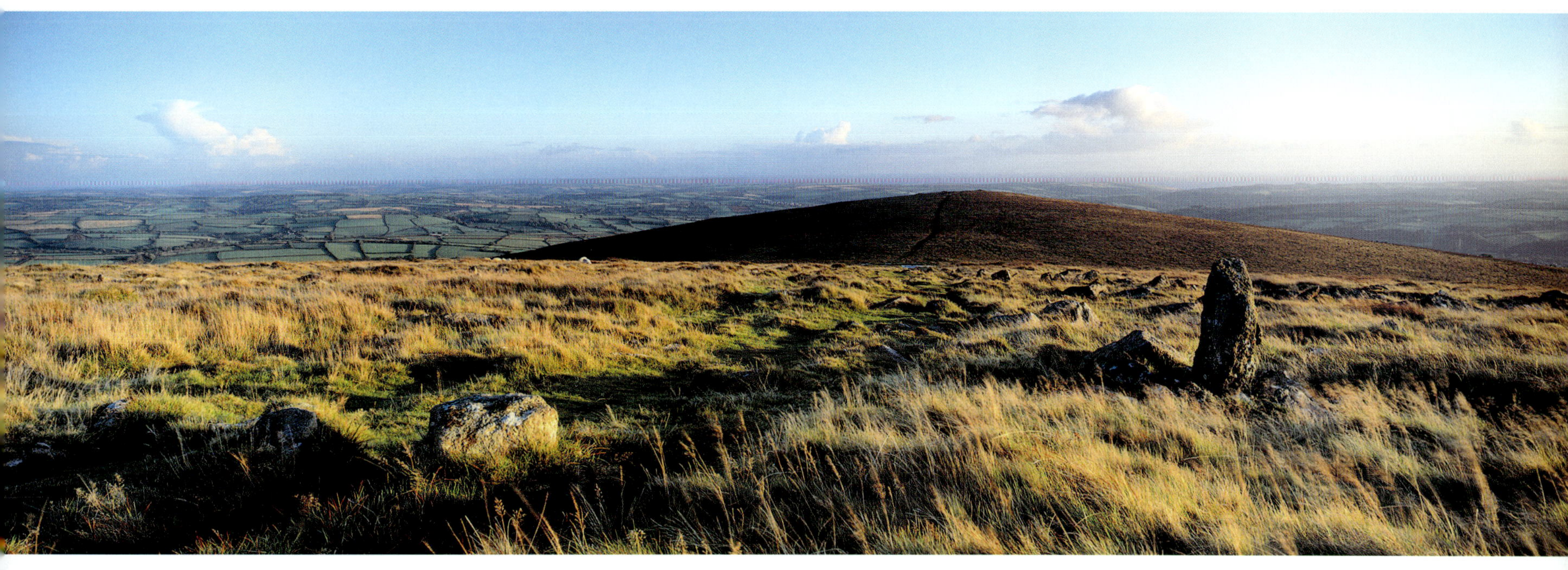

The ruins of Powder Mills, an old gunpowder factory, stand next to Cherry Brook. Situated in a remote location, presumably to reduce the risk of casualties in the event of an accident, the mill was also close to the quarries of Birch Tor, Foggintor and Merrivale, which all needed gunpowder to blast. The walls of the buildings were constructed using heavy granite slabs, built to withstand an explosion should one occur. The roofs, by contrast, were made of light wood so they would blow off rather than collapse inwards onto the workers. Closed in 1897, the mill was again used during the Second World War when American soldiers stationed there used the area to practice for the D-Day landings.

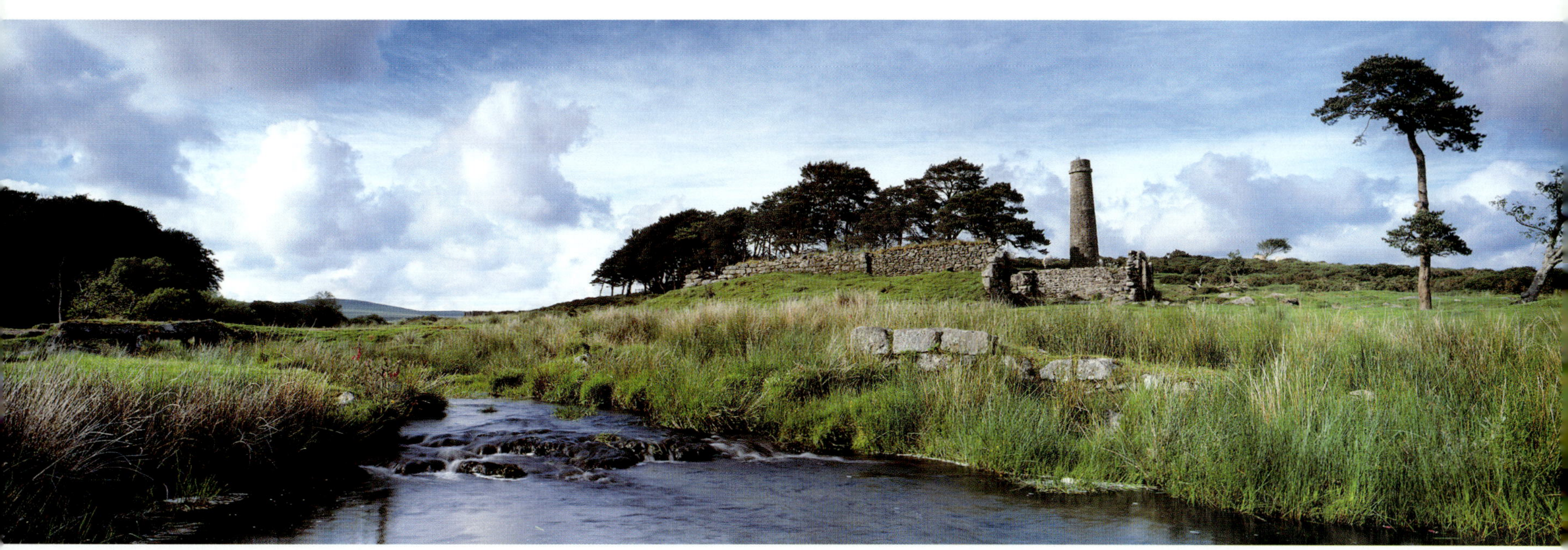

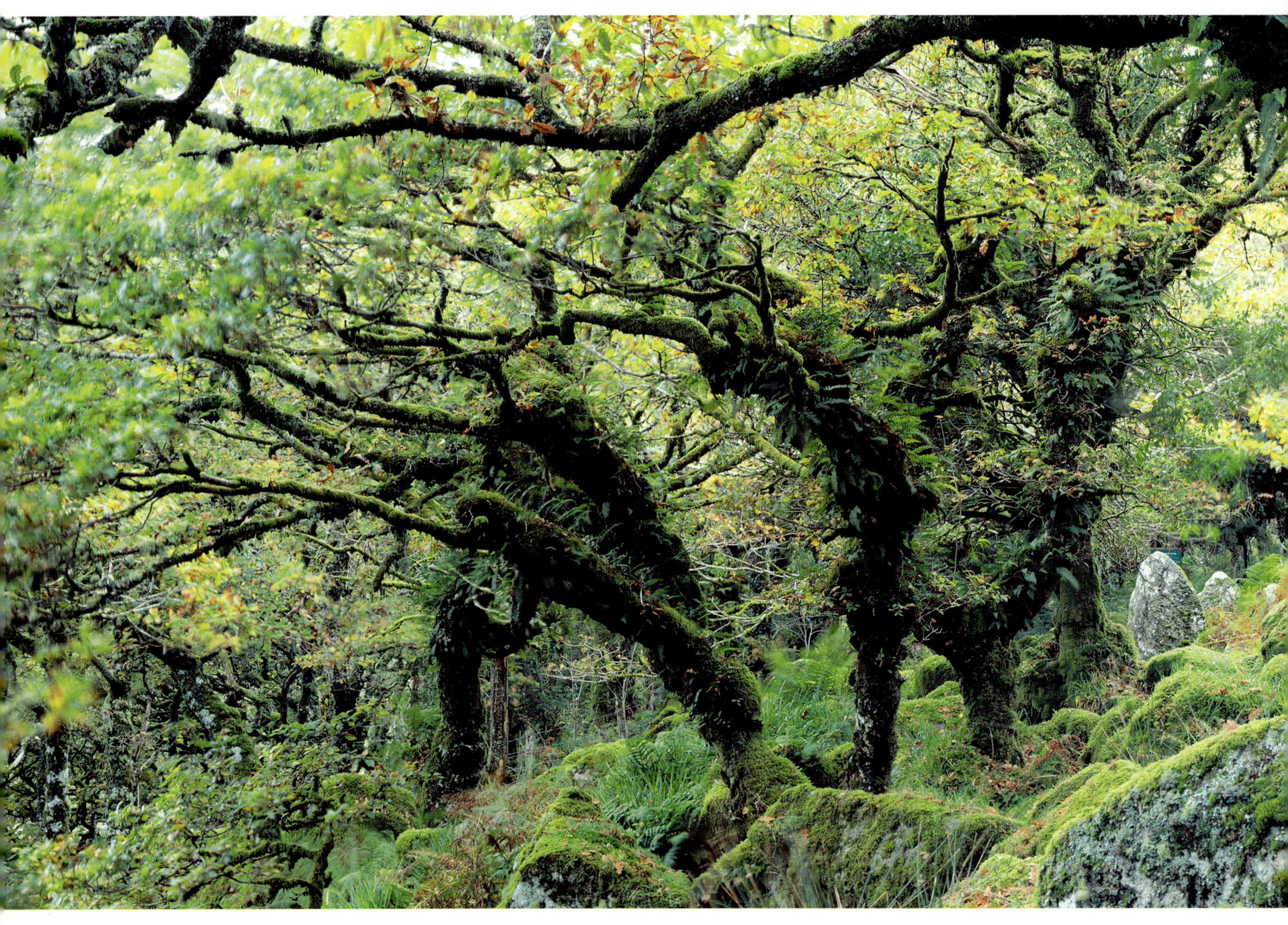

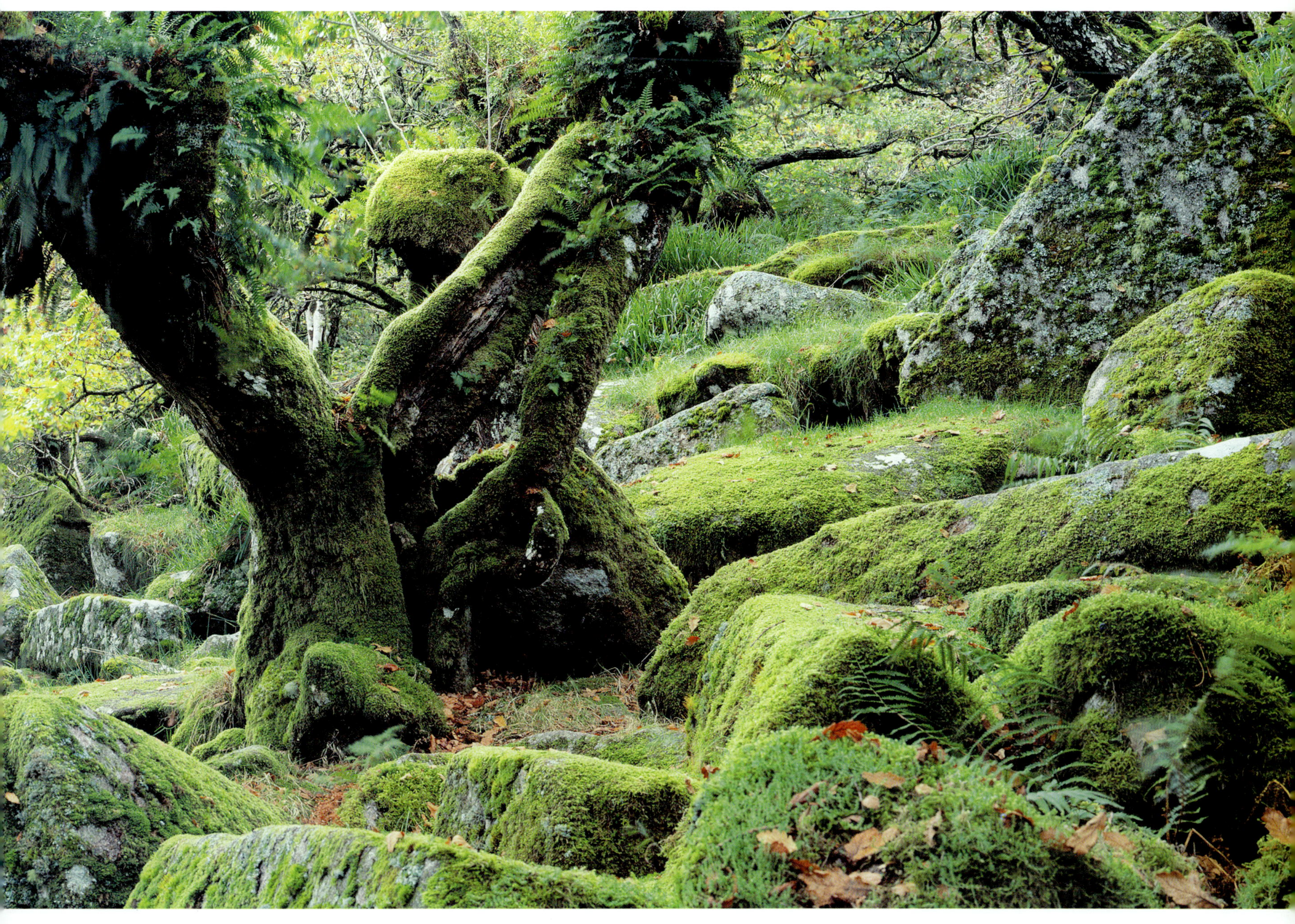

Wistman's Wood is a fascinating ancient forest, characterised by its gnarled, moss-covered oaks. Occupying a small area next to the West Dart and surrounded by moorland, the wood was once much larger, covering most of the valley where it now sits. Devon's oldest woodland, it is home to 47 species of moss and over 100 types of lichen covering the twisted trees and rocks. There is much speculation as to the reason for the trees' dwarfed stature, which creates a distinctive and sometimes eerie environment, particularly when fog descends.

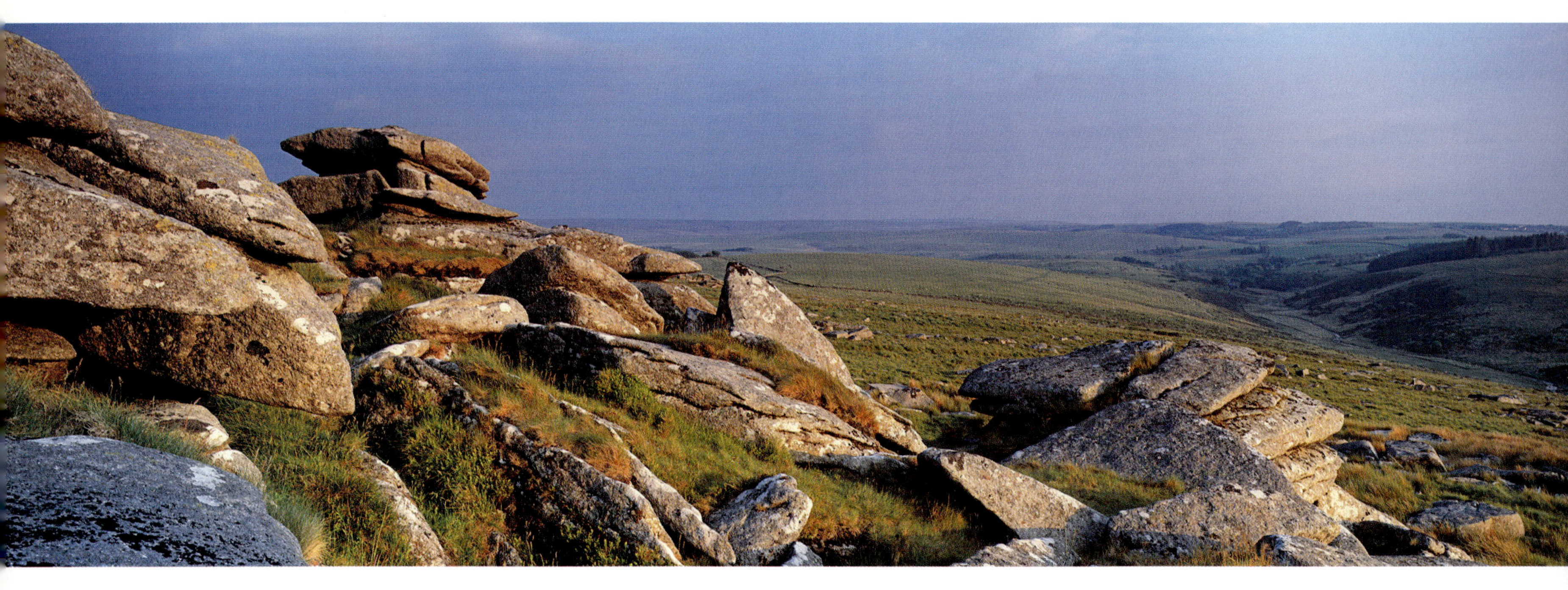

The river Meavy tumbles and flows across the moor from Princetown to Burrator Reservoir.

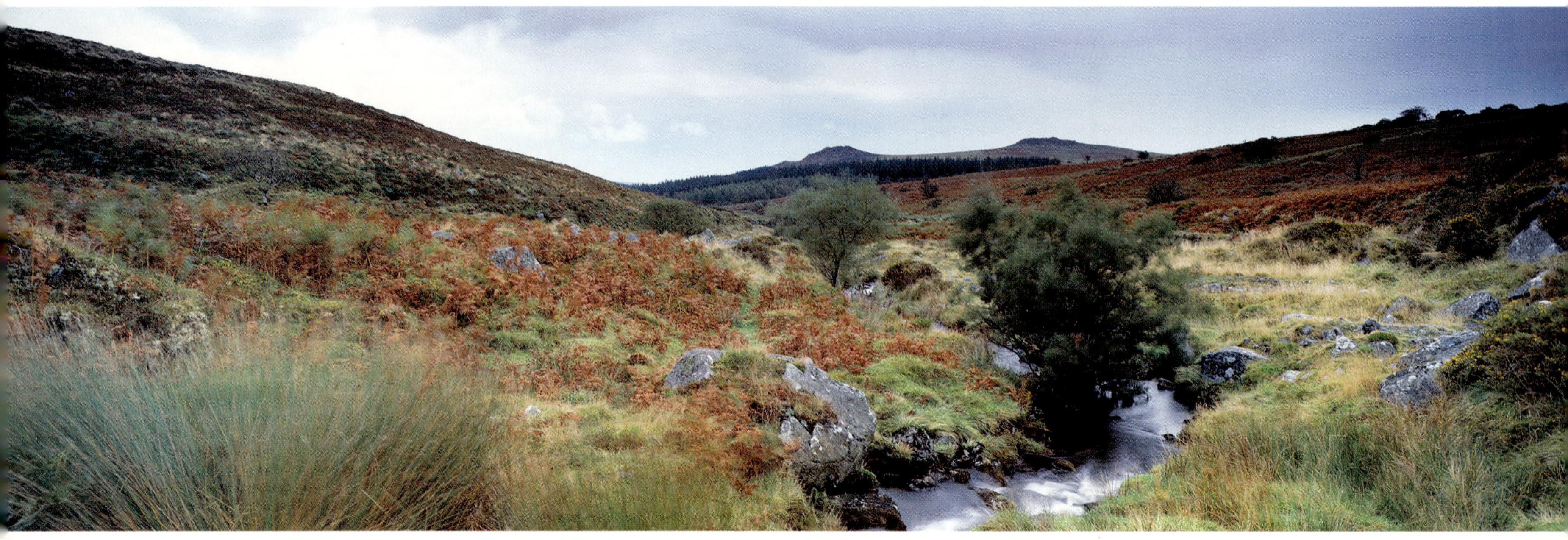

The lichen-covered granite rocks of Littaford Tor are warmed by the summer sunlight.

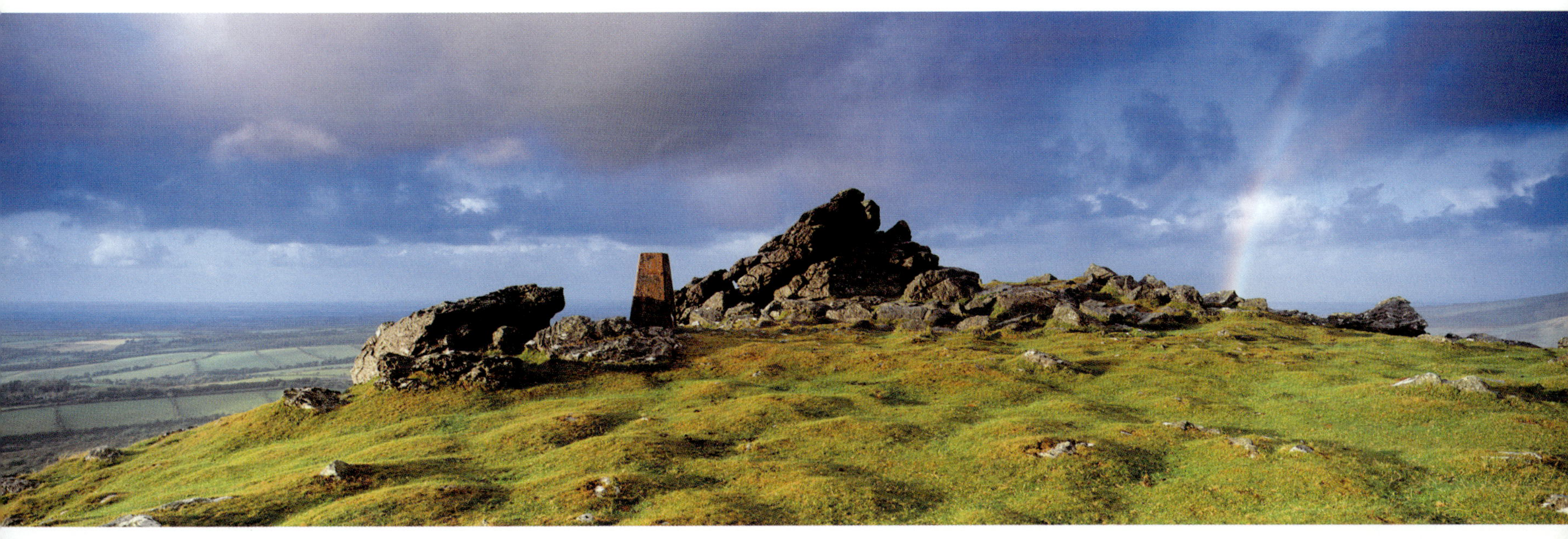

A fleeting rainbow appears next to the trig stone on Sourton Tor near Okehampton. Like much of Dartmoor, the tor offers far-reaching views across the patchwork of fields on the plains of Devon below.

The river Plym flows through Dewerstone Woods near Shaugh Prior on its way to Plymouth and the sea.

Grazing ponies wander across the slopes of Leeden Tor on a summer day. Once over 30,000 ponies lived on Dartmoor, but that number has fallen to under 3,000 today. Extensively used during the tin-mining boom of the 1800s to carry the tin to town, they were later released and now wander the moor in groups.

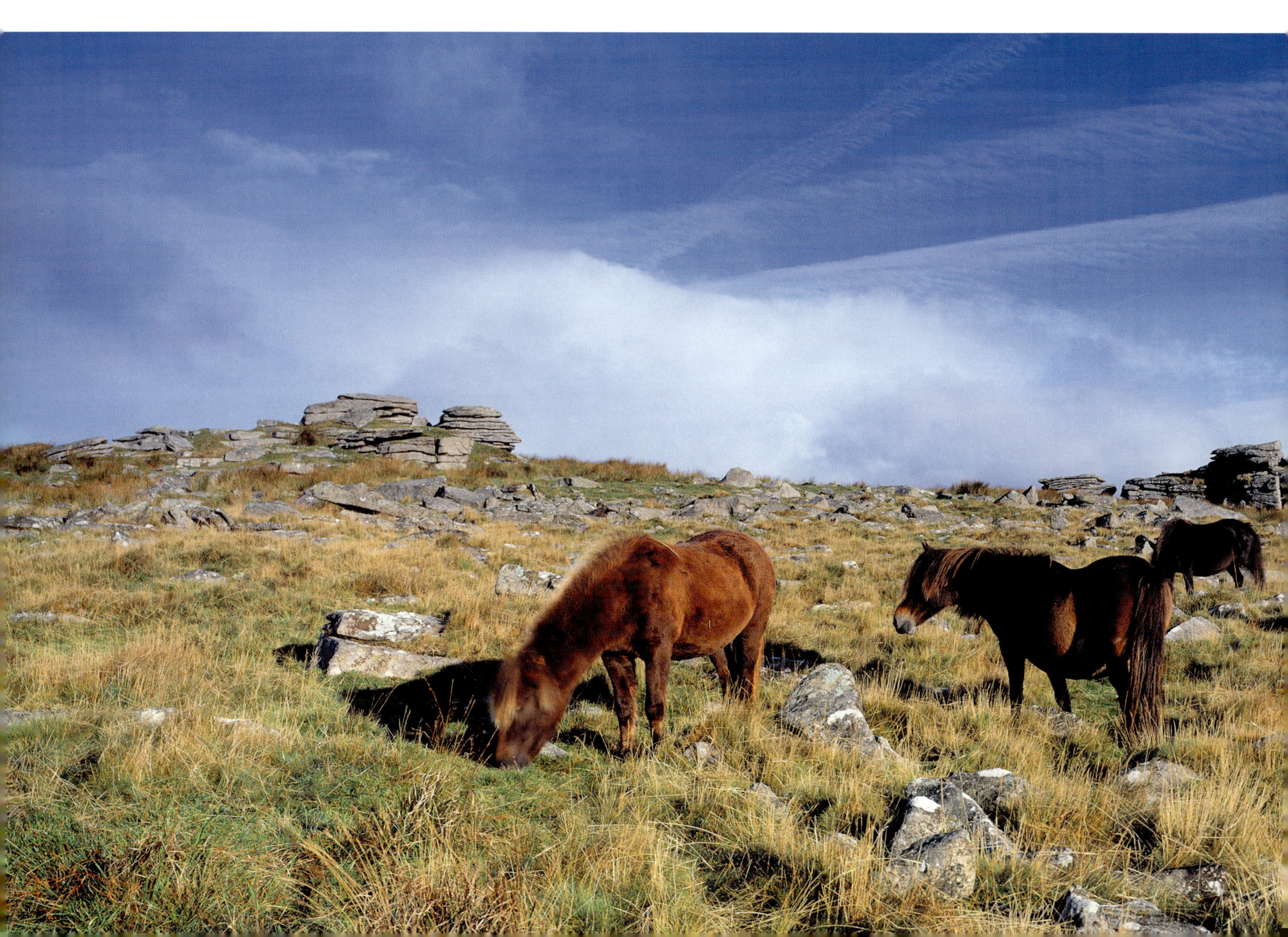

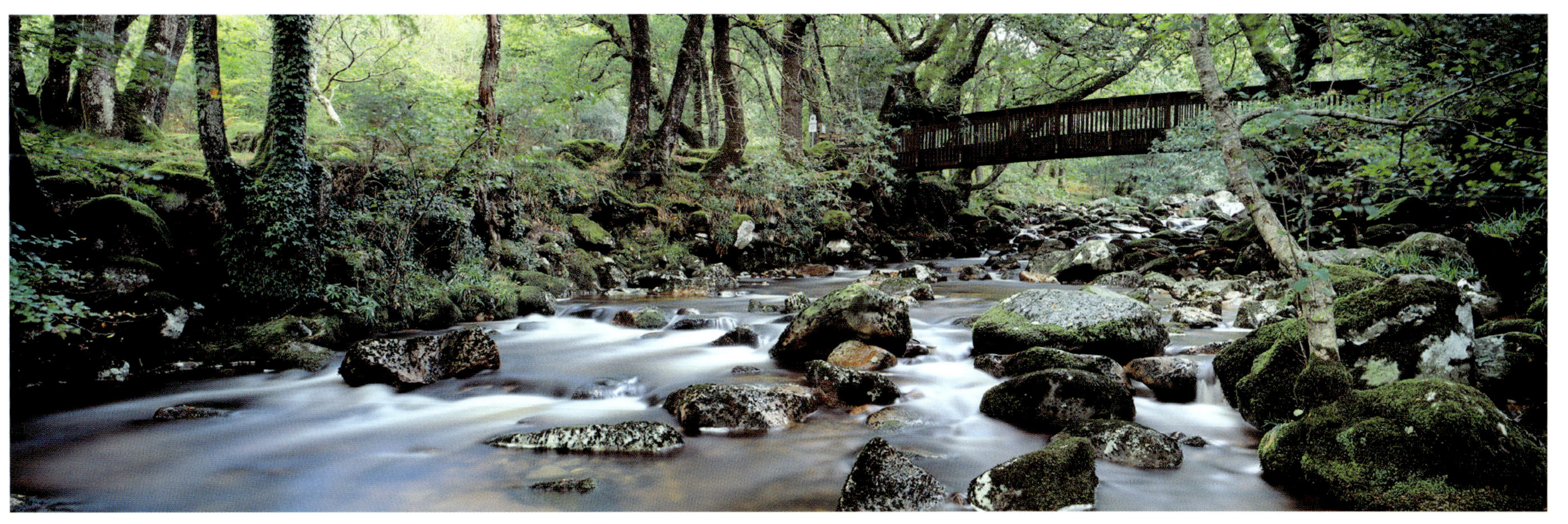

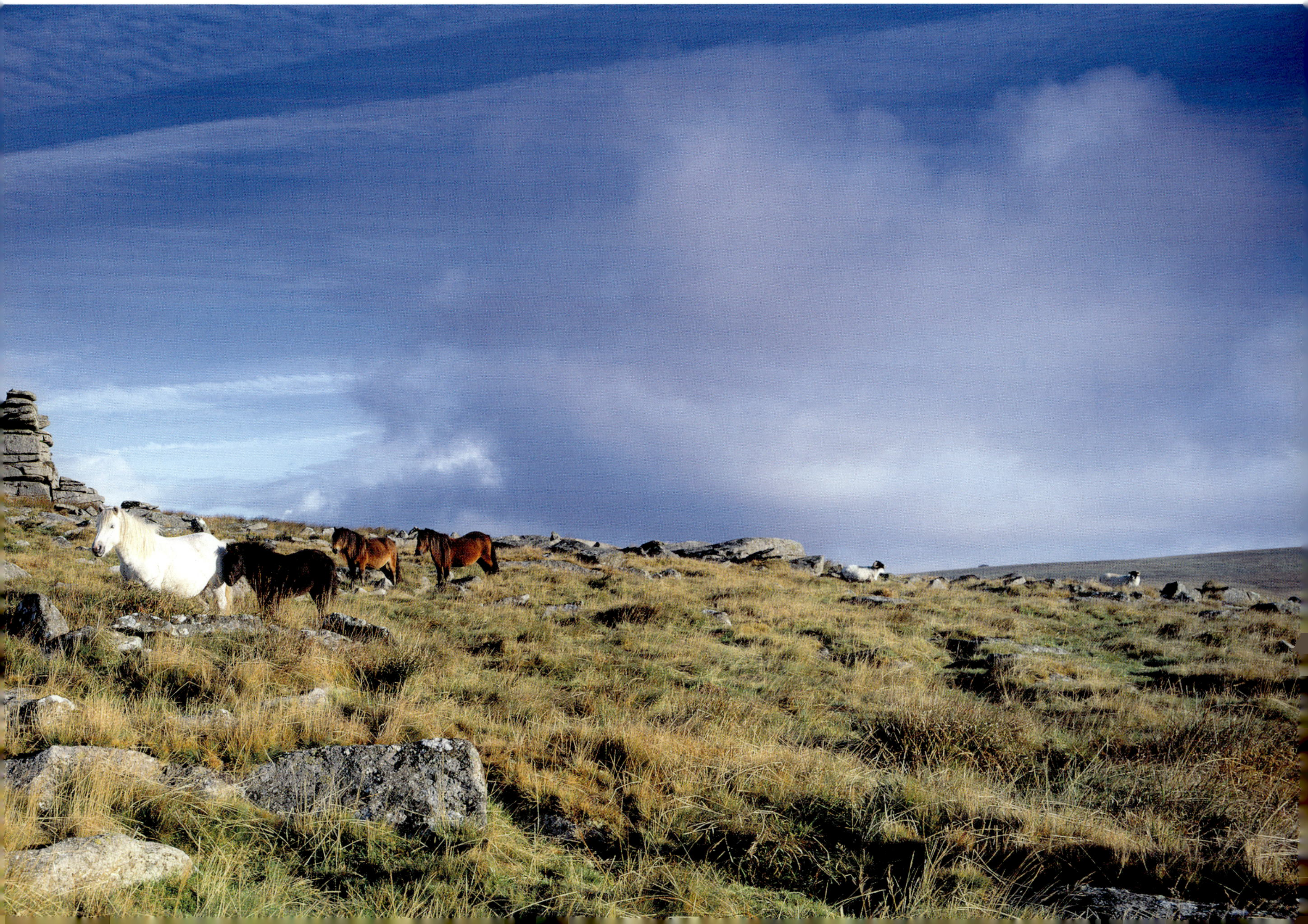

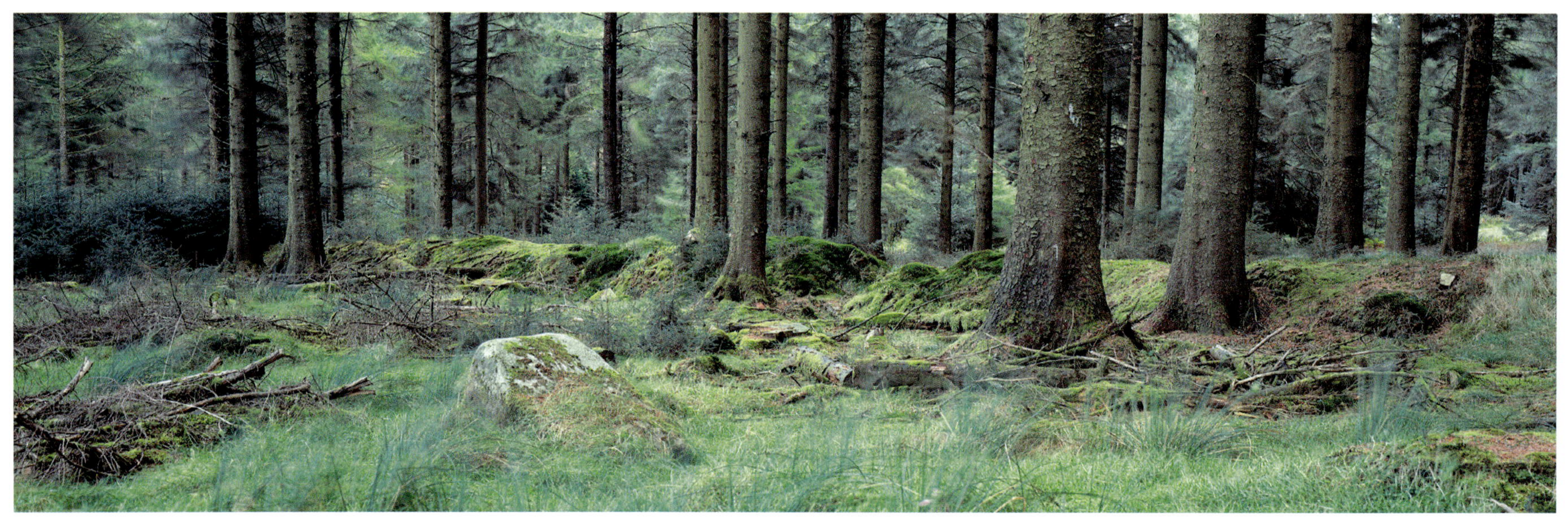

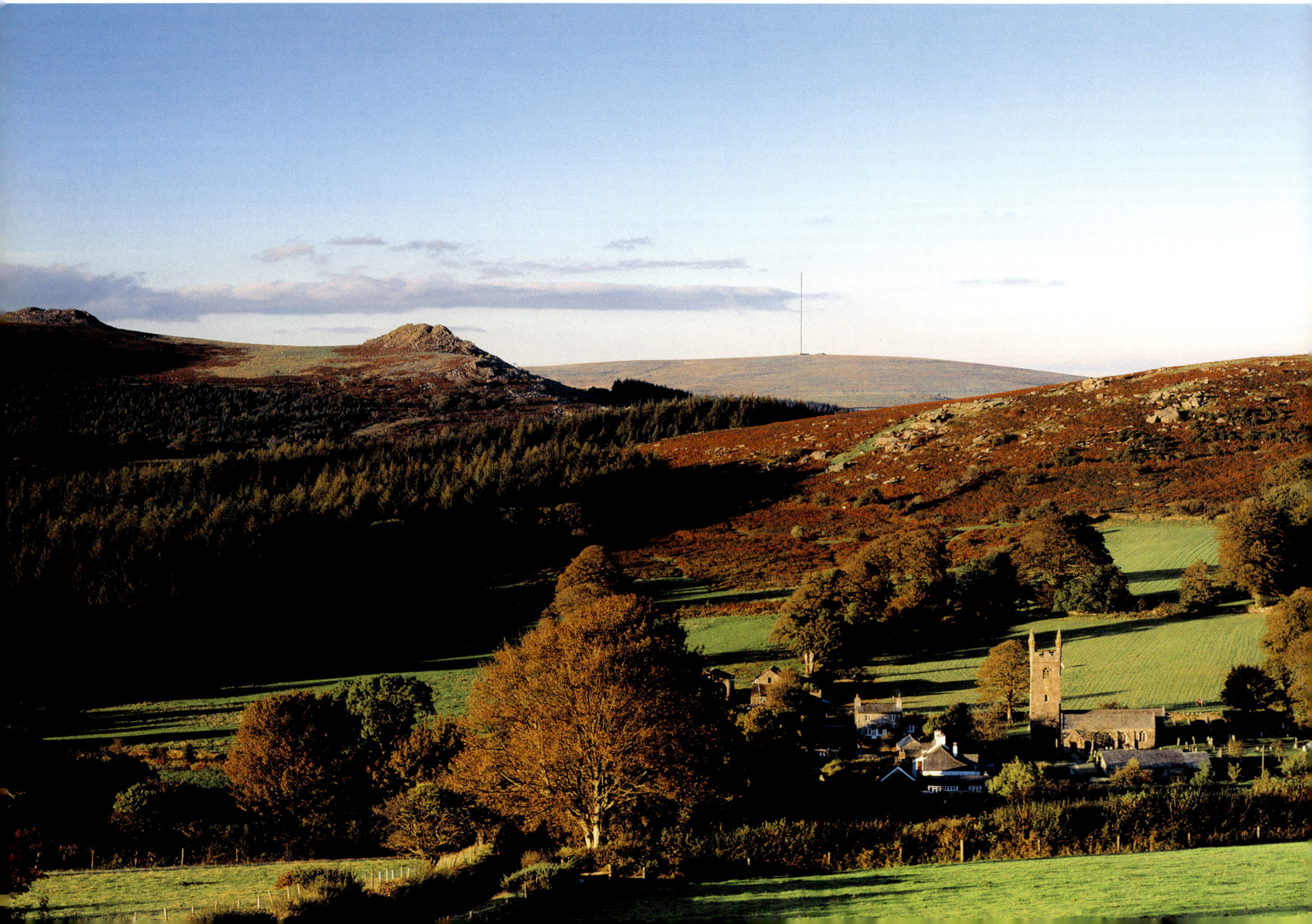

The trees in the wooded Stanlake plantation grow tall beside Devonport Leat, which channels water to Burrator Reservoir.

The picturesque church at Sheepstor catches the last rays of sunlight, as does the tor above which gives the hamlet its name.

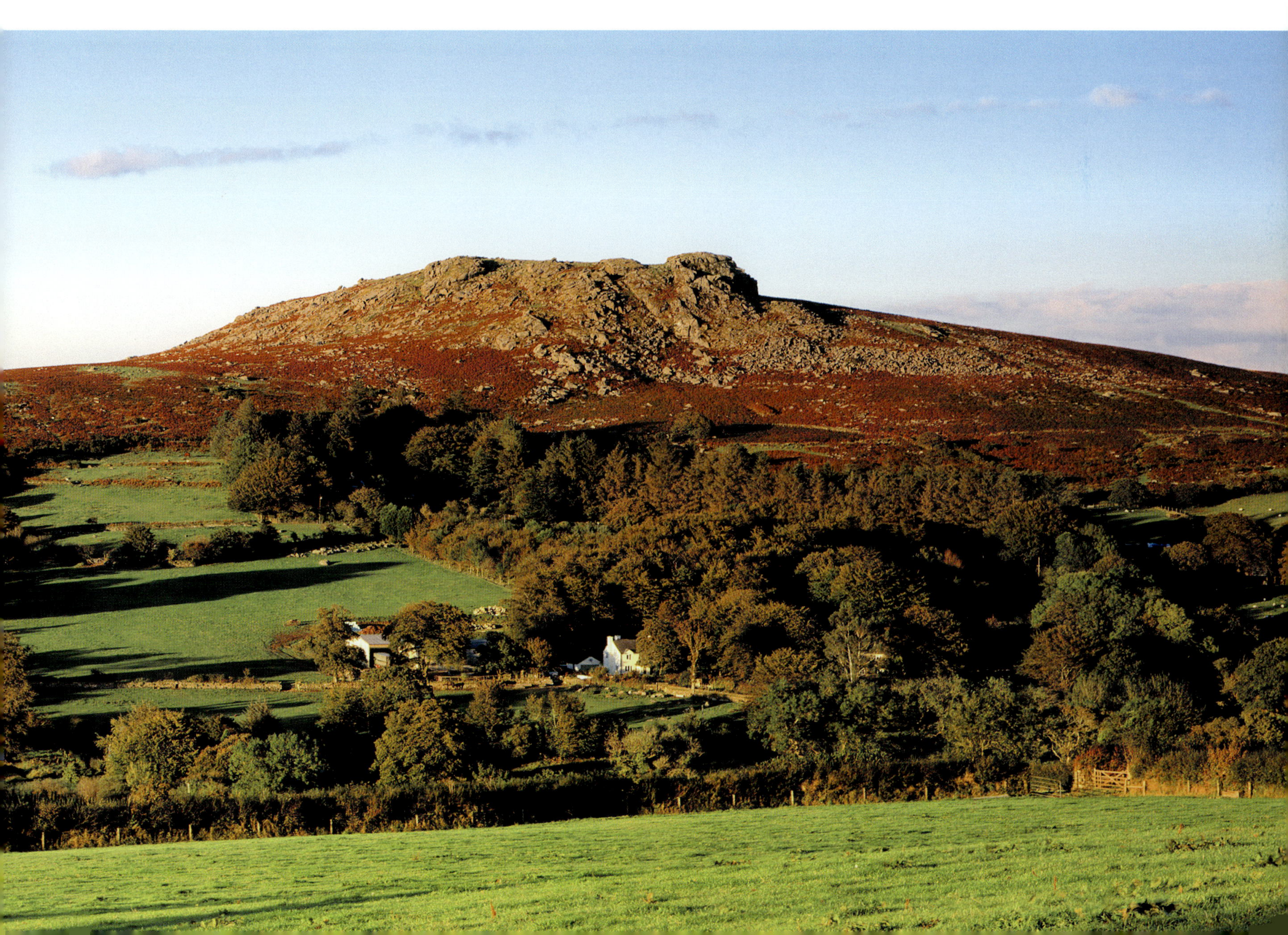

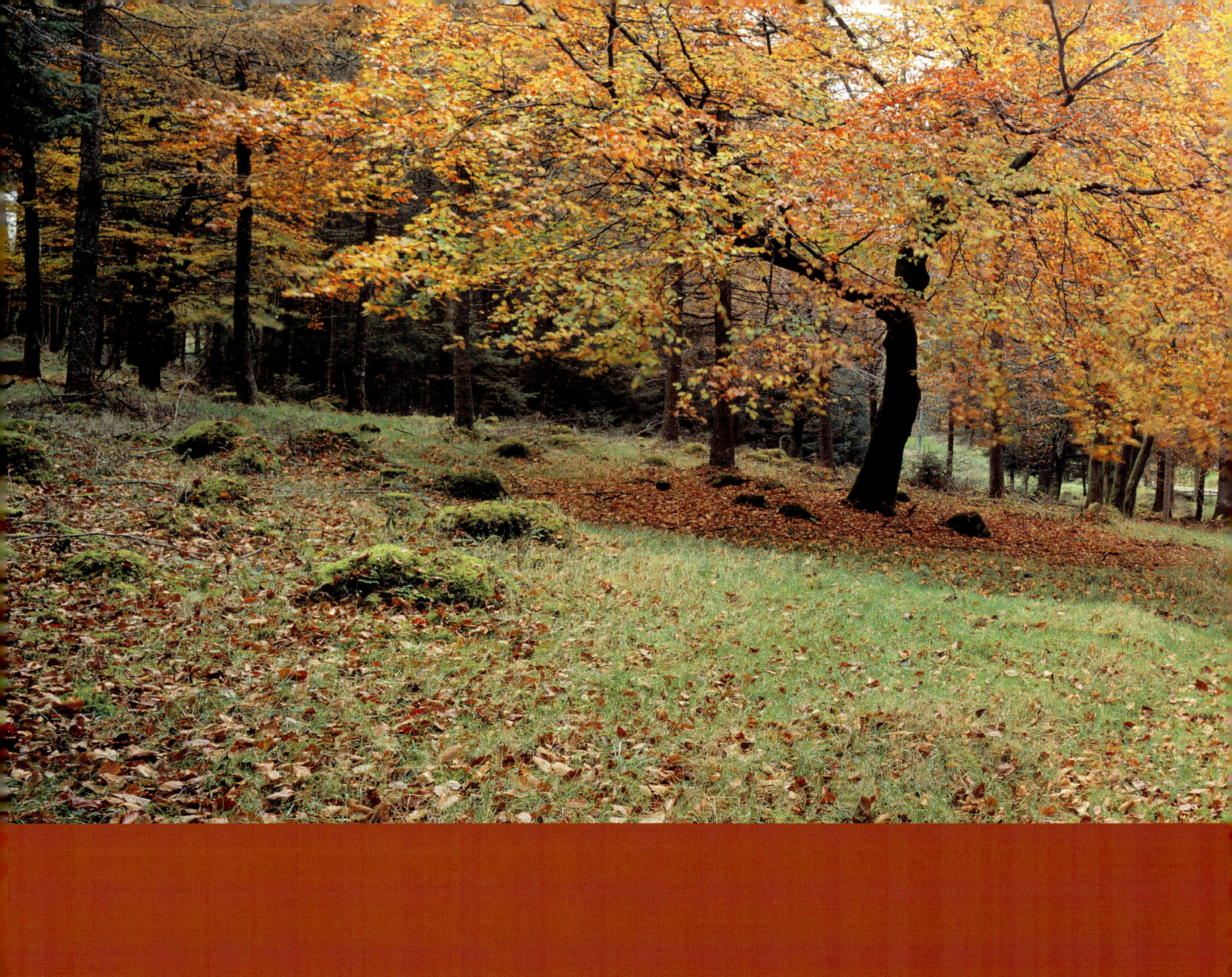

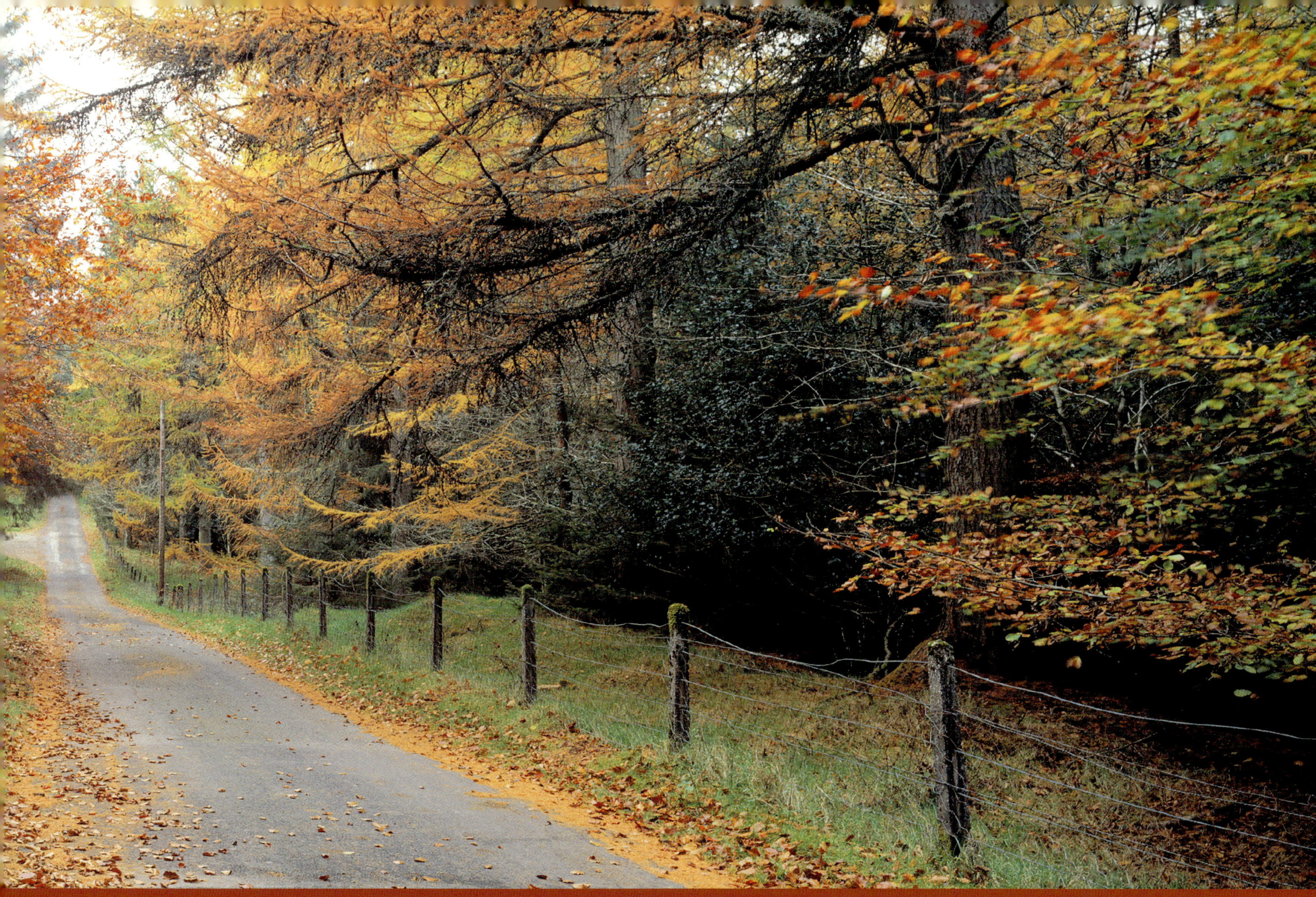

Autumn

Trees lining the single-track road beside Fernworthy Reservoir display the vibrant orange colours of autumn.

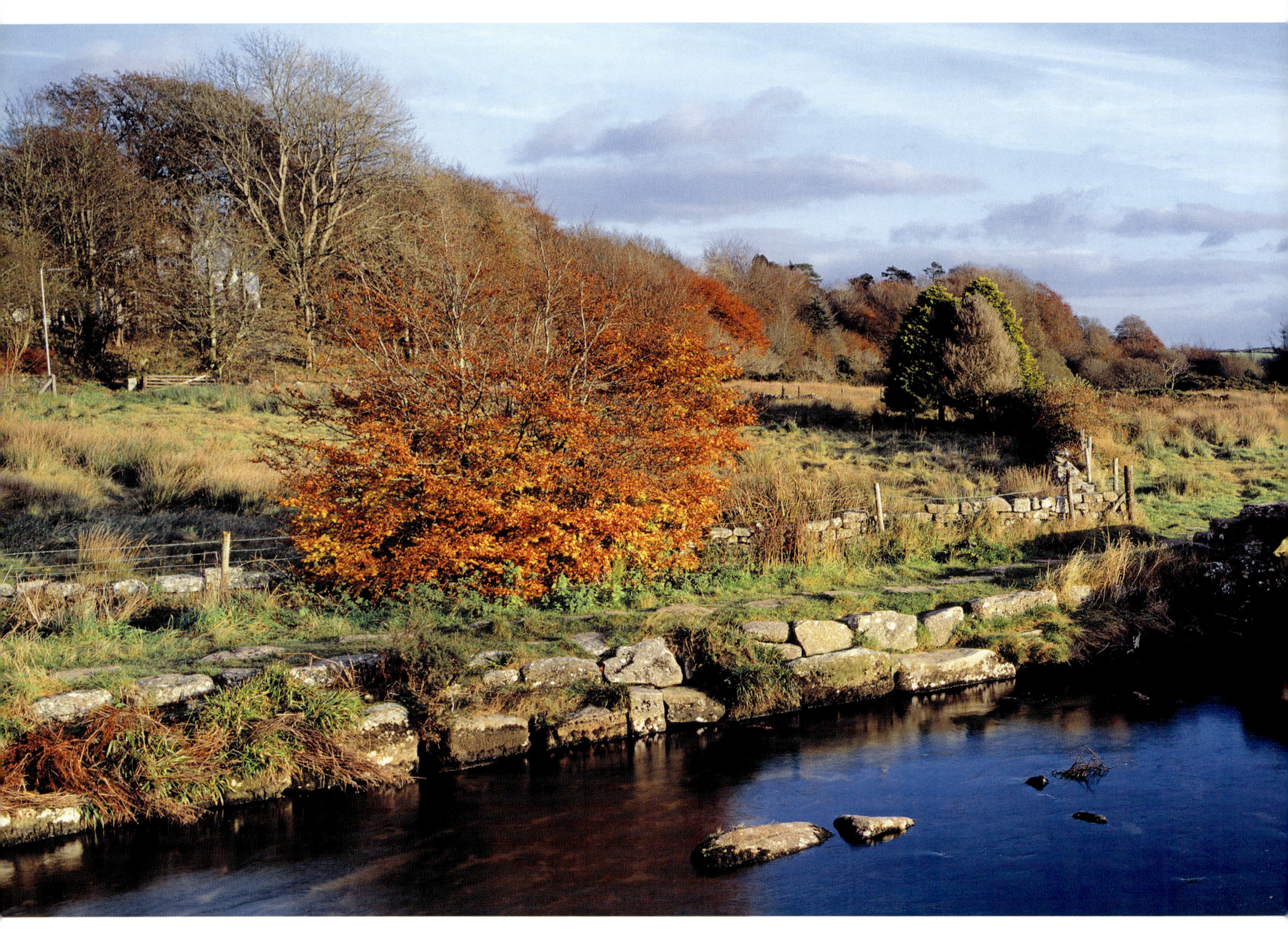

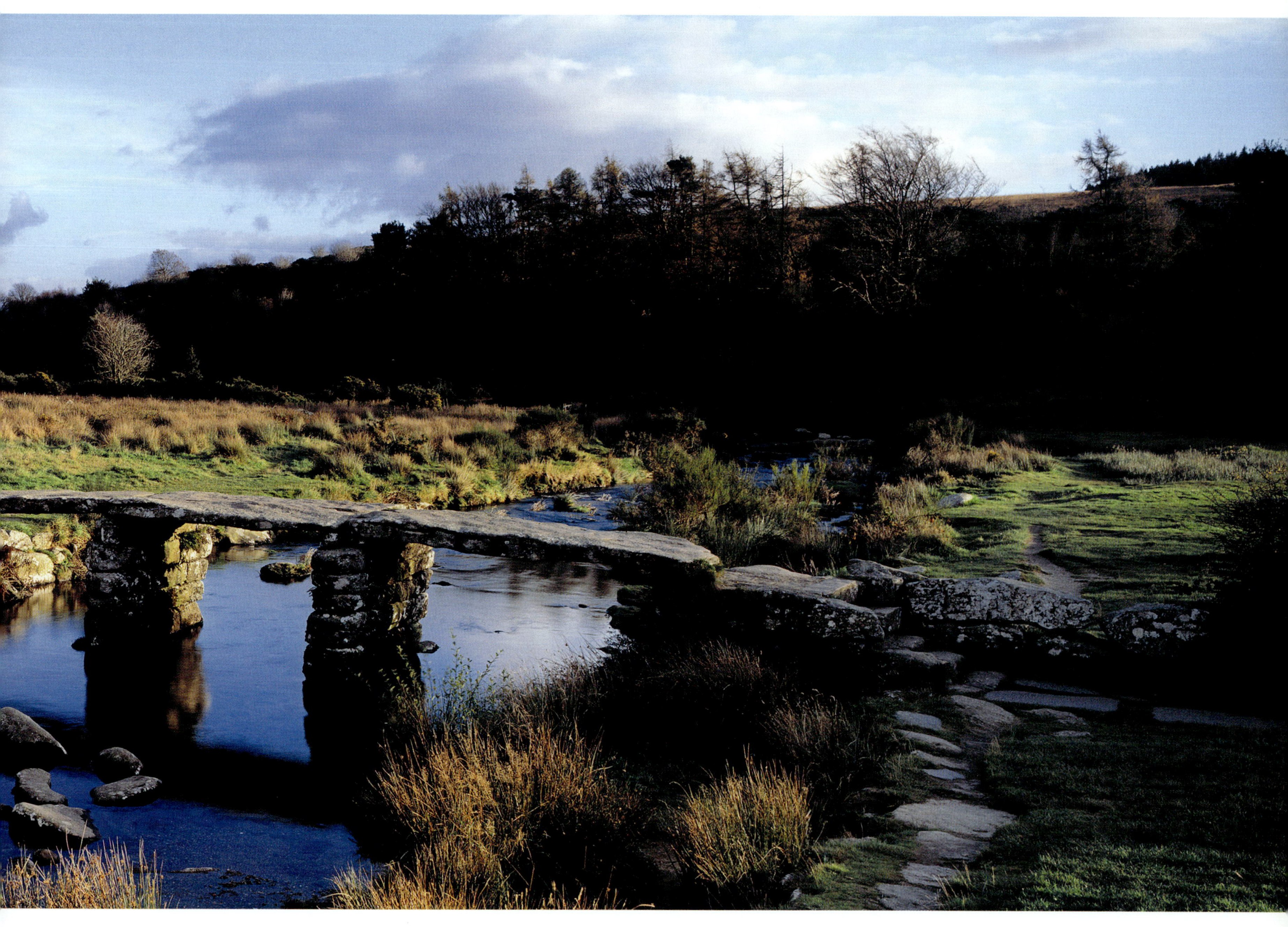

The late afternoon sunlight shimmers on the water of the East Dart as the leaves turn in autumn. Situated in the village of Postbridge deep in the centre of Dartmoor, this clapper bridge dates back to medieval times. Now a more recent humpback bridge alongside reminds us that the moor still provides a home and livelihood to some. Clapper bridges were constructed with large rocks, usually granite, spanning stepping stones in the river. The rocks that span the East Dart here weigh over 8 tonnes and are large enough for carts to cross.

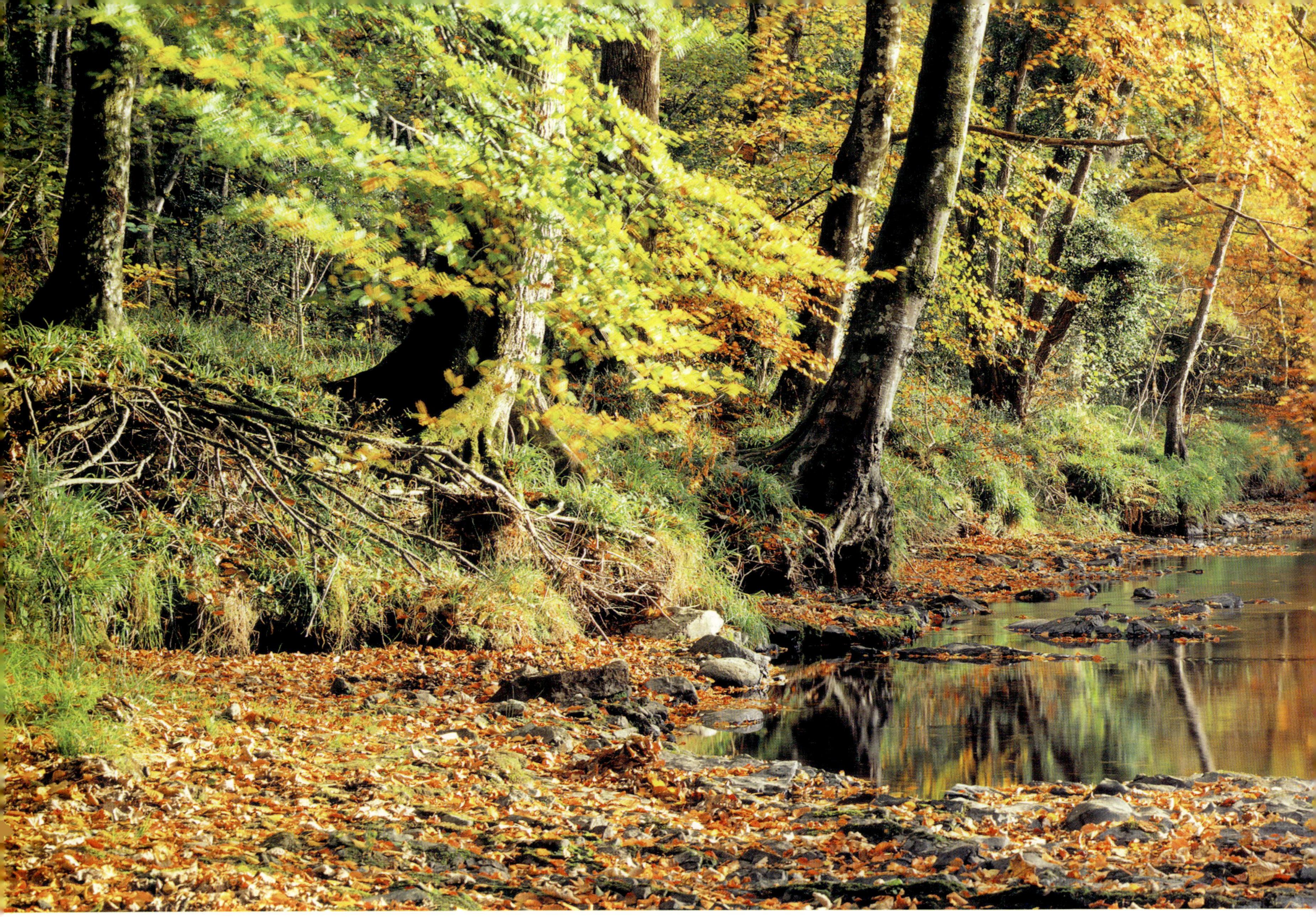

The mirrored surface of the river Teign near Dunsford reflects a beautiful display of autumn colours in the afternoon sunlight.

A carpet of fallen leaves covers the footpaths alongside the banks of the fast-flowing river Teign.

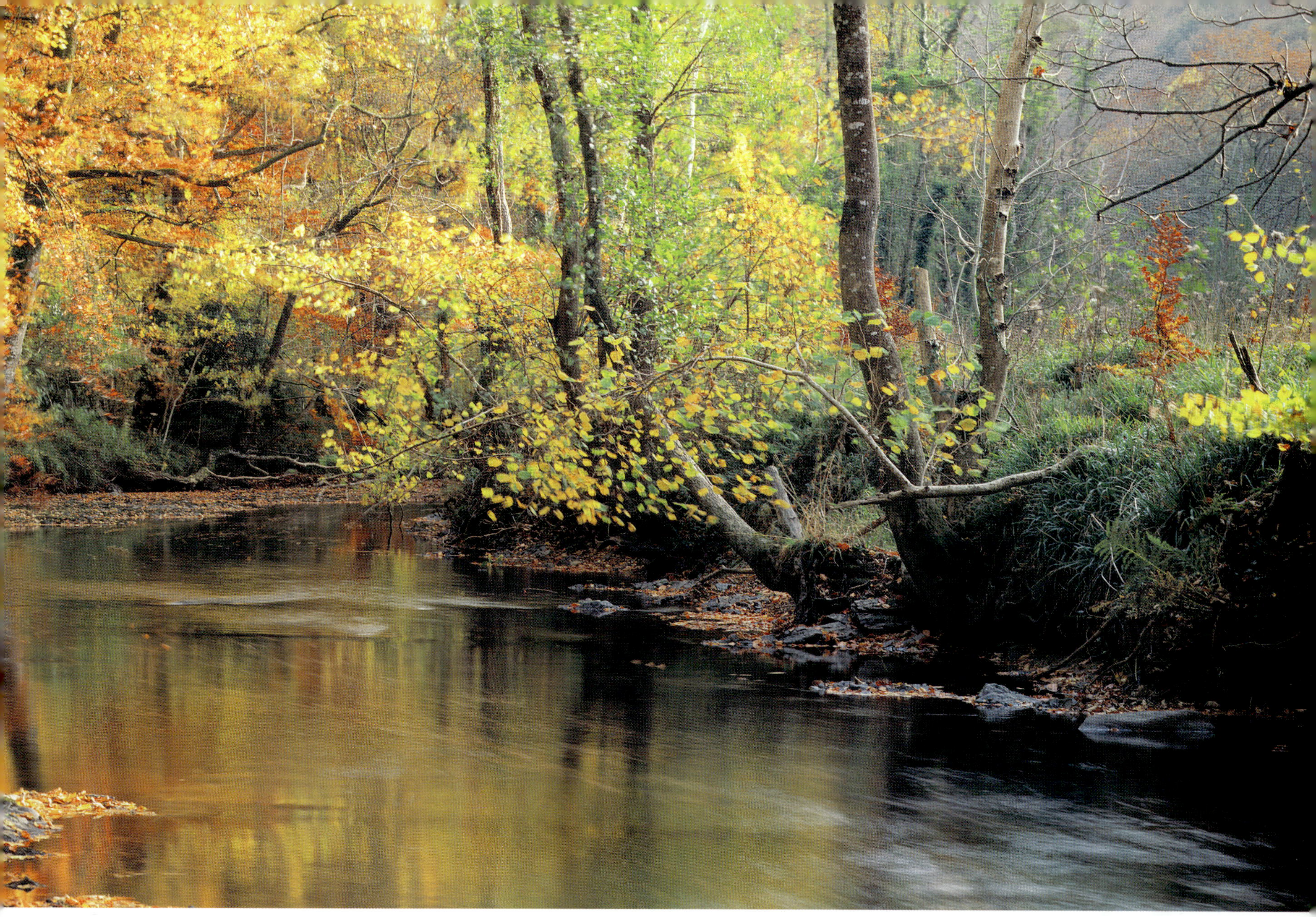

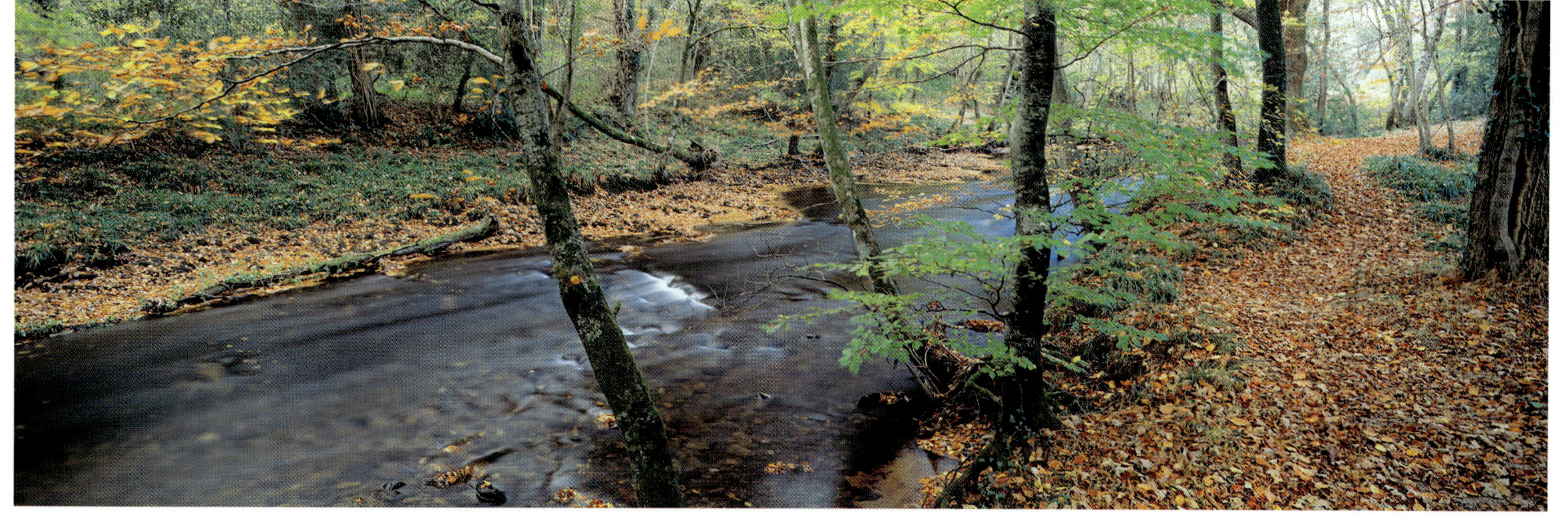

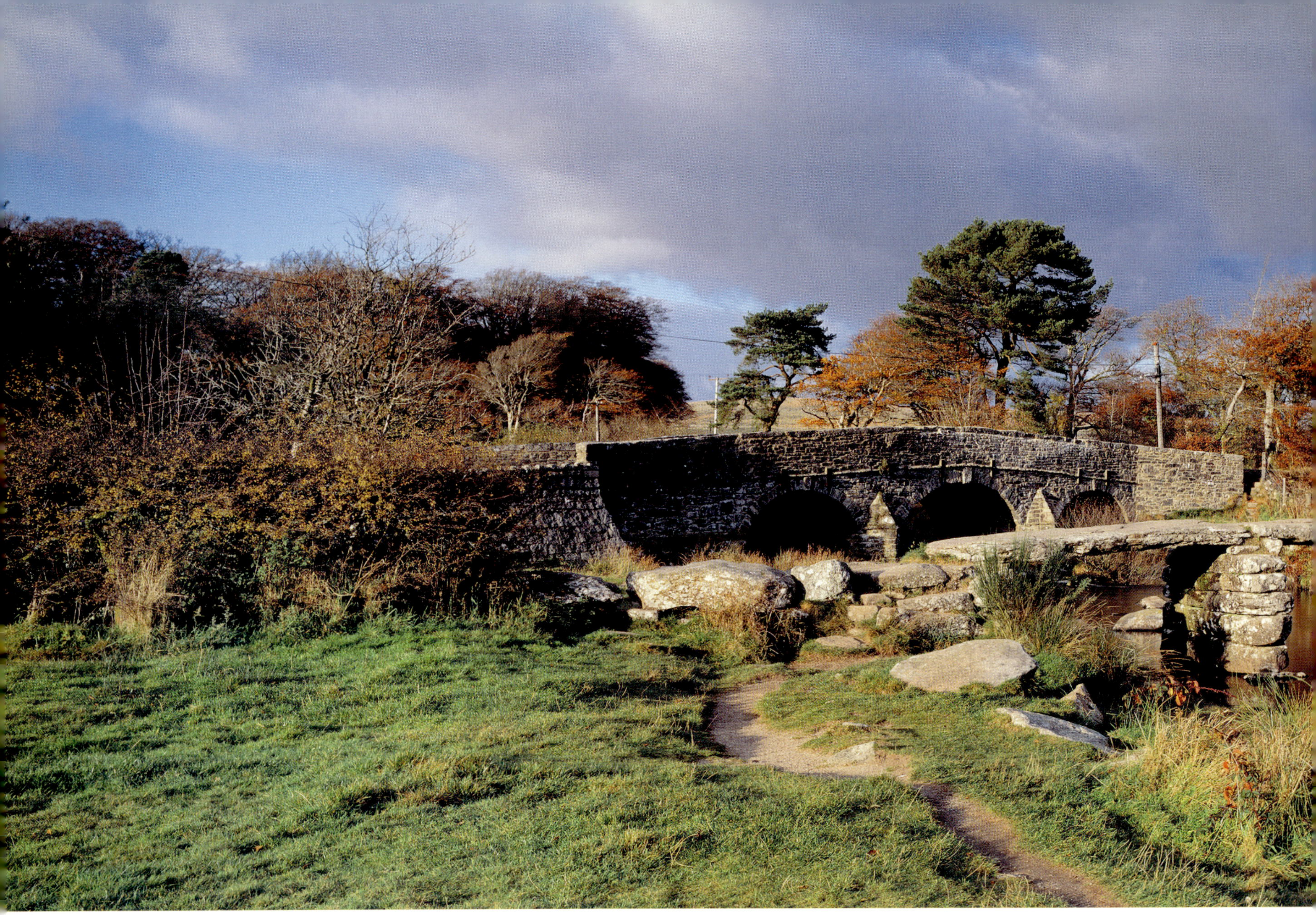

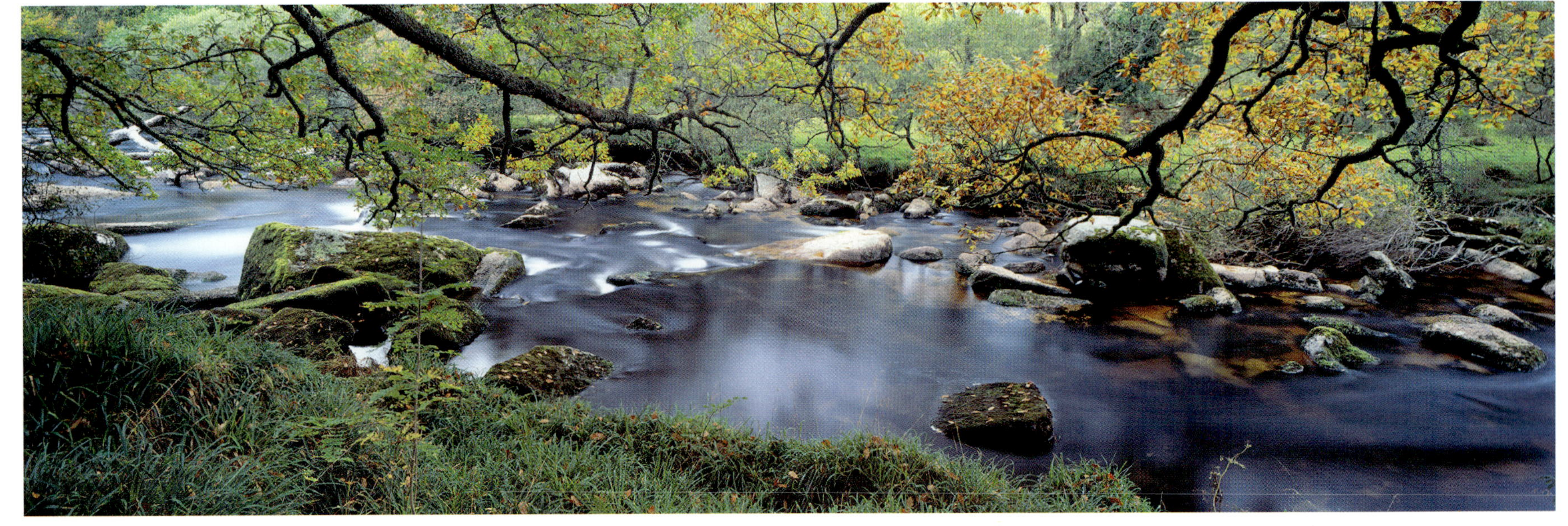

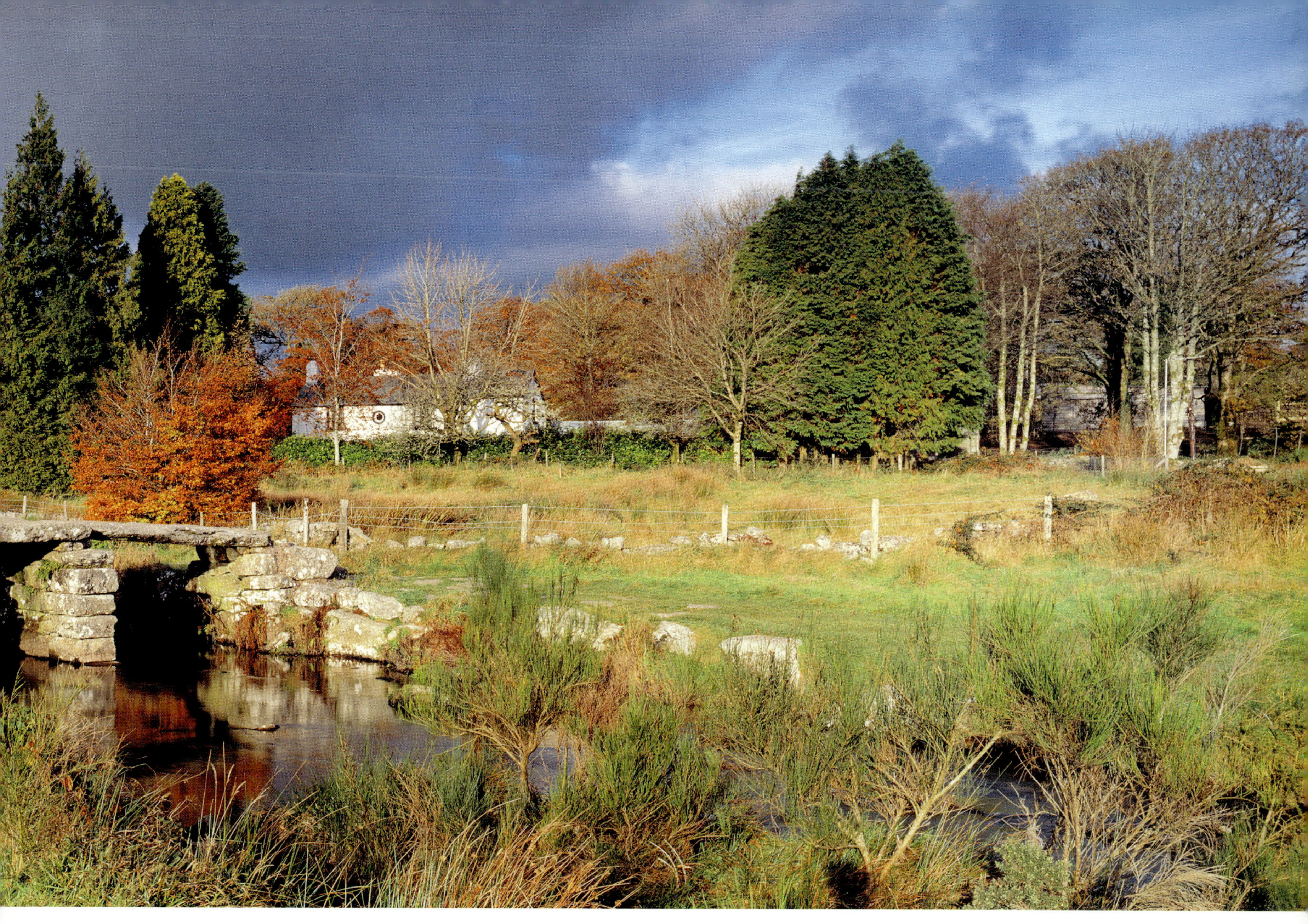

The arched stone road bridge sits next to the ancient clapper bridge at Postbridge.

The Dart flows past low overhanging branches near Hexworthy Bridge.

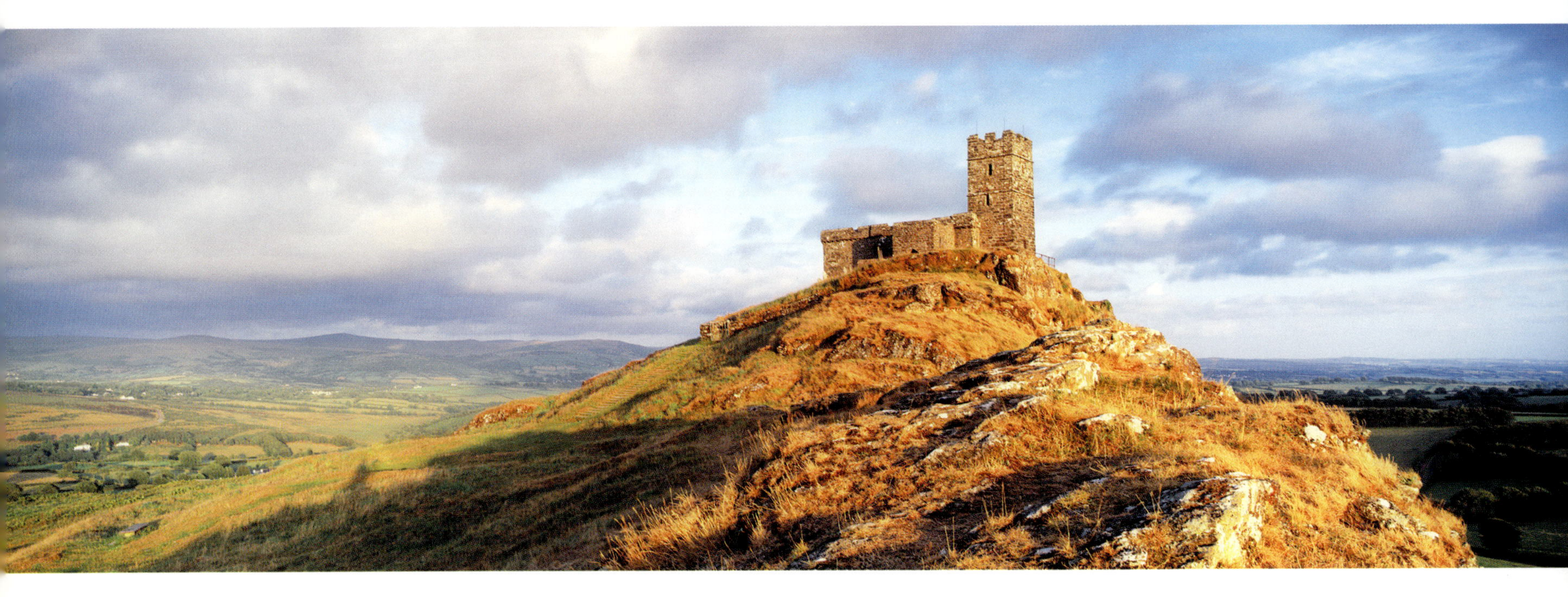

Brentor church under a moonlit sky at dusk.

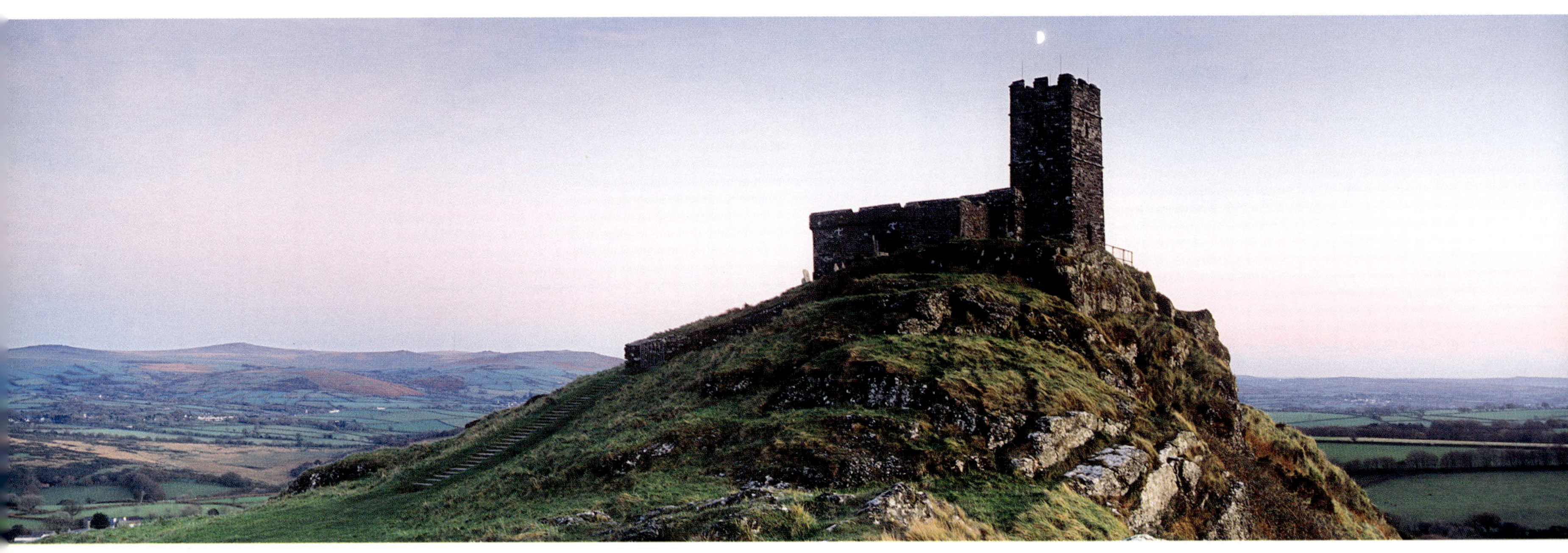

Dramatically perched upon Brent Tor, the tiny church of St Michael de Rupe dominates the landscape. Breathtaking views stretching east across Dartmoor, west towards Cornwall and south towards Plymouth reward the walker who ascends the short but steep climb. Open for services once a year at Easter, the church can be used in all seasons for prayer. It makes for a striking photographic subject as the evening sun bathes the hillside in warm light.

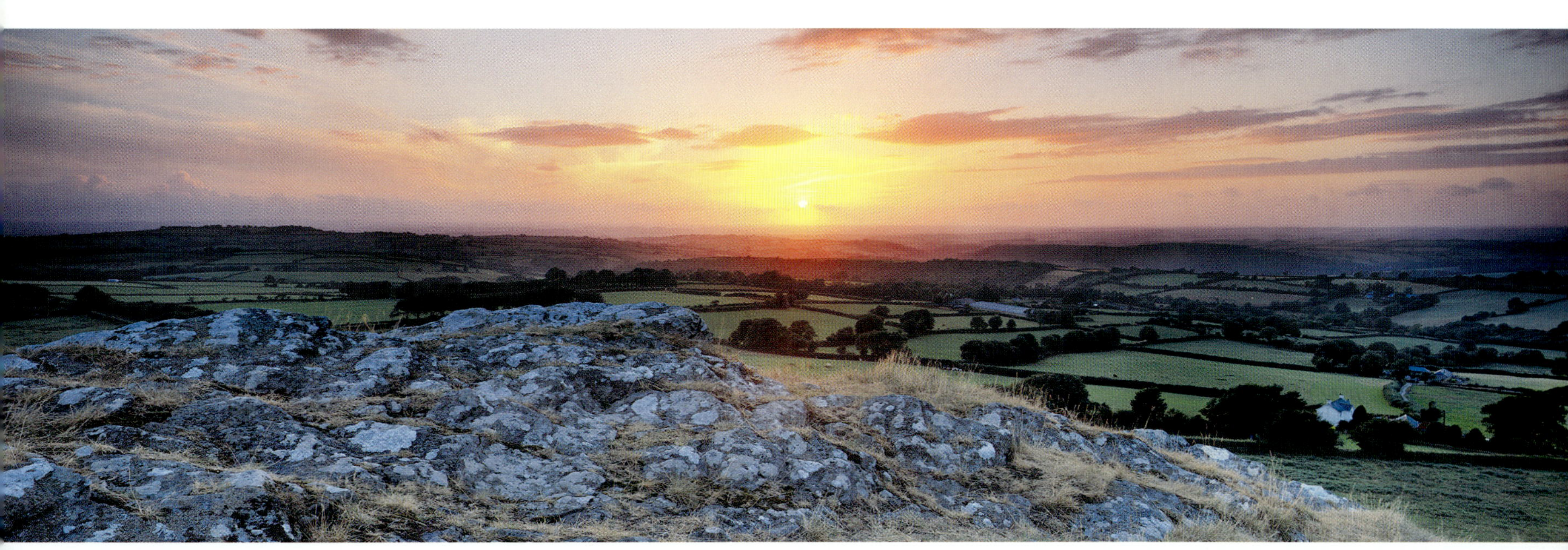

Looking west from Brent Tor over Devon fields and trees towards the setting sun.

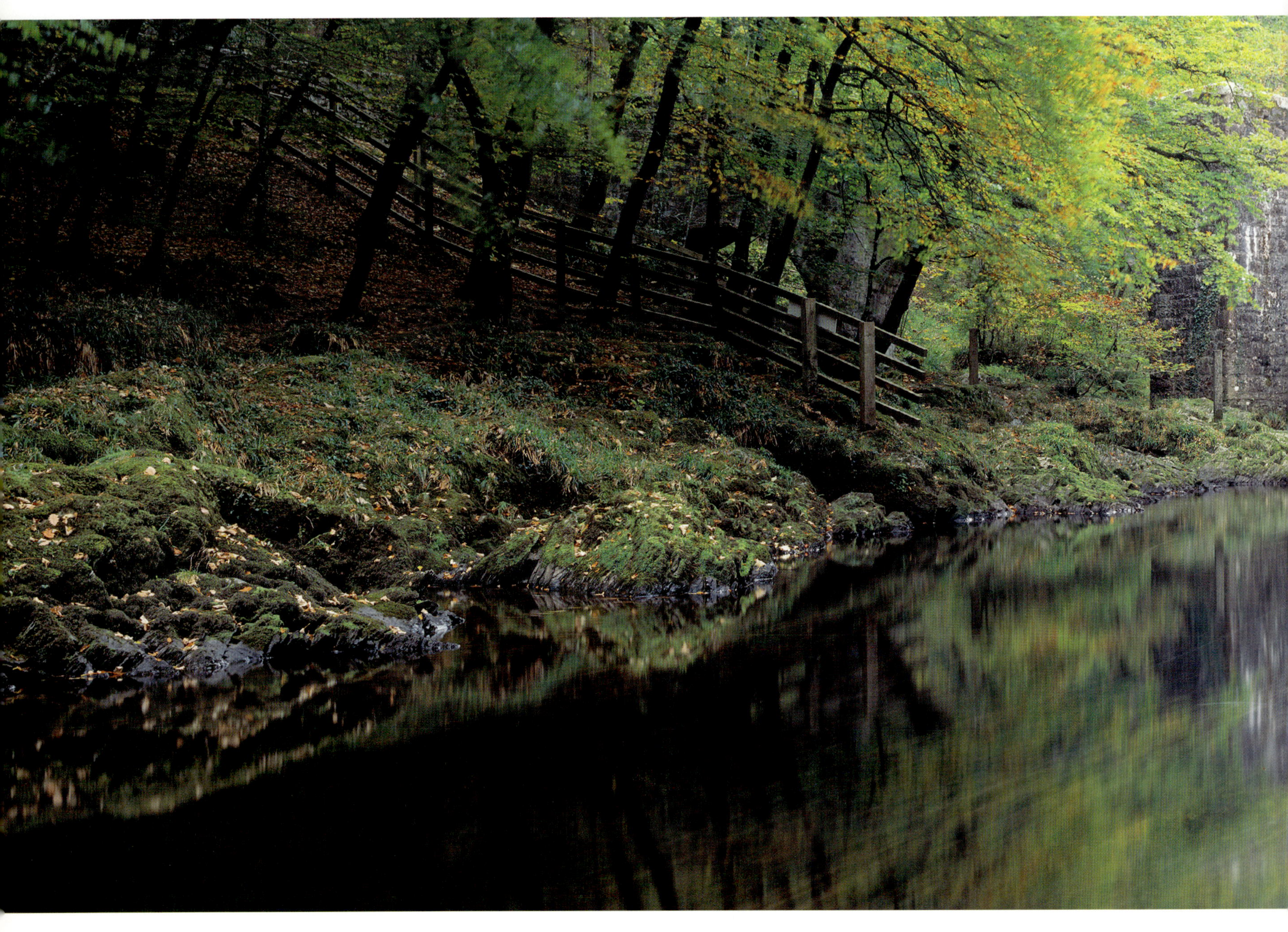

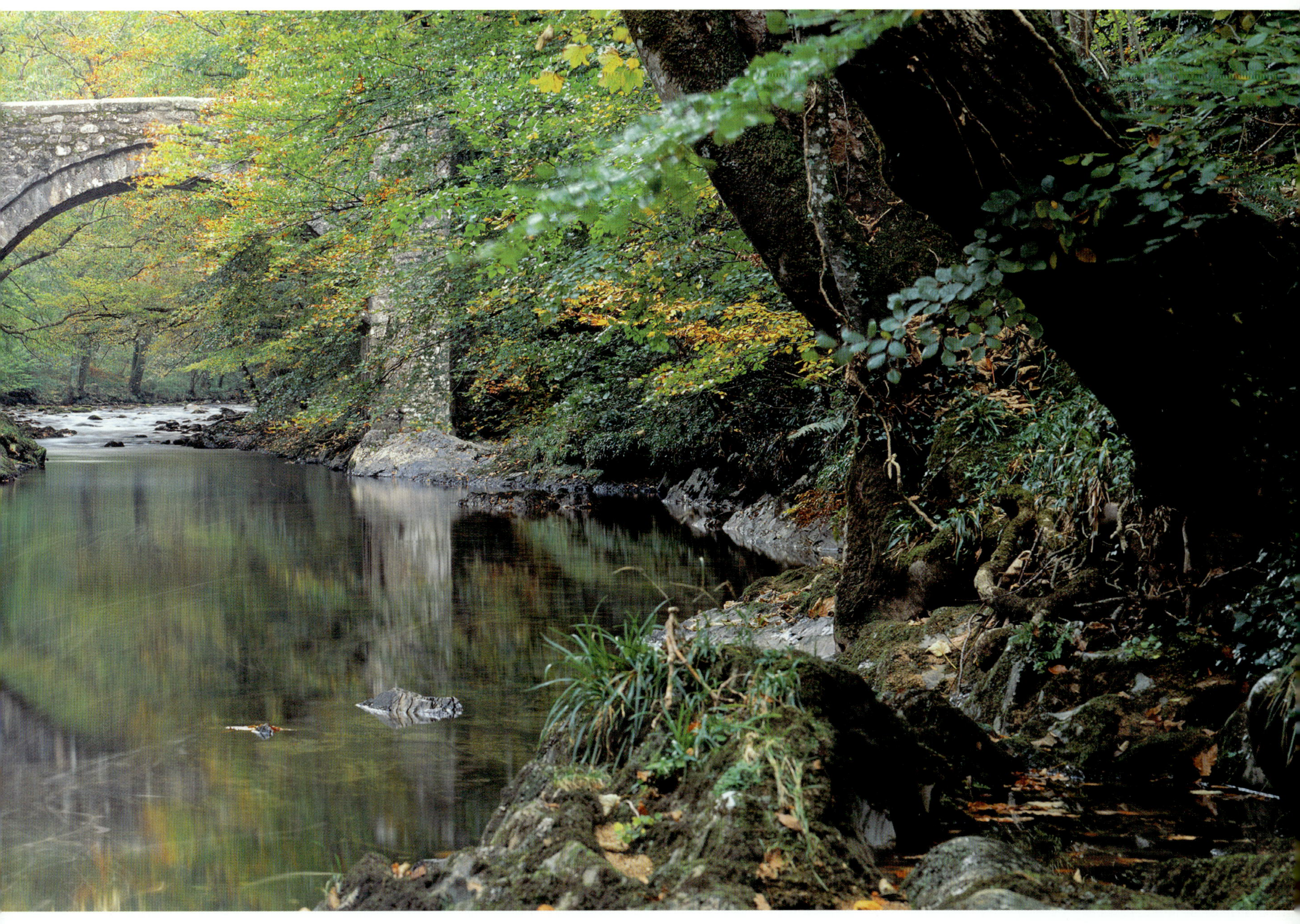

Holne Bridge, near Ashburton is one of two medieval bridges spanning the Dart. The original was destroyed by flood in 1413 and replaced with the bridge which stands today. It has pedestrian recesses built into its sides, originally to escape the hooves of packhorses. Useful today to avoid cars.

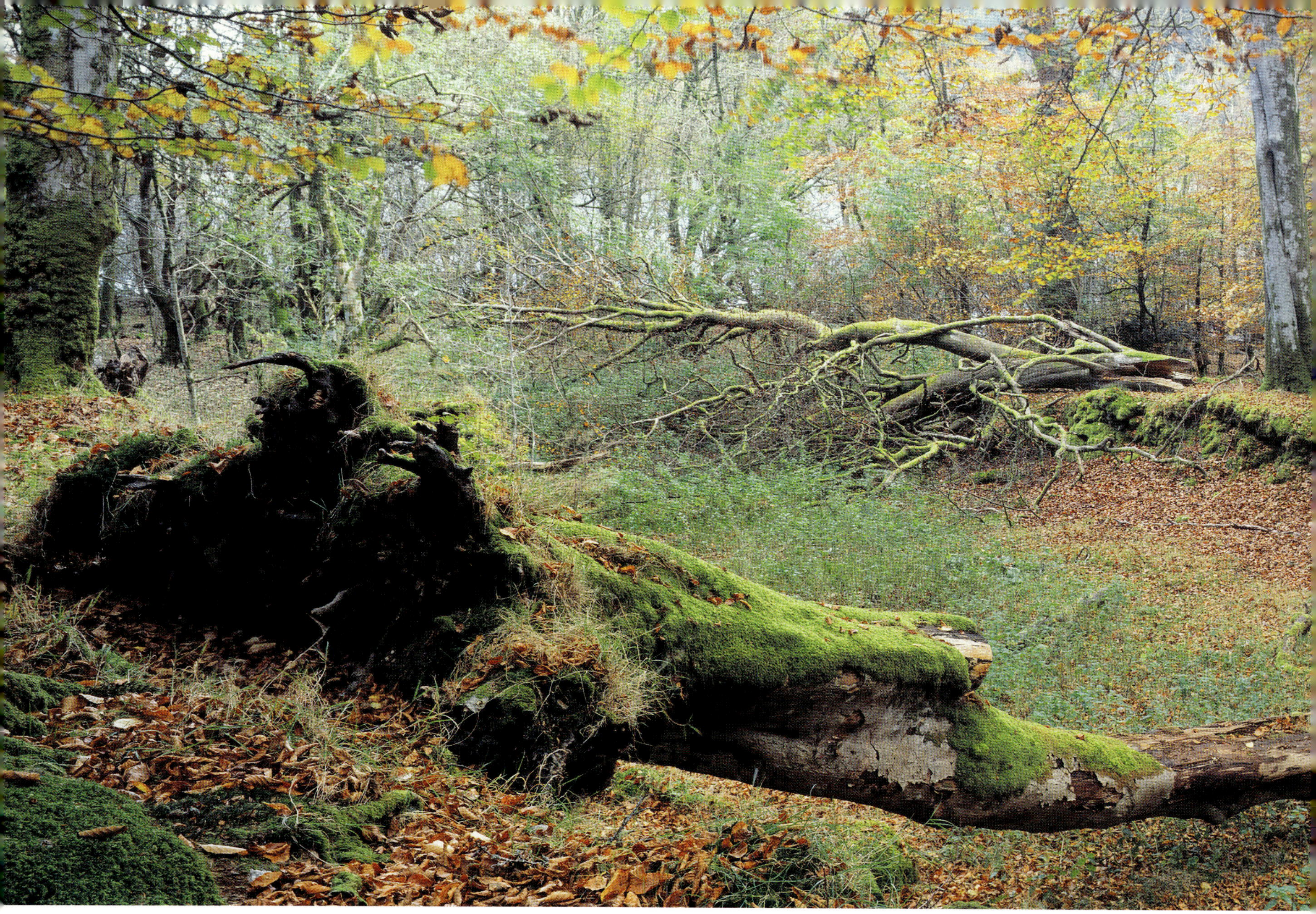

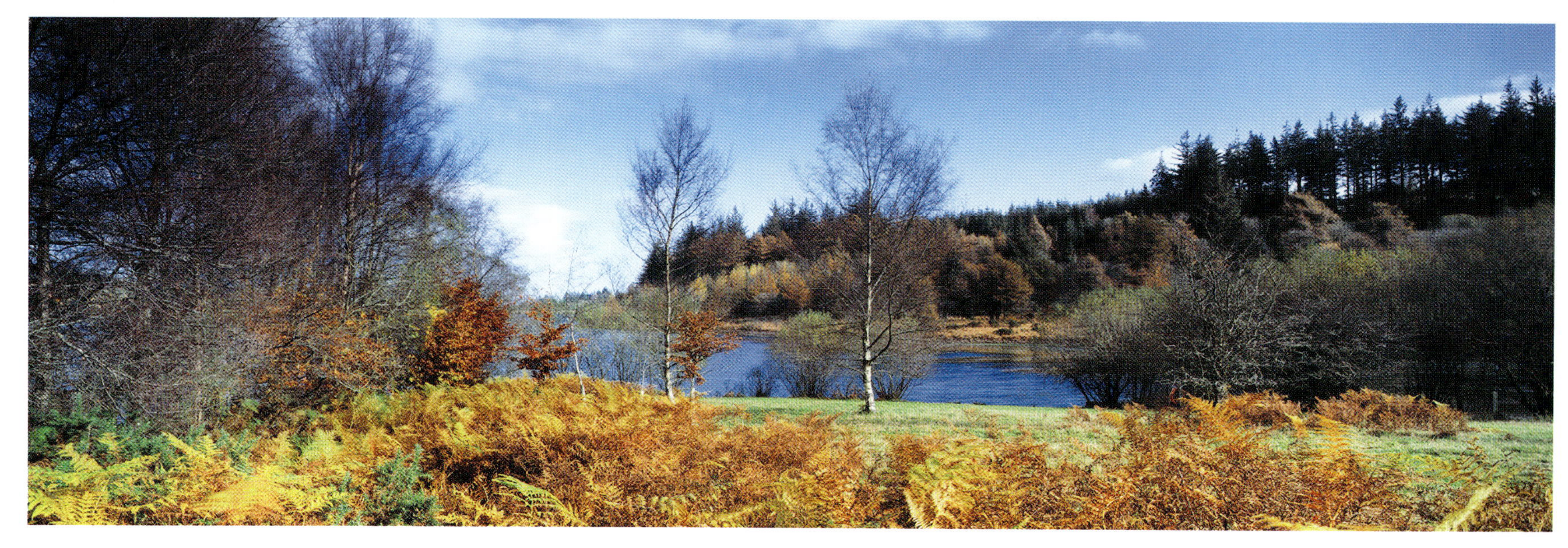

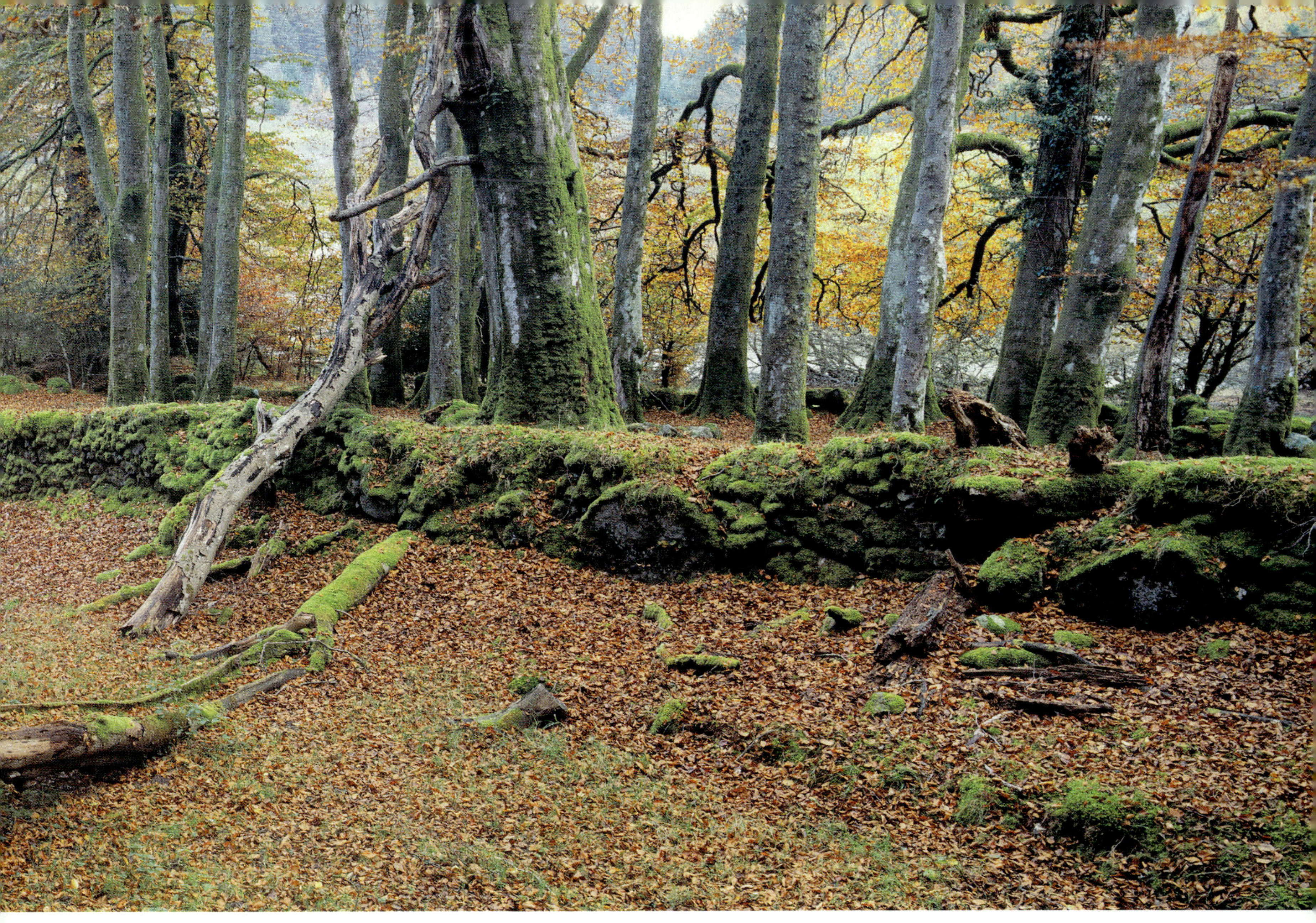

Trees lie exactly where they fall, becoming a home for wildlife and insects as decay takes hold. The surrounding trees provide a seasonal carpet of fallen leaves in this copse on the edge of Fernworthy Reservoir.

Golden coloured ferns grow beside the peaceful waters of Fernworthy Reservoir.

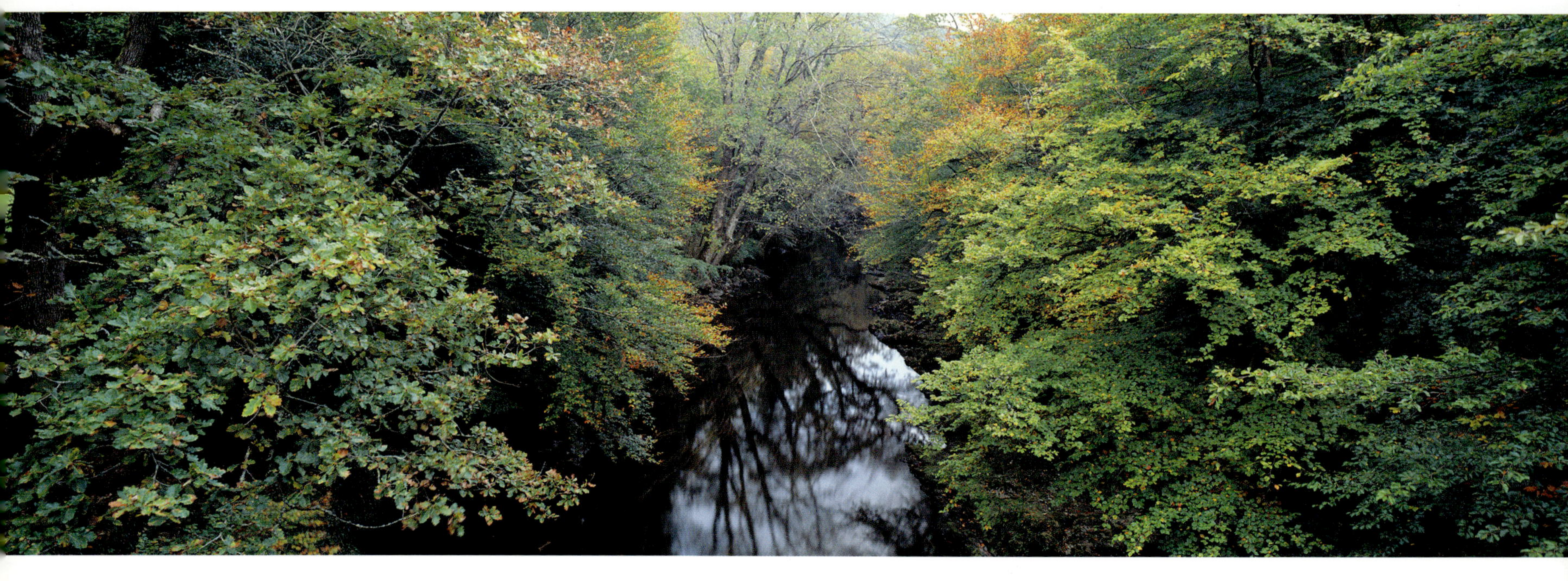

The river Lyd carves its way through the picturesque Lydford Gorge carpeted with moss and ferns.

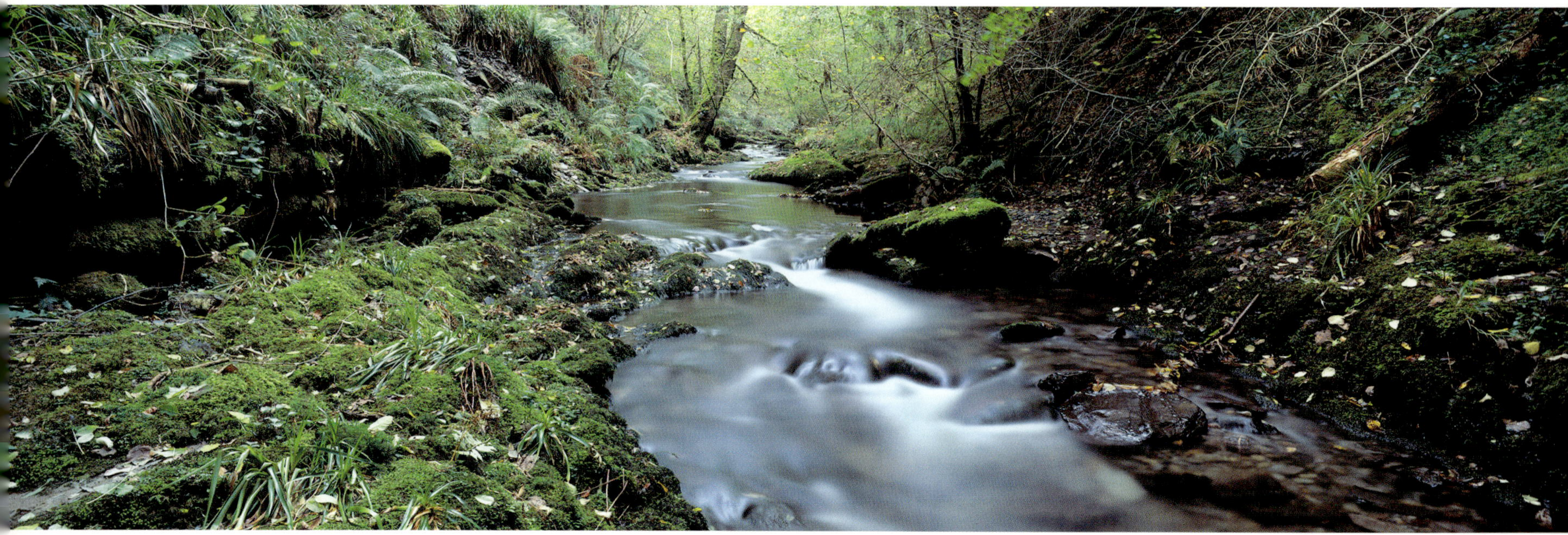

Orange and yellow start to colour the trees lining the Dart as autumn takes hold.

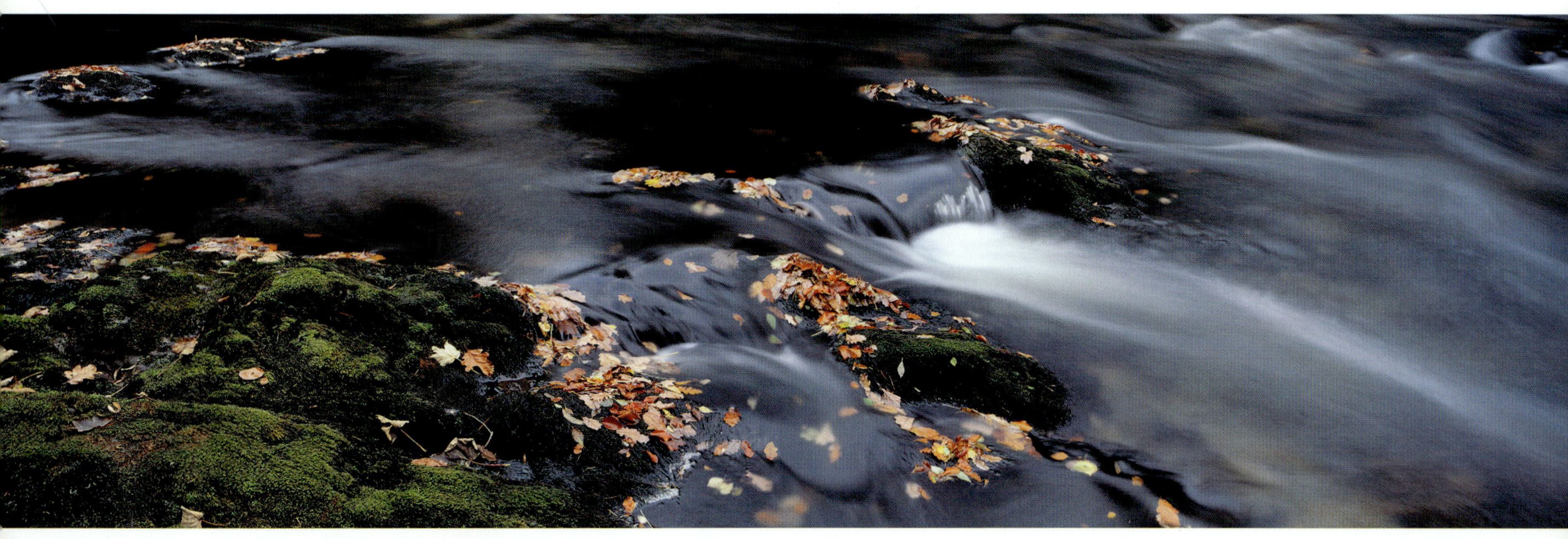

Fallen leaves collect on moss-covered rocks in the Dart as it journeys to the sea.

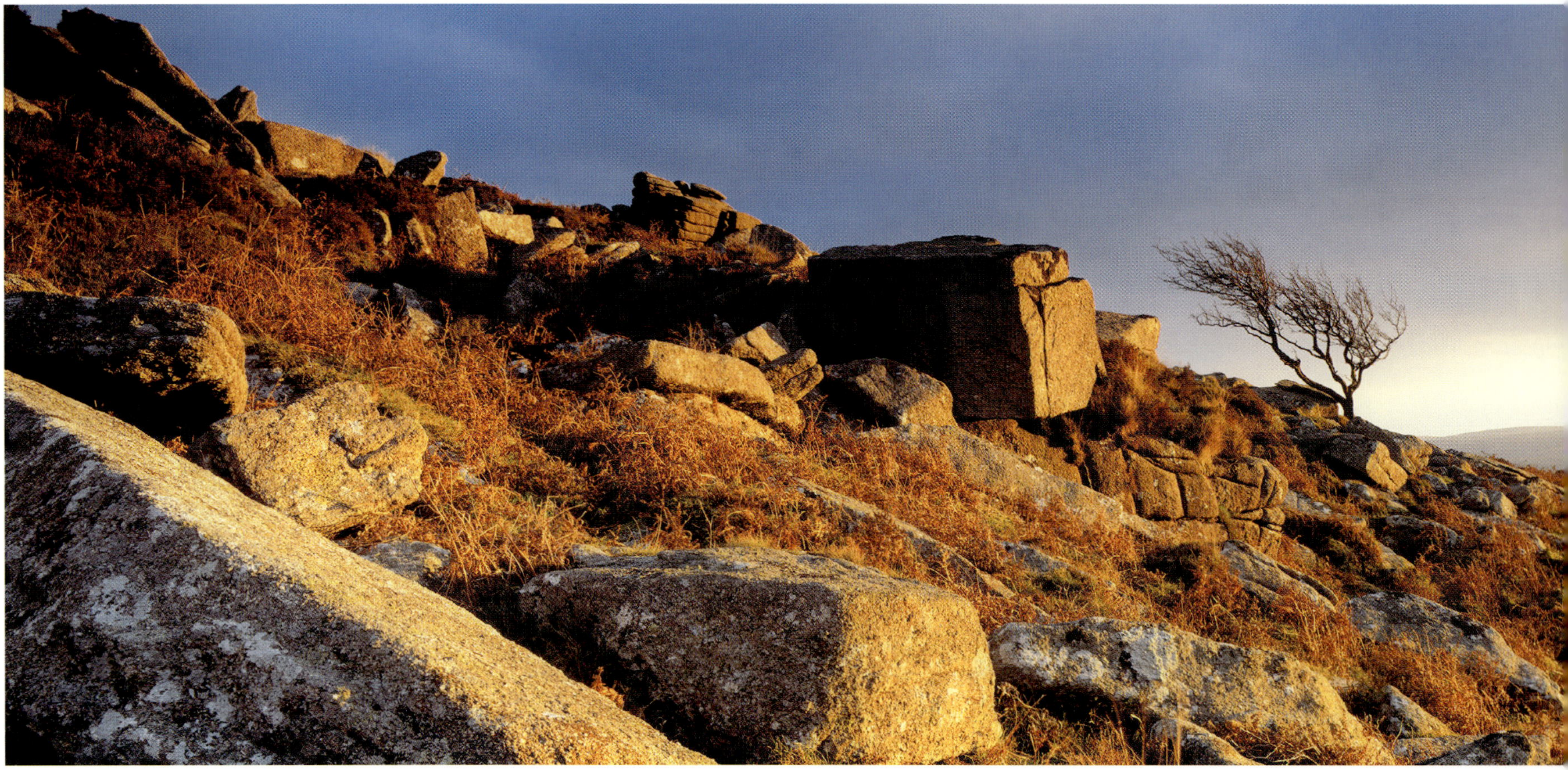

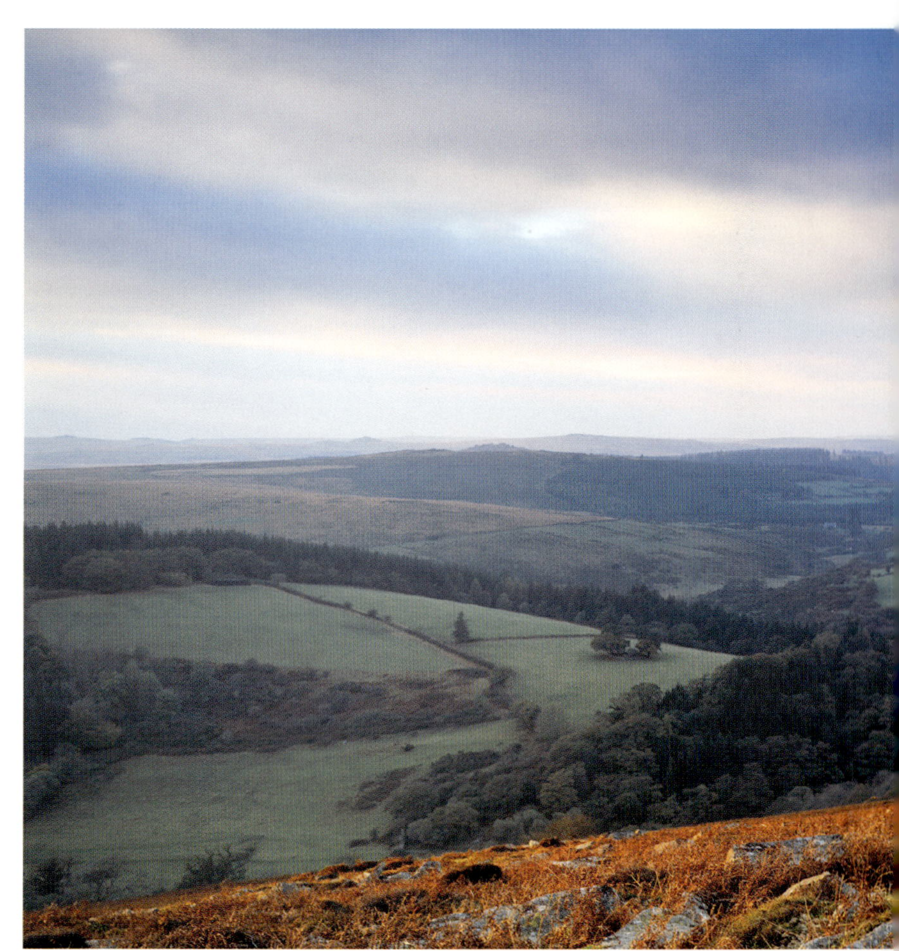

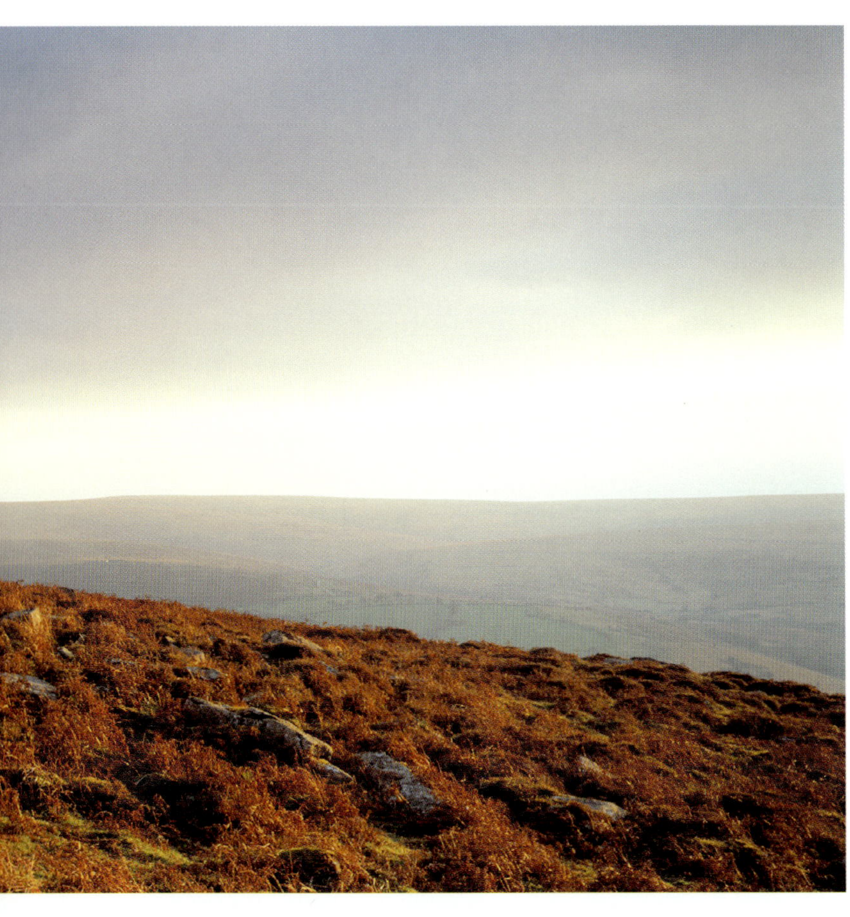

Rusty autumn ferns are softly lit by the fading sun. This windswept hawthorn tree clings to the rocky slopes of Yar Tor, looking over the forest plantations of Snider Park and Little Newtake and towards the distant Laughter Tor.

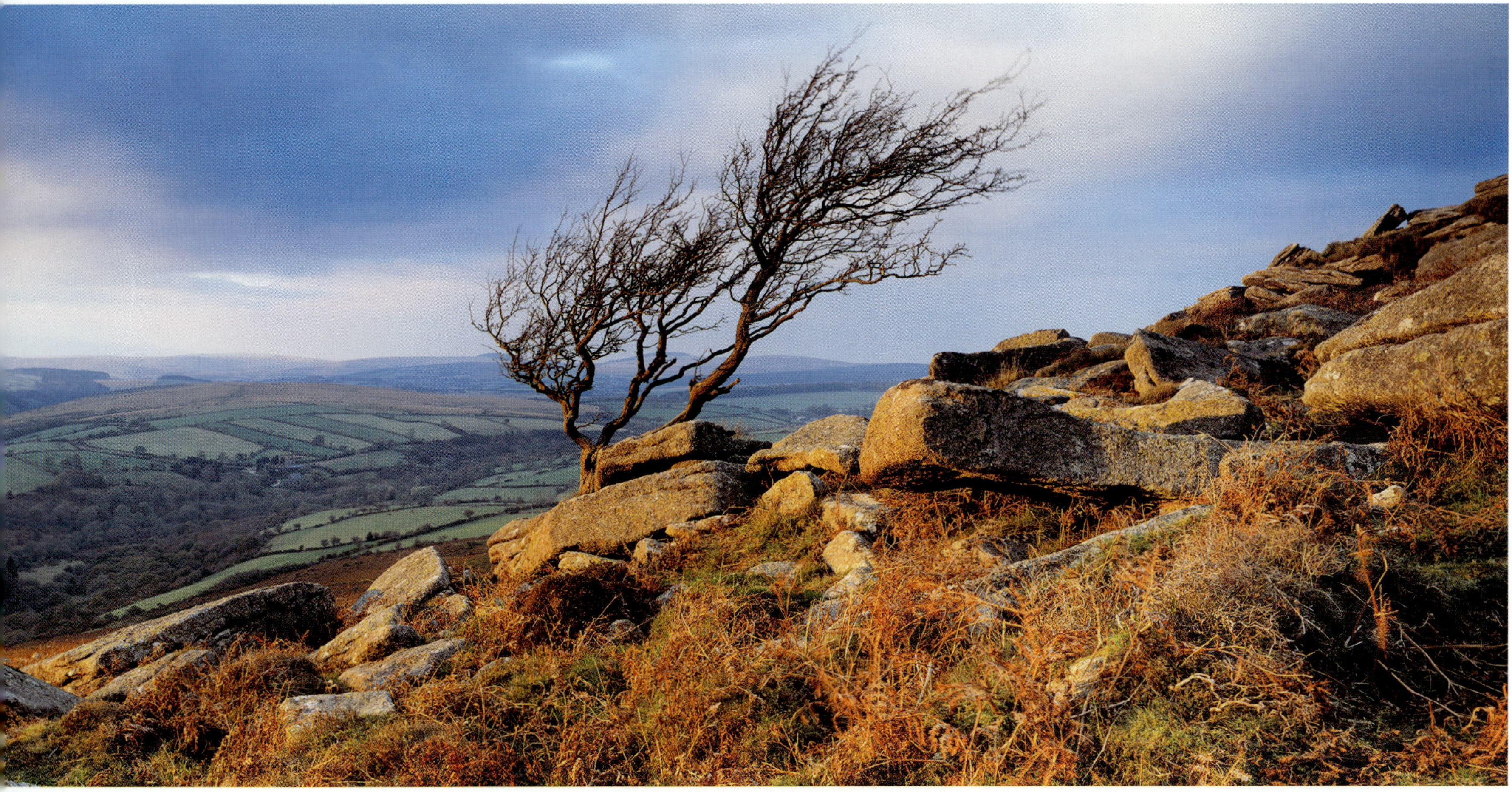

Through the heart of Rithill Wood runs the river Erme; splashing and cascading amongst the rocks, it brings a symphony of sound, drowning out all other woodland noises on approach. Leaves on the slippery rocks signal that autumn has arrived and winter is once again to grip the landscape in its icy hand.

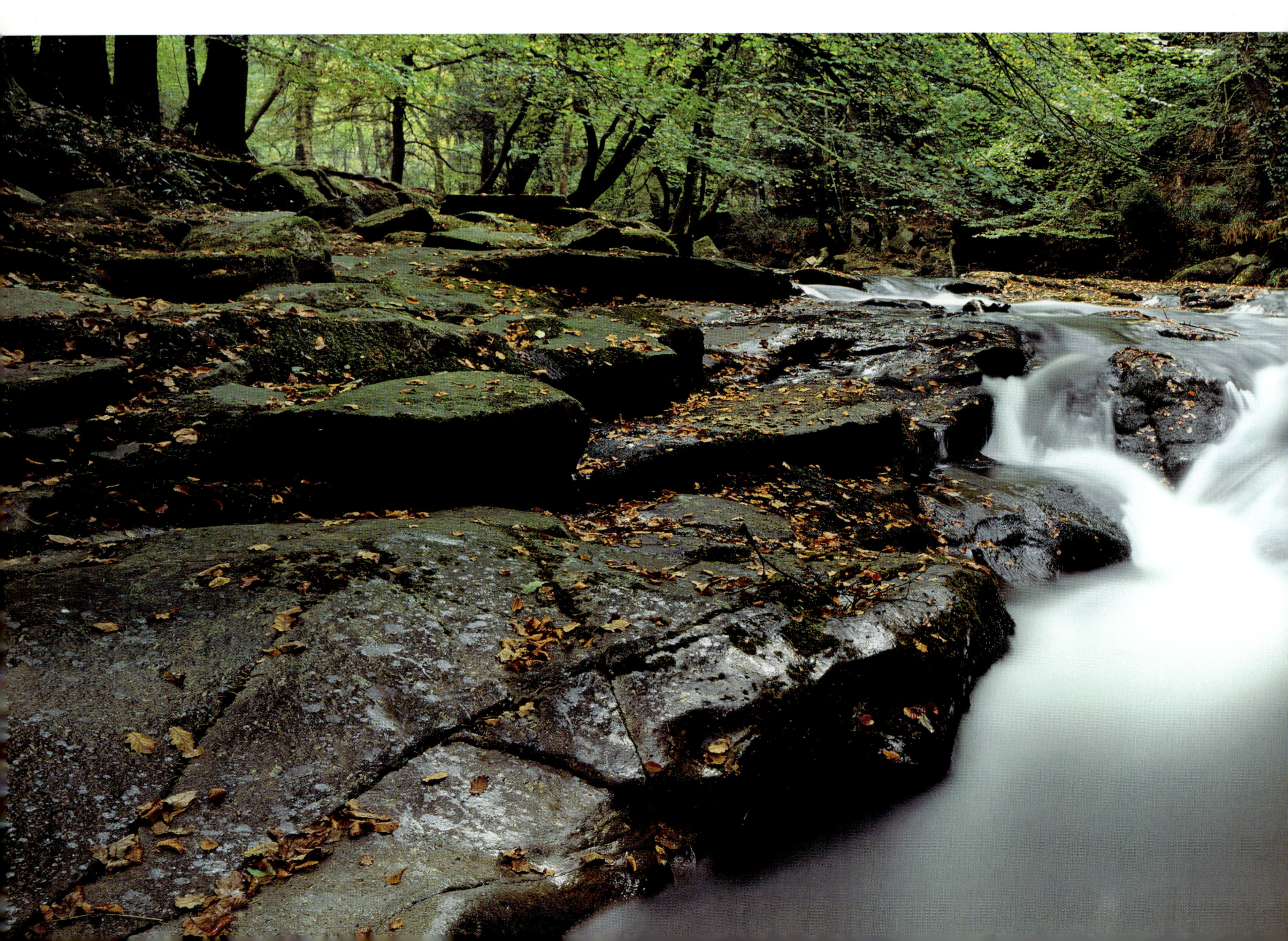

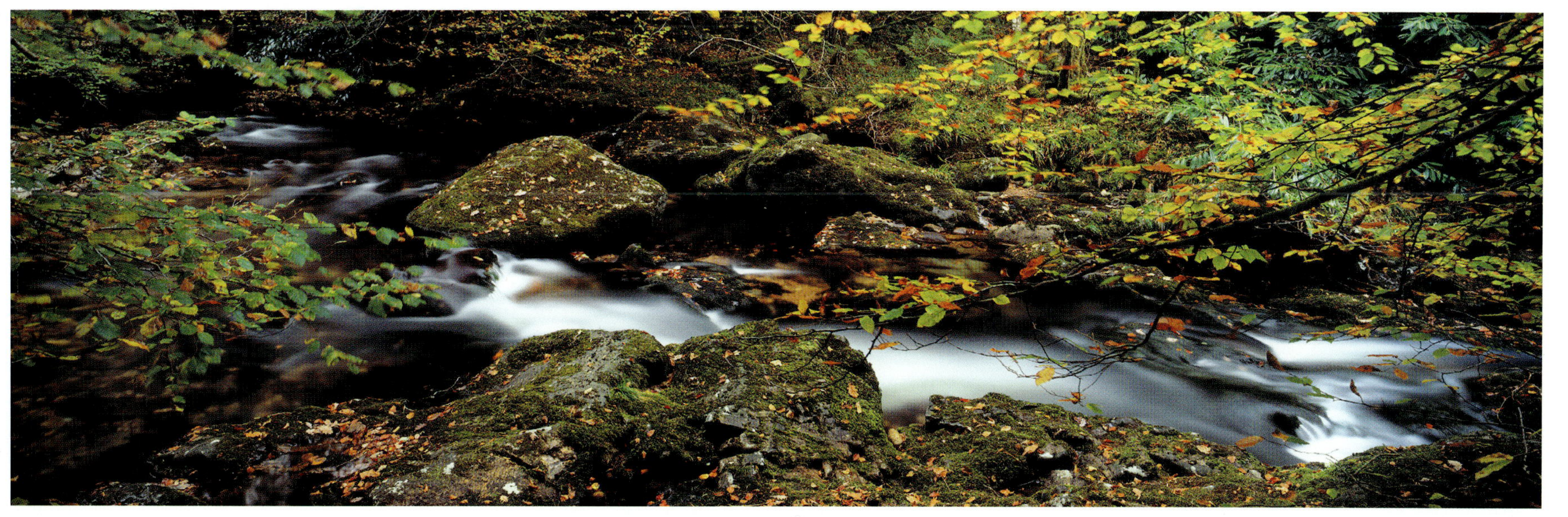

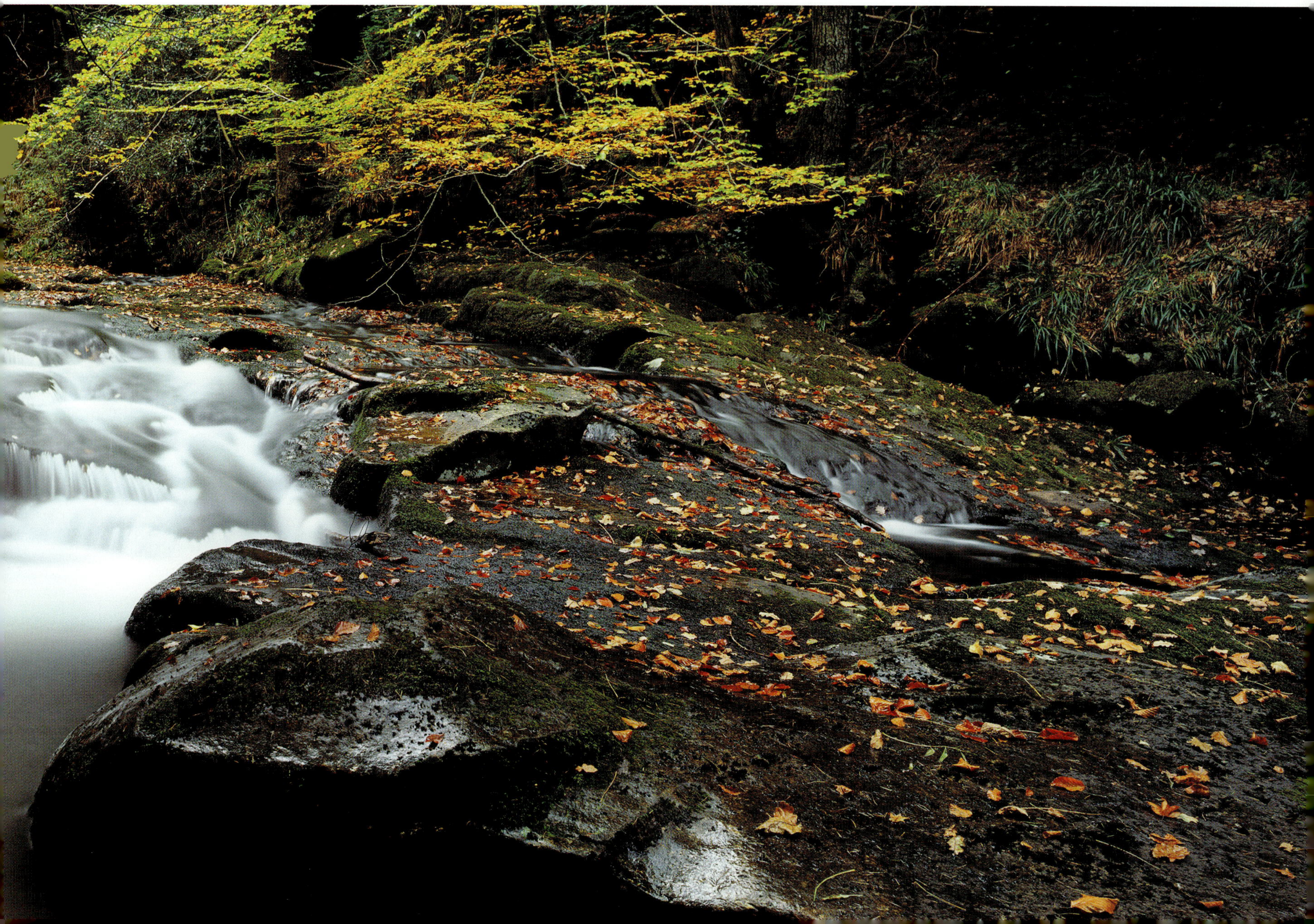

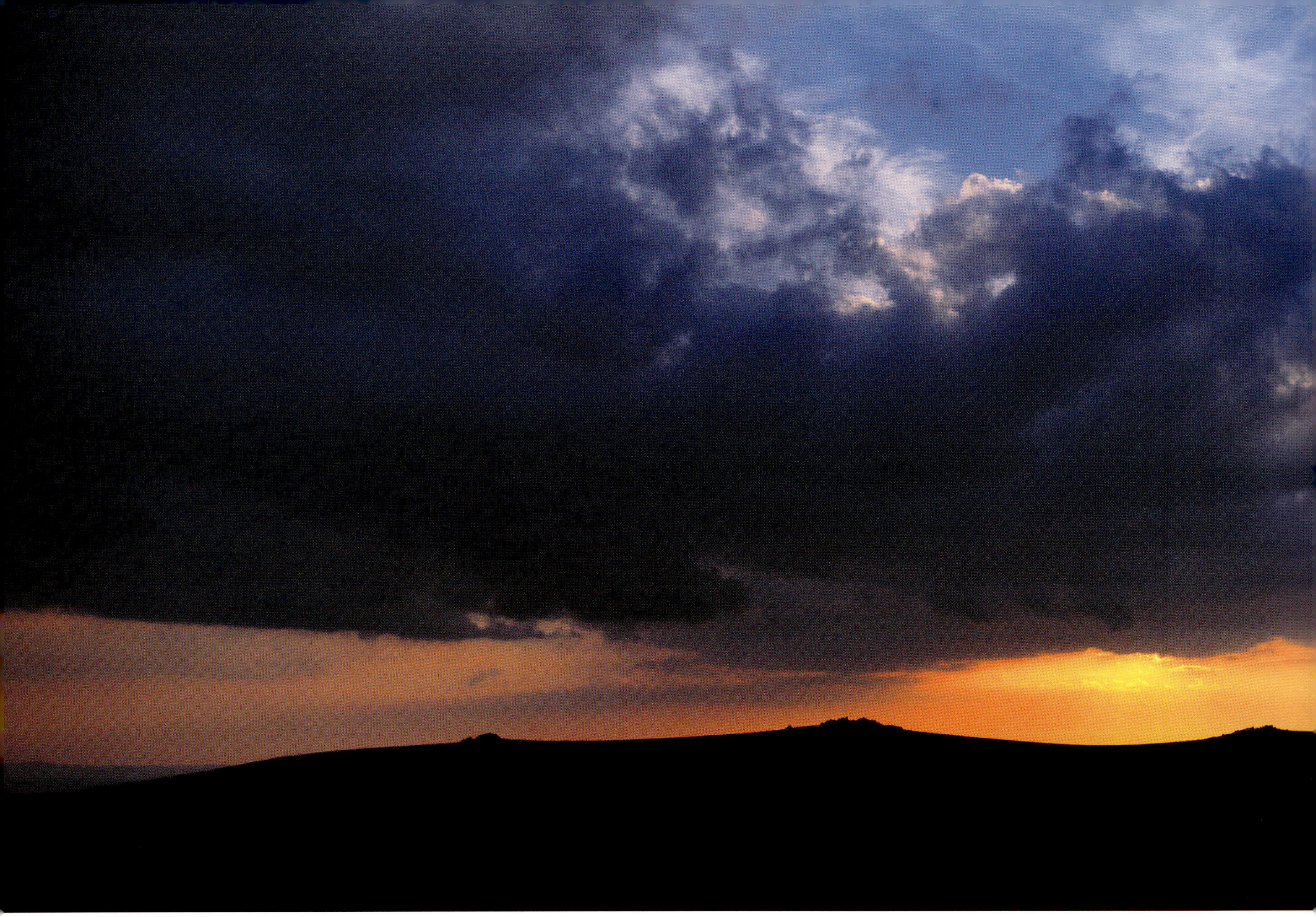

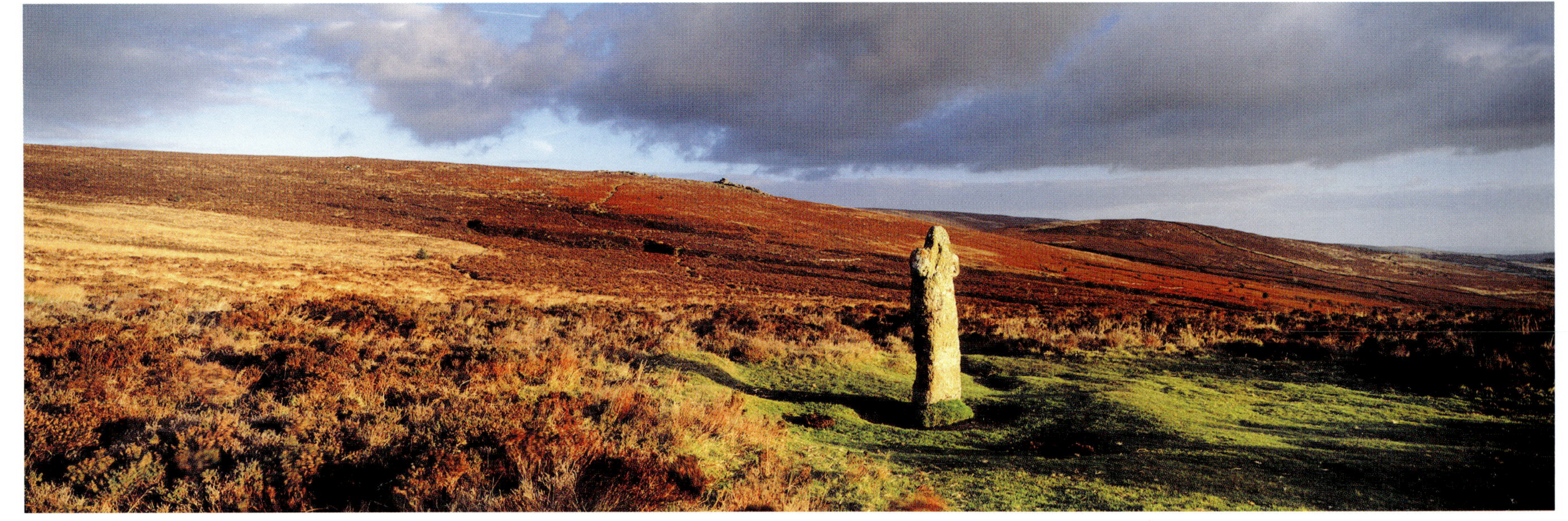

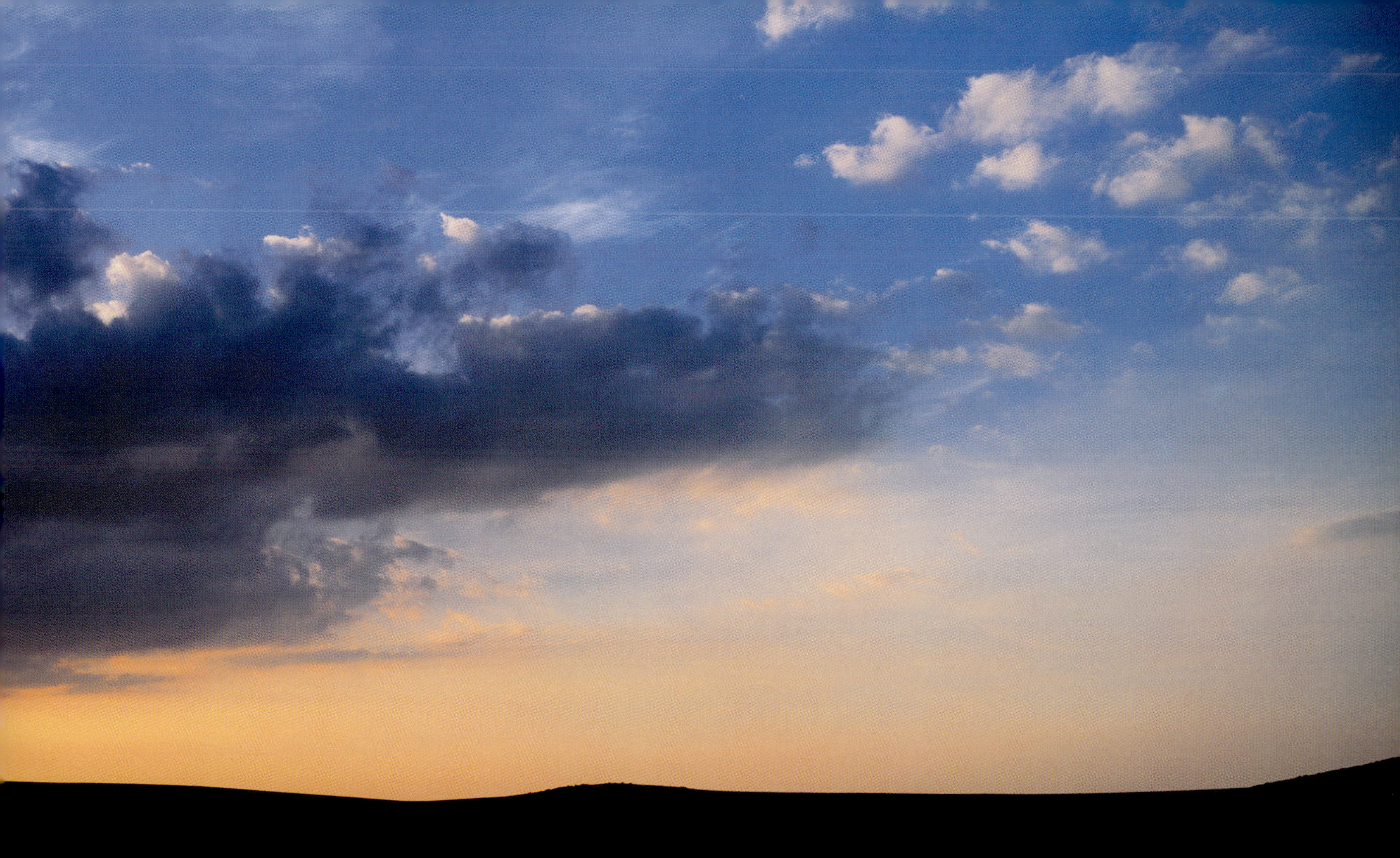

Glowing sunlight from behind dramatic clouds throws the tors of Middle Staple, Great Staple and Roos into silhouette. A scene such as this can depict the nature of Dartmoor much more clearly than a cloudless blue sky day.

The rough texture of the worn surface of Bennett's Cross is emphasised by the side-raking sunlight on an autumn afternoon. The dark rust-coloured heather mixes with the light coloured grasses on the slopes of Birch Tor, leading onto Headland Warren.

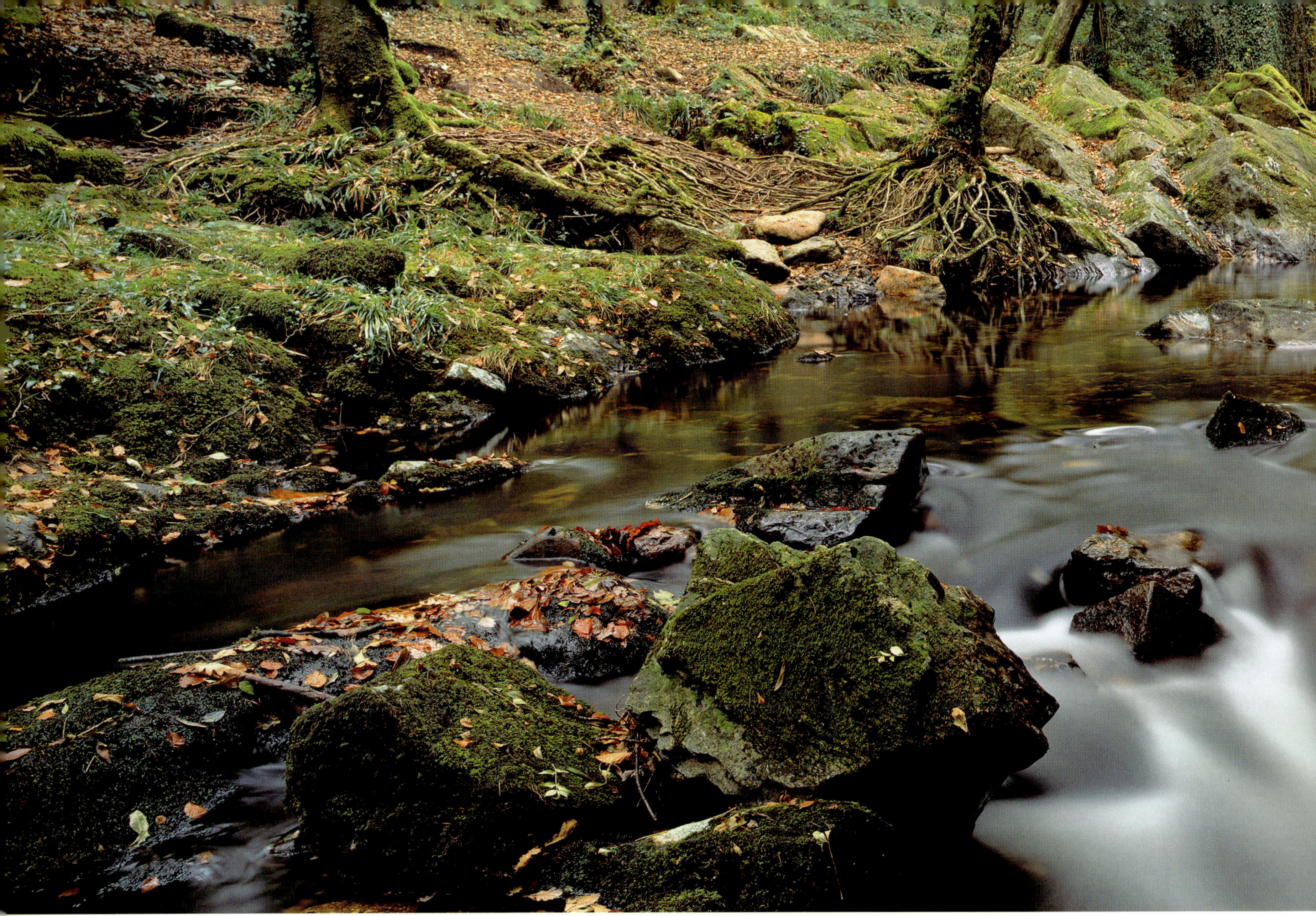

The river Erme flows past bare roots, rocks and fallen leaves. The long exposure has turned the flowing water into silk-like fabric contrasting the hard-edged rocks it surrounds.

The granite rock formation on Little Mis Tor falls into silhouette in front of a spectacular red sunset.

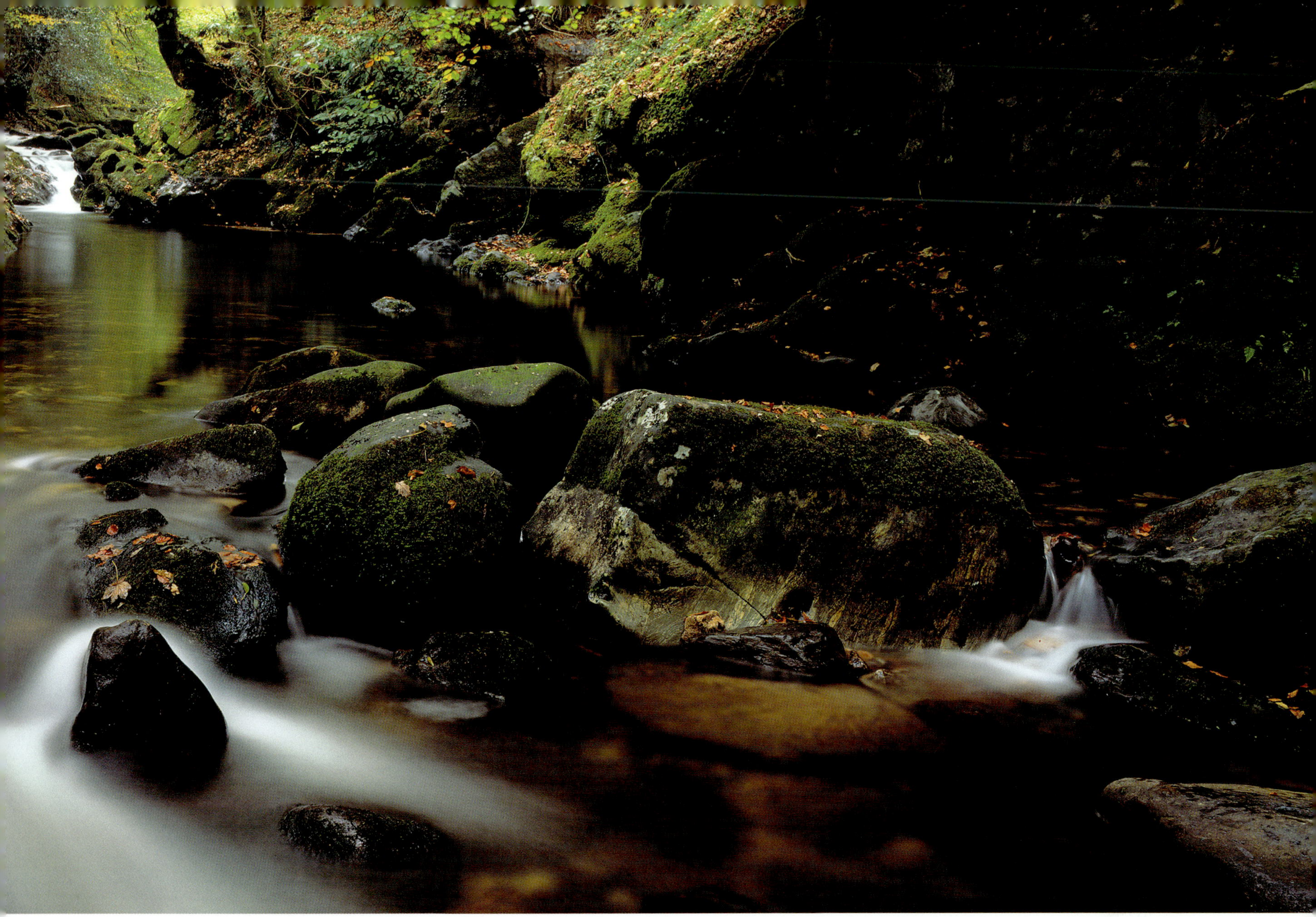

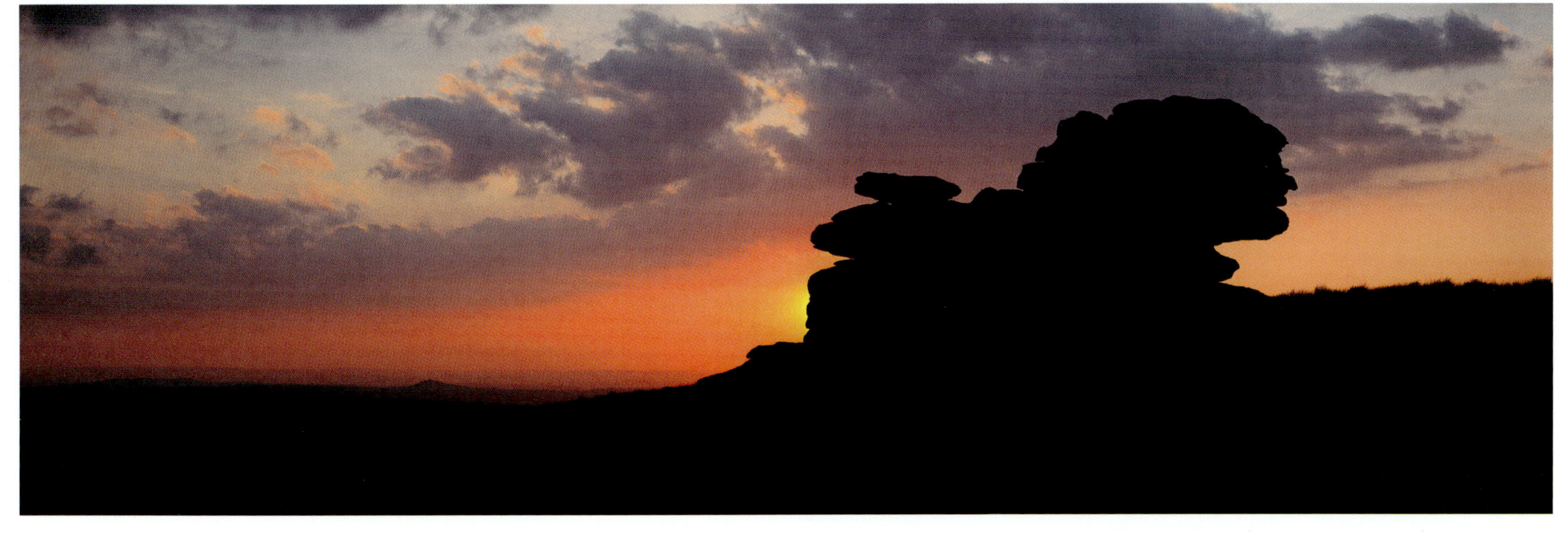

PHOTOGRAPHIC NOTES

A constant drive for quality has resulted in the Fuji GX617 panoramic camera becoming my choice of camera. A manual film camera using medium format film, each exposure is roughly 6 x 17cm in size, approximately ten times that of 35mm, producing only four photographs per roll of film.

I am often asked if I use digital, and the question is usually accompanied by a surprised reaction when I say I use film. The reason is that despite many positive features of digital photography, using film to capture panoramic landscapes simply provides the best quality I can achieve. Scanned 6 x 17cm film contains a huge amount of information, sufficient for massive enlargements in excess of 2 metres wide, making this an easy choice for me at this time.

The fully manual nature of the camera forces me to use a separate light meter to attain the correct exposure; this, together with a sturdy tripod, slows down the picture-taking process so that I feel much more of a part in making the photograph.

I use two interchangeable lenses on the Fuji, a 90mm wide angle and a moderate telephoto 180mm for selecting certain parts of the landscape. My film of choice is the excellent Fuji Velvia slide film which delivers brilliant colour and fine grain, allowing me to record my vision of the landscape on film.

When presented by spectacular displays of light on the landscape, filters must be used. The human eye is amazing in its ability to view a bright sky and a darker foreground together, but film falls short. For this reason I often use Lee Neutral Density (ND) graduate filters, which let me balance the brightness of the sky with the often darker foreground, allowing film to record it correctly.

Colin Prior and David Noton are among those who have inspired me with their amazing panoramic photography. My aim is to combine an interesting composition with great light, which sometimes can take a long time waiting for the right light or weather conditions to suit a particular location, but I hope it results in bringing some of the natural beauty of the landscape to life for the viewer.

My final piece of invaluable equipment is a campervan, which I sometimes use to sleep overnight close to where I want to be for the next morning; this way I see some spectacular sunrises I might otherwise miss!

PHOTOGRAPHIC INFORMATION

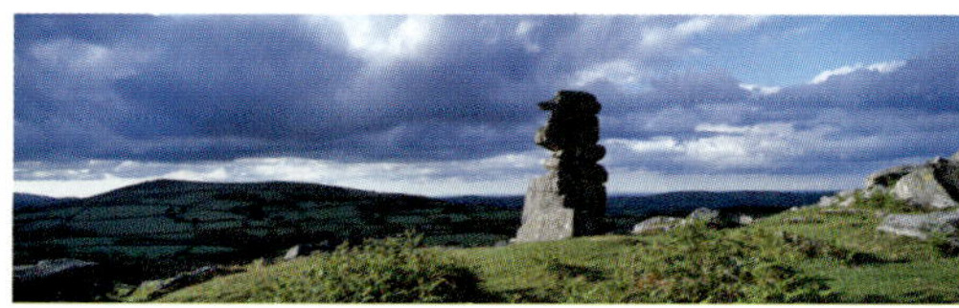

page 1
29th May 2007, 6:20pm
Fuji GX617 90mm,
Lee 0.45 ND grad, Fuji Velvia
After several past failed attempts to get a pleasing photograph of Bowerman's Nose, I finally succeeded in May. Thick clouds obscured the sun when I arrived, but after waiting for a short while the wind opened some gaps for the sun's rays to burst through, ensuring the rocks stood out against the dramatic backdrop of clouds.

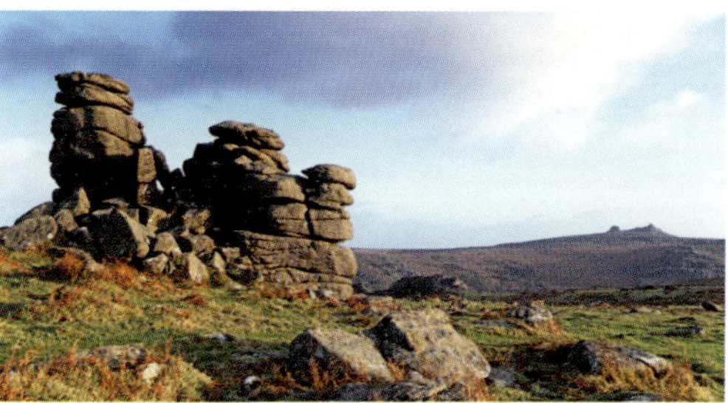

pages 2–3
2nd January 2007, 2:42pm
Fuji GX617 90mm,
Lee 0.6 ND grad, Fuji Velvia
Photographed one afternoon on a winters day, the distant view of Haytor rocks provides depth to this photo of Houndtor rocks.

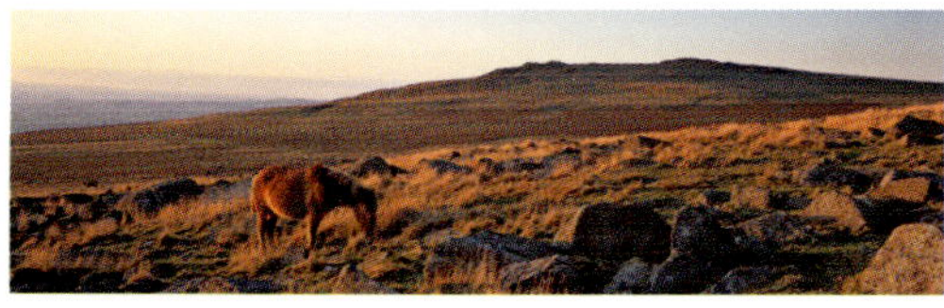

pages 4–5
19th December 2006, 3:40pm
Fuji GX617 180mm,
Lee 0.6 ND grad, Fuji Velvia
Intending to climb Staple Tor for some views from the summit, I detoured from the path when I spotted a group of wild ponies grazing the lower slopes. I spent an enjoyable time photographing the ponies as the sun faded, before finally making it to the summit and getting a couple of photographs of the Tor silhouetted by the colourful sunset.

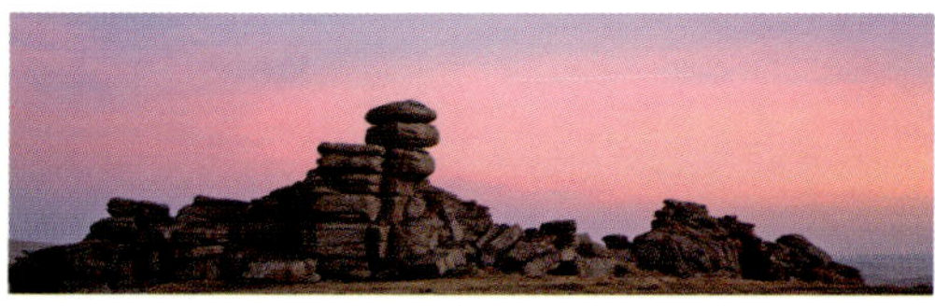

page 6
19th December 2006, 4:25pm
Fuji GX617 Fuji Velvia
Granite stacks create some interesting shapes on the summit of Great Staple Tor. Reflected light from the setting sun turns the thin cloud behind the Tor shades of pink. A long exposure was needed to record the fading light.

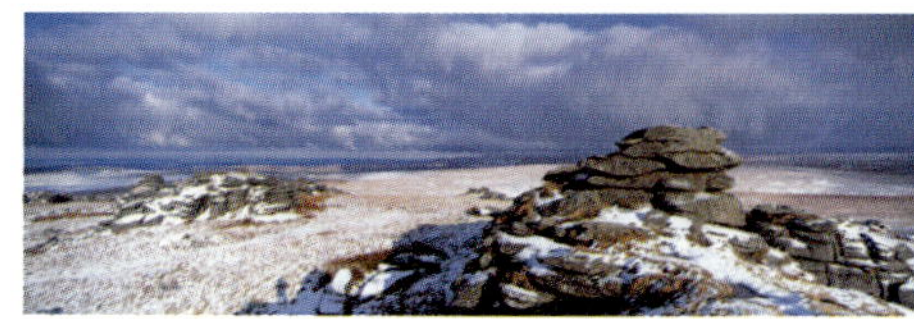

pages 8–9
24th January 2007, 10:00am
Fuji GX617 90mm, Lee 0.3 ND grad,
Fuji Velvia
A snow-covered landscape was my reward for the long early morning climb up the path to Great Mis Tor. It is higher than many of its neighbouring tors, so the overnight snowfall had stayed. A fierce wind threatened to blow over my camera on the tripod so I set up in the shelter of a rock. My preparation and cold fingers were rewarded by a brief glimpse of sun which bathed the scene in front of me as I quickly took two films - eight photos - before it was gone.

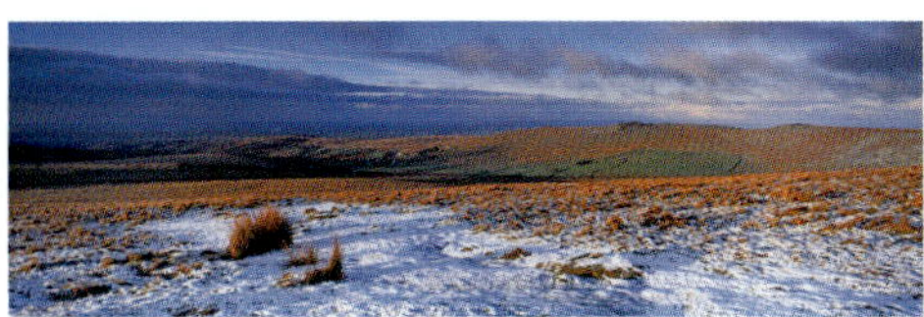

page 10
24th January 2007, 8:44am
Fuji GX617 90mm, Lee 0.6 ND grad, Fuji Velvia
Looking towards Merrivale from halfway up Great Mis Tor. The sun makes a brief appearance providing strong sidelighting to bring out the textures of the grass and snow.

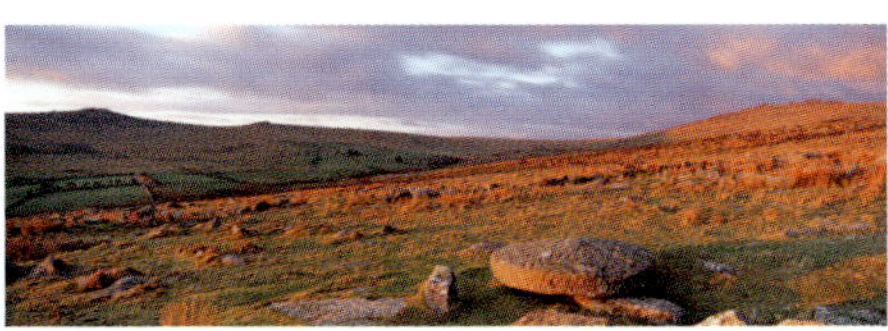

pages 10–11
24th January 2007, 4:47pm
Fuji GX617 90mm, Lee 0.6 ND grad, Fuji Velvia
Attempting to make the most of the remaining sunlight on a winter's afternoon, I headed from Sharpitor to Merrivale and the ruins of a bronze age settlement. I set up next to this huge stone disc as the sun's rays turned red.

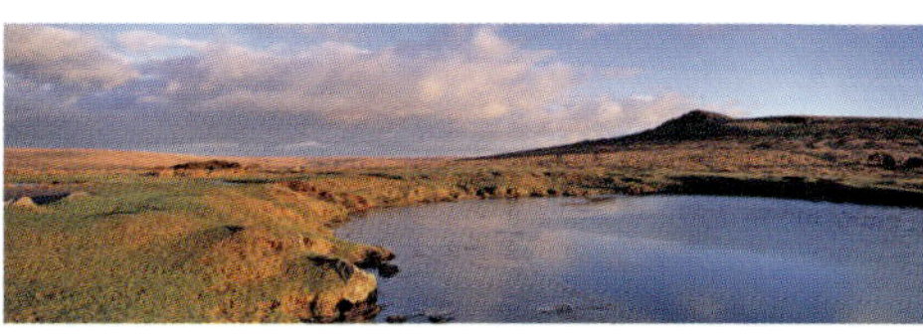

page 12
24th January 2007, 4:26pm
Fuji GX617 90mm, Lee 0.6 ND grad, Fuji Velvia
The welcome warmth of the winter sunlight brings a glow to the heavy clouds forming overhead.

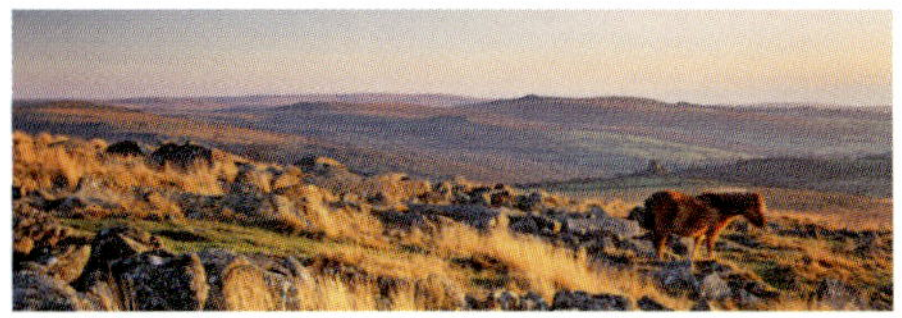

pages 12–13
19th December 2006, 3:25pm
Fuji GX617 180mm, Lee 0.6 ND grad, Fuji Velvia
Looking across Dartmoor from the slopes of Staple Tor towards Vixen Tor and the more distant peaks surrounding Burrator Reservoir. The sun's warm rays come from the right, highlighting the long grasses and textured rocks.

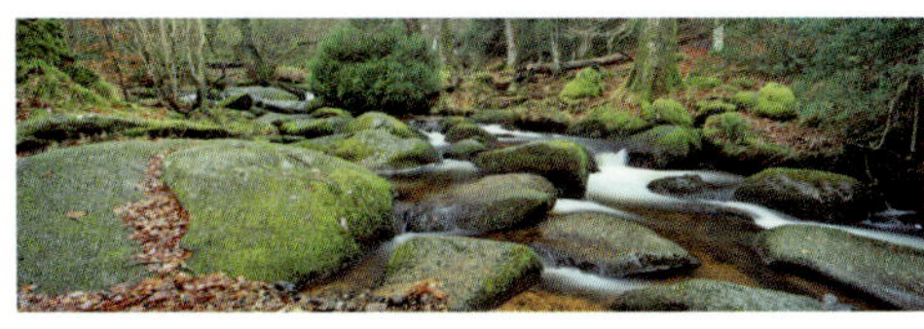

page 14
12th January 2006, 3:00pm
Fuji GX617 90mm, Polariser, Fuji Velvia
Here I used a polarising filter to reduce reflections in the wet rocks. Together with fading light in the woods beside Becka Brook this meant the exposure time ran into minutes. While the light rain was welcome for increasing the saturation of the woodland colours, it meant holding an umbrella over the camera for the length of the exposure.

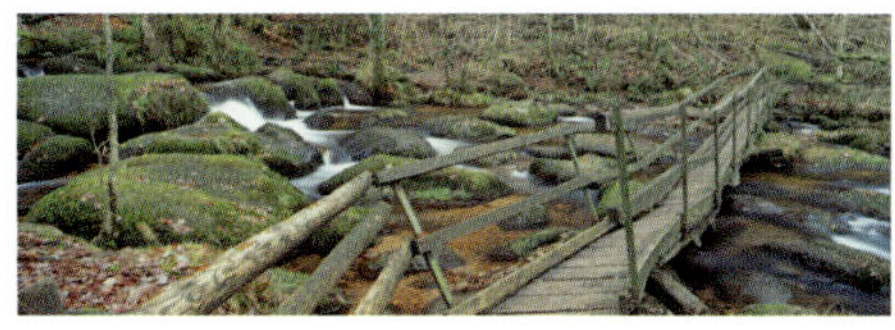

pages 14–15
12th January 2006, 2:10pm
Fuji GX617 90mm, Polariser, Fuji Velvia
While making my way across this rickety footbridge, I suddenly realised it would make a good subject. Retracing my steps, I set up beneath an umbrella and used the strong diagonal lines of the bridge to lead into the picture.

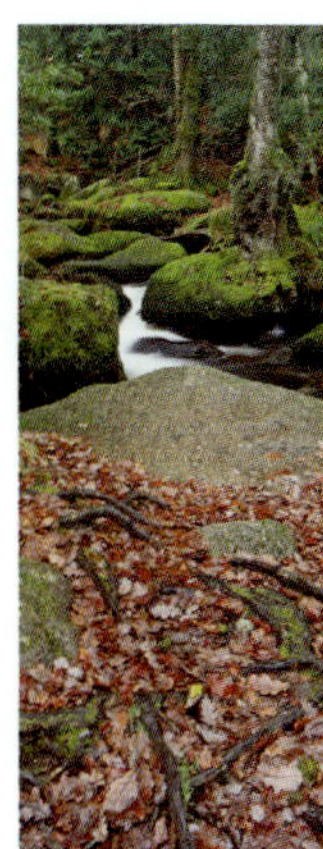

page 16
12th January 2006, 2:30pm
Hasselblad XPan 45mm, Polariser, Fuji Velvia
With a tangled web of roots and fallen leaves as foreground interest, I set up this vertical panoramic, using a polarising filter to reduce reflections in the wet leaves and saturate the colours. In addition to the roots, my interest was drawn by the tree growing over the large boulder in midstream.

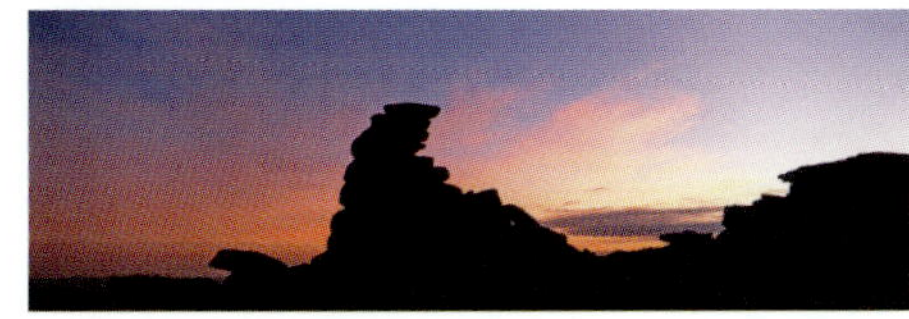

page 17
19th December 2006, 4:31pm
Fuji GX617 90mm, Fuji Velvia
A colourful display in the sky at sunset appeared just when I thought all hope of one had gone. Illuminating the clouds in shades of pink from below the horizon, the sun yet again produces a stunning display.

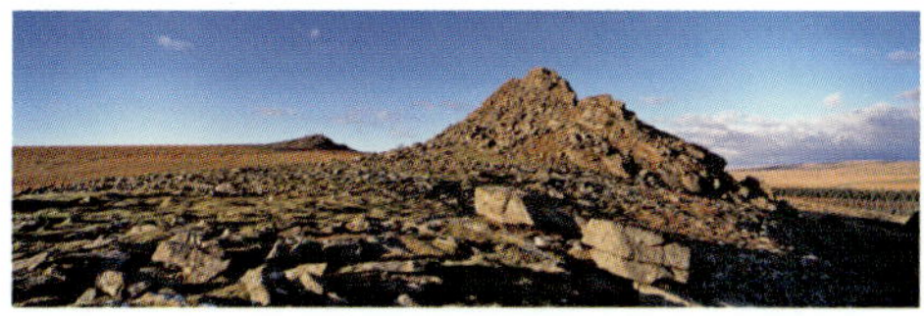

page 19
24th January 2007, 3:40pm
Fuji GX617 90mm, Lee 0.6 ND grad, Fuji Velvia
A couple of large granite boulders are picked out in the afternoon sunlight on the slopes of Leather Tor. A few wandering sheep seem to have no trouble jumping around between the rocks.

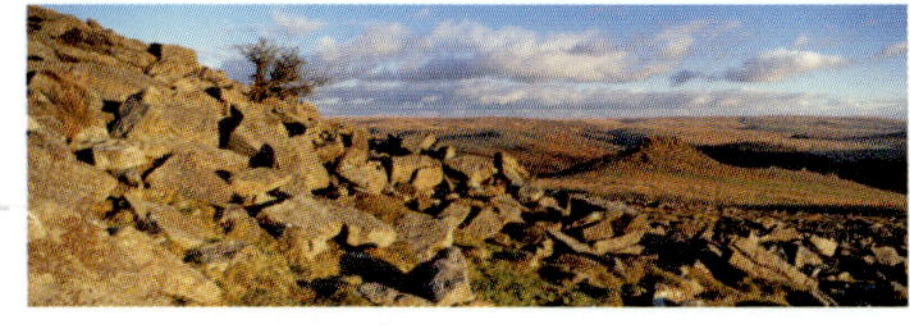

pages 18–19
24th January 2007, 4:05pm
Fuji GX617 90mm, Lee 0.3 ND grad, Fuji Velvia
A lone tree clings to life amidst the tumbled slope of granite rocks. Clouds silently move in from the north filling the sky.

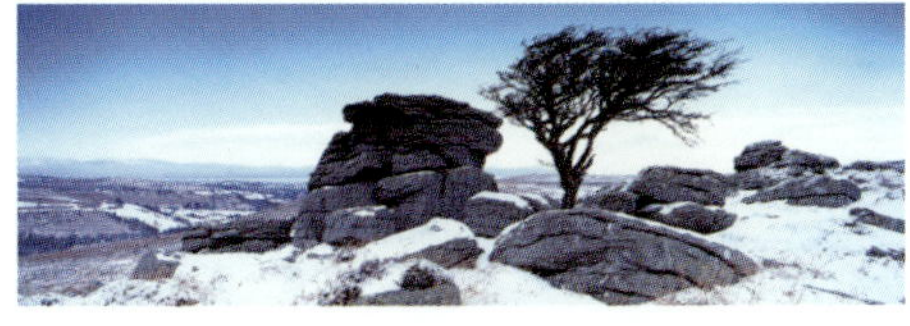

pages 20–21
25th November 2005, 2:50pm
Fuji GX617 90mm, Lee 0.9 ND grad, Fuji Velvia
After an unusually heavy snowfall the previous night, I trudged across the snowy landscape towards this windswept tree. Waiting by the tripod I was willing the sun to make an appearance, but huge dark clouds put paid to that. Still, I think the photo works well, showing something of the bleak side of the moor.

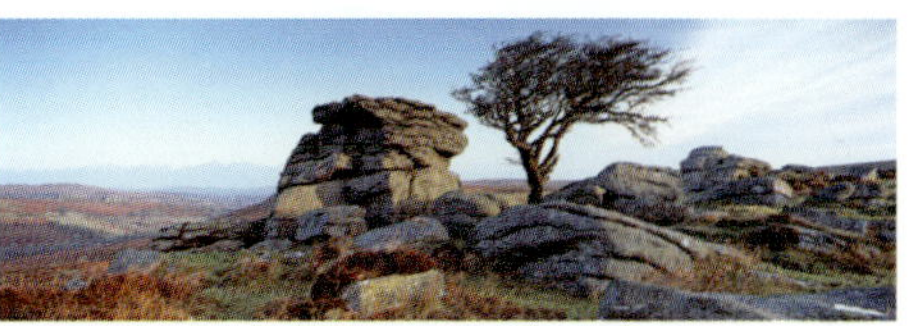

page 21
11th January 2006, 9:10am
Fuji GX617 90mm, Lee 0.6 ND grad, Fuji Velvia
An early start and a walk across the moor was rewarded by sunlight, diffused by a hazy sky, falling over the scene and providing a much needed warm glow in the cold of a January morning.

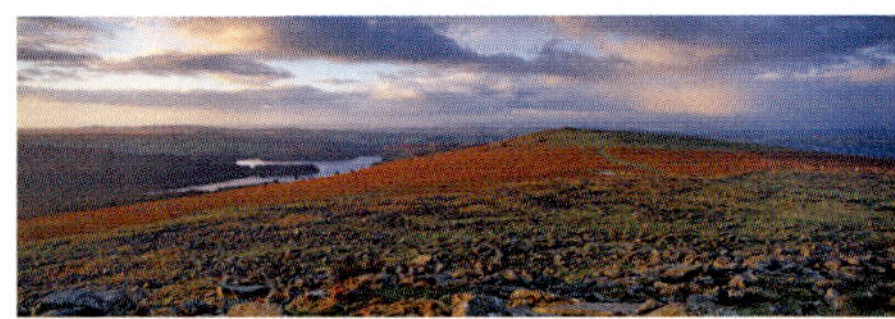

pages 22–23
22nd January 2007, 8:30am
Fuji GX617 90mm, Lee 0.9 ND grad, Fuji Velvia
Clouds above Peak Hill display the shades of a colourful sunrise with the waters of Burrator Reservoir reflecting the brightness of the sky. Using several spotmeter readings from the sky, rocks and grass to determine the exposure, I also add a neutral density grad filter to hold the detail in the sky.

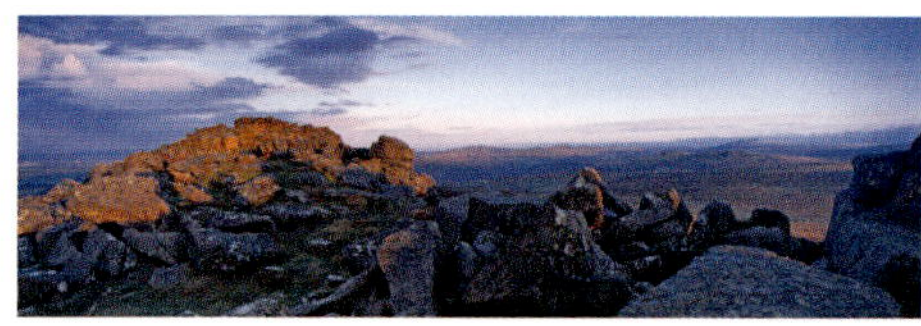

page 22
22nd January 2007, 8:20am
Fuji GX617 90mm, Lee 0.9 ND grad, Fuji Velvia
Standing on Sharpitor in the predawn light, I was greeted with a blowing gale. Battling to keep the camera upright, take exposure readings and clean the condensation from the lens, whilst freezing winds buffeted the tripod proved challenging. The resulting photograph looks deceptively peaceful as the first rays of sunlight touch the granite rocks.

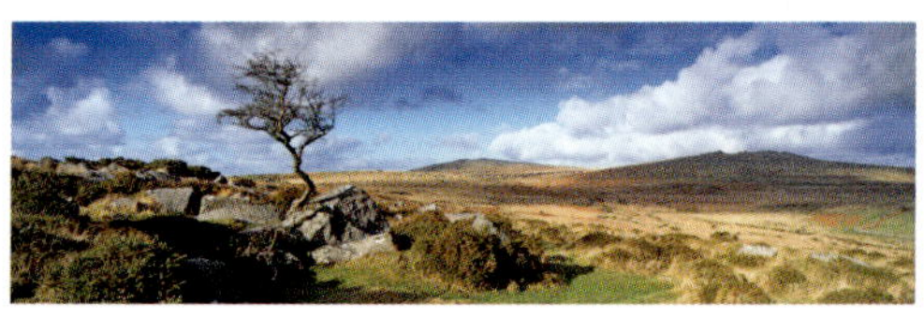

page 24
10th January 2007, 1:24pm
Fuji GX617 90mm, Lee 0.6 ND grad, Fuji Velvia
Strong winds were sweeping showers across Dartmoor on a cold day in January when I took this photograph. I like the way the clouds stretch across the sky and the contrast between the sunlit and shadow on the moor added depth to the picture. I was initially drawn to this small tree which seemed to be clinging to life in this windswept and harsh environment.

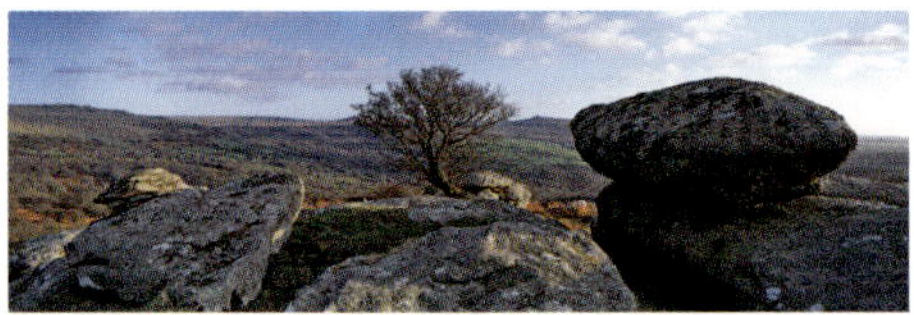

page 25
10th January 2007, 3:14pm
Fuji GX617 90mm, Lee 0.6 ND grad, Fuji Velvia
Stopping by this carefully balanced boulder, I set about finding a composition that would work. As I waited for the sun to drop, I left my camera in position and wandered off looking for other views. Suddenly I noticed several sheep climbing on the rocks around my camera. Rushing back I saw one sheep jump past my tripod, missing it by inches!

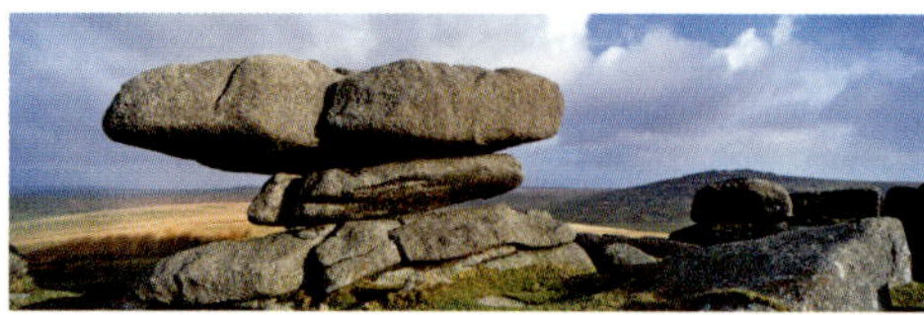

page 25
2nd January 2007, 11:23am
Fuji GX617 90mm, Lee 0.3 ND grad, Fuji Velvia
Although I had to battle to keep my camera still in high winds, the low winter sun ensured the light wasn't too harsh even close to midday. Once I had found a good view of this huge balanced rock, the usual struggle to set up my tripod in the correct position ensued. In the meantime, the sun played hide and seek behind the clouds.

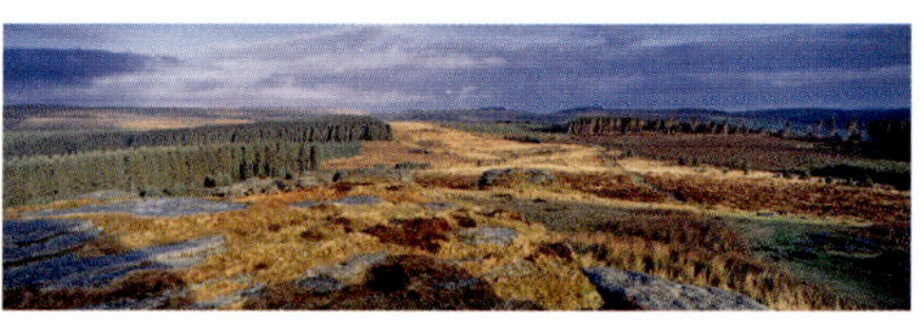

pages 26–27
14th January 2007, 9:50am
Fuji GX617 90mm, Lee 0.6 ND grad, Fuji Velvia
An early start was needed to drive to Bellever Forest and climb to the summit of the Tor by sunrise. An overcast beginning to the day left me with plenty of time to wander around and look for places to set up. I was glad of my flask of coffee as I waited, until finally the clouds broke, spilling sunlight across the moor.

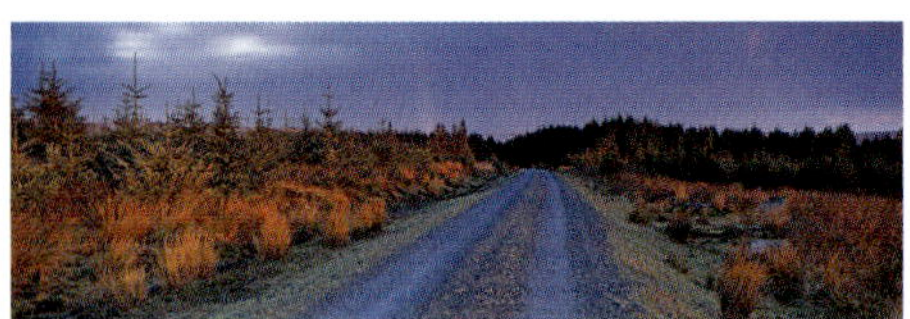

pages 26–27
14th January 2007, 8:30am
Fuji GX617 90mm, Lee 0.6 ND grad, Fuji Velvia
Without warning the sun burst through a gap in the cloud for a couple of seconds at most, and transforming this forest scene in the process. As the gorgeous light faded I was still setting up and I didn't get a second chance. Returning a few days later similar cloudy conditions prevailed, but again the sun burst through, with the addition of a fading rainbow in the distance. This time I was ready.

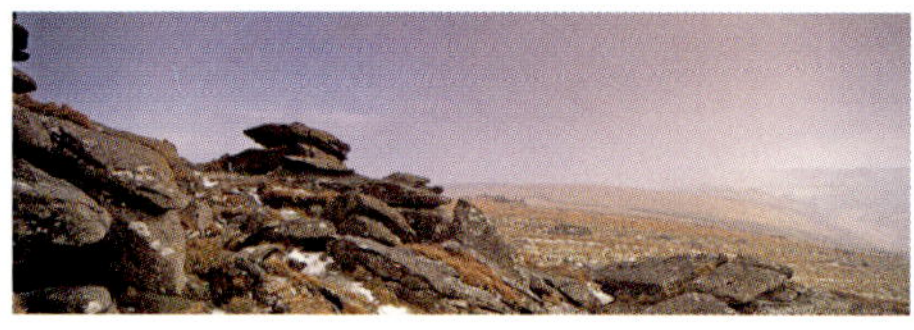

page 28
19th March 2007, 5:30pm
Fuji GX617 90mm, Lee 0.6 ND grad, Fuji Velvia
I made my way up to Littaford Tor as the weather closed in one afternoon. As I sheltered from a passing hail shower, sunlight filtered through the clouds bringing a glow to the rocks. Quickly setting up beneath an umbrella, I successfully loaded a roll of film and took four photographs before the light was gone.

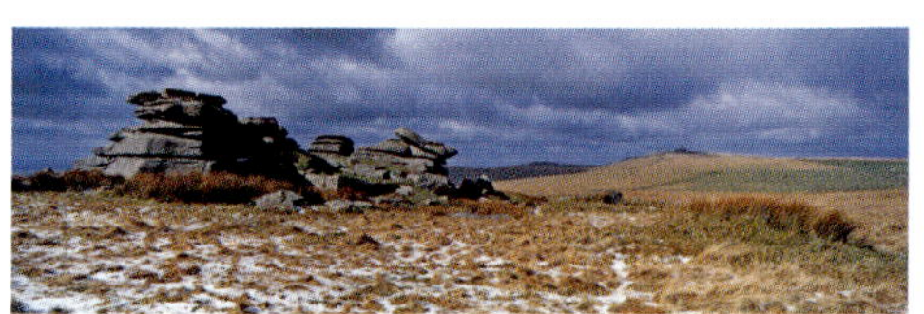

page 28
19th March 2007, morning
Fuji GX617 90mm, Lee 0.6 ND grad, Fuji Velvia
A scattering of snow lies amongst the grass at Hollow Tor near Princetown. A strong wind blows a succession of dark clouds across the sky, with occasional glimpses of the sun. I managed a couple of photographs during these short sunny spells using the tripod legs splayed wide and low to help resist the buffeting wind.

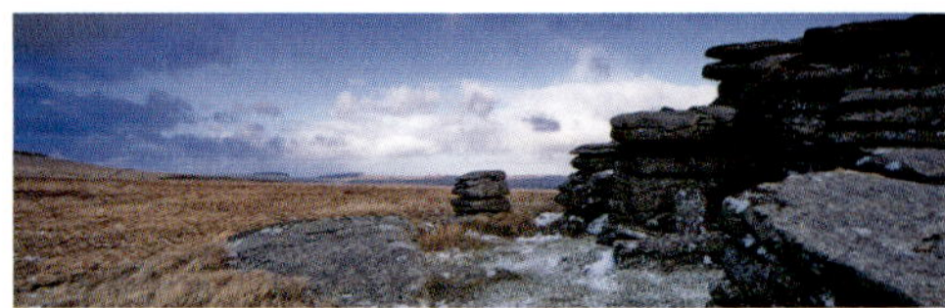

page 29
19th March 2007, 5:40pm
Fuji GX617 90mm, Lee 0.6 ND grad, Fuji Velvia
Freezing cold hailstones lie in the shadow of Littaford Tor after a passing shower. Working the tripod legs and camera controls took quite an effort in the freezing temperatures, made worse by the cold wind.

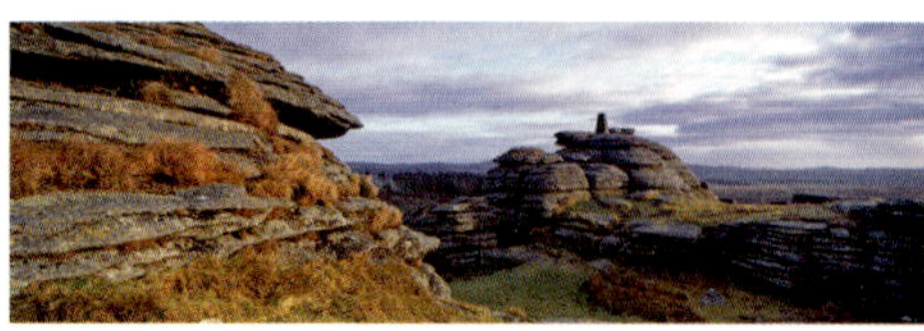

page 30
14th January 2007, 9:30am
Fuji GX617 90mm, Lee 0.6 ND grad, Fuji Velvia
I set up my camera and tripod in overcast conditions and sat down to wait. Weak sunlight bathed the scene for a couple of seconds and I missed it. Back to waiting, I double-checked all my settings and guessed what strength of grad filter to use. Watching the sunlight approach across the moor, I took my exposure reading from the sunlit distant moor and prepared myself. Sunlight bathed the scene and I managed one 5-second exposure before it disappeared.

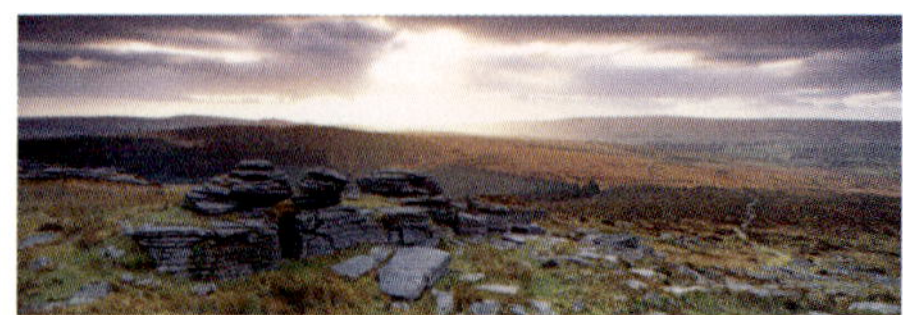

pages 30–31
14th January 2007, 9:15am
Fuji GX617 90mm, Lee 0.9 + 0.6 ND grads, Fuji Velvia
Sheltering behind a rock on Bellever Tor as the wind blew across the summit, I watched and waited as gaps in the cloud provided brief flashes of sunlight. Finally the sun came out for just long enough. I quickly took a lightmeter reading and took 4 photographs at different settings and I was left to wonder if the photo had worked. I had, unusually, used 5 stops of Neutral Density (ND) filter to balance the bright sky with the much darker foreground.

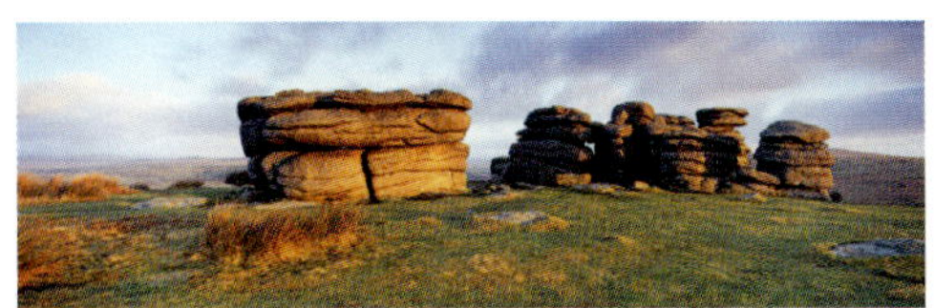

pages 32–33
12th January 2006, 8:40am
Fuji GX617 90mm, Lee 0.6 ND grad, Fuji Velvia
As a small group of cows watched on in bemusement, I set up my tripod and camera on Combestone Tor. Sunlight bathed the granite rocks and the movement of the clouds across the sky was recorded in the 6-second exposure.

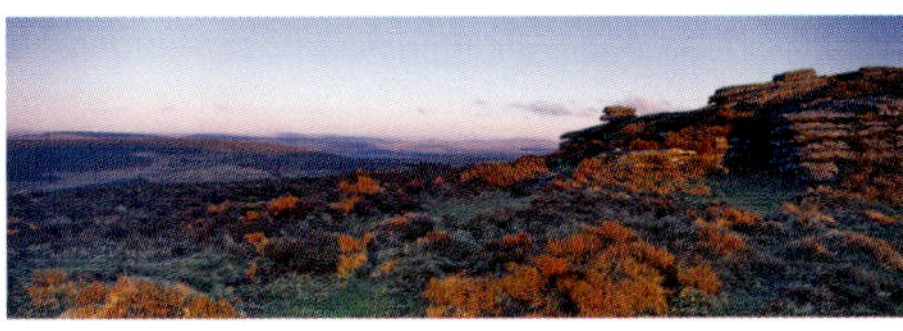

pages 32–33
23rd January 2007, 8:00am
Fuji GX617 90mm, Lee 0.9 ND grad, Fuji Velvia
Clear skies signify a cold morning on Hookney Tor above Grimspound Stone Circle. Immersed in photographing the fleeting dawn light managing to ignore the cold, I reached down to pick up my bottle of water and saw that it was full of crystals of ice which had formed in minutes.

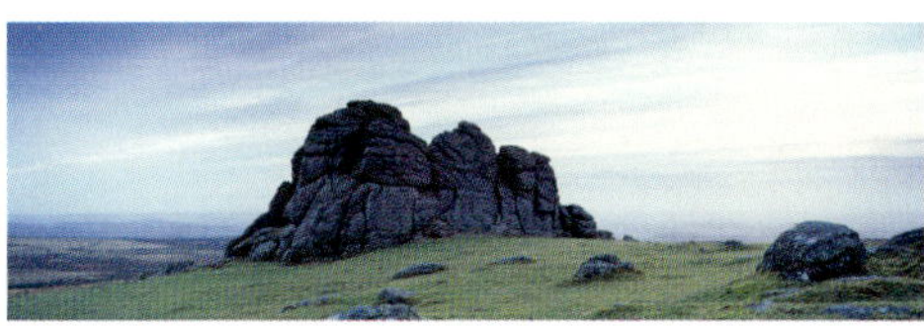

page 34
11th January 2006, 8:40am
Fuji GX617 90mm, Lee 0.9 ND grad, Fuji Velvia
After a short climb up to Haytor Rocks in soft light of dawn, I photographed the popular rocks, looking towards the East Devon coast.

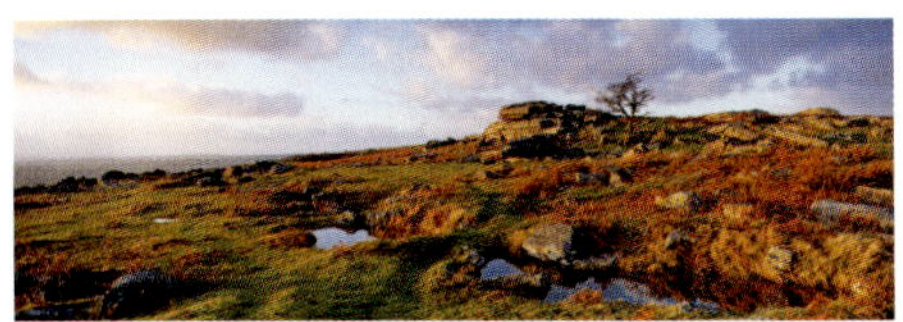

pages 34–35
10th January 2006, 4:04pm
Fuji GX617 90mm, Lee 0.6 ND grad, Fuji Velvia
As the sun dropped towards the horizon, warm light flooded across the moor on Feather Tor. I made use of small pools of water and orange ferns for some foreground interest, leading to the hardy tree and granite rock formation at the Tor. Clouds reflected the colours of the setting sun.

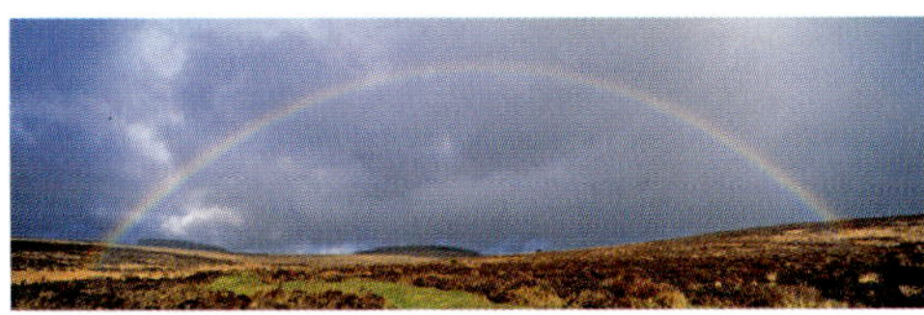

pages 36–37
10th January 2007, 11:41am
Fuji GX617 90mm, Fuji Velvia
Several heavy showers of rain had passed by during the morning and I'd seen a few rainbows. Determined to photograph one, I set up my camera using the open boot of my van for shelter. At the last possible second a rainbow spectacularly appeared and I tripped the shutter just as the rain hit and soaked me and my camera.

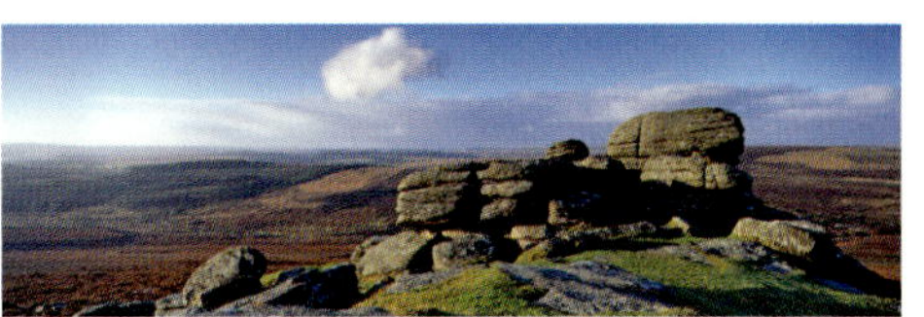

pages 36–37
10th January 2007, 9:30am
Fuji GX617 90mm, Lee 0.6 ND grad, Fuji Velvia
On the summit of Birch Tor, above Bennett's Cross, the view across Headland Warren is impressive. Another very windy and showery winter's day on Dartmoor again provided plenty of challenges for photography. The beautiful views and glimpses of sunlight more than compensated this time.

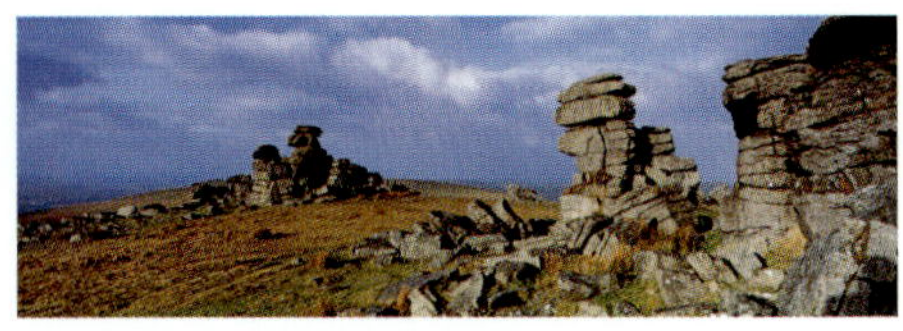

pages 38–39
2nd January 2007, 10:29am
Fuji GX617 90mm, Lee 0.6 ND grad, Fuji Velvia
A strong gust of wind had already almost knocked me and my camera over, but the same wind cleared a gap in the clouds for the sun to bring light to the interesting rocks at Staple Tor. Shielding my camera as best I could with my body, I made the exposure.

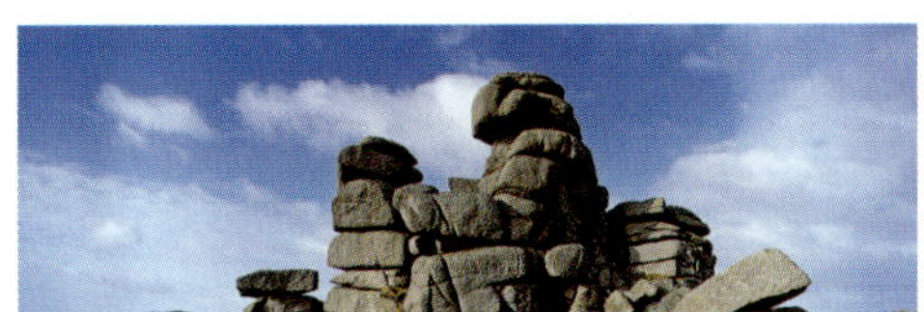

page 39
2nd January 2007, 11:46am
Fuji GX617 90mm, Lee 0.3 ND grad, Fuji Velvia
Drawn to these interesting granite rocks on Staple Tor, I moved close to the rocks using a wide-angle lens to show the shapes against the blue sky.

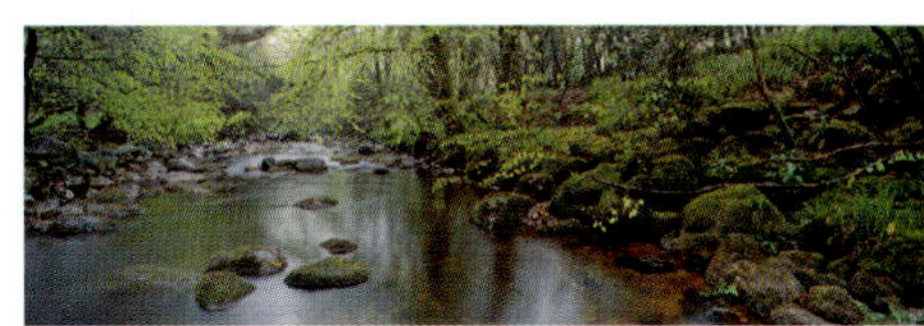

pages 40–41
23rd April 2007, 5:03pm
Fuji GX617 90mm, Lee 0.3 ND grad, Fuji Velvia
Wellington boots proved as essential as a camera on this occasion at the River Avon. Standing in the middle of the river, juggling with film, filter holders and an umbrella to shield the lens from the light but persistent rain, I must have been an unusual sight!

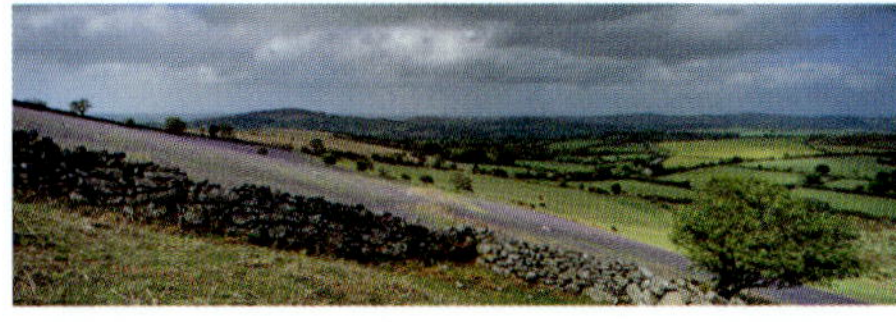

pages 42–43
18th May 2007, 3:42pm
Fuji GX617 90mm, Lee 0.6 ND grad, Fuji Velvia
On a quiet sunny afternoon, sheep grazed amongst the bluebell-covered field on the edge of the higher moor. Using a drystone wall and the tree on the right as elements of my composition, I set up looking north across green rolling fields.

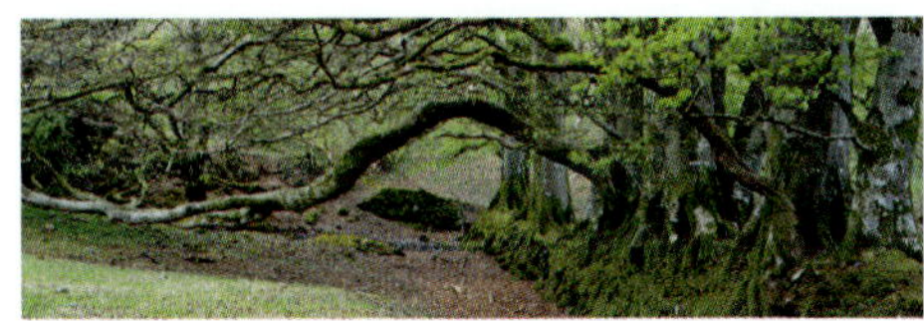

pages 42
26th April 2007, 3:37pm
Fuji GX617 180mm, Fuji Velvia
Fascinated by the line of tall trees growing atop a drystone wall, I used the extended arching branch to lead in to the view of the mossy wall. As I was midway through my roll of film, I had to switch to a telephoto lens, using a film-changing bag to change my lens, in order to stop light fogging the film.

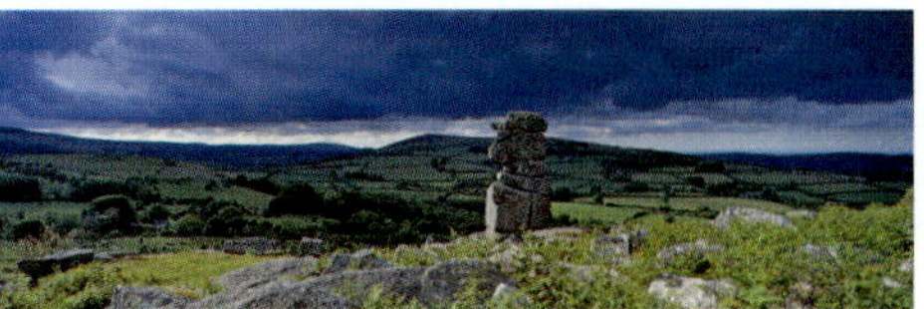

page 44
29th May 2007, 6:30pm
Fuji GX617 90mm, Lee 0.75 ND grad, Fuji Velvia
Only too aware of the often fleeting glimpses of sunlight as it streamed through cloudy skies, I hurried to set up and photograph the sudden warm sunlight bathing Bowerman's Nose. Striving to move quickly, whilst also trying to slow down and make the best use of the conditions, I set up the shot with rocks and lush ferns in the foreground. On this occasion, I was also able to walk around the hillside making several further photographs while the light lasted.

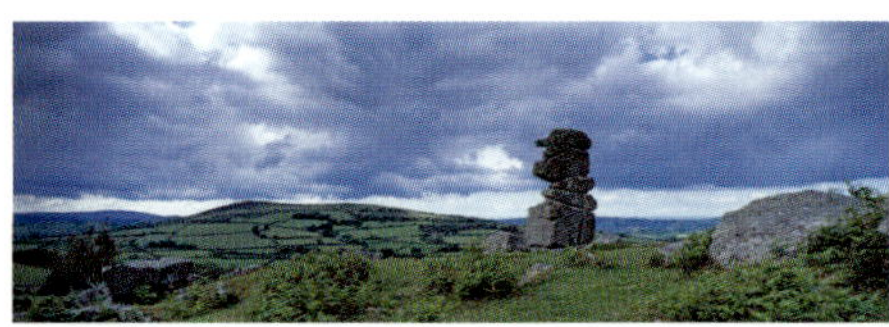

pages 44–45
29th May 2007, 5:12pm
Fuji GX617 90mm, Lee 0.75 ND grad, Fuji Velvia
I made several visits to Hayne Down, the location of Bowerman's Nose, before I took this photograph in May. I often wait for sunlight to illuminate the subject of the photo, but this photo was made with the subject in shadow with interesting clouds adding texture and drama to the sky.

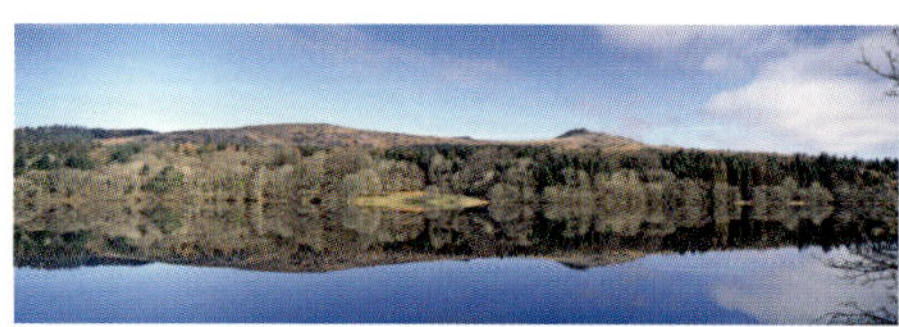

pages 46–47
14th March 2007, 9:03am
Fuji GX617 90mm, Lee 0.3 ND grad, Fuji Velvia
The still waters of Burrator Reservoir reflect the beautiful landscape in the morning. Using a Lee 0.3 ND grad filter to balance the bright sky with its darker reflection I photographed the scene in an atmosphere of almost complete silence.

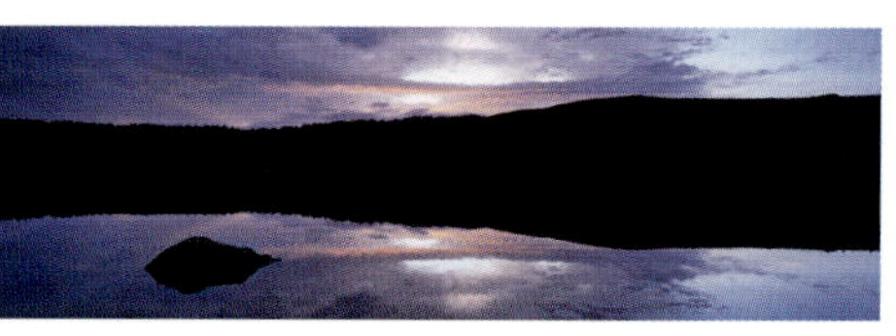

page 46
14th June 2007, 9:20pm
Fuji GX617 90mm, Lee 0.45 ND grad, Fuji Velvia
A spectacular sunset over Burrator Reservoir is reflected in the mirror-like waters. Crouched on the banks of the water and careful not to create ripples in the water, I used a Lee 0.45 ND graduated filter to balance the bright sky with the darker reflection in the water.

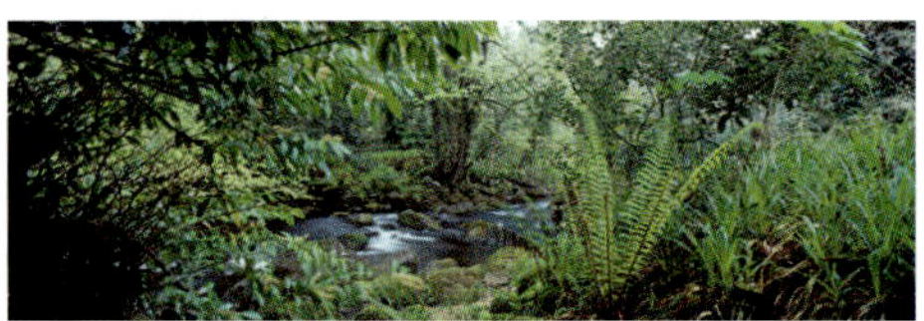

pages 48–49
23rd April 2007, 4:00pm
Fuji GX617 90mm, Polariser, Fuji Velvia
This scene reminds me of a tropical rainforest although it was taken one wet day on Dartmoor in the spring. The rain brings a vibrancy to the colours and was welcome photographically speaking, even if huddling under an umbrella and trying to keep rain off the lens was quite tricky!

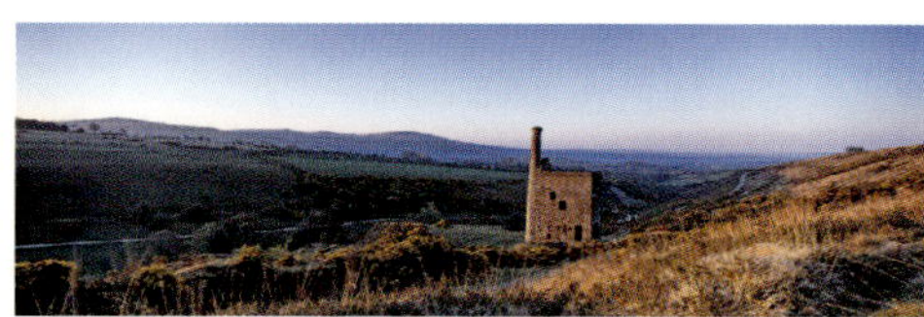

pages 50–51
20th April 2007, 6:30am
Fuji GX617 90mm, Lee 0.9 ND grad, Fuji Velvia
An early start took me to the well-preserved mine in the west of Dartmoor. Arriving in plenty of time for the sunrise, I explored the area in the intensifying morning light. Utilising long yellow grasses in the foreground and, in the middle ground, gorse bushes, I used a Lee 0.9 ND grad to hold the dawn colour in the sky.

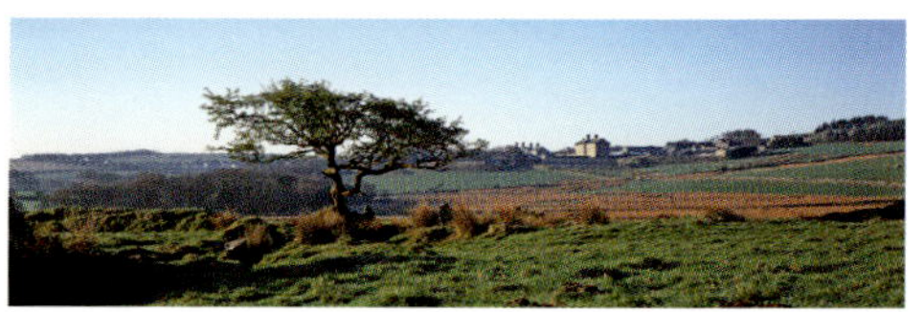

pages 50–51
20th April 2007, 7:14am
Fuji GX617 180mm, Lee 0.6 ND grad, Fuji Velvia
The early morning sunlight reflected from the granite stones of Dartmoor Prison, turning the stone almost silver in colour.

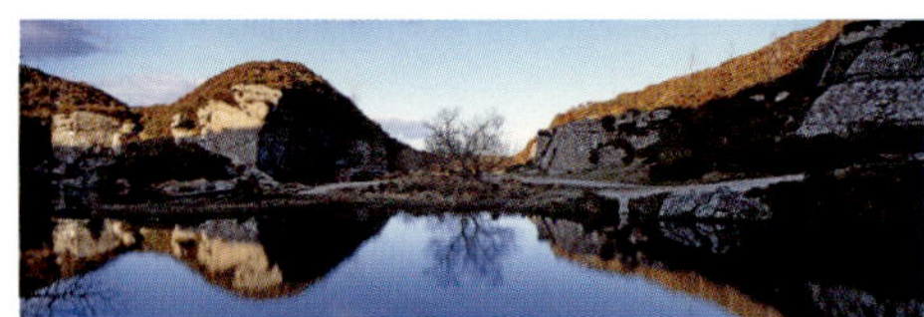

pages 52–53
13th March 2007, 4:59pm
Fuji GX617 90mm, Lee 0.6 ND grad, Fuji Velvia
The water-filled Haytor Quarry provided a mirrored surface in the stillness of the afternoon. Once a busy quarry, sending blocks of granite down a specially constructed railway track to waiting boats, there was barely a sound as the late afternoon sunlight kissed the edge of the peaceful quarry.

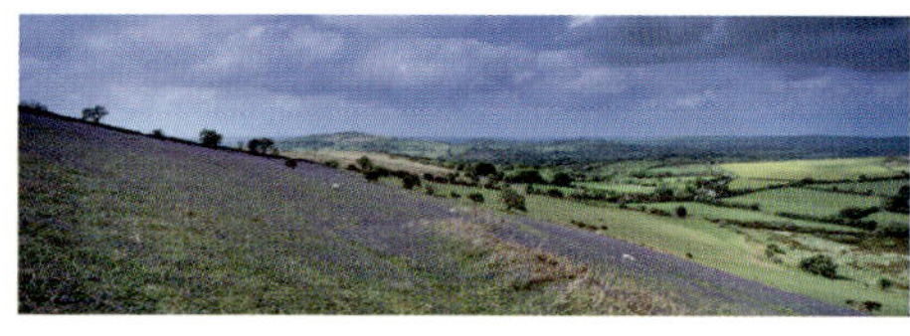

page 54
18th May 2007, 4:51pm
Fuji GX617 180mm, Lee 0.6 ND grad, Fuji Velvia
Rolling fields paint a picture of a typical English countryside scene. Enjoying the warm spring afternoon – not worrying about numb fingers or rain on the lens this time – I watched as sheep grazed amongst the bluebells.

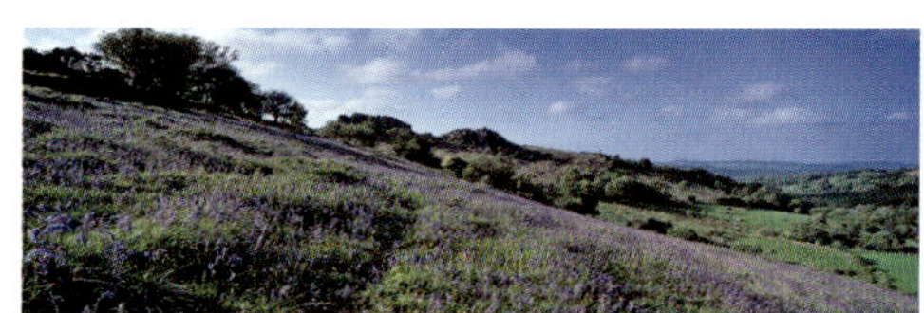

page 54
18th May 2007, 6:22pm
Fuji GX617 90mm, Lee 0.6 ND grad, Fuji Velvia
A steep hillside of bluebells lead to the rocks of Greator Rocks. As I photographed in the evening sunlight, rabbits ran across the moor, silently scurrying between warrens in the earth.

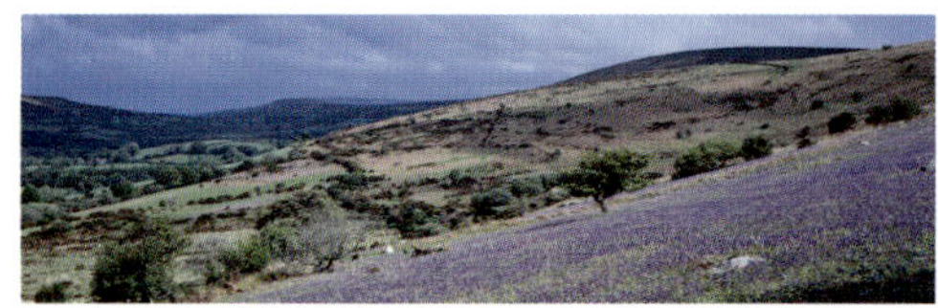

page 55
18th May 2007, 4:13pm
Fuji GX617 180mm, Lee 0.6 ND grad, Fuji Velvia
Looking across a vast covering of bluebells, I watched a sheep with its newborn lamb sitting in the shade of a hawthorn tree. As I quietly set up, the sheep wandered off, oblivious to their potentially starring role.

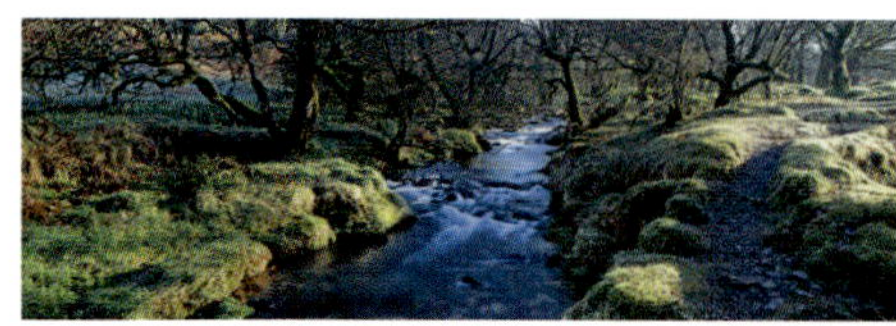

pages 56–57
14th March 2007, 8:20am
Fuji GX617 90mm, Fuji Velvia
In order to avoid lens flare from the sun, which was shining towards the camera from the right hand side, I used my body to shield the camera lens and pressed the shutter with a remote cable release to take the photograph.

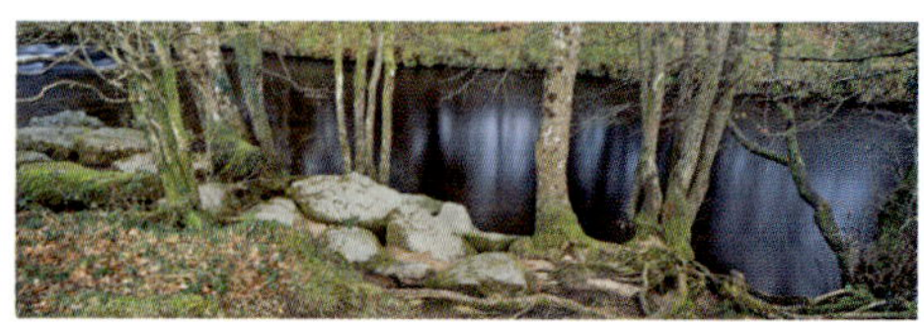

page 56
7th March 2007, 5:15pm
Fuji GX617 90mm, Polariser, Fuji Velvia
The tangled roots beside the River Dart caught my eye and I set about finding a suitable composition. Concentrating on the roots and the dark waters behind, I excluded the sky and, using a polariser, made my photograph with a long exposure in the fading light.

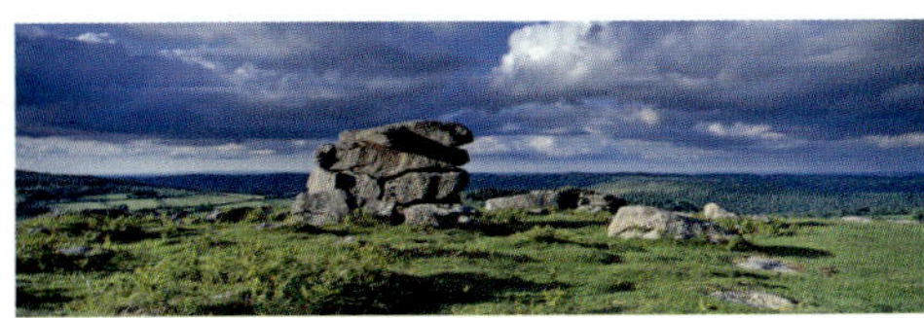

page 58
29th May 2007, 7:27pm
Fuji GX617 90mm, Lee 0.75 ND grad, Fuji Velvia
An interesting cloudscape caught my eye on Hayne Down, so I set up to photograph the rock formation using the new ferns as foreground interest. A Lee ND grad helped to keep the tones of the sky and avoid it becoming washed out.

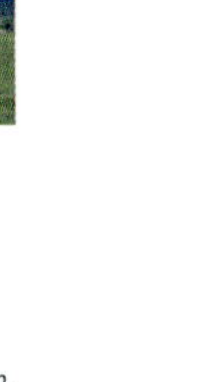

pages 58–59
13th March 2007, 5:30pm
Fuji GX617 90mm, Lee 0.6 ND grad, Fuji Velvia
After a time spent photographing Haytor Quarry, I finally emerged into beautiful afternoon sunlight, with clouds dotted across the sky. I quickly climbed up towards the popular rocks at Haytor and set up, using the contrast between the soft grass and rough granite as foreground interest.

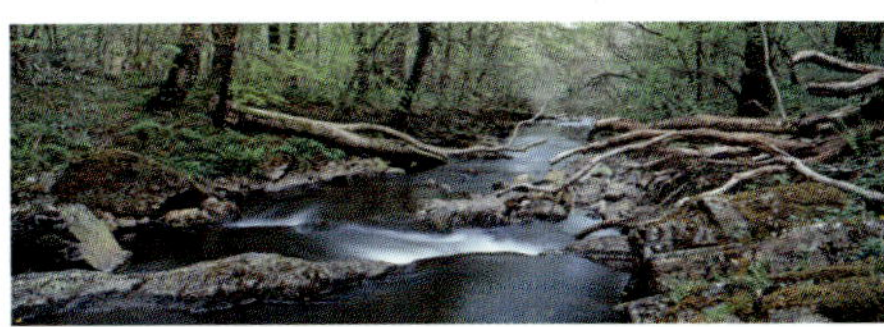

pages 60–61
26th April 2007, 4:10pm
Fuji GX617 90mm, Fuji Velvia
These fallen trees and branches lining the Okement River caught my eye as I wandered through the peaceful woods near Meldon Reservoir. I was looking for bluebells to photograph, but it was still early in the season so they would have to wait.

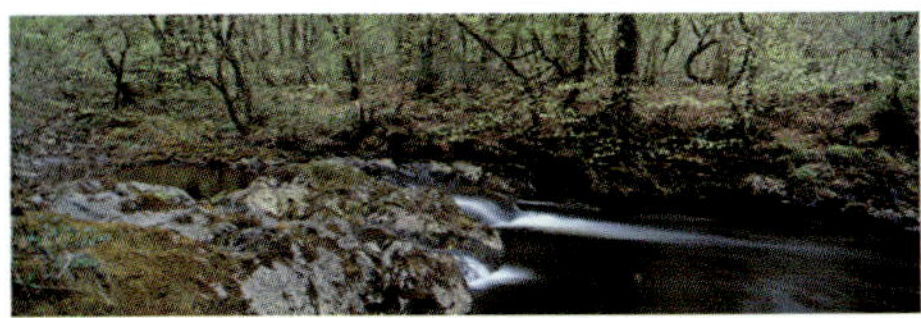

page 61
26th April 2007, 4:25pm
Fuji GX617 90mm, Fuji Velvia
The lime green leaves budding on these trees contrasted nicely with the dark waters of the Okement River in the spring. A small cascade of water is transformed into a blur with a shutter speed of several seconds.

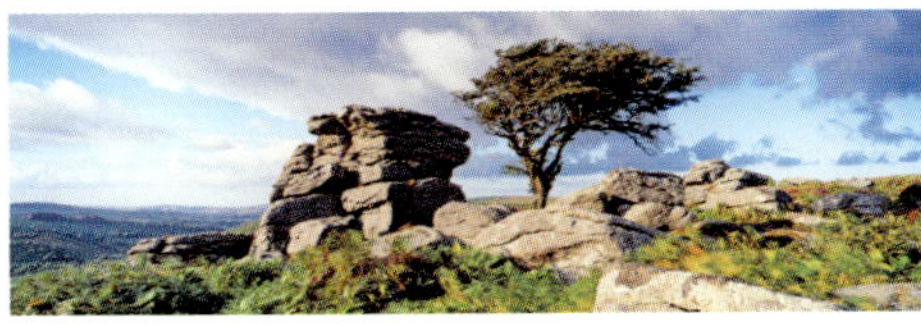

pages 62–63
12th August 2006, evening
Fuji GX617 90mm, Lee 0.6 ND grad, Fuji Velvia
A windy evening caused the trees and ferns to sway, and had the added advantage that the clouds covering the sun didn't last for long. With the sun popping in and out as the evening progressed I spent an enjoyable time on the moor photographing the scenery from different angles and trying to make the most of the lovely conditions.

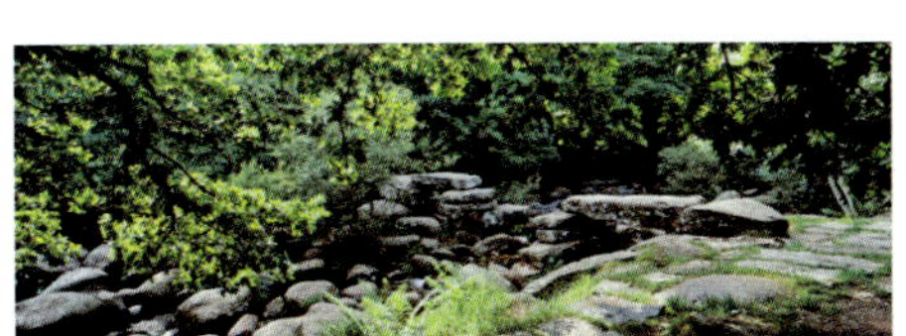

pages 64–65
14th June 2007, 3:57pm
Fuji GX617 90mm, Lee 0.3 ND grad inverted, Fuji Velvia
As I searched for an interesting view of the much photographed clapper bridge at Dartmeet, I spotted these backlit leaves and ferns taking on a luminous quality. As the sun appeared from the clouds the leaves would glow bright green. The sunlit path was almost too bright, but by using a Lee 0.3 ND grad upside down, the scene was recorded on film perfectly.

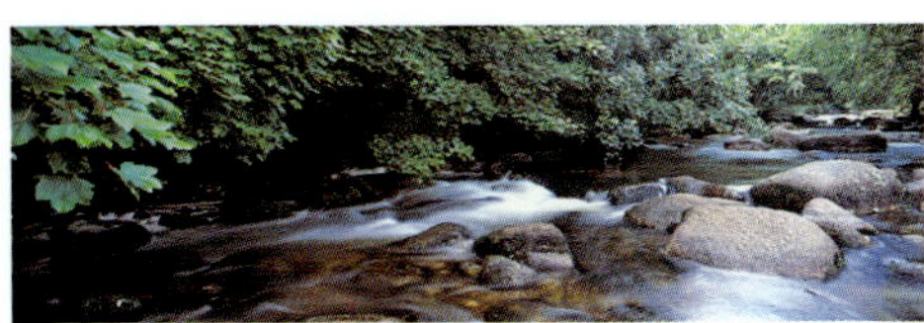

page 65
14th June 2007, 3:49pm
Fuji GX617 90mm, Fuji Velvia
Stone hopping across fast flowing rivers was a skill I quickly learned with many miles of Dartmoor's streams providing photography opportunities. With vivid green leaves bordering my shot, I carefully set up in the middle of the river, attracting curious looks from passers-by.

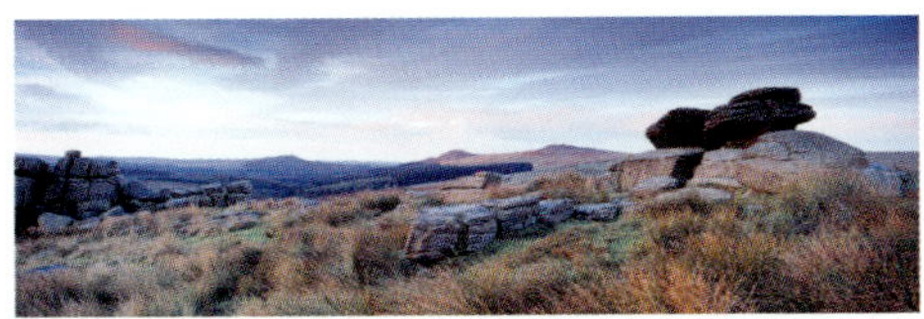

pages 66–67
26th September 2007, 7:19am
Fuji GX617 90mm, Lee 0.9 + 0.3 ND grads, Fuji Velvia
The spendour of the dawn is displayed in the sky above Black Tor with the textured granite rocks and long grasses catching some of the light reflecting from the sky above.

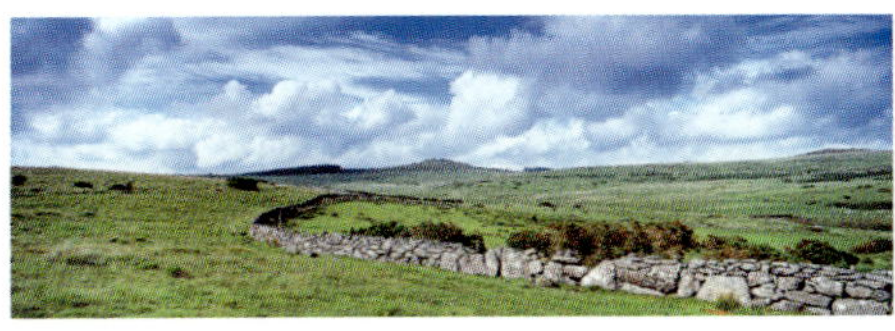

pages 68–69
14th June 2007, 5:24pm
Fuji GX617 90mm, Lee 0.6 ND grad, Fuji Velvia
The longstanding granite wall winding its way across the moor provides a perfect lead-in line towards Bellever Tor and the fluffy cumulus clouds in the sky above.

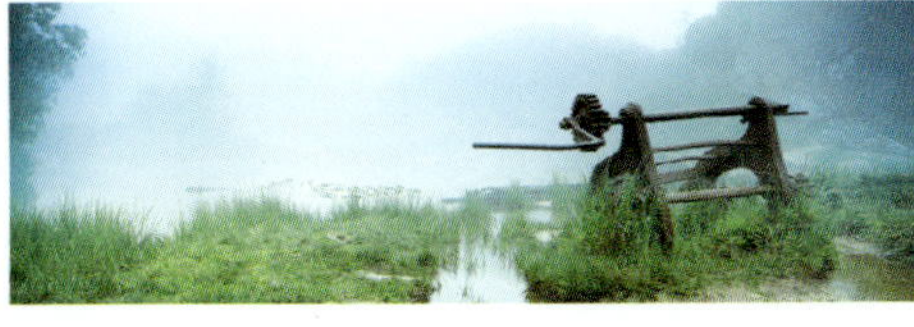

page 68
14th June 2007, 2:53pm
Fuji GX617 90mm, Lee 0.75 ND grad, Fuji Velvia
Navigating across the moor proved difficult if not dangerous when fog descended. Fortunately I remembered the path taken on previous visits to Haytor Quarry and I got there without too many wrong turns. The rusted machinery is a reminder of a bygone industry when the quarry would not enjoy the quietness surrounding it today.

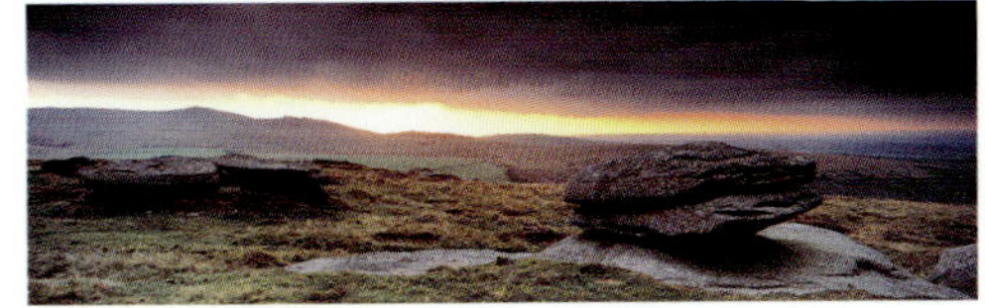

page 70
28th September 2007, 6:34pm
Fuji GX617 90mm, Lee 0.9 + 0.9 ND grad, Fuji Velvia
Looking towards Yes Tor and the setting sun, a small gap in the dark clouds provides a bright end to the day. The brightness of the sun called for the use of two strong Lee ND grads to balance it with the dark rock sitting firmly on the summit of Belstone Tor.

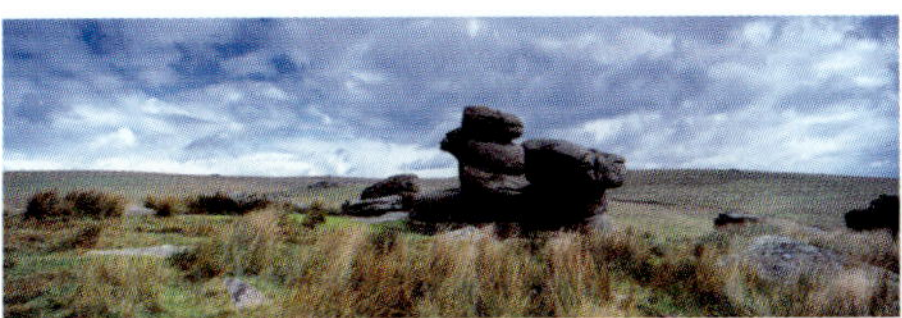

page 71
26th September 2007, 12:57pm
Fuji GX617 90mm, Lee 0.6 ND grad, Fuji Velvia
Wind rustles through the long grass surrounding Black Tor on a summer's afternoon. The cloudy sky has enough gaps for small pockets of sunlight to shine through, lifting the colours on the moor.

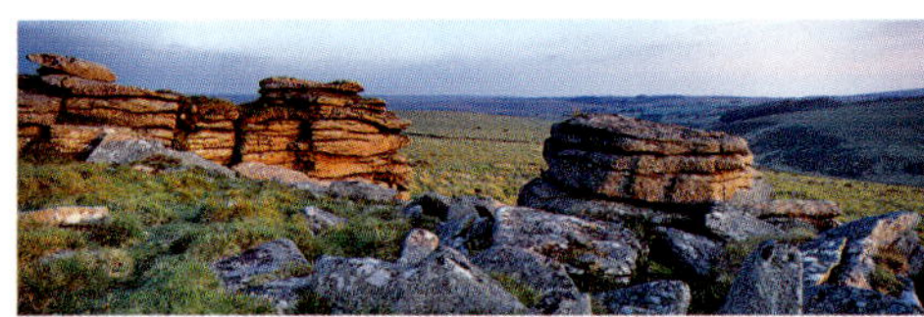

page 71
4th June 2007, 8:45pm
Fuji GX617 90mm, Lee 0.6 ND grad, Fuji Velvia
Spotting this cluster of lichen-covered granite rocks catching the fading sunlight, gave me cause to stop. With just enough time to get one quick photograph, I set up before the sun faded away, ignoring the itches from numerous midge bites suffered earlier in the day.

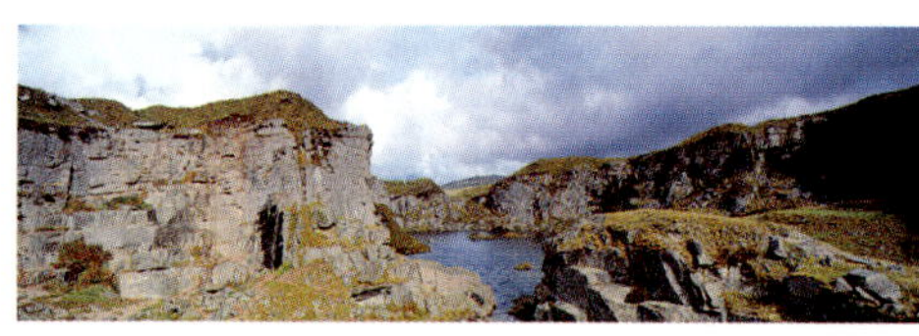

page 72
26th September 2007, 11:24am
Fuji GX617 90mm, Lee 0.3 ND grad, Fuji Velvia
I set up to photograph the abandoned Foggintor Quarry as welcome sunlight briefly flooded across the landscape. As I looked across the flooded pit towards Great Mis Tor a couple of abseilers began descending the steep cliff to my right.

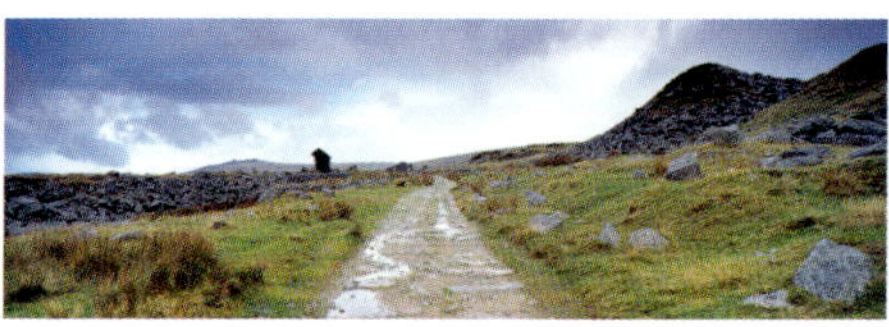

pages 72–73
26th September 2007, 11:04am
Fuji GX617 90mm, Lee 0.9 ND grad, Fuji Velvia
A wet morning walk around Foggintor Quarry tempted me to retire to a cafe. About to walk back, I instead decided to set up beneath a blowing umbrella, using the track as a lead-in line looking towards the ruined quarry buildings. As I finished photographing the scene, the day brightened and I returned to the main quarry, cafe forgotten, looking for more photographs.

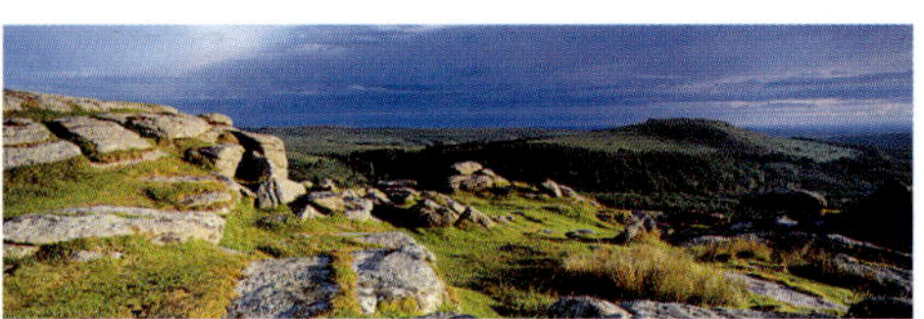

page 74
14th June 2007, 8:24pm
Fuji GX617 90mm, Lee 0.45 ND grad, Fuji Velvia
A short climb to the top of Down Tor nevertheless proved hard work in the summer sun with a heavy rucksack full of camera gear. Reaching the summit before the sun dropped behind neighbouring Leather Tor, I quickly set up. With the sun off to one side, bringing out textures and giving depth to the landscape, I photographed the scene and descended in the closing darkness.

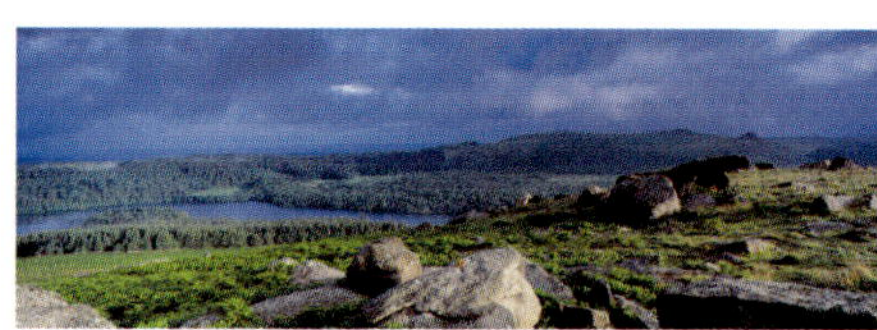

pages 74–75
15th June 2007, 6:37am
Fuji GX617 90mm, Lee 0.6 ND grad, Fuji Velvia
Climbing to the summit of Sheeps Tor, I was greeted by a blustery wind blowing across the hillside. Incredible far-reaching views stretched in every direction, making up for the cold. As sheep sheltered beside large rocks that littered the landscape, I set up my camera and loaded a film, focussing on the view across Burrator Reservoir and surrounding forest.

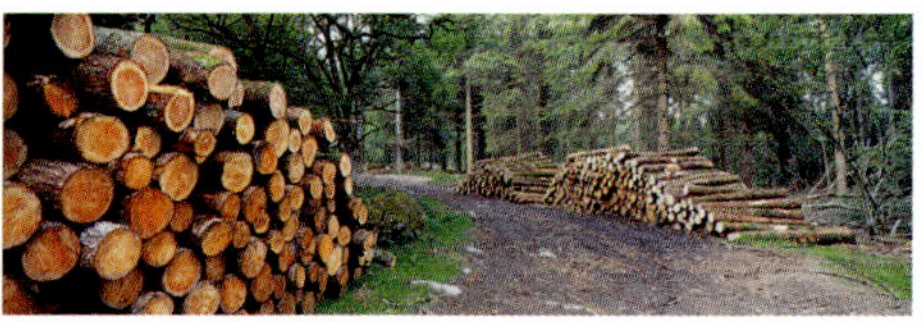

page 76
14th June 2007, 6:50pm
Fuji GX617 90mm, Fuji Velvia
Searching for the best looking, cleanest tree trunks, I moved in close to fill the frame of my panoramic camera in woods near Burrator Reservoir.

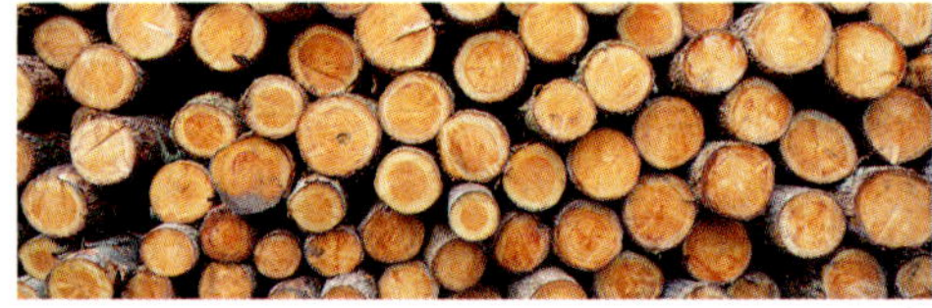

page 76
14th June 2007, 6:52pm
Fuji GX617 90mm, Fuji Velvia
Moving in close to the logs stacked to the left, I then used the forest track to lead into the scene and the next pile of logs. The uniform overcast light was perfect for softening shadows among the trees.

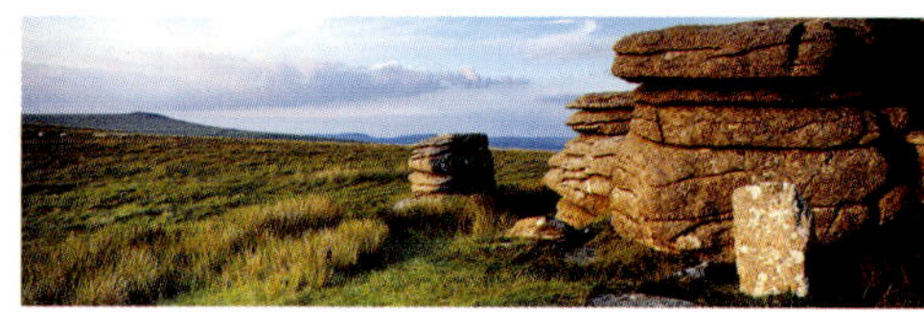

page 77
4th June 2007, 8:35pm
Fuji GX617 90mm, Lee 0.3 + 0.45 ND grads, Fuji Velvia
The warmth of colour on the moor and rocks of Littaford Tor on a summer evening are at odds with the cold winter view I witnessed here a few months earlier (page 29). Using a Lee 0.45 ND grad to hold detail in the sky, I also needed a 0.3 grad placed sideways to allow for the brightness of the sunlit granite on the right.

page 78
10th August 2005, 2:00pm
Hasselblad XPan 45mm, Fuji Velvia
Wiping spray from my lens between exposures, I was able to use the panoramic format vertically to capture the grandeur of this impressive waterfall. The greenery surrounding the fall glistened in the damp conditions, as I strained to hear the quiet sound of the shutter over the thundering sound of falling water.

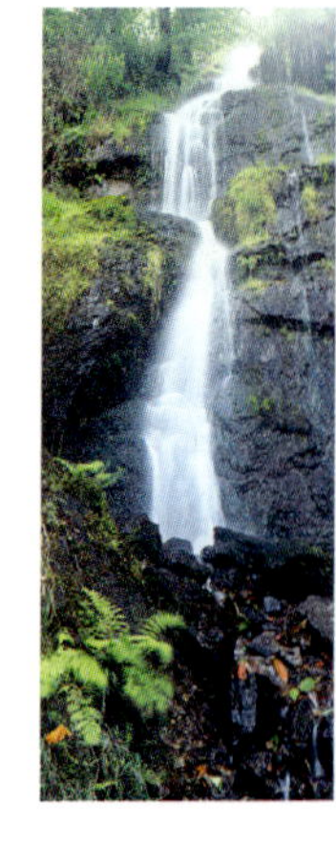

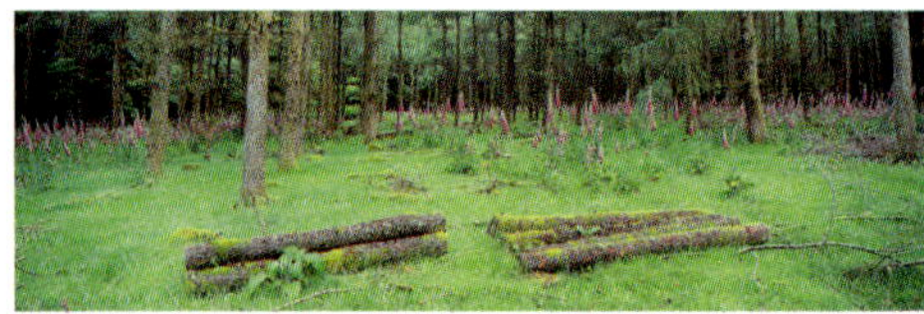

pages 78–79
16th June 2007, 5:27pm
Fuji GX617 90mm, Polariser, Fuji Velvia
I spotted this colourful display of purple foxgloves growing amongst pine trees beside Burrator Reservoir late one evening. Returning on a wet day a couple of days later, I used a polarising filter to eliminate glare and bring out the colour in the damp foliage.

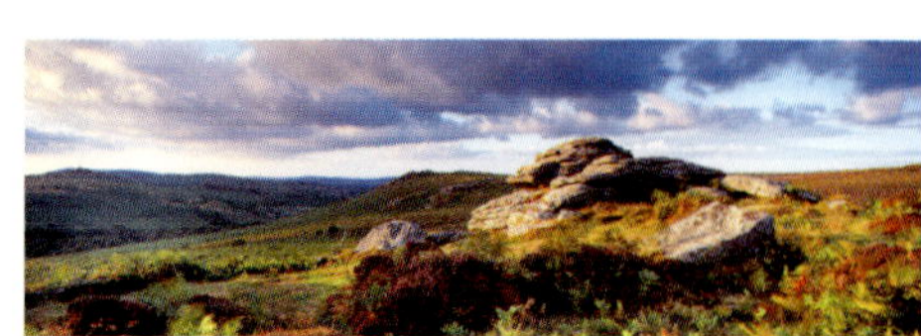

pages 80–81
12th August 2006, evening
Fuji GX617 90mm, Lee 0.6 ND grad, Fuji Velvia
Constantly changing light as the sun played hide and seek amongst the clouds made setting the correct exposure tricky. Although I managed only two quick photographs as the sunlight swept across the moor, I knew there was good potential for a dramatic image.

page 82
10th August 2005, evening
Fuji GX617 90mm, Polariser + Lee 0.3 ND grad, Fuji Velvia
Looking back towards Saddle Tor across the moor I used a polarising filter to reduce reflections in the gorse and heather and bring out their vibrant colours.

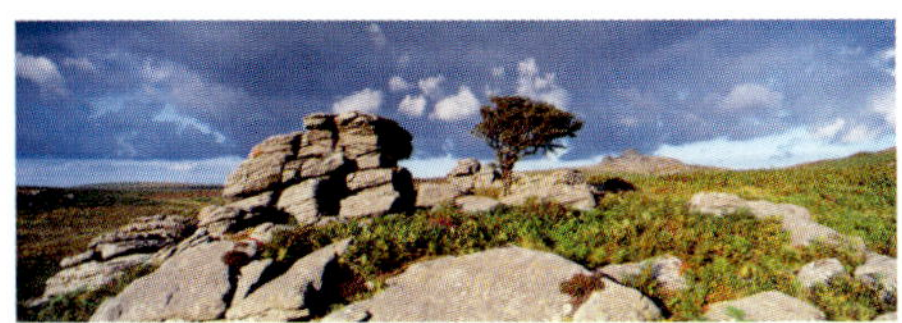

pages 82–83
12th August 2006, evening
Fuji GX617 90mm, Lee 0.6 ND grad, Fuji Velvia
A wide view shows the drama of the sky above rocks near Haytor. A Lee 0.6 ND grad holds detail in the sky, and I had climbed a nearby granite boulder which provided much-needed height to open up the view of the moor.

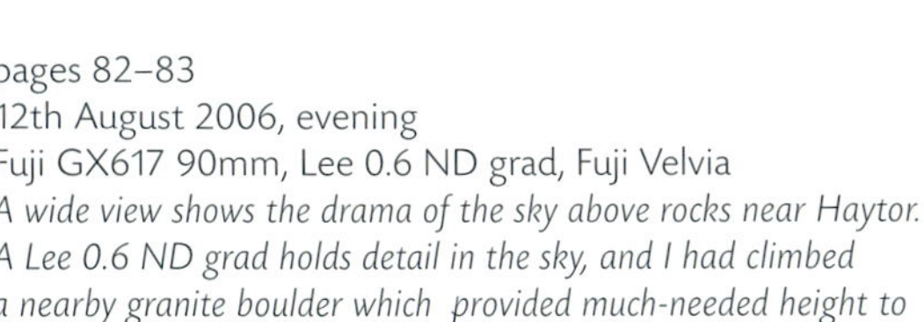

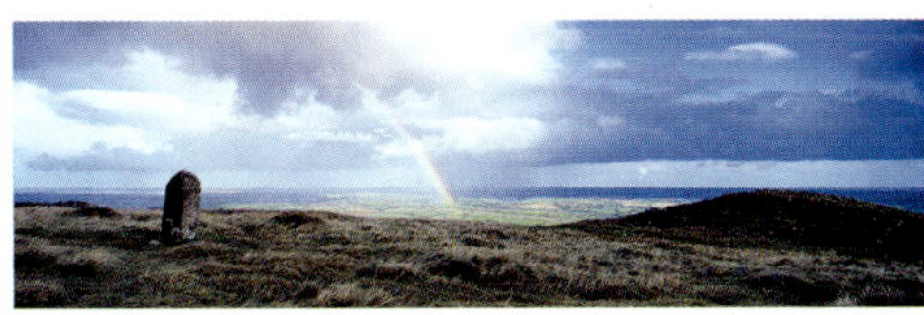

page 84
25th September 2007, 5:03pm
Fuji GX617 90mm, Lee 0.6 ND grad, Fuji Velvia
Strong winds sped heavy showers of rain across the moor above Ivybridge. Battling the wind with an umbrella held above my camera, I set up, loaded film, fitted a grad filter, took a lightmeter reading and raced to photograph the dramatic clouds and fleeting rainbow overhead.

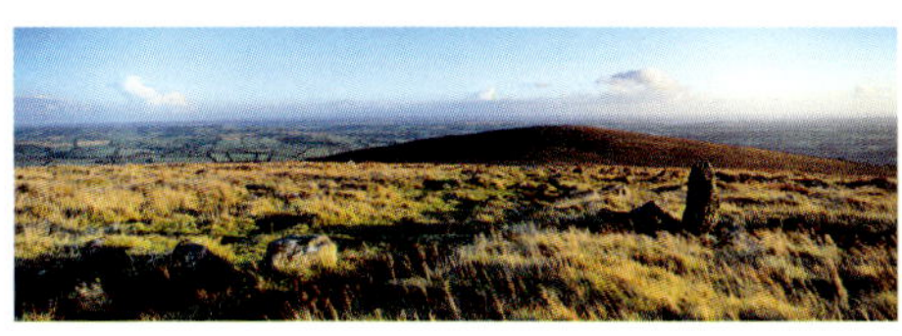

page 85
25th September 2007, 6:40pm
Fuji GX617 90mm, Lee 0.6 ND grad, Fuji Velvia
A steep climb onto the moor from Ivybridge resulted in an amazing patchwork view of the fields surrounding Dartmoor. As I set up my tripod looking back along the path I had just walked, the sun raked long shadows across the moor bringing out textures in the scene.

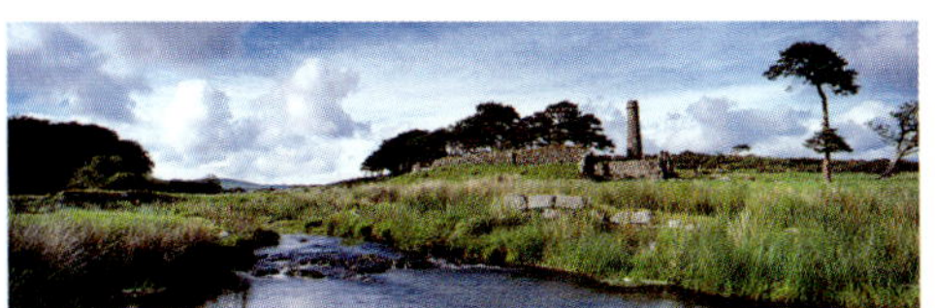

page 85
14th June 2007, 6:09pm
Fuji GX617 90mm, Lee 0.45 ND grad, Fuji Velvia
A brief glimpse of sunlight spurred me into action when I was photographing the Powder Mills ruin. I had to ignore a leaking boot as it filled with water from the deep river flowing past!

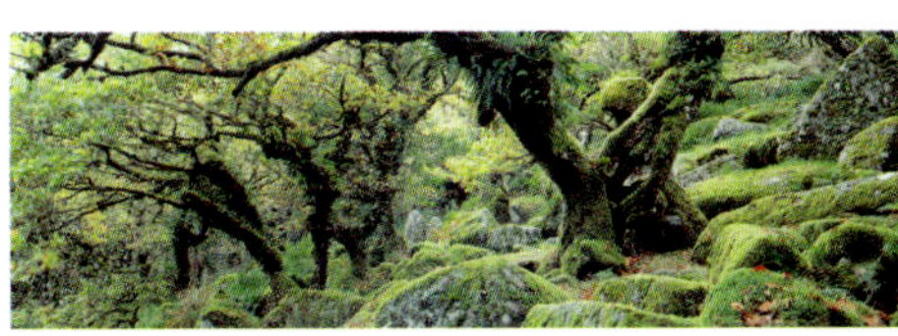

pages 86–87
3rd October 2007, 12:36pm
Fuji GX617 180mm, Polariser, Fuji Velvia
An interesting and enchanting vista of moss-covered rocks and stunted oak trees makes up the wood called Wistman. Making my way through the woods I searched for a photograph that would do it justice. Switching to a longer telephoto lens, I concentrated on this oak growing in two directions, including enough of the surroundings to show its location.

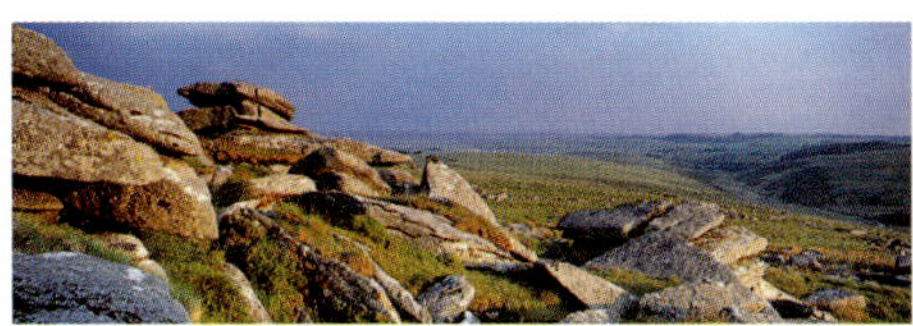

page 88
4th June 2007, 8:16pm
Fuji GX617 90mm, Lee 0.45 ND grad, Fuji Velvia
Finding the approximate position I had photographed this scene in winter (page 28) I composed this panorama in the June sunshine. Taking spotmeter readings from the rocks and grass to determine exposure, I also used a Lee 0.45 ND grad on the sky.

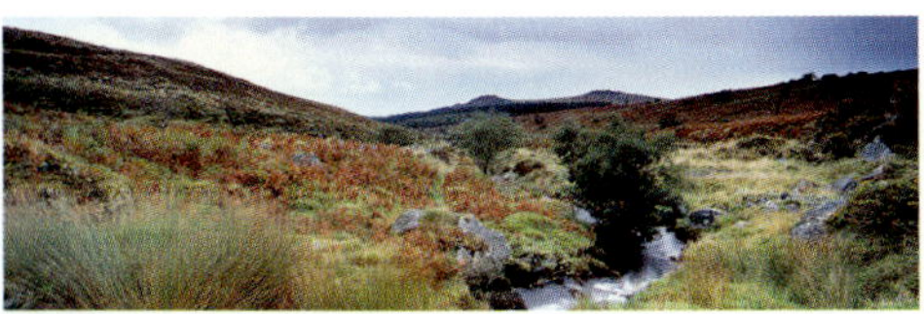

page 88
26th September 2007, 2:03pm
Fuji GX617 90mm, Lee 0.9 ND grad, Fuji Velvia
The quickly changing weather on Dartmoor brought clouds and often rain to replace blue skies and sunshine of moments before. Wiry grass and the cascading river created the depth I wanted to convey this three-dimensional landscape on film.

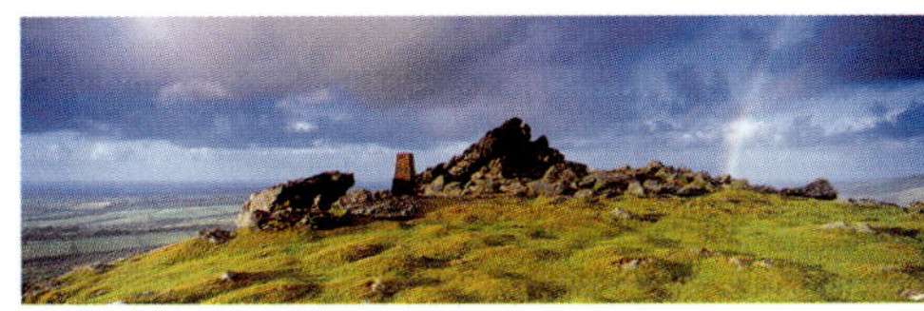

page 89
24th September 2007, 6:28pm
Fuji GX617 90mm, Lee 0.6 ND grad, Fuji Velvia
An overcast afternoon makes way for broken cloud, showers and sunlight on Sourton Tor, with a fleeting rainbow adding to the drama. Struggling to load a new film under my umbrella, it again proves its worth as a permanent fixture in my camera bag.

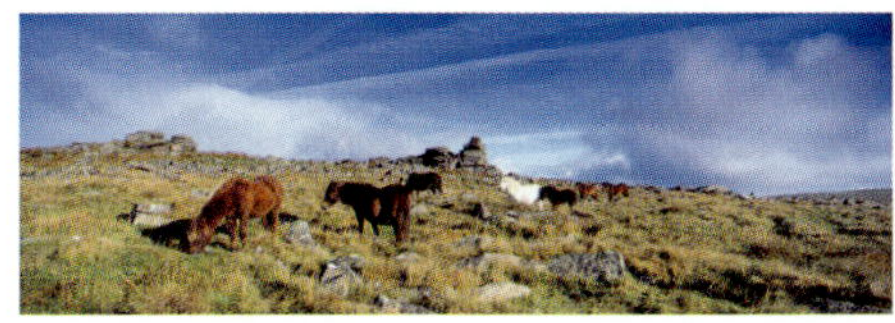

pages 90–91
26th September 2007, 8:42am
Fuji GX617 90mm, Lee 0.6 ND grad, Fuji Velvia
A small group of wild ponies wandered the slopes of Leeden Tor on a sunny morning. Working with such a large and slow-to-use camera can prove difficult when faced with moving objects. Luckily, used to the occasional presence of humans, the ponies continued grazing as I set up my tripod and took the photograph.

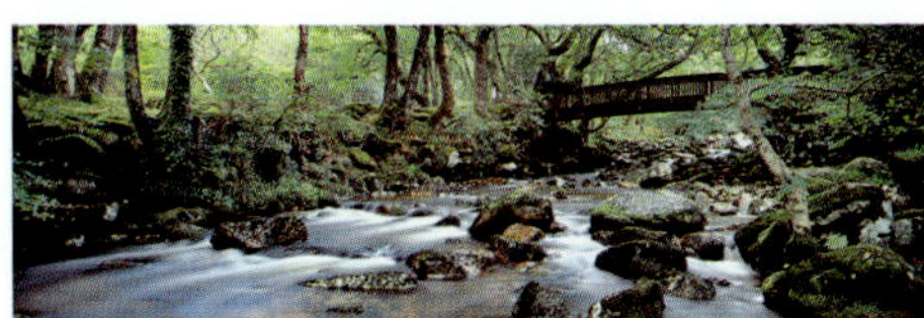

page 91
26th September 2007, 4:53pm
Fuji GX617 90mm, Polariser + Lee 0.3 ND grad, Fuji Velvia
Using the footbridge across the River Plym as a focal point, I opted for a low vantage point in order to make the most of the scattered rocks. Standing in the river beside my camera I juggled lightmeter, filters and film, hoping not to lose any in the water. A polariser was used to reduce the reflections in the foliage and a Lee 0.3 ND grad to keep detail in the bright trees.

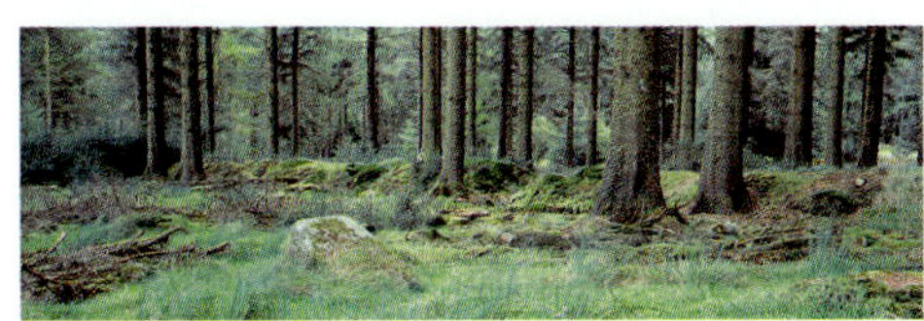

page 92
26th September 2007, 2:54pm
Fuji GX617 180mm, Polariser, Fuji Velvia
As clouds once again covered the sky over Dartmoor, I made my way into this plantation. Overcast conditions are often perfect for woodland scenes as they provide even lighting, with the clouds acting like a huge diffuser. A polariser was used to reduce reflections as I took this photograph in the stillness of the forest.

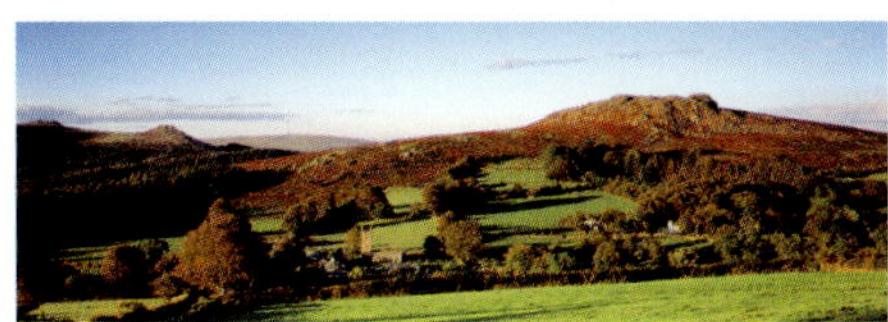

pages 92–93
26th September 2007, 6:29pm
Fuji GX617 180mm, Lee 0.6 ND grad, Fuji Velvia
The evening sunlight shone in from the left creating long shadows of trees and buildings at Sheepstor Hamlet. The use of a Lee 0.6 Neutral Density graduate filter held the bright blue colour in the sky.

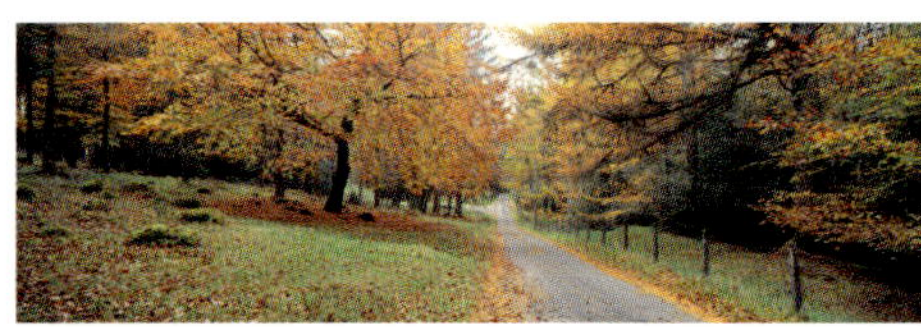

pages 94–95
6th November 2007, 11:29am
Fuji GX617 90mm, Fuji Velvia
An overcast start to this autumn day provided the perfect conditions for woodland photography. Had the sun been out, harsh shadows would have been evident, but the covering of cloud created soft light and illuminated areas of shadow nicely. I used the perspective of this single track road to lead into the photo.

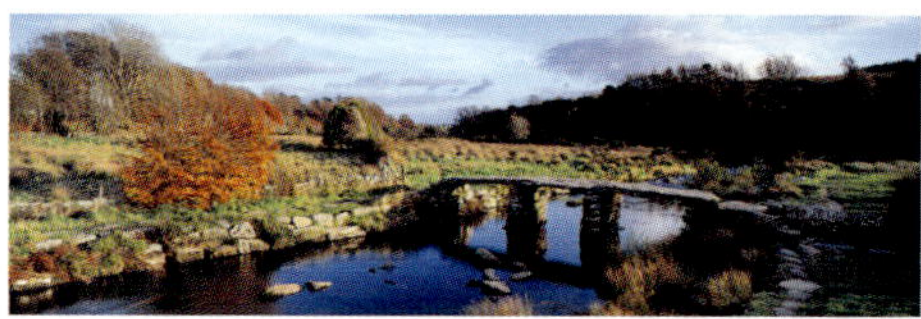

pages 96–97
6th November 2007, 3:33pm
Fuji GX617 90mm, Lee 0.6 ND grad, Fuji Velvia
An autumnal afternoon presented ideal conditions for photographing the clapper bridge at Postbridge. Several previous visits had failed to provide a picture I was satisfied with. On this occasion, it proved amazingly simple to construct a pleasing image. A Lee 0.6 ND grad retained detail in the sky and an aperture of f22 held everything in sharp focus.

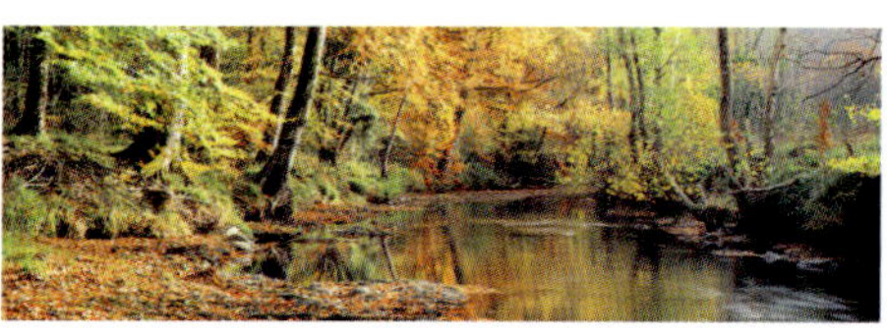

pages 98–99
7th November 2007, 2:20pm
Fuji GX617 180mm, Polariser, Fuji Velvia
Autumn promises much to the landscape photographer but often, in Britain, delivers little as the wind plucks the trees bare no sooner than they start their colourful change. This year however the colour was excellent, with sunny conditions adding to the seasonal display. As sunlight illuminated the leaves for a moment, the still water of the River Teign reflected the spectacle above.

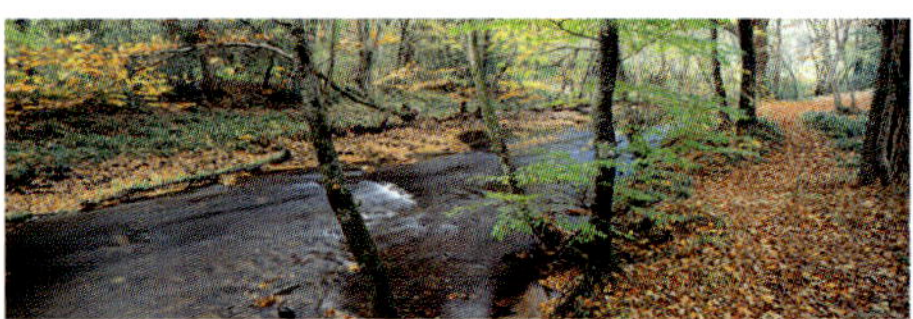

page 99
7th November 2007, 1:06pm
Fuji GX617 90mm, Polariser, Fuji Velvia
In order to gain height for this view of the River Teign, I cautiously extended my tripod as far as I dared. Using my heavy rucksack to anchor it, I was able to make the photograph using a polariser and a shutter speed of many seconds.

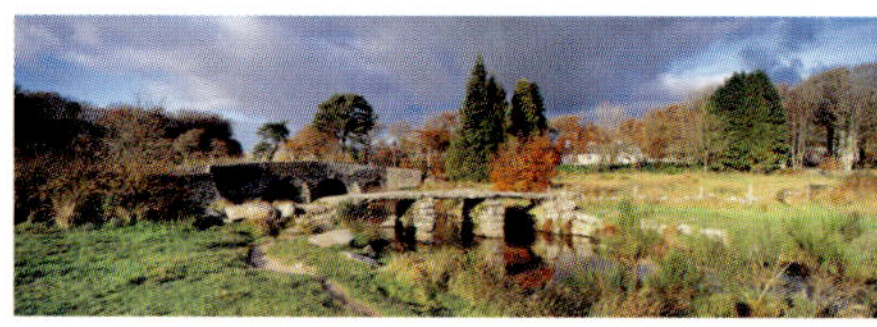

pages 100–101
6th November 2007, 3:06pm
Fuji GX617 90mm, Lee 0.45 ND grad, Fuji Velvia
A traditional view of the bridges crossing the East Dart River at Postbridge. This location is very popular with visitors but, blessed with a quiet day, I only had to wait for a short time to get an unobstructed view.

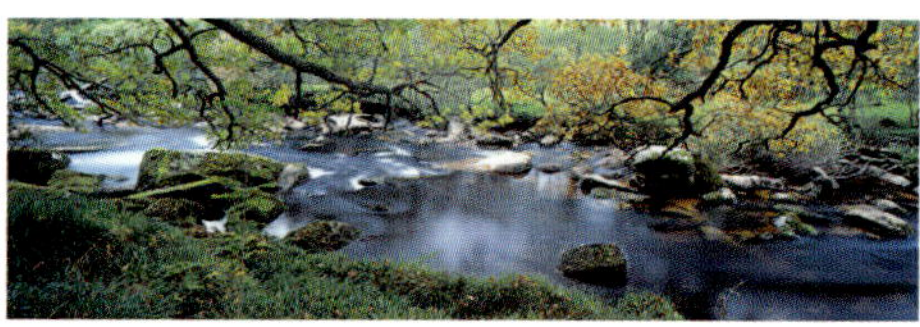

page 100
3rd October 2007, 12:10pm
Fuji GX617 90mm, Polariser, Fuji Velvia
Driving near Hexworthy Bridge, I spotted these tree limbs reaching over the River Dart with leaves tinted with the colours of autumn. Stopping to set up with a polariser to reduce glare from the riverside foliage, I photographed the panorama using an exposure reading taken from the greenery and rocks in the river.

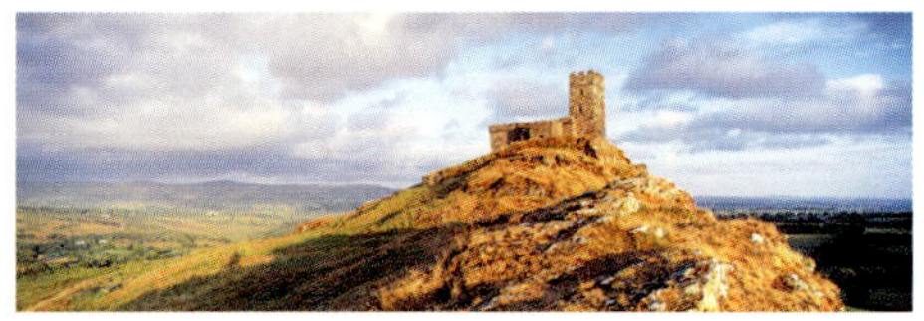

page 102
October 2006, evening
Fuji GX617 90mm, Lee 0.3 ND grad, Fuji Velvia
A windy evening scatters the clouds in the sky above Brentor Church, allowing the low autumn sun to paint the land with warm light. Perched on a rocky ridge I watched the display while families and dogs experienced the blustery conditions as they climbed the tor.

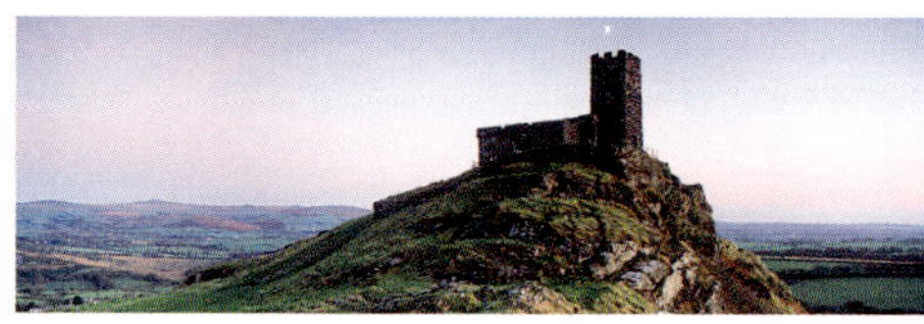

page 102
9th November 2005, evening
Hasselblad XPan 45mm, Lee 0.6 ND grad, Fuji Velvia
The sky glowed with ethereal magenta shades as evening settled over Brent Tor. The moon shone brightly in the sky above the church, and the tranquil evening was broken only by the occasional passing car on the road a short distance below.

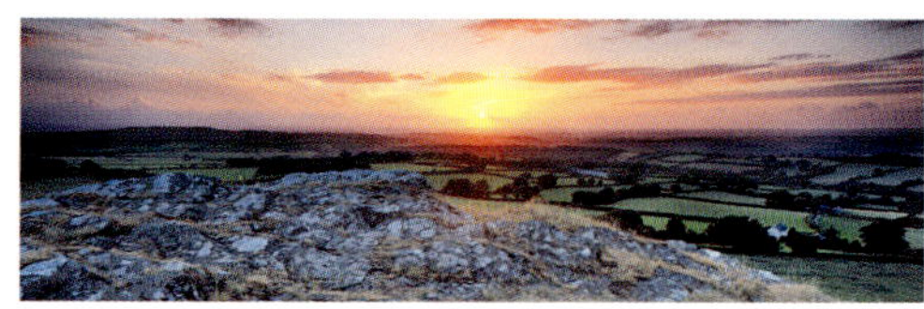

page 103
October 2006, evening
Fuji GX617 90mm, Lee 0.9 + 0.6 ND grads, Fuji Velvia
The setting sun radiated fiery red colours across the sky as I watched from the ridge beside Brentor Church. Two Lee Neutral Density filters were needed to control the brightness range of the scene.

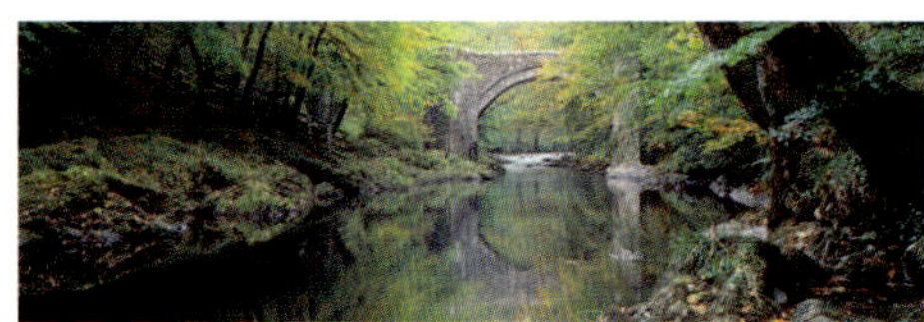

pages 104–105
24th October 2007, 4:31pm
Fuji GX617 180mm, Polariser, Fuji Velvia
The leaves had turned shades of light green and yellow, beginning their metamorphosis towards oranges and reds, beside Holne Bridge spanning the River Dart. I slowly rotated my polarising filter in order to minimise the glare of the foliage, while cautiously standing in the shallow waters alongside the calm looking river. Once there was a gap in the traffic crossing the bridge, I pressed the shutter release.

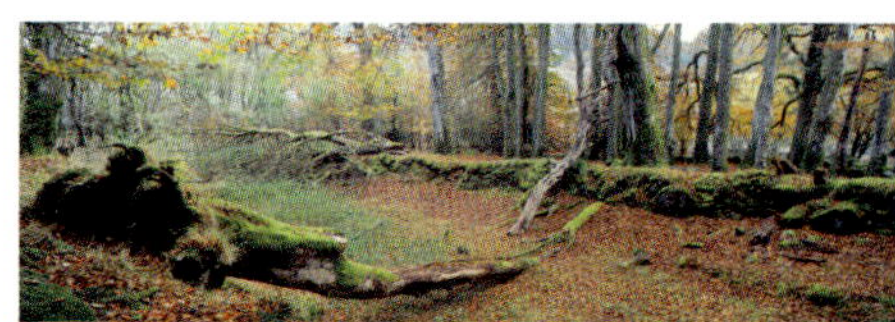

pages 106–107
6th November 2007, 12:15pm
Fuji GX617 90mm, Fuji Velvia
Composing a woodland view of fallen trees in the autumnal woods beside Fernworthy Reservoir took some time. Upon finding a pleasing panorama I set an aperture of f45, the Fuji's smallest, in order to maximize the depth of field and try and keep the roots of the fallen tree in focus, in addition to the distant trees.

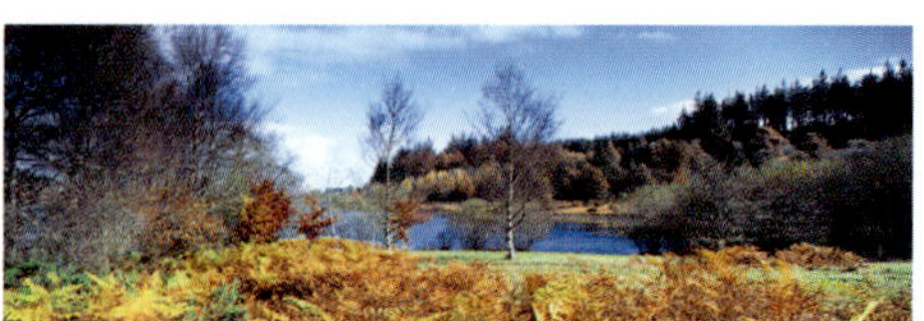

page 106
6th November 2007, 1:06pm
Fuji GX617 90mm, Lee 0.6 ND grad, Fuji Velvia
While having lunch beside Fernworthy Reservoir, as I waited for a bank of cloud to clear, I was visited by some friendly Dartmoor ponies. I managed to stop them getting too close to my tripod-mounted camera, as sunlight finally spilled onto the scene and I triggered the shutter, using a Lee 0.6 ND grad to retain the rich blue colour of the sky.

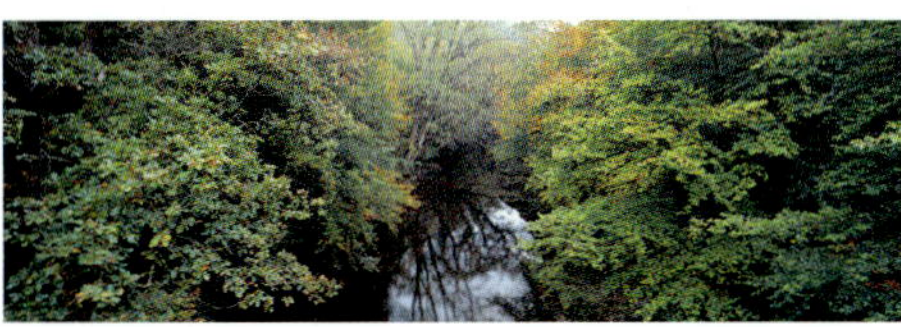

page 108
24th October 2007, 2:41pm
Fuji GX617 90mm, Polariser, Fuji Velvia
As cars passed close behind me, to some extent at odds with the peaceful view looking down the length of the river, I waited in a stone recess on Holne Bridge. I used a polariser to decrease glare from the leaves reaching across the Dart, making my exposure several seconds long.

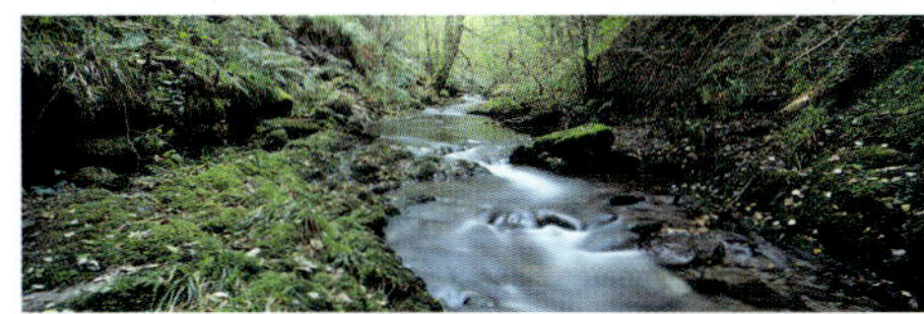

page 108
3rd October 2007, 4:48pm
Fuji GX617 90mm, Polariser, Fuji Velvia
The vibrant green foliage coupled with the winding river, carving its path through the gorge presented a rich landscape asking to be photographed. The steep rocky walls, together with a polariser and a small aperture for sufficient depth of field, meant that several minutes were needed to record the panorama on film.

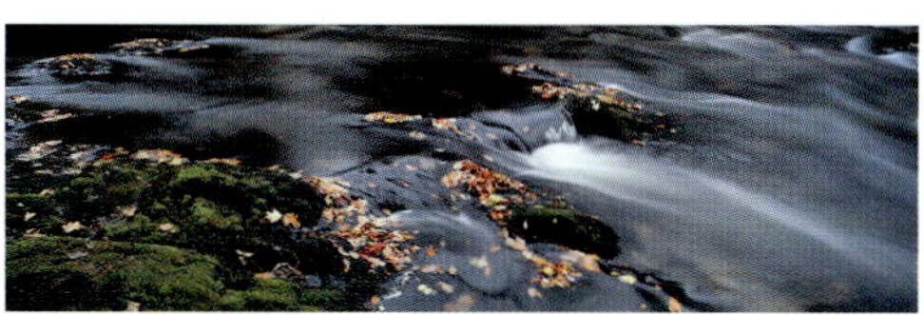

page 109
24th October 2007, 3:38pm
Fuji GX617 90mm, Fuji Velvia
The peaceful nature of the autumn afternoon was only heightened by the babbling sound of the River Dart flowing over pebbles as it journeyed east. Concentrating on the detail of fallen autumn leaves grounded by rocks, I selected a shutter speed of several seconds, softening the motion of the water.

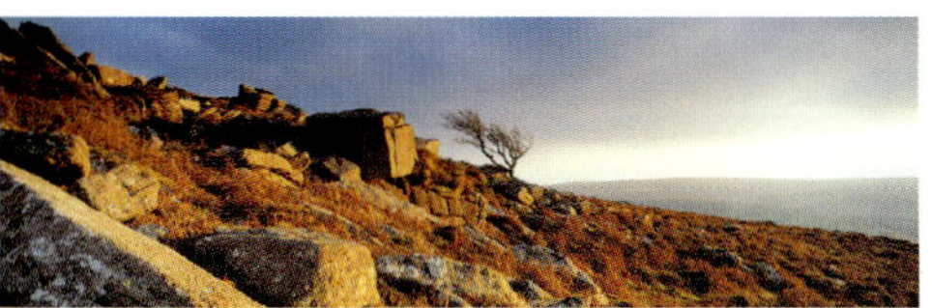

pages 110–111
24th October 2007, 5:30pm
Fuji GX617 90mm, Lee 0.6 ND grad, Fuji Velvia
An overcast afternoon dampened any prospects of a final show from the sun. Deciding to climb Yar Tor on the off chance, a friend and I watched as the sun slid into a break in the clouds, spilling warm coloured light across the moor.

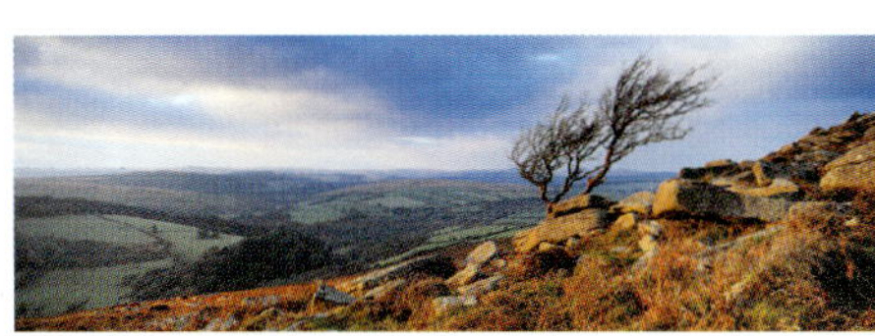

pages 110–111
24th October 2007, 5:28pm
Fuji GX617 90mm, Lee 0.6 ND grad, Fuji Velvia
As evening sunlight covered the slopes of Yar Tor, I endeavoured to produce an interesting panorama, while not delaying pressing the shutter in case the sunlight faded. Carefully loading yet another film as quickly as possible I managed to use two rolls before the sun disappeared.

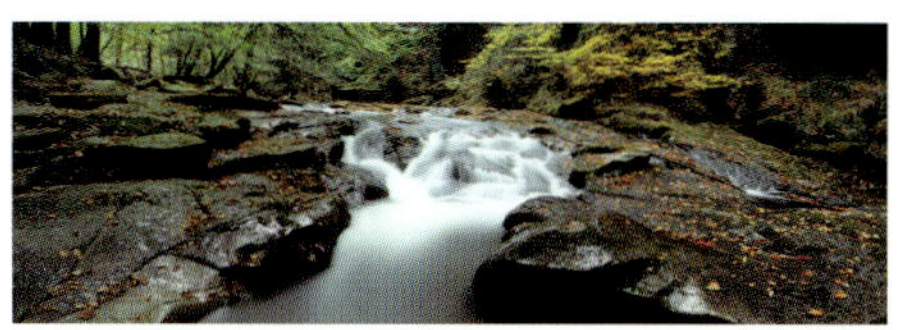

pages 112–113
26th October 2007, 3:16pm
Fuji GX617 90mm, Fuji Velvia
Slippery rocks border the cascading River Erme in the heart of Rithill Woods. The light was already fading as shortened winter days approached and dark clouds collected above. The sound of the crashing water drowned out all others as I managed only one exposure, nearly three minutes long, in the dying light.

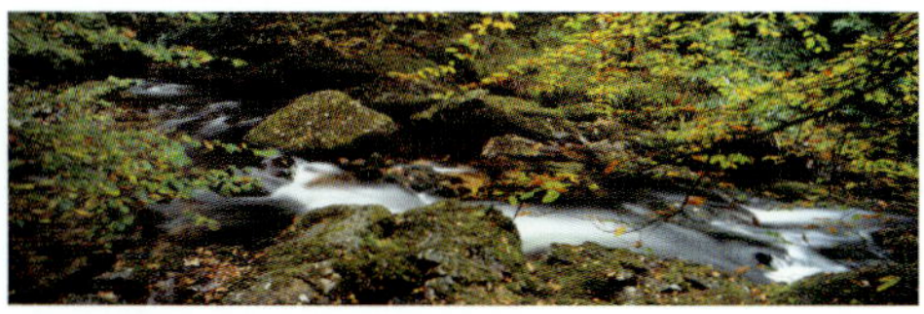

page 113
26th October 2007, 2:15pm
Fuji GX617 90mm, Polariser, Fuji Velvia
The tumbling River Erme flows past moss-covered rocks and autumnal branches north of Ivybridge, as dog walkers and families follow the woodland path alongside. The pleasing autumn display of yellow and orange leaves decorate the trees, and rocks below as they continue to fall.

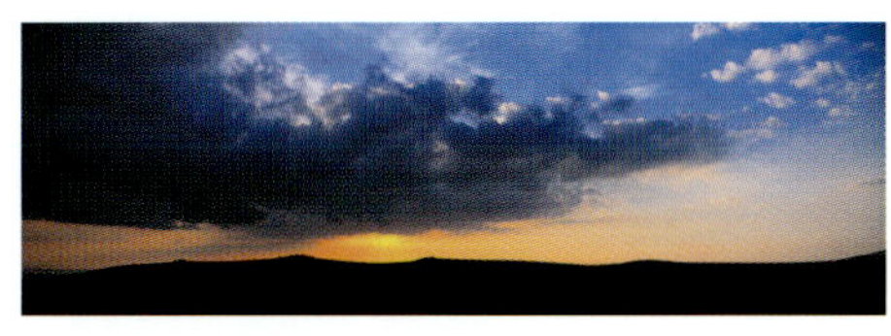

pages 114–115
October 2006, evening
Fuji GX617 180mm, Fuji Velvia
Watching dark clouds obscure the sun over Staple Tor as I climbed the track leading to Great Mis Tor, I decided to stop my pursuit of the summit and concentrate on the drama. Using a medium telephoto lens on the panoramic Fuji, the Tors were thrown into silhouette as I took my exposure reading from the bright sky below the clouds.

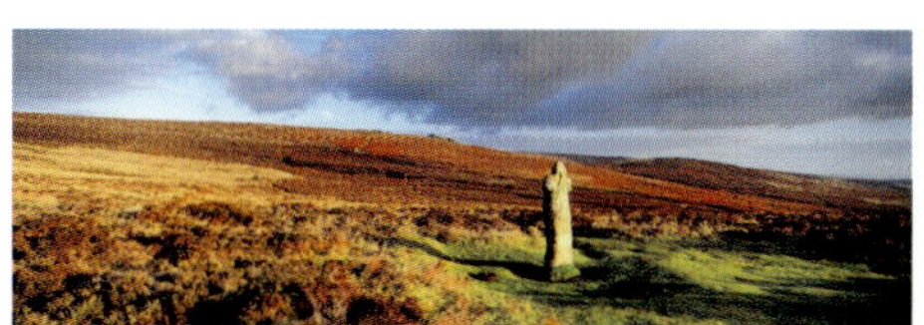

page 114
6th November 2007, 3:51pm
Fuji GX617 90mm, Lee 0.6 ND grad, Fuji Velvia
Stopping at Bennett's Cross when returning home from Postbridge, I decided to brave the strong winds. Taking a number of spotmeter readings from the grasses, heather and granite cross I worked out an average. Holding the detail in the dark clouds above with a Lee 0.6 ND grad, I took a sequence of shots slightly over and under my metered result.

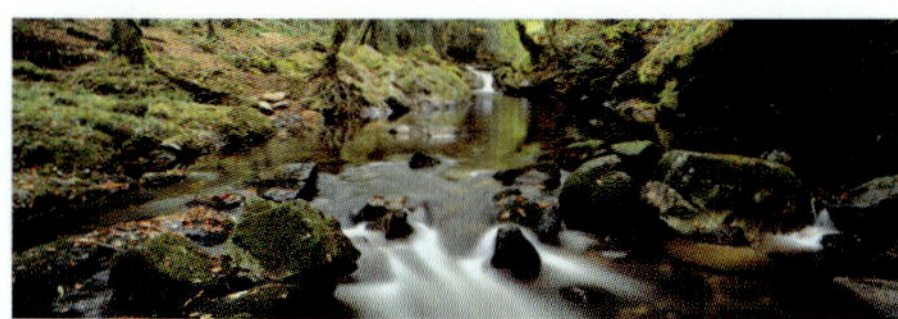

pages 116–117
26th October 2007, 1:10pm
Fuji GX617 90mm, Fuji Velvia
Intrigued by the exposed system of tangled roots that anchored a tree to the ground beside the River Erme, I decided my best vantage point was in the middle of the fast flowing river. Clambering over several unsteady rocks I balanced on a boulder and set up my tripod. Setting the correct aperture and pressing the shutter without either falling in or losing my equipment was a nerve-racking experience.

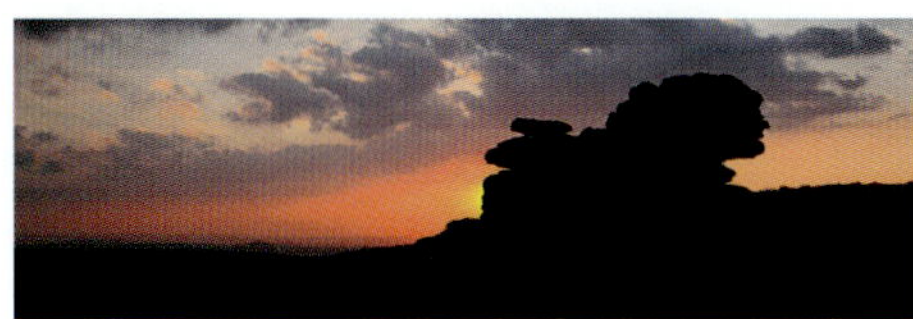

page 117
October 2006, evening
Fuji GX617 180mm, Fuji Velvia
Presented with a vivid red setting sun I decided to silhouette the rocks called Little Mis Tor. Placing the bright sun just behind one edge of the rocks to avoid lens flare, I took a spotmeter reading from a bright patch of sky and increased the reading by one stop to ensure the bright colours were faithfully produced. Not making it as far as the summit this time, I turned back down the army track, as the sun set and darkness rapidly descended.

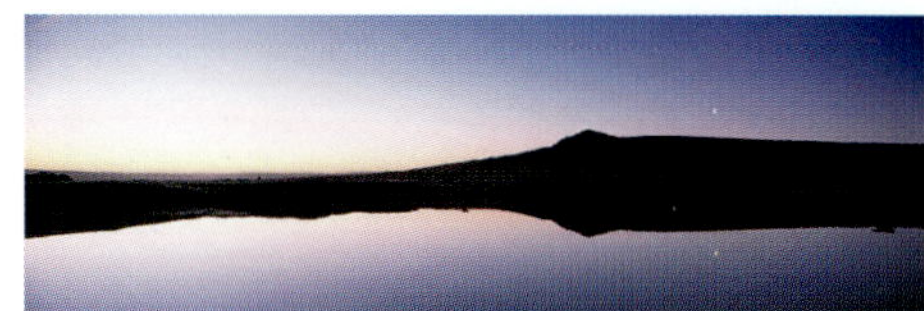

page 128
14th March 2007, 6:09am
Fuji GX617 90mm, Lee 0.3 ND grad, Fuji Velvia
Travelling towards Burrator reservoir in the pre-dawn light, I spotted this still pond reflecting the moon and the rapidly lightening horizon beside Sharpitor. Quickly making my photographs in the crisp cold morning before the colours disappeared, I then continued on my journey to photograph nearby Burrator reservoir.

ACKNOWLEDGEMENTS

I would like to thank the following people who have helped me in the making of this book:

Fran and David Cripps
Mark Denton
Richard Downer
Jane Entrican
Sarah Hamer
Ian Hunt
Graham Merritt
John Nicoll
Colin Prior

Thanks also to the person who had faith in my photography and bought me a great camera.

David Entrican's images are distributed by Panoramic Images Inc (Chicago) at www.panoramicimages.com and by www.orange-skies.com.

For prints, commissions, photo sales and any other enquiries please visit www.orange-skies.com or contact David at dave@orange-skies.com and on 07816 362068.

Moon reflection, Sharpitor,
Dartmoor.

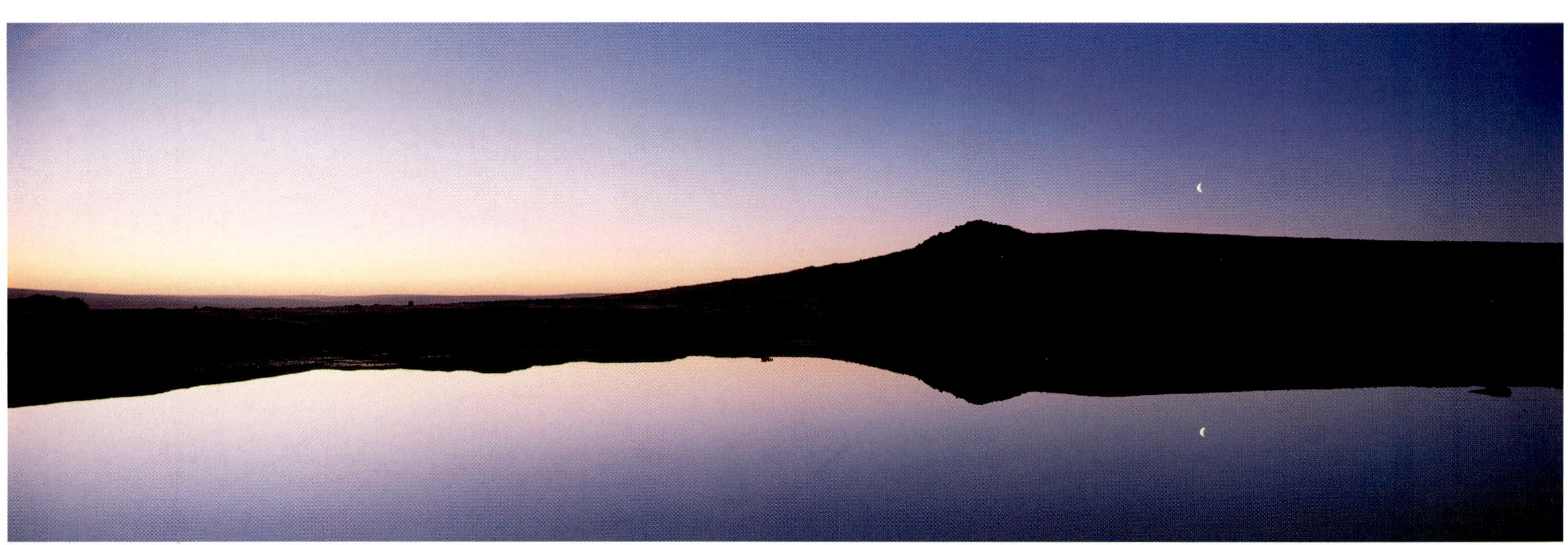